Rabbi Adin Steinsaltz

Hebrew text edited by Meir Hanegbi

Translated by Rabbi Yaacov Tauber

—⁓— Opening the *Tanya*

Discovering the Moral and Mystical Teachings of a Classic Work of Kabbalah

An Arthur Kurzweil Book

JOSSEY-BASS
A Wiley Imprint
www.josseybass.com

Published by Jossey-Bass
A Wiley Imprint
989 Market Street, San Francisco, CA 94103-1741   www.josseybass.com

Jossey-Bass books and products are available through most bookstores. To contact Jossey-Bass
directly call our Customer Care Department within the U.S. at 800-956-7739, outside the U.S. at
317-572-3986, or fax 317-572-4002.

Jossey-Bass also publishes its books in a variety of electronic formats. Some content that
appears in print may not be available in electronic books.

Library of Congress Cataloging-in-Publication Data

Steinsaltz, Adin.
[Be'ur Tanya. English]
    Opening the Tanya: discovering the moral and mystical teachings of a classic work
of Kabbalah / Adin Steinsaltz; Hebrew text edited by Meir Hanegbi; translated by
Rabbi Yaacov Tauber.
        p. cm.
    "An Arthur Kurzweil book."
    Includes bibliographical references and index.
    ISBN 0-7879-6798-X (alk. paper)
    1. Shneur Zalman, of Liadi, 1745-1813. *Likkutei Amarim.* 2. Hasidism. 3. Cabala.
I. Shneur Zalman, of Liadi, 1745-1813. *Likkutei Amarim.* English. II. Hanegbi, Meir.
III. Title.
BM198.2.S563S7413 2003
296.8'332—dc21   2003001614

Printed in the United States of America

FIRST EDITION
HB Printing   10 9 8 7 6 5 4 3 2 1

Contents

———∿∿∿∿———

Opening the Tanya

is dedicated to the memory of

Reb Yehoshua Shneur Zalman Serebryanski ז״ל

A Chasid and Emissary of the Rebbe

An initiator and founder of learning institutions

Principal founder of Chabad Institutions in Australia

A teacher and mentor of many

A loving husband and father

"הֶעֱמִידוּ תַּלְמִידִים הַרְבֵּה" (אָבוֹת א,א)

—Nechama and Nathan Werdiger and children

Melbourne, Australia

—⁓— Acknowledgments

This commentary comprises an "oral Torah" that emerged from a series of weekly classes in Chabad Hasidism and—in a different fashion—from *Tanya* classes broadcast over *Kol Yisrael,* the Israeli state radio station, and informal conversations.

Great thanks are due to Meir Hanegbi, who took all of this oral material and turned it into a book, adding many comments, explanations, source references, and an extensive glossary.

Thanks also go to Rabbi Yaacov Tauber, who translated *Opening the* Tanya; to Yehoshua Fieldsteel, who translated the glossary; to Yehudit Shabtai, for her proofreading acumen; to Margy-Ruth Davis, for her help and good advice; and to Jeff Burt, for his legal skill, support, and friendship.

Last but not least, the participants in the *Tanya* classes added so much—through their questions, their comments, and even their very listening. For all the many ways they have enriched me and my classes, I am deeply grateful.

Rabbi Adin Steinsaltz

Special thanks are due the Lubavitch publishing house, Kehot Publication Society, for its permission to use its acclaimed English translation of the *Tanya* text (Brooklyn, NY 1962). *Lessons in Tanya: The Tanya of R. Shneur Zalman of Liadi* (5 vols. Brooklyn, NY 1982), also by Kehot, is an additional important resource for those seeking to explore the *Tanya* in greater depth.

~~~ A Note About Gender

This book was written using male pronouns to refer to individuals not because it is a book for men only—which it is not—but because that is the way in which it is usually expressed in Hebrew. Hebrew does not have the neutral gender; thus, most nouns are, by default, in the masculine gender.

Furthermore, the *Alter Rebbe* did not address female audiences during his lifetime, and so his writing assumed a male readership and reflected men's way of life (making frequent reference, for example, to *mitzvot* that are performed by men only, such as the wearing of the *tefillin*). However, the assumption was that women would receive the teachings of this book through their husbands—as indeed they often did.

We have used neutral language wherever possible when it did not interfere with the accuracy or clarity of the content.

─w─ Preface

Over 250 years ago, a revolutionary movement arose at the center of the Jewish world. With remarkable speed, the Hasidic movement spread throughout Eastern Europe and White Russia (now Belarus). Hasidism had a profound—and continuing—impact on Jewish spiritual thought and practice, changing it as no other movement has.

What is Hasidism? What is its innovation? Hasidism strives for consciousness of one's inner essence and simplicity—in relation to Torah, man, and divinity—and for this, there are no adequate words or direct definitions. Initially, Hasidism was an all-encompassing approach to life, a distinct way of praying, studying, and living that emphasized cleaving to and serving God with joy. Because it deals with man's inner essence, Hasidism defies easy definition or description. Our understanding is further complicated by the fact that the first generations of Hasidic masters, on principle, wrote little or not at all. Even the few writings we do have tend to be secondary sources, often fragmented and unsystematic, and are idiosyncratic to the specific environment in which they arose. Thus, they provide faint illumination, while essentially leaving us in the dark.

The *Tanya* does not purport to provide a comprehensive definition or explication of Hasidism. Nevertheless, it is the first—and in many ways, the only—systematic book of the Hasidic movement.

The *Tanya* is a small book, and it is not encyclopedic, yet it is—in a particularly Jewish sense—all-inclusive. The Written Torah is considered to be the ultimate source of the many details of Jewish thought that continually emanate from the Oral Torah. So, too, the leaders of the Chabad branch of Hasidism called the *Tanya* "the Written Torah of Hasidism," the repository—in potential, in essence, and in full—of the whole of Hasidism.

The author of the *Tanya*, Rabbi Schneur Zalman, was born in 1745 in the small town of Liozna in White Russia. At a young age, he became a prominent disciple of the Rabbi Dov Ber of Mezherich

(1704–1773)—known as the Maggid ("preacher")—who was the successor of the founder of Hasidism, the Baal Shem Tov (ca. 1700–1760). The Maggid recognized Schneur Zalman's greatness in Torah and his unique talent for systematic organization; he gave him the task of compiling, organizing, and recording all of the Jewish laws up to his day. (The Chabad Hasidim fondly refer to him in Yiddish as the *Alter Rebbe*.)

Rabbi Schneur Zalman's compilation, known as *The Rav's Shulchan Aruch*, the first volume of which was published when he was in his late twenties, was such a tremendous achievement that it established him as a great Torah luminary even among Hasidism's detractors. It was only natural for Schneur Zalman to apply these same talents to the elucidation of the fundamentals of Hasidic teachings.

At first glance, the *Tanya* seems to affect the style of an ordinary book of *mussar*, practical advice intended to direct people in the path of God's worship and of self-perfection. In fact, it takes an original approach to the basic issues of self-improvement, applying the principles of Hasidism to reveal the root causes of human failings and to devise comprehensive solutions.

The central innovation of the book was the creation of an original conception of the ideal to which a person should aspire: the *beinoni*. (Indeed, the *Tanya* is referred to as the Book of the *Beinonim*.) Historically, the *beinoni* represented a turning away from the predominant ideal of the Jew in the existing *mussar* literature to something more attainable, if no more closer to the abilities of the average person.

A *beinoni* is not righteous or evil, nor is he precisely something in between. This state of the *beinoni* is a condition of ongoing tension and struggle, but this fight—and our ability to conduct our lives within it—are the very purpose of the creation of humankind. As the *Tanya* explains it, this status is not simply the confrontation between good and evil, but rather the ongoing encounter between the two components of the human soul: the animal and the divine. The tension is between the part of the soul that draws us downward toward the earth and the part that aspires upward toward the divine.

The conflict, then, is not a war of annihilation, in which man seeks to destroy certain parts of his soul; rather, it is an effort to educate all the parts of the human soul, to create within them a consciousness and a feeling—until their aspirations merge with those of the divine soul, so that the person reaches a state of perfect harmony between body and soul, the earthly and the divine.

A companion message of the *Tanya* is the attainability of this goal. The *Tanya* seeks to demonstrate to the "average" man or woman that knowledge of God is there for the taking, that spiritual growth to ever higher levels is real and immanent, if one is willing to engage in the struggle. "For it is exceedingly near to you, in your mouth and in your heart, to do it" (Deuteronomy 30:14).

The *Tanya,* then, does not create a system; instead, it clothes the essence of the system in structures that bring them to a level that is both higher and more revealed than anything that a story, a Hasidic maxim, a feeling, or a personal relationship could ever do. This, then, is how we should interpret the reaction of Rabbi Zusha of Anipoli, upon receiving this book: "I wonder how he managed to put such a great and awesome God into such a small book!"

Because this book is a "written Torah," it requires, in every generation, an "oral Torah" to accompany it and to serve as an usher and guide. This is especially true in our generation, in which so many people grew up without any contact with the Hasidic world and are unable to access this book.

It is for this generation, and for these people, that this commentary to the *Tanya* is written. The book contains the precise text of the *Tanya* as it was written by the *Alter Rebbe,* along with its authorized translation, and a full commentary that provides source references. I have added extensive explanations of basic Hasidic concepts, theoretical background, metaphors and parables from daily life, and stories from the past and present lives of the Hasidim. The book also contains an expanded Glossary defining and expounding on various important terms and concepts.

This book is intended for all of those who have the mind and the will for it, who desire to access this world and grow through it.

⟨⟩ Introduction

THE AUTHOR

The author of *Tanya,* Rabbi Schneur Zalman of Liadi, was born on the 18th of *Elul* 5505 (1745), in the town of Liozna in White Russia (now Belarus). His father was Rabbi Baruch, a descendent of the famed Maharal, Rabbi Loewe of Prague. From his early childhood, Rabbi Schneur Zalman's genius and prodigious Torah knowledge were widely recognized. A few years after his marriage in 1760, he decided to study Torah at one of the great Torah centers. The two centers he considered were Vilna, home to Rabbi Elijah, the famed Gaon of Vilna; and Mezherich, where the great Maggid ("preacher"), Rabbi Dov Ber, successor to the Baal Shem Tov, founder of the Hasidic movement, taught. Feeling that he knew a little about how to study Torah but virtually nothing about how to pray, he decided to go to Mezherich.

Rabbi Schneur Zalman arrived in Mezherich in 1764. Despite his student's youth, the Maggid soon counted him among the inner circle of disciples. The Maggid greatly appreciated his talents and Torah knowledge, giving the young man the task, in 1770, of compiling a new and updated *Shulchan Aruch* (Code of Jewish Law). Rabbi Schneur Zalman labored at this task for many years (parts of it underwent two drafts), but tragically, most of the work was destroyed by fire. Only a part of it (most of *Orach Chaim* and a few chapters from the other three sections) survived and was published after his death. The book, which is not a specifically Hasidic work, is known as *The Rav's Shulchan Aruch;* it is a tremendous halakhic ("relating to Torah law") achievement, adapting and condensing the gist of Torah law up to that time. The author's use of the Hebrew language is outstanding: he explains things concisely and clearly, in depth but without unnecessary complexities. His halakhic approach is similar, in many ways, to that of the Gaon of Vilna. Still, the work has earned an honored status among halakhic authorities all over the Jewish world, and it serves as the basic halakhic source for Hasidim in general and Chabad Hasidim in particular. Were it not for the violent opposition to Hasidism that prevailed at the time, it would doubtless have earned even a more central position in halakhic literature.

In 1767, Rabbi Schneur Zalman was appointed Maggid in his hometown of Liozna; beginning in 1772, highly talented young men began to come to him for instruction in Torah and the service of God. Rabbi Schneur Zalman arranged these disciples in three *chadarim* ("rooms" or classes), instructing each according to his level. According to Chabad tradition, Rabbi Schneur Zalman began to consolidate his unique Chabad philosophy and approach in this same year, which is thus considered the founding year of Chabad Hasidism.

In 1774, Rabbi Schneur Zalman and his teacher-colleague, Rabbi Menachem Mendel of Vitebsk, went as a Hasidic delegation to Vilna in an attempt to come to an understanding with the Vilna Gaon, the leading figure in the opposition against the Hasidic movement. But the Vilna Gaon refused to receive them.

In the same year, following the death of the Maggid, the Hasidic community accepted the central leadership of Rabbi Menachem Mendel of Vitebsk. But in 1777, under the pressure of persecution and excommunication by the opponents of Hasidism, which were directed mainly against the Hasidim of White Russia, Rabbi Menachem Mendel and a large group of Hasidim emigrated to the Land of Israel. Rabbi Schneur Zalman, who was initially in the group, was persuaded to return home and became one of the leaders of the Hasidic community in White Russia, together with Rabbi Israel of Plotsk and Rabbi Issachar Dov of Lubavich. In 1788, Rabbi Menachem Mendel, in a letter from the land of Israel, appointed him as the sole leader of the Hasidim in this region. This, however, was merely a confirmation of the de facto state of affairs, because Rabbi Schneur Zalman's comprehensive educational endeavor, both written and oral, and his impressive success in many public debates with Hasidism's opponents (including the famous disputation in Minsk in 1783), had made him the most important Hasidic leader in White Russia. Moreover, by this time, his teaching had also consolidated into a unique system within Hasidism, the system of Chabad (an acronym for *Chokhmah, Binah, Daat;* see Chapter 3).

Rabbi Schneur Zalman's influence continued to grow. Copies of his writings on Hasidic teaching circulated widely, and his published works, initially published anonymously, added considerably to the spread of the Chabad approach and to the author's reputation. If his *Hilchot Talmud Torah* (Laws of Torah Study, published anonymously in 1794) demonstrated his knowledge of halakhah and of Torah in general, his *Tanya* (published in 1797) was a lucid and systematic articulation of the fundamentals of Hasidic teaching.

His influence spread not only throughout White Russia but increasingly also in Lithuania and even in Vilna itself, to the extent that several community leaders in this bastion of opposition to Hasidism were among his followers. This aroused the wrath of the *mitnagdim* ("opponents" of Hasidism), who, finding their old recourse of excommunication ineffective, availed themselves of their last remaining weapon: informing against him to the Russian government, which had recently annexed White Russia and Poland. The Rabbi of Pinsk brought a formal complaint to the Russian authorities, accusing a number of Hasidic leaders, and in particular Rabbi Schneur Zalman, of various offenses, both religious and political: sending money to the sultan of Turkey (actually funds he raised for the support of the Hasidic community in the Holy Land, then under Turkish rule) and the creation of a new religious sect, which Russian law strictly forbade. In 1798, as a result of these accusations, Rabbi Schneur Zalman was arrested and brought as a capital offender to Petersburg. After a secret trial, whose details we do not fully know to this day (though a number of authenticated documents and a great deal of legendary material are connected with it), he was exonerated of all charges and released from prison on the 19th of *Kislev* of that year. This day came to symbolize the public victory of Hasidism over its opponents and was established, in the lifetime of Rabbi Schneur Zalman, as the Festival of Redemption.

Historically, that 19th of *Kislev* represents a watershed in the development of Hasidism: from that point, it grew stronger, accelerated its spread, and gained tens of thousands of new followers. The date also is said to hold a deeper, spiritual significance. Hasidim came to see Rabbi Schneur Zalman's arrest, trial, and liberation as the earthly reflection of a heavenly trial, in which God was judging his activities and approach. To what extent ought the teachings of Hasidism to be publicized and disseminated? Is the generation capable of receiving these revelations? Would it uplift them spiritually, or would it perhaps cause more harm than good? The Russian authorities' verdict was, in its inner essence, the supernal verdict; the earthly court's decision to free Rabbi Schneur Zalman merely echoed the decision of the heavenly court, expressing the supernal vindication of Hasidism. Thus,

Chabad Hasidim celebrate the 19th of *Kislev* as the New Year's Day for Hasidism to this day.

The 19th of *Kislev* also marks a new period in Rabbi Schneur Zalman's teachings and works. The period before his imprisonment is known as "before Petersburg," and the period following it as "after Petersburg." Before Petersburg, Rabbi Schneur Zalman did not convey his esoteric teachings openly and clearly, leaving much to allusion. After Petersburg, the trickling wellspring became the great river of Chabad Hasidism, because Rabbi Schneur Zalman then felt that there was no longer any divine impediment to the teaching of Hasidism, and the time had come to elaborate on it and disseminate it without inhibition.

Following further slanderous accusations, Rabbi Schneur Zalman was summoned to a second interrogation in Petersburg in 1800, and after a lengthy imprisonment, though under much easier conditions, he was finally released by command of the new czar, Alexander I. On his return from prison, he moved to the town of Liadi and thus came to be known as the Rav of Liadi.

After Rabbi Schneur Zalman had largely overcome the opposition to Hasidism from without, a bitter dispute broke out within the Hasidic community, mainly over the intellectual nature of the Chabad system. The leader of the dispute, which also involved personal elements, was Rabbi Abraham of Kalisk, a disciple of Rabbi Menachem Mendel of Vitebsk, who was later joined by Rabbi Baruch of Mezhibuzh, the Baal Shem Tov's grandson. This dispute caused Rabbi Schneur Zalman deep sorrow, but it did not affect his standing, instead actually highlighting the uniqueness of his personality and his philosophy.

When Napoleon invaded Russia in 1812, Rabbi Schneur Zalman was among the fiercest opponents of the French conquest. He feared that French rule would grant emancipation to the Jews and accelerate assimilation; he therefore supported Russia with all his power. As the French army advanced, he was forced to flee behind the Russian army to the interior of the country. He fell ill on the journey and on *Tevet* 24, 5583 (1812), died in the remote village of Pyern; he was buried in the nearby town of Haditz.

Rabbi Schneur Zalman was among the greatest Jewish personalities of his time: great in Torah, both in its exoteric or "revealed" aspect (that is, Talmud and halakhah) and in its esoteric dimension. He was learned in secular knowledge, a virtuoso of the Hebrew language, a master writer and editor, a born leader and superb administrator—in addition to being a charismatic leader, an ecstatic mystic, and a composer of music. In each of his creative fields, he wrote books of permanent value that have become the basis of the Chabad Hasidism for all generations.

THE *TANYA*

The *Tanya* is not only one of the fundamental works of Hasidism, it is also one of the greatest books of moral teaching (*mussar*) of all time. Although the author modestly describes himself as a "compiler," this is a most original work, both in its basic premise as well as in the many ideas and insights it expresses parenthetically. And though the author repeatedly notes that the book is intended for a select audience, for "those who know me personally," it strives to solve the dilemmas with a most broad and comprehensive approach—an approach that is not specific to a particular person, time, or outlook.

Most moral works address themselves to personal problems and to the ways that a person can attain specific goals in specific areas. The advantage in such an individualized approach is that it deals with the specific questions that a person might ask himself; the answers supplied are likewise specific and definitive. On the other hand, the book is limited to the specific problems it raises and is thus of actual help only to specific individuals. Others might be impressed that the book is indeed a great and profound work, yet they will always feel that, as a book of moral teaching, it does not speak to them. It fails to answer their problems or to take into account their specific personalities and circumstances.

Tanya, by contrast, does not, in the main, address specific problems but delves into their root causes, seeking to distill the predicaments of humankind down to their most elementary maxims and to solve them in the most comprehensive way. The crux of the book is an in-depth summation of the workings of the inner soul and an analysis of good and evil in general and as fundamental forces at play in the soul and the primary sources of its dissonance. *Tanya* trains its students to see the many thousands of complexities, doubts, and drives within them as expressions of a single basic problem: the struggle between the good and evil in the human soul.

Although the book is written with great restraint, it energetically and dramatically depicts human life as an immense battle between good and evil that one endures throughout one's lifetime, a battle between the forces that drag the soul down and the forces that strive heavenward. Each chapter develops from the previous one, and all are interconnected, progressively leading their student to recognize the inner soul, its intrinsic duality, the array of conflicting forces within it and their respective strengths and weaknesses, and the battle's nature and vicissitudes.

In describing this battle, the author offers a completely new approach. The battle in a person's soul is actually not between good and evil (expressions he rarely uses, except when he needs to clarify a point by using the ordinary semantics of these terms) but between the two elements within the human soul: the Godly soul and the animal soul. The *Godly soul* is that part of the soul that aspires to the divine, in all its connotations. The *animal soul* is the part that relates to one's physical identity and one's involvement in the material world. These are not merely alternative terms for "good" and "evil" or for "body" and "soul"; they draw a far subtler distinction. The animal soul is not negative in essence, nor is it necessarily hedonistic. The animal soul can become refined and wise and achieve much in the life of the spirit yet remain animal. The animal soul is the soul of a human being as a biological creature, as a specific level of development in the zoological system. Even in this sense, humans are superior to other creatures in our ability to attain great heights in the realms of thought and feeling; still, we remain an animal among animals. It is in the Godly soul, in its aspiration to the divine, that man's uniqueness lies. The Godly soul yearns to cleave to and be absorbed by the divine, and only by this aspiration, by the constant struggle of the Godly soul to transcend its needs and its very self in order to attain identification with the divine light, does one achieve a true identity as a human being.

It is from this definition of the inner struggle of the soul that the appropriate solution emerges. This is not a war to the death, in which a person tries to destroy and obliterate a part of the self. As the animal soul is not fundamentally evil, the battle against it is essentially a battle of education. A person's task is to train the animal soul, to elevate it to a higher level of awareness and understanding, until it is unified, both in its objectives and in its aspirations, with the Godly soul. Thus, one achieves full harmony of body and soul, of earthliness and transcendence.

The perpetual battle in the human soul, which stems from its dual nature, also has moral and pragmatic implications. The teachers of *mussar* have always recognized the almost vital need for a person to achieve total inner identification with his deeds and actions. The assumption is that a purely mechanical act has a low moral and spiritual value. However, few individuals are capable of truly attaining such an inner identification. This leaves to most the choice of either giving up the spiritual struggle or descending to hypocrisy and self-delusion. The *Tanya,* by delving into the nature of the relationship between a person's two souls, finds an approach that is very different, indeed revolutionary. It readily acknowledges that not everyone is able to achieve complete victory for the Godly soul over the animal, but not everyone is required to do so. A state of war within the human soul, says the *Tanya,* is not a negative thing. A person might achieve perfection with respect not only to deeds but also to speech and even to inner thoughts—without achieving complete perfection within the soul. The *Tanya* requires a person to achieve perfection in the "garments" of the soul (thought, speech, and action) but not in the soul's essence.

Thus, the *Tanya* removes the veil of hypocrisy that has cloaked many a soul as a result of the demand to elevate us beyond our capacity. The recognition of the intrinsic duality of the soul enables a person to understand that his moral imperfection need in no way impede his aspiration and ability to fulfill his divinely ordained role. Once we know that our undesirable lusts and thoughts emanate from a fundamental source within ourselves that might not be within our power and duty to uproot, their presence within us is not tragic, nor will it necessarily bring about an unsolvable inner crisis. On the contrary, a person can achieve perfection precisely through this knowledge. One can be righteous in all particulars of one's life and at the same time be engaged in the constant struggle within one's soul. *Tanya* assigns to this spiritual persona a new moral status—that of the *beinoni,* the "intermediate." The intermediate is the hero of this book: the book addresses him, discusses him, and carries his name (one of the titles the author gave *Tanya* is the Book of *Beinonim*). The intermediate is the "one who serves God," whose entire life is a perpetual battle for the sake of the divine, whose inner struggle is a hymn of praise to his Creator. The concept of the *beinoni* as an ideal to which every person should aspire opens the door to everyone, regardless of spiritual status, to be counted among those who aspire for true greatness—those who serve God in truth.

But these points, despite their centrality to the work, do not summarize the *Tanya.* This is a book in which the incidental ideas, as well as the supporting chapters surrounding the central theme, are no less important than the main topics. The more one reads this book, the more one discovers illuminating thoughts and ideas, a comprehensive outlook on life, insight into the structure of Jewish history, and moral guidance on countless problems. This short book encapsulates an entire philosophy and guide to life. As Rabbi Zusha from Anipoli expressed it: "How did he put such a great and awesome God into such a small book?"

If it is at all possible to define a work such as the *Tanya*, then its best description lies in the words of the previous Lubavitcher Rebbe, who said: "*Tanya* is the 'Written Torah' of Chassidim, and studying it is like studying *Chumash:* everyone studies it, from the greatest scholars to the most simple of folk; each, according to his level, understands what he understands, and no one understands it at all."

A NOTE TO THE READER

The *Tanya* is indeed a short book, in terms of the number of words, but considering its wealth of expressions and numerous innovative ideas, it is a very long book. Together with the English translation and the commentaries, the *Tanya* is grand in its simplicity, multitude of terms, and explanations, yet it is also like a gigantic mountain soaring in the distance that cannot be encompassed in a single glance. This was not the author's original intent. Just as we will state about the *beinoni,* we may state about the Book of the *Beinonim:* its goal is not only to extract the truth but to extract that truth that the reader may transfer, absorb, and implement. Therefore, to preserve the spirit of the writing, to present clear methodology and understanding, and to allow the reader to grasp the ideas both intellectually and consciously, this volume provides the reader with only part of the manuscript, a single concise unit composed of the introduction and the first twelve chapters of the *Tanya*. In this unit, Rabbi Schneur Zalman, the *Alter Rebbe,* reveals the *beinoni,* augurs his existence and essence and exposes him, chapter after chapter, until in the twelfth chapter the *beinoni* is fully displayed and revealed.

The subsequent chapters of the *Tanya* delve deeply into the development and implementation of the ideas and are essential for the reader interested in reaching the later stage of the book. However, as the author mentions in the beginning of the *Tanya,* its path is a "long-short way." Long, indeed, but short in relation to what one may accomplish now. What the reader may accomplish now is to study and teach the ideas that these initial chapters present.

And if God so wills it, may He grant us the merit of continuing our studies until such time as the long and lofty path in the heavens will be also the earth upon which we are privileged to walk.

The *Tanya*

The Title Page

Book of
Collected Sayings
Part One
entitled
The Book of *Beinonim*
Gleaned from books and sages, exalted and holy, whose souls are in Eden;
based on the verse, "For it is exceedingly near to you, in your mouth and
in your heart, to do it"—to explain clearly how it is exceedingly near,
in a long and short way, with the help of God, blessed be He.

COMMENTARY

Study of the *Tanya* customarily begins with the title page, both
because the author himself wrote it and because it largely defines the
essence of the work.

Book of Collected Sayings, Part One

The *Tanya* has been traditionally published as a work consisting of
five parts. The author called the first part *Likkutei Amarim* (Collected

Sayings) and *Sefer Shel Beinonim* (Book of the Intermediates) as he indicated on the title page of the book, but even in his lifetime it came to be called *Tanya*, after its opening word in Hebrew ("It has been taught"). This part, the first to be published, is the most central and important part of the book, by whose name the entire work is known, and it is also the most complete, containing fifty-three chapters. Hasidim consider the *Tanya* to be the "Written Torah" of Hasidism, its fifty-three chapters plus the author's preface corresponding to the fifty-four *sidrot* ("weekly portions") of the Torah.

The second part is *Sha'ar haYichud v'haEmunah* (The Gate of Unity and Faith) also called *Chinukh Katan* (A Minor's Education). The author intended this to be equal in extent to the first part, about fifty-three chapters, but for various reasons never completed it. This section deals mainly with the concept of "Particular Divine Providence" (*hashgachah p'ratit*): the premise that God permeates the entirety of existence and that the exclusion of something—anything—from the providence of God is contrary to the most basic truth of the divine reality. This section consists of twelve chapters.

The third part, *Iggeret haTeshuvah* (A Letter on Repentance), deals with the subject of repentance. The author never completed Part Three, which, like Part Two, contains twelve chapters.

The fourth part, *Iggeret haKodesh* (The Holy Letter), is a collection of thirty-two letters written by the author and edited and published posthumously by his sons. Most are open letters to all of the *Alter Rebbe*'s disciples; only a few are addressed to specific individuals. Most of these letters are not reproduced in full; we are given only those parts that are pertinent to Hasidic thought and life.

The fifth part, *Kuntras Acharon* (Concluding Pamphlet), contains notes and an addendum to subjects mentioned in the first four parts that were not included there so as to avoid disrupting the flow. Here they are clarified comprehensively and in detail.

Although the five parts differ in structure and content, they have a common theme: the inner battle of man with his self and soul. The subjects with which the book deals, from the palpable predicaments of the human soul to the sublime conception of the process of creation and the spiritual infrastructure of reality, are never abstract philosophizing. This book does not deal with others' problems; there is nothing in it about which one could say: "This is not for me; this does not pertain to my path in life." Throughout the work, the subject is—

directly or by inference—the survival of the Jewish soul in its inner struggles and its possible victory.

entitled, The Book of *Beinonim*

Beinonim means "intermediates." This title, which the author gave to the book, indeed expresses its uniqueness: the introduction of the concept of the intermediate is doubtless the essential innovation of the *Tanya*. Although not a new term, it appears here in a new connotation and spells a fundamental departure from the basic premises of most systems of the moral teaching (*mussar*). The aim of the *mussar* books, and the ideal to which they strive to elevate the human being, is the ideal of the *tzaddik*, "the perfectly righteous individual"; they assume that it is attainable. In contrast, *Tanya* was written for intermediates, for those who have not attained the station of *tzaddik*, though they are not transgressors (*resha'im*, "wicked persons"). The ideal of the *tzaddik* is, in a certain respect, withdrawn as a mandatory attainment for everyone—not everyone can achieve this, and not everyone is expected to. Instead, the *beinoni* is presented as the ideal that everyone can and must attain.

The persona of the *beinoni* acquires a new definition. The intermediate person is not merely the median, the halfway point between utter evil and utter goodness; neither a compromise nor a composite, the *beinoni* is in a class alone. The *mussar* books that discussed this rank saw it as a temporary stage that one must surpass, as a spiritual dissonance to be stabilized and resolved. But the *Tanya* sees the state of *beinoni* as a legitimate, ongoing one, describing a person whose inner essence and spiritual path is the subject of a lifelong struggle—a struggle that might never reach decisive resolution. It describes this person as an elevated individual—as one who, in a certain sense, is comparable to the perfect *tzaddik*—who at the same time is engaged in an ongoing struggle and endures the perpetual pain of imperfection. The *beinoni* is not a *tzaddik*, for he is unable to maintain an immutable state of holiness and control over his passions; nevertheless, the *beinoni* attains a state of *d'veikut*, "attachment to God." When in a state of *d'veikut*, this is his truth of truth; when he falls from *d'veikut*, this too is his truth of truths.

Unlike the *tzaddik*, who is in a state of constant stability, the *beinoni's* state is not inherently stable. We can say that the *Tanya's* purpose is to show the *beinoni* how to maintain balance, how to remain in a state where, although the temptation to do wrong exists, one does not sin—neither in deed, word, nor thought.

The concept of the *beinoni* is the focal point of the book (and of the entire philosophical system that is predicated upon the *Tanya*), the cornerstone from which it springs and to which it returns. This does not make it an easy book to understand, but as a book of moral teaching, it has a totally different outlook, one that is easier to apply.

Gleaned from books and sages,[1] exalted and holy, whose souls are in Eden;

With the characteristic modesty of authors of Torah works, Rabbi Schneur Zalman does not say that he has written a book, rather that he has merely compiled one. Nonetheless, this book is manifestly not a compilation, with its originality and its minimal quotation of source-texts. Of course, everything the author writes has its source, but the sources are presented here in a new context—at times in a completely original one—to be understood as they have never been understood before. But the author's description of his book, both on the title page and in his preface, reflects not only his humility but also a core truth in his philosophy: that it is of the utmost importance to eliminate all "bumps" of personality—all that extends outward to make an impression but has no basis within.

Which "books and sages" is Rabbi Schneur Zalman referring to? A tradition among Hasidim is that the books, apart from the basic sources (Bible, Talmud, *Zohar, Shulchan Aruch,* and the Kabbalistic works of Rabbi Isaac Luria, who is known as the Holy Ari), are the works of the Maharal, Rabbi Loewe of Prague, of whom the author is a seventh-generation descendant. Rabbi Schneur Zalman does not quote directly from the Maharal's books, but their influence is strong: Hasidism explains, gives form to, and applies nearly all of the Maharal's innovations, both his moral system and his unique approach to Torah exposition. Additional books are Rabbi Isaiah Horowitz's *Sh'nei Luchot haBrit* and Rabbi Elijah de Vidas's *Reshit Chokhmah.*

"The Sages" are a reference to Rabbi Schneur Zalman's teachers. Hasidim count three mentors. The first is the Maggid of Mezherich, who was Rabbi Schneur Zalman's primary teacher, and many of whose oral and written teachings are incorporated in *Tanya.* The second is the Maggid's son Rabbi Abraham, known as the angel, who was both teacher and colleague to the author. The Maggid instructed the two to teach each other: Rabbi Schneur Zalman, already a prodigious scholar in the exoteric parts of Torah (Talmud, halakhah, and so on) when he came to Mezherich, gave lessons in these to Rabbi Abraham, who in turn tutored him in the esoteric teaching of Kabbalah and Hasidism. Rabbi Schneur Zalman would later say that he received the teachings of Hasidism from the Maggid and his son, who taught him the inner content of these teachings as a father would teach his son. He enjoyed a profound and intimate friendship with Rabbi Abraham, one of mutual love and mutual learning—a friendship that gave him a sense of almost familial relationship with the Maggid. The flow of wisdom the author received from the Maggid was complemented by Rabbi Abraham's interpretations of and elaborations upon his father's teachings.

The author's third teacher was Rabbi Menachem Mendel of Vitebsk, who in a sense succeeded the Maggid as leader of the Hasidic movement.[2] When Rabbi Menachem Mendel emigrated to the land of Israel, he appointed the author to take his place in the region of White Russia. This region was near Lithuania, the stronghold of the *mitnagdim* ("opponents," that is, opponents of Hasidism). Thus, the greatest opposition to Hasidism fell mainly on the Hasidic leaders living in Lithuania and White Russia. (Persecution by the *mitnagdim* forced Rabbi Levi Yitzchak of Berdichov, then rabbi of Pinsk, to flee the city. Rabbi Menachem Mendel of Vitebsk and Rabbi Abraham of Kalisk, both great scholars, emigrated to the land of Israel partly because they could not hold out against the pressure of the opposition.) Therefore, the question of who would stand as the leader of the Hasidim in this region was extremely important. Even if he could not prevent the opposition, he had to be someone whose greatness in Torah even the opposition could not deny. (For this reason, prior to publishing the *Tanya,* the author wrote a short book on laws of Torah study and another on blessings and benedictions; he distributed both anonymously so that the rabbis who granted their "approbations" to them—and who would never have publicly endorsed a work by a Hasid—would not be able to retract their words. This is why the first editions of the *Tanya,* too, appeared anonymously (note also that the approbations to the *Tanya* do not mention the author's name).[3] Indeed, *Tanya* was largely designed to deal with the special difficulties encountered by Hasidim in those regions, by establishing Hasidism as a systematic and soundly based doctrine rather than the isolated and abbreviated sayings by which it had spread until that time.

Some also count Rabbi Israel Baal Shem Tov, founder of the Hasidic movement, among the sages to whom the author refers. Though the author did not study under the Baal Shem Tov, he considered him his spiritual grandfather (because he was the teacher of his teacher) and also saw him as one whose teachings he received as from the mouth of a sage and not as one learns from books.

based on the verse, "For it is exceedingly near to you, in your mouth and in your heart, to do it"

This verse (Deuteronomy 30:14) is the motto of the entire book. More than an epigraph, a pertinent quote to decorate the beginning of the book, it is the book's very heart, the central theme that runs as a thread through every chapter and every page. The verse expresses the *Tanya*'s fundamental optimism: the premise that the realization of Torah's program for life is possible to achieve, and not only possible but near at hand, not only the realization but also the closeness to the divine. Anyone can, "with his mouth and his heart," generate within himself the loftiest emotions and experiences, remaking his soul along a new path.

to explain clearly how it is exceedingly near,

The word of God and God Himself are very near, specifically to humankind. The *Tanya* will show that it is possible to attain great heights in self-elevation and attachment to God via the particular path of divine service described in this book.

in a long and short way

The author defines this path in three Hebrew words: *derekh arukkah u'ktzarah* ("a long and short way"). These three words are perhaps the most concise definition of the author's system. The phrase is borrowed from the well-known Talmudic story about Rabbi Joshua ben Hananiah, who said, "No one ever got the better of me, except for one woman, one boy, and one girl."[4] The boy was a child he once met at a crossroads and asked about the way to the city. The boy pointed to the two paths and said, "This is a long and short way, and this is the short and long way." Rabbi Joshua chose the "short and long" way and discovered that it was indeed the shorter route, but that at the end, he could not actually reach the city because orchards and gardens obstructed his path. He was forced to retrace his steps and choose the "long and short way." The "short and long" path seems, at first glance, to be a shortcut, but it is full of obstacles that make it all but impassable. The "long and short" way seems, at the outset, to be a more winding and difficult path, but ultimately it turns out to be a sure way to reach the destination.

The path in serving the Almighty that the author presents in this book is a "long and short" way. Theoretically, there are shorter ways—spiritual shortcuts—by which one might surmount certain gaps and cover tremendous distances. But these shortcuts are not reliable. Some are as dangerous as can be; others are purely theoretical and simply impassable in practice. Sometimes a specific shortcut appears practical, but many have tried it and failed due to unforeseen pitfalls; or a person might generate an inner flame of enthusiasm that goes out just as quickly as it flares, leaving him back where he started. The path that *Tanya* offers is a long way, one that does not promise an immediate feeling of spiritual elevation; it is not a path of jumping from level to level, of leaping from state to state, that might instantly transform a person from an ordinary individual to an elevated one. Rather, it is a path that involves hard work, learning, training, and very little pure emotion; it is a path of laboring with the *chokhmah, binah,* and *daat* of one's mind to build the edifices of awareness and feeling. This is a path that involves working from the bottom up and does not rely on inspiration from above. This way, systematic yet complex and complicated, is indeed the long way, but because its structure is well founded, it is ultimately the short way.

The author calls this the "long and short way," taking us full circle back to the quote at the beginning of his statement: "For it is exceedingly near to you." Although it is very near, the shorter way is the longer way.

The "long and short way" permeates the very style of the book. *Tanya* contains very few passages that fire the soul and create an instant feeling of exhilaration. The words appear simple and gray by design. There are no flashes of color that elicit a response: "Beautiful! Tremendous!" The student discovers the inner and outer beauty of *Tanya*'s words only when he delves deeply into them over and over again. The restrained style reveals the depth of content and feeling it hides only after great effort. Studying the book a second time reveals more than it did the first time, and the third time reveals even more.

The power and beauty of the book are submerged in a style of writing that is reminiscent of that of Maimonides: very simple writing, little use of technical terms (except where the content demands it), yet behind the words is lucid depth and powerful, oscillating, spiritual emotion. The book contains no overflowing expressions of elation, not because they are not there but because the author hides them within the words and allows only the barest hint to seep out. To a large extent, the book is built on the attitude of Hillel when he followed his summary of the Torah with the remark "and the rest is exposition— go and study it!"[5] The reader is called on to apply the words within himself and allow them to penetrate his soul; when they have become an integral component of his psyche, they will begin to acquire increased depth and meaning each time he ponders them.

The author often said that he expended considerable toil in formulating not only the content of *Tanya* but also the finer points of its precise wording. There are stories of how long he sat contemplating each letter, considering carefully whether to add or omit the word *and* (which in Hebrew is a single letter and is often optional) or even whether or not to insert a comma or period. This excessive care indeed shows itself in the form of loaded or awkward language, but it also obliges the student to delve deeply, for one can appreciate the ultimate meaning and significance of the *Tanya*'s words only by studying its choices of synonym and phrasing and by contemplating what is not said no less than what is. This style of writing is one of classical, well-refined beauty—beauty that one must study to appreciate.

with the help of God, blessed be He.

This is usually understood as referring to the author's earlier words, "to explain clearly," that is, the author will explain these concepts with the help of God. A deeper significance to these concluding words is that they refer to the immediately preceding ones, namely, that the "long and short way" is traversed with the help of God. The way is long: the requirements are clear and precise, and one must work diligently, step after step. Nevertheless, from time to time one does resort to God's help. This path through life is not marked exclusively by the toil and struggle of solitary labor but also contains flashes of encouragement and assistance from above.

The Approbations

APPROBATION

By the famous rabbi and [Hasid], Godly man, of saintly renown, our teacher RABBI MESHULLAM ZUSIL of ANIPOLI:[1]

I have seen the writings of this rabbi and *gaon,* Godly man, saintly and pure, lucid speculum; and well he did; God in His wonderful kindness having put into his pure heart to accomplish all this in order to show the Godly people His holy ways.

It was [the author's] intention not to publish these writings in print, since it is not his custom. However, because these pamphlets (*kuntresim*) have spread in the midst of all Israel in numerous copies by sundry copyists, and, as a result of the many transcriptions, the copyists' errors have multiplied exceedingly, he was impelled to bring these pamphlets to the printing press.

And God has aroused the spirit of the [two] partners, the outstanding and distinguished scholar R. SHOLOM SHACHNE,[2] the son of R. NOAH, and the outstanding and distinguished scholar R. MORDECHAI, the son of R. SHMUEL HALEVI, to bring these pamphlets to the printing house in Slavita. So I said of this good deed, More power to you. However, they were apprehensive of

11

the growing number of printing establishments which are wont to cause damage and ruin to the accredited ones. In view of this, we have resolved to give this approbation so that no man should dare lift his hand and foot to cause any damage, heaven forfend, to the said printers by encroaching upon their exclusive right in any manner. It is to restrain any person from reprinting this book without the knowledge of the said printers for a period of five full years from the date below. He who will heed these my words will be blessed with good. These are the words of one who demands this for the glory of the Torah, this day, the third [of the week], twice blessed with "it is good,"[3] of the weekly portion *Tavo,* in the year 556.[4]
—The insignificant MESHULLAM ZUSIL of Anipoli

APPROBATION

By the famous rabbi and [Hasid], Godly man of saintly renown, our teacher Rabbi Yehuda Leib haCohen:[5]

The wisdom of the man illumines the face of the earth[6]—on seeing the work of the saintly hands of the author, rabbi and *gaon,* Godly man, saintly and pure, pious and humble, whose hidden [powers] had been revealed long ago, when he dwelt in the council of the wise with *our lord, master, and teacher,* the *world gaon,*[7] and drew water from *the well of living waters.* Now, *Israel*[8] shall rejoice as his saintly words are revealed in this compiled work which is about to go to press, to teach the people of God the ways of holiness, as anyone can see in the inwardness of [the author's] words.

That which is common knowledge requires no proof. Only because of the apprehension of a wrong, lest a loss be caused to the printers, I come to confer sanction and prohibition, that no man lift up his hand or foot to reprint this work for a period of five years from below date. Whoever will heed these my words will be blessed with good.

These are the words of one who speaks for the glory of the Torah, this third day of the weekly portion *Tavo,* 556.[9]
—YEHUDA LEIB HACOHEN

APPROBATION

By the rabbis, long may they live, the sons of the gaon the author, of blessed memory, whose soul is in Eden:

Whereas it has been agreed by us to give authorization and prerogative to bring to the printing press, for a remembrance unto the children of Israel, the written words of uprightness and truth, the words of the Living

God, authored by our lord, father, teacher, and master, of blessed memory, recorded personally in his saintly expression, whose words are all burning coals to set the hearts aflame to bring them closer to their Father in heaven; they are entitled *Iggeret haKodesh* (Holy Epistle), being mostly epistles sent by his holy eminence, to teach the people of God the way by which to walk and the deed which they should do;

And inasmuch as he has made references, in many places, to the book *Likkutei Amarim,* since the words of the Torah are scanty in one place and ample in another,[10] especially also as he introduced new material in the *Kuntres Acharon* on certain chapters which he wrote when he composed the book *Likkutei Amarim,* profound discussions on passages in the *Zohar, Etz Chayyim,* and *Peri Etz Chayyim,* which [passages] appear contradictory to one another, but he, with his inspired perception, has reconciled them, each statement in its own manner, as he has written in the *Likkutei Amarim,* we have seen fit and proper to join them with the *Sefer Likkutei Amarim* and *Iggeret haTeshuvah*[11] of his saintly eminence, our lord father, teacher and master of blessed memory;

[Therefore], we come to place a great fence and the rabbinical injunction of *NChSh*[12] ("excommunication") for which there is no remedy, that no man lift his hand to reprint them in their present form, or in part, for a period of five years from the date below.[13]

However, this should be made known: to our misfortune, the manuscripts written by his personal saintly hand which were composed with great punctiliousness, without a superfluous or deficient letter, have become extinct; only this little has remained from the abundance, and it has been carefully collected one by one from the copies spread among the disciples. Should, therefore, an error be discovered—"Who can be wise to errors?"[14]— the evident error will be identified as a scribe's error, but the meaning will be clear.

Declared by DOV BER, the son of my lord father, teacher and master, *gaon* and [Hasid], saint of Israel, our teacher and master SCHNEUR ZALMAN, of blessed memory, his soul rests in the hidden treasures of heaven.

Also declared by CHAIM ABRAHAM, the son of my lord father, teacher and master, *gaon* and [Hasid], saint of Israel, our teacher and master SCHNEUR ZALMAN, of blessed memory, his soul rests in the hidden treasures of heaven.

And also declared by MOSHE, the son of my lord father, teacher and master, *gaon* and [Hasid], saint of Israel, our teacher and master SCHNEUR ZALMAN, of blessed memory, his soul rests in the hidden treasures of heaven.

COMMENTARY

A *haskamah*, or "approbation," is a letter of endorsement and recommendation by a leading Torah sage that is printed in the beginning of a book. By common practice, Torah works, especially those by unknown authors, require such approbations as affirmation that their content and spirit are faithful to Torah and Jewish tradition. The approbations for *Tanya*, which are traditionally included in the study of the book, were written by two of the author's colleagues, disciples of the Maggid of Mezherich. Interestingly, the author turned specifically to them for endorsements to publish his book, although they were not among the most famous of the Maggid's disciples.

The approbations do not mention the name of *Tanya*'s author, because the book initially appeared anonymously, for two reasons: the author's humility and because the author feared that the dispute between Hasidim and their opponents might prevent people from studying the book. However, if his name was not mentioned, readers would judge the book by its contents. Indeed, readers held the book in great esteem from its very first editions, when many had no knowledge of who wrote it. Only beginning with the eighth edition (Shklov, 1814), two years after the author's death, was his name mentioned on the title page. It was in this edition that the "Approbation by the Author's Sons" first appeared.

Compiler's Preface

*B*eing a letter sent to the communities of our faithful (*may the Almighty guard them*).

To you, worthy people, do I call. Listen to me, you who pursue righteousness, who seek the Lord, and may God hearken to you, both great and small, all our faithful in our land and those adjacent to it. May each in his place achieve peace and eternal life, for ever and ever. Amen, may this be His will.

It is a common saying among our faithful that hearing words of *mussar* is not the same as seeing—reading—them in books. For the reader reads after his own manner and mind, and according to his mental reach and grasp at that particular time. And if his mind and conceptions are confused and wander about in darkness regarding the service of God, he finds difficulty in seeing the light "that it is good" that is concealed in books, even though the light is sweet to the eyes and a balm to the soul.

Apart from this, books on piety that are built upon human understanding certainly are not equally suited for all people, for not all intellects and minds are alike, and the intellect of one man is not affected and excited by what affects [and excites] the intellect of another. As our Sages, of blessed memory, have said with reference to the blessing of "Wise One in Secrets" upon [beholding] six hundred thousand Jews, "Because their minds differ from each other . . . "; and as Nacmanides explains there in his *Milchamot,* elaborating on the commentary of the *Sifri* regarding Joshua of whom it is said "a man in whom there is spirit"—"A man who can attune himself to the spirit of each and every one . . ."

But [this is the case] even with books on piety whose foundation is in the peaks of holiness, the Midrashim of our Sages, of blessed memory, through whom the spirit of God speaks and His word is on their tongue. [For although] the Torah and the Holy One, blessed be He, are one, and all the six hundred thousand general [souls] of Israel with their individual off-shoots, and the offshoots of their offshoots, down to the "spark" in the most worthless and least estimable members of our people, the children of Israel, are thus bound up with the Torah, and the Torah binds them to the Holy One, blessed be He, as is known from the holy *Zohar*—this pertains only in a general way to the community of Israel as a whole. [As for the individual,] although the Torah was given to be interpreted *klal u'frat* ("general and specific") down to the most particular detail, to [apply to] each individual soul of Israel, which is rooted in it, nevertheless, not every person is privileged to recognize his individual place in the Torah.

Even in the case of the laws governing the prohibited and permitted, which are "revealed to us and to our children," we find and witness differences of opinion among *tanna'im* and *amora'im* from one extreme to the other. Indeed, "these as well as these are the words of the living God (*Elokim chayyim*)"—the plural being a reference to the source of life for the souls of Israel, which are generally divided into three categories, right, left, and center, namely *chessed, gevurah,* etc.; those souls rooted in the attribute of *chessed* are likewise inclined in their behavior toward benevolence, to be lenient, and so on, as is known. All the more so in the case of "the hidden matters [belonging] to the Lord our God," these being the awe and love that are in the mind and heart of "each and every one according to his measure," [that is,] according to his heart's estimation, as explained in the holy *Zohar* on the verse, "Her husband is known in the gates (*she'arim*). . . ."

I speak, however, of those who know me well, namely, each and every one of our faithful who lives in our country and in the lands adjacent to it, with whom words of affection have been frequently exchanged, and who have revealed to me all the secrets of their heart and mind in the service of God which is dependent on the heart. To them does my word percolate, and my tongue be a scribe's pen in these pamphlets that are entitled

Likkutei Amarim (Collected Sayings), which have been gleaned from books and Sages, exalted and holy, whose souls are in Eden; [sayings] that are widely known amongst us, and some of which are hinted to the wise in the holy letters from our teachers in the Holy Land, may it be built and established speedily in our days, Amen, and some of which I have heard from their saintly mouths when they were here with us. All of them are responses to the many questions which all our faithful in our country have constantly asked, seeking advice, each according to his quality, so as to receive spiritual advice in the service of God. For time no longer permits replying to each and every one individually and in detail on his particular problem; also, forgetfulness is common. I have therefore recorded all the replies to all the questions, to be preserved as a signpost and to serve as a visual reminder for each and every person, so that he will no longer press for admission to confer in private (*yechidut*) with me. For in these [writings], he will find peace for his soul and true counsel on every matter that he finds difficult in the service of God. His heart will thus be firmly secured in God, who completes for us.

As for him whose mind falls short in the understanding of the counsel given in these pamphlets, let him discuss the matter with the eminent ones of his town, and they will elucidate it for him. And I beg of them not to lay their hand on their mouth, to conduct themselves with false meekness and humility, God forbid. It is known what bitter punishment is his who "withholds grain," and the greatness of the reward [in the opposite case], from the saying of our Sages on the verse, "God illuminates the eyes of them both," for God will cause His face to shine upon them, with the light of the countenance of the Living King. May the Giver of Life to the Living merit us to live to see the days when "No longer shall one man instruct the other . . . for all shall know Me . . . ," "For the world shall be full of the knowledge of God . . . ," Amen, may this be His will.

Since the said pamphlets have been disseminated among all our faithful, as mentioned above, by means of numerous transcriptions by the hands of various and sundry scribes, the multitude of transcriptions brought about an exceedingly great number of copyists' errors. Therefore, the spirit of the noble men, named on another page, has generously moved them to a personal and financial effort, to have the said pamphlets published, cleared of chaff and errors and thoroughly proofed. I congratulate them on this worthy deed.

And inasmuch as there is an explicit verse, "Cursed be he that encroaches upon his neighbor's domain"—and "cursed" includes both damnation and shunning, God forbid—therefore, "like Judah and scripture in addition", I come to invoke a strict prohibition on all publishers against printing the said pamphlets, either themselves or through their agency, without the authority of the above-named, for a period of five years from the day that this printing is completed. And it will be well with those who conform, and they will be blessed with good.

These are the words of the compiler of the said *Likkutei Amarim*.

COMMENTARY

Compiler's Preface, being a letter sent to the communities of our faithful, may the Almighty guard them.

The preface consists of two parts. The first part (up to the words "her husband is known in the gates") explains why it is not sufficient to learn moral teaching from written books, and why Hasidim therefore travel to their rebbe. The second part (commencing "But to those who know me") explains why, despite this, the author has written this book.

This "letter," like many of the author's letters, is directed both externally and internally within the Hasidic community, for the *Tanya* had aroused a certain degree of disapproval among his Hasidic colleagues as well. Objections were raised not only about the method, which many considered too rational, but also about the very act of formulating the words and putting them in writing. The Hasidic movement is structured upon a direct and personal relationship between master and disciple, and many saw any attempt to put Hasidic teaching into writing as detrimental to this special relationship. There is something dead about the written word, and that makes it unfit for solving the real problems of the soul. Even preparing a lecture in advance is considered an act of petrifaction. Hasidim used to interpret the verse, "And you shall investigate well, and if it is true and the thing is correct, this abomination has been done in . . . Israel,"[1] as follows: even if the *drashah* ("lecture," a play on the word *v'darashta*, "And you shall investigate") is well delivered, even if there is truth in it, but it was prepared in advance (a play on the word *nachon*, "correct," which also means "prepared")—an abomination has been done in Israel!

It is told that the Baal Shem Tov once dreamed that he saw a demon walking with a book in his hand. He asked the demon, "What book are you holding?" The demon replied, "This is the book that you wrote." The next day, the Baal Shem Tov assembled his disciples and demanded of them: "Which of you has been putting my teachings into writings?" One of his disciples admitted that he had collected his teachings and written them down. The Baal Shem Tov asked him to show him the writings; he looked at them and said, "There is not one word here of what I said!" It was for fear of such that both the Baal Shem Tov and the Maggid of Mezherich (and likewise many Hasidic masters to the present day) refrained almost completely from writing. They felt that the written word is not the medium for conveying messages from soul to soul, that writing might be appropriate for other subjects but not for Hasidism.

This preface tells us that the decision to write a book did not come lightly to the author. In compiling the theory of Hasidic moral teaching as a structured philosophy, he is conscious of inherent limitations and dangers, and, as will become clear, he does this in a way that will address some of them.

Maimonides did something similar with his book *Mishneh Torah.* He wrote a book that is not constructed as thoughts on the weekly Torah reading portion or as a commentary on an earlier work, as virtually all Torah works were constructed, but a book that states directly and systematically what he wants to say. However, there is a great difference in the approach. Maimonides, in his introduction to *Mishneh Torah,* writes that now, "a person can first read the Written Torah and then read this work—and from it he will know all the Oral Torah, without the need to read any other book in between." The author of the *Tanya,* by contrast, is apologetic. He discusses the difficulties and problems in writing as he did and why he is nevertheless compelled to do so.

This preface is from "a letter sent to the communities of our faithful, may the Almighty guard them": a public letter, addressed to all Hasidim.

To you, worthy people, do I call. Listen to me, you who pursue righteousness, who seek the Lord, and may God hearken to you, both great and small, all the faithful in our land and those adjacent to it. May each in his place achieve peace and eternal life, for ever and ever. Amen, may this be His will.

As this commentary will explain, this book is intended for a specific community, and the author does not know if it will be as effective with people from a different background. So it is addressed to "our faithful in our land and those adjacent to it," namely, to the Hasidim of

White Russia and the neighboring areas, a community that at that time was defined only vaguely as Chabad Hasidim.

It is a common saying among our faithful that hearing words of *mussar* is not the same as seeing—reading—them in books.

The Talmudic adage "hearing should not be given greater importance than seeing"[2] was turned around in a Hasidic adage regarding words of *mussar* ("moral teachings") that come to arouse the heart to God's service. The Talmud expressed the truth that seeing something makes a greater impression than hearing about it. This Hasidic saying applied the difference between hearing things and seeing them in an opposite manner, by maintaining that hearing words of *mussar* face-to-face is much more effective than seeing them in a book. This is why it is not sufficient to read the writings of the *tzaddikim* ("righteous persons") and of the leaders of each generation and why a person must go to a contemporary sage to hear words that, in essence, have been said since the beginning of time.

For the reader reads after his own manner and mind, and according to his mental reach and grasp at that particular time.

No book, however great and holy, can adapt itself to each reader. It is the reader who decides what he reads, how he reads it, and what he understands.

The reader has two basic limitations. First, he reads a book "after his own manner and mind." A person does not read passively; he takes in the words according to his own understanding and interpretation of them, which depends on his spiritual inclinations, his mood, and his situation at the time of reading the book. A book is never the same to two different people; two people reading the same words will be influenced by them in different ways. Each reader has his own inclinations, attitudes, and perspective, in light of which he reads the words. It is impossible to disregard these ideological and emotional prejudices.

The second limitation is that the reader reads "according to his mental reach and grasp." Even if his mind is properly attuned to the matter, his ability to receive the message in the appropriate manner is limited by the extent of his intellectual ability.

And if his mind and conceptions are confused

Apart from limitations of intelligence, additional factors might limit the reader's ability to properly assimilate the words he sees in a book, such as "if his mind and conceptions are confused." These are two kinds of confusion. Confusion of the mind is a defect or kink in one's thought process, which can lead even an intelligent person to a distorted conclusion. A confusion of conceptions is distorted viewpoints and perspectives that mislead a person in his understanding of who and where he is, what he is searching for, and what paths he should follow.

and wander about in darkness regarding the service of God,

A person might be clever, intelligent, even brilliant in other matters yet be confused in mind and conceptions regarding the service of the Almighty. To know how to serve God is not merely a matter of learning and intelligence; it involves the most sublime heights and the most sensitive depths of the soul. These are matters in which a person can easily err and deceive himself; they are extremely involved and complex, so the slightest deviation in the soul or mind can leave a person in complete darkness. In these matters, one requires a great deal of effort and much help from above in order to reach the merest point of light.

he finds difficulty in seeing the light "that it is good" that is concealed in books, even though the light is sweet to the eyes and a balm to the soul.

Although *Tanya* is very sparing in its use of quotations, the author makes considerable use of expressions borrowed from the Torah and the words of the sages, thereby setting them in different contexts and alluding to additional layers of significance. Here, for instance, the expression "the light 'that it is good' that is concealed in books" is a reference to the Midrashic statement that God concealed the light of the six days of Creation[3]—light that the Torah refers to as "that it is good"[4]—for the righteous. The author also hints at the Baal Shem Tov's explanation of this: that God hid this light in the Torah.[5] This means that the sacred books of Torah contain a great light, the divine light of the creation, but this light is concealed therein in a way that is not always discernible. A person who studies books sees the words according to his knowledge and understanding; if he has an impediment, he will not see this light, even if the light itself is "sweet to the eyes."

Words written in books, even if they are holy themselves, will not arouse the reader if he distorts them; he will not find in them the sweetness and the spiritual balm that people seek in these books. The problem lies at the point of transfer from the book's abstract subject to the person's individual applications of it, not so much in understanding the theory (though this itself can also be a problem) but in how one relates to it and implements it in practice.

The student of books is necessarily bound by the limitations of his subjective experience. A person is blind to his own shortcomings and therefore unable to find the remedy to his ills. How can he find the way if he does not know how he went wrong? But when a person hears the teacher's words, the teacher can adjust and present them in the way that the particular listener needs to hear them at that time. Furthermore, the teacher can be asked for clarification. By contrast, if a reader does not understand, he is not always aware that he did not understand, so he does not notice when he errs and strays from the path. The reader is therefore liable to remain as he was, and the light from the book does not bring him the benefit and change that it might have.

Apart from this,

Apart from these limitations, there is a deeper, inherent problem. Even if the person is a proper "receptacle" to the light in the book, the very nature of this light contains a limitation that may prevent him from properly receiving it.

books on piety that are built upon human understanding

Many books of *mussar,* even great and important ones, are essentially philosophical works, based on human reason. These include major works such as *Chovat haLevavot,* which is built largely on the understanding and ideas of the author.

Such books

certainly are not equally suited for all people, for not all intellects and minds are alike, and the intellect of one man is not affected and excited by what affects [and excites][6] the intellect of another.

Theoretically, every intellectual concept is intelligible, and everything logical can be understood logically. But the difference between one human being and another is not in the concept itself but in the relationship between the person and the concept. As we said, concepts do not affect people in a uniform way. An idea may appeal to the mind and heart of one person and not say anything to another. What brings one person to the peak of excitement and exaltation of the soul may well leave another totally unmoved.

A book of moral teaching or philosophy may be a great work in itself, but the questions it asks and the problems it discusses are not necessarily the questions and problems of the reader of another period or culture; however true, however beautiful in themselves, the book's words might not touch him, might not arouse his soul, and so will not move him to change on their account. Maimonides' book *Mishneh Torah* contains a section that is an example of "a book of piety based on human understanding." In *Laws of the Fundamentals of Torah,* Maimonides gives us two chapters on astronomy and then says: "When a person considers these things and comes to know all creations . . . , his love of God increases, and his soul thirsts and his flesh yearns to love God."[7] Indeed, some people—including individuals such as Einstein or, in a different manner, Kant—who the more they contemplate "Your skies, the work of your fingers"[8] and the more they comprehend nature, the more their soul dissolves in yearning for God. But many others study astronomy, and their flesh does not yearn to love God. It seemed to Maimonides that these things cannot but arouse the heart to love of God, but many a reader does not feel this. This in no way undermines the holiness of these books; it is only that these books have an inherent limitation. A book based on human reason speaks to the author and to people who are attuned to him, to a lesser or greater degree. Others, who may be wise and righteous, are not moved at all—not due to any deficiency on their part but because human beings are different, also in the way in which words influence them.

As our Sages, of blessed memory, have said with reference to the blessing of "Wise One in Secrets" upon [beholding] six hundred thousand Jews, "Because their minds differ from each other . . . ";

The Talmud instructs that one who sees six hundred thousand Jews assembled in one place makes a special blessing:[9] "Blessed are You God

... the Wise One in Secrets." The meaning of this blessing, explains the Talmud, is praise of the Almighty, who created so many people whose "minds each differ from each other";[10] only He, the "Wise One in Secrets," knows the mind of each.

What this means is that among six hundred thousand individuals, no two are alike. Six hundred thousand individuals represent six hundred thousand mind-sets, approaches, and opinions, all different. So no book based on human reason can relate to the six hundred thousand souls of Israel. At most, it can relate to a limited number of individuals at a specific place and time.

and as Nachmanides explains there in his *Milchamot,* elaborating on the commentary of the *Sifri* regarding Joshua of whom it is said "a man in whom there is spirit"—"A man who can attune himself to the spirit of each and every one . . ."

In *Milchamot Hashem,*[11] Nachmanides illuminates another side to the blessing, "the wise one of secrets." The Talmud, following the discussion related earlier, cites a story concerning Rabbi Haninah, who recited this blessing upon seeing Rav Papa and Rav Huna, implying that the blessing may also be recited on seeing a great scholar and leader in whom all the diverse minds of Israel are included. Although Nachmanides does not accept this as law, he says it contains "a hint from the foundations of wisdom," for it reflects a truth expressed by the Torah. In Numbers 27:18, Moses asks God to appoint as a leader for Israel "a man with spirit in him." The *Sifri* explains this phrase to mean "A man who can attune himself to the spirit of each and every one," who can address himself to each one, grasping the spiritual character, the outlook, and the attitude of each individual. This is the true definition of a leader of Israel: the man who can relate to each of the six hundred thousand souls of Israel.

The author's point in all this is that people differ from one another, and saying something that will be acceptable to all is impossible. However, a speaker who directly addresses a live listener can adjust his delivery so as to overcome their initial incompatibility. The teacher of Torah and *mussar* must not only say things that are correct but also attune himself to his listener; otherwise, he has not fulfilled his task. He needs to know the listener's preconceptions and the flaws in his thought process so that the listener should find the words acceptable and understandable within the context of his own mind-set, opinions, and current state of mind and soul. Thus, it is immeasurably more difficult to speak to two people than to one. To speak to a crowd—and certainly to write a book—one needs to be, in this sense, a "leader for Israel," who can speak simultaneously in all languages, so everyone can relate to his teachings.

Solomon Maimon tells an interesting story (and the fact that he was a complete heretic makes this testimony of his doubly reliable). He visited the Maggid of Mezherich when the Maggid was receiving guests. The Maggid sat at the head of the table and addressed each guest by name and town, then asked each to quote any verse that happened to come to mind. Each one did so. The Maggid then thought a moment and delivered a discourse that bound all those verses together. The amazing thing was that each listener was certain that the Maggid was talking only about his own verse and referring only to his own life and problems. The important point of the story is not that the Maggid knew the names of all the guests but that he was able to speak in such a way that each guest heard what he was supposed to hear and particularly what the speaker had wanted him to hear. A leader of Israel can speak to fifty or even a thousand people and still speak to each one individually about what affects and concerns him personally.

This cannot be done in a book. No book can bridge the gaps of time, place, and culture. Even the wisest of authors writes from his own point of view and from his appreciation of the people he knows, who are close to him in time, place, and outlook. To them, he can perhaps communicate his ideas. Others will find themselves strangers to his words, unable to identify with them and truly relate to them.

The limitations of human diversity exist not only in books that are based on human knowledge and intelligence,

But [this is the case] even with books on piety whose foundation is in the peaks of holiness, the Midrashim of our Sages, of blessed memory, through whom "the spirit of God speaks in them and His word is on their tongue."

According to our belief, the words of the sages are more than words of profound wisdom; they are words generated, to a certain degree, by *ruach haKodesh* ("[revelation of the] divine spirit"):[12] a divine voice speaks from their throats and is implicit in their words. Furthermore, this is true not only concerning the words of the *Rishonim* ("the early post-Talmudic sages") but also those of the *Acharonim* ("latter sages").

The Baal Shem Tov is quoted as saying that all Torah works, up to and including the *Maharsha*,[13] were written with divine inspiration. Although one cannot delve into or derive rulings from each individual word, the gist of our sages' words, even in the later generations, is said with an inspiration of holiness. When a person devotes himself utterly to the Torah and his sole objective is for the sake of heaven, "the spirit of God speaks in them and His word is on their tongue."[14] Not every opinion or ruling expressed by a Torah sage comes to constitute halakhah and to be implemented in common practice, but "these and these are the words of the living God":[15] all valid Torah views are expressions of the word of God spoken to Moses at Sinai.

[For although] the Torah and the Holy One, blessed be He, are one, and all the six hundred thousand general [souls][16] of Israel with their individual offshoots, and the offshoots of their offshoots,

Six hundred thousand, the number of Israelites who left Egypt, is the overall number of Israel: the whole of Israel constitutes six hundred thousand "general souls." These general souls are the roots, the spiritual prototypes of Israel, and subdivide into offshoots and offshoots of offshoots of individual souls to eternity.[17] So although there are only six hundred thousand souls in Israel, we have the prophesy that "they shall be too numerous to be counted,"[18] for many souls are not "new souls" but individual fragments of the "general souls."

down to the "spark" in the most worthless and least estimable members of our people, the children of Israel,

The six hundred thousand souls include all Israel, from the leaders to the "spark" that provides life for the "least estimable"—the person who has neither wisdom, piety, nor good deeds.

are thus bound up with the Torah, and the Torah binds them to the Holy One, blessed be He,

All six hundred thousand souls and their offshoots are connected to their source in God through the Torah. Some are manifestly connected by the Torah; their every endeavor and thought are of Torah. But the emphasis here is that all, even the lowliest—even those who take no interest in Torah, who perhaps do not want Torah—are connected via the Torah. For all of them, the Torah is the means of connecting to the Almighty, and thus do all of them at least have a connection to the Torah.

as is known from the holy _Zohar_—

The _Zohar_ states: "Three levels are bound one with the other: God, the Torah, and Israel."[19] The Torah, being God's Torah, is connected to God and is of the divine essence (see Chapter 4). At the same time, the Torah is one with the essence of Israel and thus connected to (and binding upon) each individual Jew, whoever and wherever he may be. The Torah is thus the medium through which every Jewish soul is bound to God.

For this reason, words of Torah—be it the words of the Scriptures, those of the Oral Torah articulated by the sages, or the teachings arising from them—are not a personal expression of their authors but are words deriving from the divine source of Torah, to which all the souls of Israel relate and through which they are united. So a book deriving from Torah, "whose basis is in the peaks of holiness," should apply equally to every soul, because every Jewish soul is bound to the Torah, and no one, not even the lowliest of them, can say, "The Torah is not for me, the Torah does not speak to me."

this pertains only in a general way to the community of Israel as a whole.

Nevertheless, the connection between the Torah and Israel is a general connection: the entire Torah is connected to the whole of Israel. The 613 _mitzvot_ ("commandments") of the Torah are a general list of all the _mitzvot_ commanded to the totality of Israel; it is not a specific list for any specific individual, for there is no individual to whom all 613 apply. Some _mitzvot_ apply only to _kohanim_ ("priests"), and some apply only to one who is not a _kohen_ ("priest"); some _mitzvot_ apply only to men, and some only to women; some _mitzvot_ apply only to a king; and so on. The Torah speaks in general terms to the community as a whole, and all the people of Israel are connected to the entire Torah. But each Jew, as an individual, is connected only to part of it.

So we pray, "grant us our portion in the Torah,"[20] our own individual part in the Torah.

[As for the individual,] although the Torah was given to be interpreted *klal u'frat* ("general and specific"), down to the most particular detail, to [apply to] each individual soul of Israel, which is rooted in it,

Klal u'frat ("general and specific") is one of the thirteen rules of homiletic exposition of the Torah. Here, the author borrows this halakhic term to express the idea that the Torah has both general and specific applications. It is not just for people in general but also for specific individuals.

The soul of every Jew is connected to the Torah, which is his source of nurture and the very essence of his life. Thus, the Torah, in addition to its general application to the community of Israel, addresses him personally and individually, wherever he may be, according to his nature and his situation.

nevertheless, not every person is privileged to recognize his individual place in the Torah.

Despite the fact that the Torah speaks to each of us individually, addressing our every experience, every event to befall us, our every metamorphosis of being, not everyone is privileged to understand the Torah on such a personal level. Not everyone merits to recognize the way in which Torah speaks to his individual mind, heart, and personality.

A person needs to recognize what belongs to him, which aspects of Torah are relevant to his life, which part he is to implement at any given moment. But not everyone knows this. Some individuals (even great ones) were said to have been told to concern themselves only with a particular aspect of the Torah and no other. It is told that following the death of Rabbi Moses Cordovero, Rabbi Joseph Karo went to learn Kabbalah from Rabbi Isaac Luria (known as the Holy Ari) and kept falling asleep when the Ari was speaking, until the latter told him that this was not his portion in the Torah, that the Holy Ari's Kabbalah was not for him. The Ari also is said to have told Rabbi Moses Alshech that he should not involve himself in Kabbalah but in homiletic discourse, as this was his portion in the Torah, and Rabbi Alshech indeed wrote his book *Torat Mosheh* in this genre of Torah learning.

Some explain the prayer, "grant us our portion in the Torah," as a request not only to be granted a portion in Torah but also to be granted the knowledge of which portion is ours. Every Jew can and must study Torah, but if he concerns himself with aspects of Torah that are not truly his, then, although he has certainly fulfilled the commandment to study Torah, he fails to realize the ultimate potential of his soul in regard to Torah study.

Even in the case of the laws governing things prohibited and permitted, which are "revealed to us and to our children,"[21] we find and witness differences of opinion among *tanna'im* and *amora'im* from one extreme to the other.[22]

Even regarding the concrete laws of the Torah, which can be defined, discussed, and debated much more definitively than the spiritual dilemmas of the soul, we find disputes between Talmudic sages whose views are diametrically opposed. Regardless of whether these disputes concern general principles or specific laws, fundamental matters of belief or legal details, two people contemplating the same Torah passage can disagree even on matters that belong to the exoteric or revealed part of Torah and disagree in ways that result in diametrically opposed conclusions. For example, in the case of "a daughter's rival wife,"[23] the sages of the School of Shammai rule that marrying a certain woman is a *mitzvah* and obligation, whereas the House of Hillel interprets the law to say that doing so is strictly forbidden.

Indeed, "these as well as these are the words of the living God (*Elokim Chayyim*)"—the plural being a reference to the source of life for the souls of Israel, which are generally divided into three categories, right, left, and center, namely *chessed, gevurah,* etc.;

This regards the differing rulings by the Schools of Shammai and Hillel that the Talmud states: "These and these are both the words of the living God."[24] The author renders the expression *Elokim Chayyim* ("living God") as "vitalizing God," so that it describes God not only as Possessor of Life but as Granter of Life. This is why the word *chayyim* is in the plural,[25] because the life God bestows through the Torah is not uniform; rather, each soul receives it in a different manner, as befits its source and basic nature.

On a very general level, the souls of Israel and their variant "categories" in Torah are divided into three "columns." Kabbalistic teaching describes the ten divine attributes (*sefirot*) as being configured in three vertical "lines" or columns: *chokhmah, chessed,* and *netzach* are in the right column; *binah, gevurah,* and *hod* are in the left; and *daat, tiferet, yesod,* and *malkhut* are in the center. The attributes in each column have a common character: *chessed,* the attribute of "closeness and attraction," being the pervading nature of the right column; *gevurah,* "severity and rejection," of the left; and *tiferet,* "harmony," which is the synthesis of *chessed* and *gevurah,* of the center.

those souls rooted in the attribute of *chessed* are likewise inclined in their behavior toward benevolence, to be lenient, and so on, as is known.

In the most simple sense, a sage who rules to forbid something under Torah law—for example, if he rules that an ox is forbidden for consumption—is being harsh, causing a fellow Jew financial loss or other hardship. Such a tendency would therefore be associated with a soul that derives from the column of *gevurah,* the attribute of law, retraction, and restriction.

But the concept of prohibition also has a much broader scope and significance. As the author discusses in Chapter 7 of *Tanya,* the halakhic term for "permissible" is *mutar,* which literally means "unbound" or "released," whereas the term for "forbidden," *assur,* means "bound." In other words, when a halakhic authority permits something, he in effect releases it from the sphere of impurity and un-Godliness, allowing it the potential to be elevated through its use toward a holy end. In contrast, when a halakhic authority forbids something, he binds and imprisons it in the sphere of impurity, in effect condemning it to spiritual death. The story is told about a certain rabbi who once ruled that a slaughtered ox whose *kashrut* (kosher status) was in question is permissible, contrary to a ruling by the *Siftei Cohen.*[26] When asked how he dared to rule contrary to the view of one of the greatest halakhic authorities, the rabbi replied: "When I reach the World of Truth, and I shall stand trial over the ruling I gave, I prefer to defend myself against the *Siftei Cohen* than against the ox." The critical aspect of the halakhic ruling is not the butcher or the purchaser of the meat but the piece of meat (or other item whose permissibility is in question) itself. Is it to be forbidden and condemned to eternal disgrace, or is it to be permitted, released from fetters of *kelipah* ("husk" or the negative elements of creation; see Chapter 1) and included in the sphere of holiness? Here, the author states that it is a soul's nature and root that leads a Torah scholar to tend in general toward leniency or strictness. If his soul is rooted in *gevurah*—the attribute of law, restriction, and limitation—he tends to be strict. If it is rooted in *chessed*—kindness and expansiveness—he tends to be lenient. In actuality, no soul is purely of *chessed* or purely of *gevurah* but of a particular composite of the two attributes such as *chessed she-b'gevurah* (*chessed* of *gevurah*), or *gevurah sheb'chessed* (*gevurah* of *chessed*). Thus, despite the fact that the School of Shammai usually puts forth the stricter view and the School of Hillel is usually lenient, the School of Shammai is in some cases more lenient and the School of Hillel stricter. Indeed, we often find halakhic authorities known for their stringency who often hand down lenient rulings where others are stricter.

The essential point is that even in matters with a rational consideration, the nature of a person's soul tends to impel him in one direction or the other. One person sees the argument one way, and another sees it another way.

All the more so in the case of "the hidden matters [belonging] to the Lord our God,"

If in the revealed part of Torah, where all factors are out in the open, unambiguous, and rationally debatable, we find such disagreement in outlook and in practical legal decisions, how much more so must we expect to find that regarding the tenuous and nebulous matters of the soul, "the hidden matters belonging to God,"[27] each individual has his own unique path, and it is entirely impossible to deal with such matters by generalities.

these being the awe and love that are in the mind and heart of each and every one according to his measure, [that is,] according to his heart's estimation, as explained in the holy *Zohar* on the verse, "Her husband is known in the gates (*she'arim*). . . ."

The *Zohar* interprets the verse "her husband is known in the gates"[28] to say that the degree of a soul's love and fear of God depends on the extent to which God ("her husband")[29] is known to it, the measure of its perception of Him. (*She'arim*, "gates," also means "estimations" or "measures." Thus, "Her husband is known in the gates" can be interpreted as "The measure of a soul's knowledge and perception of God determines the nature of her relationship with Him as her husband.") A heart's measure of God is not something that can be taught or communicated but is inherent to its individual nature and perception.

A great man once said that in the verse "I know that God is great,"[30] the word *I* should be understood as an emphasis: *I* alone know how great God is to me; only *I* know and nobody else can. Not that I am greater or lesser than anyone else, just that I am different. And because I am different, I alone know my individual recognition of God's greatness.

The revealed elements of Torah can be passed along, argued, and discussed also with individuals who differ in their way of thinking. In contrast, a person's mental and emotional measures of God's greatness, as well as what one thinks—even in Torah matters—are, like the quintessential root of his soul, unique and incommunicable.

To summarize, in this part of the preface, the author has explained why the "internal" elements of Torah cannot be acquired from books. Even if they are indeed "the words of the living God," they cannot address themselves along the precise individual "line" of each reader. A person can study books on the intimate soul of Torah and drown in them, without ever reaching *his* Torah and his individual path in the service of God. He must therefore go to a teacher; and it is that living, speaking teacher who can address the needs of his student and shape his words according to what the student needs to hear.

Having explained at length why not to write books on moral teaching, the author goes on to explain why he nonetheless wrote this book.

I speak, however, of those who know me well, namely, each and every one of our faithful who lives in our country and in the lands adjacent to it, with whom words of affection have been frequently exchanged, and who have revealed to me all the secrets of their heart and mind in the service of God which is dependent on the heart.

As the author stated earlier, the first limitation of any book is that the writer is essentially talking to himself; he cannot specifically address the reader because he does not know him. But in this case, states the author, I wrote the book because I speak to my intimates and "to those who know me well." *Tanya* was for a specific audience— the author's closest Hasidim, whose inner selves were no mystery to him, for they had already come to consult with him on the most intimate matters of their souls. They had poured out their hearts to him, telling him not so much their material cares (as Hasidim did even then, a phenomenon that the author later denounces),[31] but mainly the inner problems of the heart, problems of how best to serve and attain a relationship with God. (Hasidim, however, insist that not only the Hasidim of his time but all who study and will study the *Tanya* in all generations are included among Rabbi Schneur Zalman's intimates and "those who know me well"; all will be able to find in this book the answers to their individual questions.)

To them does my word percolate, and my tongue be a scribe's pen in these pamphlets that are entitled *Likkutei Amarim* (Collected Sayings), which have been gleaned from books and Sages, exalted and holy, whose souls are in Eden; [sayings] that are widely known amongst us, and some of which are hinted to the wise in the holy letters from our teachers in the Holy Land, may it be built and established speedily in our days, Amen, and some of which I have heard from their saintly mouths when they were here with us. All of them are responses to the many questions which all our faithful in our country have constantly asked, seeking advice, each according to his quality,

Tanya, then, is essentially a compilation of answers to questions, the common questions that each person asks concerning his spiritual problems, his troubles, and his struggles to reach God.

Many such questions were posed to the author by his Hasidim, who numbered in the many thousands. Each asked in accordance with his level: a person of spiritual stature—one who has already achieved certain things within his soul—does not ask the same questions as a simple man who is only beginning to struggle to attain a measure of himself and perceive the divine light.

so as to receive spiritual advice in the service of God.

The road leading to the service of God is a tortuous one, strewn with pitfalls in matters of practical law and particularly in questions that touch on the life of the soul. How is a person to address his problems and questions regarding the pains of his soul? A substantial part of the rebbe's job was to give spiritual advice in matters of how best to serve God.

For time no longer permits replying to each and every one individually and in detail on his particular problem;

At first, when the number of Rabbi Schneur Zalman's Hasidim was small, each was able to enter into *yechidut* ("private audience") with the rebbe; present his questions and dilemmas at length and in detail; and receive a systematic, personal answer. But when the number of Hasidim greatly increased, it was no longer possible to spend so much time with each visitor.

also, forgetfulness is common.

This refers to the listener's forgetfulness. What the rebbe says to a Hasid in *yechidut* is highly condensed. Every word, every point, every shade of phrasing has its meaning. The full implications are not always apparent at the time; much can be understood only later, sometimes years later. As a result, the listener, unable to appreciate all aspects of what the rebbe said to him, is likely to forget some of the details that have no immediate relevance. Thus, there is also a certain shortcoming to advice obtained in private.

I have therefore recorded all the replies to all the questions,

This suggests that *Tanya* is a collection of answers the author gave to questions that various individuals asked over a period of time. But even a cursory examination of the book will reveal that it is much more complex than that. Indeed, the book in no way resembles a book of questions and answers, nor can it be described as an ingenious tapestry of various topics. Rather, it is constructed as a broad and systematic work of *mussar*. It considers abstract problems from all aspects of a person's outer and inner struggles to achieve love and fear of God, and it carefully constructs the edifice of concepts in which they find their resolution. However, this structure is but a cloak covering its more inner contents, which, as the author states, are the answers to very specific questions posed by specific individuals. In this, the author sees the uniqueness of the book; it is not a "book" at all in the sense that its audience is universal and its content an abstract philosophy that a person generated on his own (and which, to a great extent, is but the expression of his own self) but an intersection of specific, highly sensitive answers to extremely private questions. At the same time, the questions being many, the answers must also be understood in a way that is general and universal.

For this reason, the questions are not always apparent, nor are the answers clear to every reader. One must search for the points that translate the general approach into a private answer. But the great strength of the book is that despite its classical universal style, despite the logical structure that develops a series of points toward an all-inclusive edifice, this is all but the external format, within which lies the inner format, which remains a personal response to personal questions.

The purpose of the book is not the development of a philosophical, theological, or moral theory. It aspires to a far greater task: to address specific spiritual problems connected to a soul's endeavor to serve its Creator. Unlike standard books of moral teaching, *Tanya* is not written from the author to a general audience, dealing in the abstract with general problems relating to the public at large, but as a response to real problems—not the author's problems, but those of the readers. The reader searches for the answer to his own personal problem, and he is sure to find it: sometimes in a single sentence, sometimes in a string of sentences scattered in different parts of the book, and sometimes only in the wording or context in which a thought is presented.

to be preserved as a signpost and to serve as a visual reminder for each and every person, so that he will no longer press for admission to confer in private (*yechidut*) with me. For in these [writings], he will find peace for his soul, and true counsel on every matter that he finds difficult in the service of God.

The book is appreciated when the reader realizes that it is the answer to a question. One to whom the question is not clear, who is not troubled and pained by it, cannot understand and relate to the answer. But this drawback of the book is also its greatest merit. For it is more than a book, it is the author's conversation with real live people; it is an intimate *yechidut* of a rebbe with his Hasidim. In the words of Rabbi Shalom DovBer of Lubavitch (the author's great-great-grandson and the fifth rebbe of Chabad), to study *Tanya* is "to speak with the rebbe" (that is, Rabbi Schneur Zalman).[32]

His heart will thus be firmly secured in God, who completes for us.

This is not just a phrase. Note that the author is not saying simply to trust in God but in "God who completes for us." It means that in whatever concerns service of God, one is not to rely on divine help (compare the Talmudic saying, "Everything is in the hands of heaven except fear of heaven").[33] One may look to God for help and illumination, but one may not expect God to do the job for us. We can expect, at most, that He will "complete for us"—if we begin.

Until now, the author has explained why this book was written. It is intended to replace a personal audience, the *yechidut* with the rebbe. The reader needs to see it as the beginning and the continuation of a private talk, to define the problems that trouble him and discover the answers that are implicit in the book. But because the answers are buried in the format of a book, a book that contains much difficult language and deals with esoteric subjects, the reader may at times be unable to discover his personal connection with the words. The author therefore adds the following section:

As for him whose mind falls short in the understanding of the counsel given in these pamphlets,

Had the book been arranged as a list of questions and answers, certain people could perhaps more readily draw from it the personal advice they require. But this would mean that the author would have to enter into all the details of the problem, to the point that his answers would become increasingly detailed and personal, and thus appropriate for only one person, on a single issue and on a particular occasion. To make it meaningful to a greater variety of people and situations, the book has been arranged in another way. Different people often ask in different ways and with considerable variation of detail what really amounts to the same basic question, and they need the same answer. The external format of the book is that of generalized answers. The questions remain in all the detail and particularity of an individual's inner dilemmas as played out in his own time and place, but it is the answers, not the questions, that the book presents. The difficulty is that the reader has to find for himself the route from his personal problem to the written answer, and not everyone can find the connection between the words in the book and the question that is burning inside him now. The difficulty, however, is not one of essence, because the answer is in the book, but rather a literary one: of categorizing the private answer one seeks from within the overall structure. The author advises the reader how to overcome this difficulty.

let him discuss the matter with the eminent ones of his town, and they will elucidate it for him.

Whoever feels that the book does not directly answer his problem should discuss it with the leading Hasidim in his community, who will provide him with the tools that will enable him to understand and find the answer to his questions independently.

And I beg of them not to lay their hand on their mouth, to conduct themselves with false meekness and humility, God forbid.

The author explains, I tell the leading Hasidim: when you are approached by a questioner, do not be silent and say you do not know. If one is capable of teaching others and says, "How dare I, a lowly and insignificant man, presume to explain things to others?" one may consider this to be humility, but it is false humility. Inner humility is a virtue, and there is not a book of *mussar* that does not praise it. But when a person behaves with outward humility—when he knows the answer to a question and does not reply because he thinks that it will appear to others as arrogance—this is not true humility, for it is contrary to the truth. Humility must never prevent a person from contributing what he is able to contribute. Genuine humility lies in assessing one's true potential and recognizing what he has and what he has not attained with his particular capabilities. If he possesses the capability to explain to his companion what the other cannot understand on his own, he is obliged to do so, not as an honor to which he is entitled but as a duty imposed on him. He has no right to evade his responsibilities with pretensions of humility.

It is known what bitter punishment is his who "withholds grain," and the greatness of the reward [in the opposite case],

The Talmud declares that when someone withholds a teaching from a pupil, even unborn children in their mothers' wombs will curse him, as in the verse, "He who withholds grain, a nation shall curse him."[34] Whoever withholds the nourishment of the Torah, the bread of Torah, from those to whom he can impart it, is severely punished. But great is the reward, continues the Talmud, of the one who dedicates his life to teaching those who know less than he.[35]

from the saying of our sages on the verse, "God illuminates the eyes of them both," for God will cause His face to shine upon them, with the light of the countenance of the Living King. May the Giver of Life to the Living merit us to live to see the days when "No longer shall one man instruct the other . . . for all shall know Me . . . ,"[36] "For the world shall be full of the knowledge of God . . . ,"[37] Amen, may this be His will.

In another place, the Talmud interprets the verse, "When a pauper and a teacher meet, God illuminates the eyes of both."[38] When a pupil goes to his teacher and requests of him, "Teach me Torah," and he teaches him, then "God illuminates the eyes of both." Not just the "pauper's" eyes are illuminated but also the eyes of the teacher, as a reward for illuminating the eyes of the pupil.

To summarize: the Compiler's Preface explains why the author wrote the book and how it is unique among books of moral teaching. As we said, the preface is divided into two main parts. The first explains why the Hasidic outlook shrinks from studying books of moral teaching and sees them as an inadequate substitute for a live teacher. The author of such a book, even when he derives its contents solely from the Torah itself, expresses them in his own way; indeed, it is not only legitimate but also inevitable that a person should understand and create according to his own personality and the nature of his soul. So every book expresses, to a significant extent, the personality and spirit of its author. As a result, the book remains closed to the outside reader, not because it is difficult to understand but because these matters are inherently "hidden matters belonging to God." It is impossible to relate oneself to them and experience them, because this experience is so individual, so unique to each person, that it cannot be generalized. Consequently, however important and holy these books may be, they do not serve the purpose of granting a true and direct perception; they cannot touch that fine, unique, and sensitive point that defines each individual.

Nonetheless, states the author in the second part of the preface, this book, intended to serve as a substitute for a private conference with the rebbe, aspires to be something different. The author writes it not out of his own experience but for other, specific people whom he knows intimately and of whose specific problems he has firsthand knowledge. The book is, in essence, a response to their questions. The response is generalized and constructed within a profound philosophical framework, but it remains a response to personal questions by real individuals. Therein lies the strength of the book as well as the difficulties in understanding it: the need to study it over and over again in order to arrive at the precise phrasing of the question (which the student must do) and comprehend the individualized answer.

At the same time, adds the author, in order that the response should indeed reach every individual, the book requires the aid of a personal touch, of live contact between teacher and pupil. Whoever is capable of studying and finding answers in the book is obligated to assist others in discovering how its words personally and specifically relate to them.

This preface also served as a general introduction to a number of books written in this style: as Oral Torah in written form, a form that remains a personal and intimate oral conversation between the rebbe and the Hasid, something that retains the life and vibrancy of interpersonal contact.

Since the said pamphlets have been disseminated among all our faithful, as mentioned [earlier], by means of numerous transcriptions by the hands of various and sundry scribes, the multitude of transcriptions brought about an exceedingly great number of copyists' errors. Therefore the spirit of the noble men, named on another page, has generously moved them to a personal and financial effort, to have the said pamphlets published, cleared of chaff and errors, and thoroughly proofed. I congratulate them on this worthy deed.

And inasmuch as there is an explicit verse, "Cursed be he who encroaches upon his neighbor's domain"[39]—and "cursed" includes both damnation and shunning,[40] God forbid—therefore, "As in Judah and Scripture in addition"[41] I come to invoke a strict prohibition on all publishers against printing the said pamphlets, either themselves or through their agency, without the authority of the above-named, for a period of five years from the day that this printing is completed. And it will be well with those who conform, and they will be blessed with good.

These are the words of the compiler of the said *Likkutei Amarim.*

The author explains that the existence of a large number of manuscript copies has led to many mistakes and errors, and he has therefore given license to print the book, with the usual warning about respecting the printers' copyrights and not causing them loss by other printings. This last clause was the common text of approbation for a book. In fact, however, the book had already been printed in tens of thousands of copies, and a different edition was printed elsewhere within the five-year period.

Chapter 1

It has been taught (*Niddah,* end ch. 3): "An oath is administered to it, 'Be a *tzaddik* ("righteous person") and do not be a *rasha* ("wicked person"). And even if the entire world tells you that you are a *tzaddik,* regard yourself as if you were a *rasha.*'"

This requires to be understood, for it has been taught (*Avot,* ch. 2), "And do not be a *rasha* in your own eyes." Furthermore, if a man considers himself to be wicked, he will be grieved at heart and depressed, and will not be able to serve God joyfully and with a contented heart; on the other hand, if he is not perturbed by [his self-appraisal] at all, it may lead him to irreverence, God forbid.

But the matter [will be understood by first prefacing the following]:

We find in the Talmud five distinct types: "A *tzaddik* to whom is good," "a *tzaddik* to whom is evil," "a *rasha* to whom is good," "a *rasha* to whom is evil," and the *beinoni* ("intermediate"). It is there explained that the "tzaddik to whom is good" is the perfect *tzaddik;* the "tzaddik to whom is evil" is the imperfect *tzaddik.* In *Ra'aya Mehemna (Parashat Mishpatim),* it is explained that the "*tzaddik* to whom is evil" is one whose evil nature is subservient to his good nature, and so on. And in the Talmud (end ch. 9, *Berachot*), it is stated: "*Tzaddikim,* their inclination for good judges them . . .

resha'im, their inclination for evil judges them . . . *beinonim* are judged by both. . . . Rabbah declared: 'I am an example of a *beinoni.*' Said Abbaye to him: 'Master, you do not make it possible for anyone to live. . . .'"

The above requires a thorough understanding. Also [requiring understanding is] what Job said (*Bava Batra,* ch. 1), "Master of the universe, You have created *tzaddikim,* You have created *resha'im* . . ."—for do we not know that he does not proclaim *"tzaddik"* or *"rasha"*? It is also necessary to understand the essential nature of the level of *beinoni.* For surely the *beinoni* is not one whose deeds are half virtuous and half sinful, for if this were so, how could Rabba err in classifying himself as a *beinoni*? It is known that his mouth never ceased from study, so much so that the Angel of Death could not overpower him; how, then, could he err in [thinking that] half of his deeds were sinful, God forbid?

Furthermore, when a person commits sins, he is deemed a complete *rasha* (and when he repents afterwards, he is deemed a complete *tzaddik*). Even he who violates a minor rabbinical prohibition called a *rasha,* as it is stated in *Yevamot,* ch. 2, and in *Niddah,* ch. 1. Moreover, even he who has the opportunity to forewarn another against sinning and does not do so is called a *rasha* (ch. 6, *Shevuot*). All the more so he who neglects any active *mitzvah* which he is able to fulfill, for instance, whoever is able to study Torah and does not, regarding whom our Sages have quoted, "Because he has scorned the word of God . . . [that soul] shall be utterly cut off . . . "—obviously such a person is considered a *rasha,* more than he who violates a rabbinical prohibition. If this is so, we must conclude that the *beinoni* is not guilty even of the sin of neglecting to study the Torah. So how could Rabbah have mistaken himself for a *beinoni*?

Note: As for what is written in the *Zohar* III, p. 231, "He whose sins are few is classed as a *'tzaddik* to whom is evil'"—this is the query of Rav Hamnuna to Elijah. But according to Elijah's answer [on the same page], the meaning of "a *tzaddik* to whom is evil" is as stated in *Ra'aya Mehemna* on *Parashat Mishpatim,* which is quoted [earlier]. And the Torah has seventy faces.

As for that which is generally said, that one whose deeds and misdeeds are equally balanced is called a *beinoni,* while one whose virtues overweigh his sins is called a *tzaddik*—these are only borrowed terms in regard to reward and punishment, because a person is judged according to the majority of his [deeds] and is deemed *"tzaddik"* (righteous) in his verdict when he is acquitted by law. But concerning the true definition and quality of the distinct levels and ranks of *tzaddik* and *beinoni,* our Sages have said that "*Tzaddikim,* their inclination for good [alone] judges them," as it is written, "And my heart is void within me,"—that it is void of an evil inclination, because he had slain it through fasting. But whoever has not attained this level, even if his virtues exceed his sins, cannot at all be reckoned to have ascended to the rank of *tzaddik.* This is why our Sages have declared in the Midrash, "The Almighty saw that *tzaddikim* are few, so He planted them in every generation . . . as it is written, 'The *tzaddik* is the foundation of the world.'"

The explanation [of these questions] is to be found in the light of what Rabbi Chaim Vital writes in *Sha'ar haKedushah* (and in *Etz Chayyim,* Portal 50, ch. 2) that in every Jew, *tzaddik* and *rasha* alike, are two souls (*neshamot*), as it is written, "The souls (*neshamot*) which I have made," [that is] two souls (*nefashot*).

One soul originates in *kelipah* and *sitra achra.* This is the soul that is clothed in the blood of human being, giving life to the body, as it is written, "For the fleshly soul is in the blood." From it stem all the [person's] evil characteristics, deriving from the four evil elements which are contained in it. These are: anger and pride, which emanate from the element of Fire, the nature of which is to rise upwards; the lust for pleasure from the element of Water, for water makes to grow all kinds of enjoyment; frivolity, causticity, boasting, and idle talk from the element of Air; and sloth and melancholy from the element of Earth.

From this soul also derive the good characteristics that are to be found in the innate nature of every Jew, such as compassion and charity. For in the case of the Jew, this soul of the *kelipah* is derived from *kelipat nogah,* which also contains good, as it originates in the esoteric "Tree of Knowledge of Good and Evil."

The souls of the nations of the world, however, derive from the other impure *kelipot* which contain no good whatever, as it is written in *Etz Chayyim,* Portal 49, ch. 3, that all the good that the nations do, is done from selfish motives. As the Talmud comments on the verse, "The kindness of the nations is sin"—that all the charity and kindness done by the nations of the world is only for their own self-glorification and so on.

COMMENTARY

As is the case with all classic Hasidic works and discourses, the *Tanya* opens with a selection of citations from Torah sources and raises a series of questions regarding these source-texts; the author then proceeds to build his thesis. Although the author's purpose is not to explain the source-texts but to present an approach to life, he nevertheless structures his work as an explanation of the sources. This is to establish the validity of the work as more than a particular individual's philosophy, as something that is predicated upon Torah sources and derives from them.

It has been taught (*Niddah,* end ch. 3): An oath is administered to it,

"It has been taught" to the soul before its descent into the body.

"Be a *tzaddik* ("righteous person") and do not be a *rasha* ("wicked person"). And even if the entire world tells you that you are a *tzaddik,* regard yourself as if you were a *rasha."*

This oath has two parts: (1) to be a *tzaddik* and not to be a *rasha;* (2) to consider oneself a *rasha,* even if the entire world says that one is a *tzaddik.*

Rabbi Schneur Zalman's grandson, Rabbi Menachem Mendel of Lubavitch, raises the question: What is the purpose of this oath? Does not the soul desire only good? Only the human being, saddled with a physical body and nature, is susceptible to evil, not his spiritual essence. So why administer this oath to the soul? Rabbi Menachem Mendel explains that this oath represents not only a promise but also an empowerment. Every soul possesses the necessary powers to overcome the evil inclination and "not be a *rasha*"; however, these powers reside in the transcendent essence of the soul, where they are often beyond the reach of its conscious, experiential self. The oath that the soul takes has the effect of stimulating these potentials and making them accessible to its everyday life. Indeed, the Hebrew word *mashbi'in* ("he is made to swear") can also read as *masbi'in,* "he is fortified."

This requires to be understood,

The question is, of course, on the second part of the oath: Why is the soul forced to take this oath—namely, an irreversible divine command—to consider oneself a *rasha?*

for it contradicts the Mishnaic dictum (*Avot,* ch. 2), "And do not be a *rasha* in your own eyes."

Thus, we have a seeming contradiction between two Talmudic statements: the quote from *Niddah* relates that the soul is commanded by oath to regard itself as a *rasha*, "even if the entire world tells you that you are righteous," whereas the Mishnah in *Avot* enjoins a person *not* to regard himself as a *rasha*.

Furthermore, if a man considers himself to be wicked, he will be grieved at heart and depressed, and will not be able to serve God joyfully and with a contented heart; on the other hand, if he is not perturbed by [his self-appraisal] at all, it may lead him to irreverence, God forbid.

In other words, aside from the problem of resolving two contradictory statements by our sages, the issue presents a dilemma in its own right. For if a person were to regard himself as wicked and deficient, he would inevitably fall into depression; and depression, as the author elaborates in Chapter 26, is a grave handicap to a person's inner struggle with his negative inclinations. On the other hand, when one is not critical of oneself or when one's self-critique tends to attribute all failings to the fact that someone else, society, or God has done wrong, the result is a disavowal of responsibility for one's actions and the neglect of one's duties to God and humankind.

So what we have here is not only an inconsistency between two source-texts but also a fundamental question: How should a person perceive himself? Should he see himself as perfect, imperfect, or surely lacking? For a person's self-vision is not subjective. On the contrary: the manner in which society defines a person—as a *tzaddik, rasha,* and so on—is never accurate, because others have only partial knowledge of his public self and virtually no knowledge of his inner self; only the person himself is in the position to make a true judgment. A person's self-definition, when he rises above his prejudice and judges himself by objective criteria, is far more valid and significant than any definition that society might confer on him.

But the matter [will be understood by first prefacing the following]:

Before we can discuss what a person's self-perception should be, we must first define the concepts *tzaddik* and *rasha*. The author will now proceed to cite a number of passages from the Talmud, *Midrash,* and *Zohar,* from which he will derive a concise definition of these terms, as well as of a third category, the *beinoni* ("intermediate" individual). He will then employ these definitions as the basis of man's approach to the fulfillment of his mission in life to serve the Creator.

We find in the Talmud five distinct types: "A *tzaddik* to whom is good," "a *tzaddik* to whom is evil," "a *rasha* to whom is good," "a *rasha* to whom is evil," and the *"beinoni."*

Two Talmudic passages, taken together, yield a total of five categories of individual. In *Berachot* 7b, we find four categories: "a *tzaddik* to whom is good," "a *tzaddik* to whom is evil," "a *rasha* to whom is good," and "a *rasha* to whom is evil." A fifth category, the *beinoni* ("intermediate man"), is discussed in *Berachot* 66a.

It is there explained that the *"tzaddik* to whom is good" is the perfect *tzaddik;* the *"tzaddik* to whom is evil" is the imperfect *tzaddik.*

In *Berachot* 7b, the first four categories are described in terms of the correlation between their virtue and their material fortunes. "A *tzaddik* to whom is good" is a righteous individual who enjoys good fortune also in the material sense; "a *tzaddik* to whom is evil" is the righteous individual who suffers bad fortune in his material life; "a *rasha* to whom is good" is the wicked individual who prospers materially; and "a *rasha* to whom is evil" is the wicked individual who suffers material misfortune.

At first glance, these seem superficial distinctions, relating not to the inner quality of men but to the circumstances of their material lives. However, the Talmud goes on to explain that "a *tzaddik* to whom is good" is a completely righteous individual, whereas "a *tzaddik* to whom is evil" is an incompletely righteous individual. The same applies to the two categories of *rasha:* a *rasha* who prospers is one who is not completely wicked, whereas the utterly evil individual has it bad materially as well.

Hence, these four categories reflect intrinsic differences between different types of people. Together with the *beinoni,* they constitute the five quintessential categories of human being, embracing all inhabitants of earth.

In *Ra'aya Mehemna (Parashat Mishpatim)* it is explained that the *"tzaddik* to whom is evil" is one whose evil nature is subservient to his good nature, and so on.

The *Ra'aya Mehemna,* a component of the Kabbalistic work *Zohar,* offers a deeper level of interpretation of the Talmud's words. According to the *Zohar,* the phrases "a *tzaddik* to whom is good," "a *tzaddik* to whom is evil," and so on refer not to a person's material circumstances but to the state of his inner self. "A *tzaddik* to whom is evil" is a person whose evil (his negative traits and inclinations) is "to him"— subject to, and dominated by, his righteous self. Therefore, the Talmud also refers to him as "incompletely righteous"; some evil still remains in him, though he has subjugated it to himself. Conversely, "a *rasha* to whom is good" describes the wicked individual who has good in him, but this good is "to him"—overpowered by his wicked self. He is thus an "incompletely wicked" individual: basically, he is wicked, but there is good in him also. In the same vein, "a *tzaddik* to whom is good" is a "perfectly righteous" individual—only good inhabits his soul— whereas the reverse is true of the "*rasha* to whom is evil."

And in the Talmud (end ch. 9, *Berachot*) it is stated: "*Tzaddikim,* their inclination for good judges them . . . *resha'im,* their inclination for evil judges them . . . *beinonim* are judged by both . . ."

Man has two internal judges—as derived from the verse "He stands to the right of the pauper, to save him from the judges of his soul":[1] his good inclination and his evil inclination. The difference between the *tzaddik* and the *rasha* lies in which judge has the decisive voice, regardless of what other members might be on this internal tribunal. With the *tzaddik,* only the good inclination has a say, whereas the arbiter who holds sway in the *rasha*'s heart is his evil inclination. With the *beinoni,* the situation is far more complex, as later chapters will explain.

The Talmud continues:

"Rabbah declared: 'I am an example of a *beinoni.*' Said Abbaye to him: 'Master, you do not make it possible for anyone to live . . .'"

The *tzaddik* and the *rasha* are the more clearly defined categories, whereas the *beinoni* is an intermediate state and thus more complex and difficult to understand. Therefore, Rabbah offered himself as an example, so that his students might grasp the concept of *beinoni.* But Abbaye, Rabbah's nephew and disciple, found this self-categorization of Rabbah's difficult to accept. "Master," he objected, "you do not make it possible for anyone to live!" Rabbah was no ordinary individual; he was one of the great *amora'im* ("Talmudical sages") of Babylonia,

the dean of the illustrious academy of Pumpedita, a man so saintly
that the Talmud relates that when his time came, the Angel of Death
was powerless to take his soul! If you are a *beinoni*, Abbaye said to him,
then your criteria for righteousness leaves no room for anyone else; if
you are a *beinoni*, no man on earth can be a *tzaddik*.[2] Or as the famed
Hasidic teacher, Rabbi Shmuel Grunem Estherman, put it: if you are
beinoni, we are all *resha'im* ("wicked persons").

The above requires a thorough understanding.

"The above" refers to this division into the different kinds of *tzaddik, rasha*, and *beinoni*, as well as how all these definitions touch upon
the fundamentals of the way to worship God and the opening questions that a person should pose to himself when setting out to choose
his own path of worship.

**Also [requiring understanding is] what Job said (*Bava Batra*, ch. 1), "Master
of the universe, You have created *tzaddikim*, You have created *resha'im* . . ."—
for do we not know that he does not proclaim *"tzaddik"* or *"rasha"*?**

The Talmud describes Job taking issue with God not only over his
personal misfortunes but also over what he saw as a fundamental
injustice in God's creation. "Master of the Universe," Job protested,
"You created an ox with cloven hooves ([that is,] as a kosher animal),
and You created the donkey with non-cloven hooves; You created paradise, and You created hell; You created *tzaddikim*, and You created
resha'im."[3] Job's argument is that God imparts positive potential to
some of His creatures and negative potential to others; each creature
is thus ordained to be and act in accordance with its predetermined
nature. Thus, Job argued, "sinners are compelled" to sin;[4] a person is
born a *tzaddik* or a *rasha*, and he cannot be reproached for being what
he intrinsically is.

How, asks the author, does this fit in with the Talmud's account of
the formation of man? The Talmud relates how "the angel in charge
of conception" takes a drop of semen, places it before the Almighty, and
inquires: "Master of the Universe, what is the fate of this drop? Will it be
strong or weak? wise or foolish? wealthy or poor?" However, the Talmud adds, the question "Righteous or wicked?" is not posed by the
angel or determined by the Almighty; for "Everything is in the hands
of Heaven, except for the fear of Heaven."[5] A person is given the fac-

ulties, talents, and nature that cause him to excel in certain areas but do poorly in others; but he is also given a particular life trajectory that will determine whether he enjoys material abundance or suffers poverty and whether he succeeds or fails in other areas. But as far as the choice between good and evil is concerned, a person retains absolute freedom at all times. God created the ox kosher and the donkey nonkosher, and neither can change its spiritual status. But there is nothing that determines the righteousness or wickedness of men.

So what did Job mean when he said, "Master of the Universe, . . . You created *tzaddik*im, and You created *resha'im*"? Did he not know that "wicked or righteous" is the one factor that is *not* determined from above?

It is also necessary to understand the essential nature of the level of *beinoni*.

The emphasis is the *beinoni*, though we have enumerated five distinct classes of man, from the complete *rasha* to the complete *tzaddik*. For, as we have discussed in our commentary on the *Tanya*'s title page, the *beinoni* is the focus of the entire book. The author of the *Tanya* calls it The Book of *Beinonim*, and it is primarily devoted to explaining "the essential nature of the level of *beinoni*." As we shall see, there is a marked difference between the *beinoni*'s "essential nature" and his "level." Indeed, one can say that the entire book deals with the tension between the essential nature and the level of the intermediate man.

For surely the *beinoni* is not one whose deeds are half virtuous and half sinful,

The concept of an intermediate in any sphere is no simple matter. One cannot, in all cases, speak of a middle between two extremes; not everything lends itself to such categorization. Certain things are either one thing or the other, without any intermediary state. One of these things is the righteousness or wickedness of a person's behavior, as will be explained later in this chapter. Although the term "intermediate" is sometimes used to describe a person whose virtues balance out his sins, this is only a borrowed or figurative term. As far as the definitive terms for a person's essential moral and spiritual state are concerned, defining the *tzaddik* as one who is completely virtuous, the *rasha* as one whose deeds are wholly wicked, and the *beinoni* as "half and half" is completely out of the question, as the author proceeds to prove from several sources.

for if this were so, how could Rabbah err in classifying himself as a *beinoni?*

If the *beinoni* were one whose deeds are half virtuous and half sinful, he is certainly a person who has sinned perceptibly. So the term surely cannot be applied to Rabbah, a man who was among the greatest and most pious of his generation.[6]

Nor can it be said that Rabbah referred to himself as a *beinoni* out of humility. Humility is not falsehood or self-deception. A tall person who says that he is short is not being humble; he is not telling the truth. By the same token, a righteous man who says that he is a sinner is just as untruthful as is a sinner who proclaims himself righteous. The humble person might underestimate himself but only regarding matters that are subjective and nebulous, not empirical facts. True humility is a person's acknowledgment of his insufficiency before God or his insufficiency before his own potential. Such humility can be found only among the truly great—those who are aware of the loftiness of their own soul, who know the true extent of their capacity, and who understand how distant is the actual from the potential. Such subjective self-judgment is the source of true humility; humility has no place, however, regarding things that are measurable by objective criteria. Furthermore,

It is known that his mouth never ceased from study, so much so that the Angel of Death could not overpower him; how, then, could he err in [thinking that] half of his deeds were sinful, God forbid?

Indeed, the Talmud relates that when the Angel of Death was sent to take Rabbah's soul, he was unable to approach him, because Rabbah did not cease studying Torah for a single moment; only when the Angel of Death succeeded in causing Rabbah to pause in his study was he able to take his life.[7] (The author's son, Rabbi DovBer of Lubavitch, explains this, based on the statement by our sages that when the Jewish people received the Torah at Mount Sinai, they were liberated from all constricting influences, including death itself; only because they were tainted by the sin of the golden calf did they again become subject to the mortality of man. Thus, concludes Rabbi DovBer, death cannot touch one who studies Torah pure of the slightest taint of sin.)

Furthermore, when a person commits sins, he is deemed a complete *rasha* (and when he repents afterwards, he is deemed a complete *tzaddik*).

From Rabbah's self-categorization as a *beinoni*, taken together with what we know of his person and deeds, it is obvious that a *beinoni* is not half sinful. Clearly, the *beinoni* is similar enough to the *tzaddik* that people can confuse the two terms. But the problem of defining the *beinoni* runs deeper than that. Because we are dealing here not with an external definition of one's actions and deeds but rather with a true definition of one's inner essence, it would seem that there can be no intermediate state between the state of *tzaddik* and the state of *rasha*. For we know that the moment a person commits a sin—an express violation of the divine will—he is at that moment a *rasha*, regardless of the degree of his prior merits, as the following paragraph will establish. Conversely, if a person truly repents his sins, he immediately assumes the status of a *tzaddik*, regardless of his previous station.[8] So when is a person a *beinoni*?

Even he who violates a minor rabbinical prohibition is called a *rasha,* as it is stated in *Yevamot,* ch. 2,[9] and in *Niddah,* ch. 1.[10]

One might posit that this applies only to severe prohibitions. The *beinoni* might be one whose good deeds are unspectacular and his iniquities minor. But the Talmud clearly states that even the violation of a minor clause in a rabbinical prohibition renders one a *rasha*.

Moreover, even he who has the opportunity to forewarn another against sinning and does not do so is called a *rasha* (ch. 6, *Shevuot*).[11]

Furthermore, a person becomes a *rasha* not only through an active violation of the divine will but also by passively allowing the evil deeds of others. One who is in a position to protest and perhaps prevent an evil act and fails to do so is a *rasha*.

All the more so he who neglects any active *mitzvah* which he is able to fulfill, for instance, whoever is able to study Torah and does not, regarding whom our Sages have quoted, "Because he has scorned the word of God . . . [that soul] shall be utterly cut off . . ."—obviously such a person is considered a *rasha,* more than he who violates a rabbinical prohibition.

If the *beinoni* has no sins, could it be that he is distinguished from the *tzaddik* by his inadequate performance of *mitzvot* ("commandments")?

Again, the answer is no: failure to perform a *mitzvah* properly—even if one commits no transgression at the time of not performing the *mitzvah*—also places one in the category of *rasha*. A prime example is the status of one who neglects the study of Torah when he has the opportunity to do so, even if he spent his time involved in morally neutral pursuits. Regarding such an individual, our sages[12] apply the verse: "For he has scorned the word of God and broken His commandment, that soul shall be utterly cut off, his sin shall be upon him."[13] Obviously, one who is the object of such severe reprimand and punishment is no less a *rasha* than the violator of a rabbinical decree or the passive bystander to evil.

If this is so, we must conclude that the *beinoni* is not guilty even of the sin of neglecting to study the Torah. So how could Rabbah have mistaken himself for a *beinoni*?

One who commits a grave sin is a *rasha;* one who commits a minor sin is a *rasha;* one who neglects to prevent another's sin is a *rasha;* one who fails to use an opportunity to perform a *mitzvah* is a *rasha.* It follows that the *beinoni* is one who has no sins and who fulfills all the *mitzvot* he is capable of fulfilling; a man who, as we shall see, is utterly perfect in thought, speech, and action. That much we have ascertained from the sources quoted. So the *beinoni* is obviously not the "normal" person or the "median" in the statistical sense; he is a very special—indeed, unique—individual. The question remaining is: Why do we call him the "intermediate"? What does he lack that he is not a *tzaddik*?

As we shall see, the *beinoni*'s lack is not in his behavior—his deeds, his speech, or even his thoughts—but relates to the inner recesses of his soul. There, in a place invisible to all but himself and his God, lies the distinction between the *beinoni* and the *tzaddik*.

Note: As for what is written in the *Zohar* III, p. 231: "He whose sins are few is classed as a '*tzaddik* to whom is evil'"—this is the query of Rav Hamnuna to Elijah. But according to Elijah's answer, [in the same place], the meaning of "a *tzaddik* to whom is evil" is as stated in *Ra'aya Mehemna* on *Parashat Mishpatim,* which is quoted above. And the Torah has seventy faces.

In this gloss, the author quotes a passage from the *Zohar* that seems to contradict what he has said. The *Zohar* cites an exchange between

Rav Hamnuna and Elijah the Prophet, in which Rav Hamnuna posits that "a *tzaddik* to whom is evil" is "one whose sins are fewer than his merits," and Elijah responds with the definition cited here, namely that "a *tzaddik* to whom is evil" is not one who actually sins but one "whose evil nature is subservient to his good nature."

But the very fact that Rav Hamnuna could even consider such a definition—even though it has not been accepted—means that we must take his words into account. If, as the author has demonstrated, it is impossible to credit even the title *beinoni* to one who transgresses even once, how could Rav Hamnuna have held such an opinion in the first place? Was he unaware of the numerous sources quoted by the author that seem to utterly disqualify such a view?

The answer is that "There are seventy faces (*panim*)[14] to the Torah." The Torah has numerous modes of interpretation; a single word or phrase will have many meanings, all true, for it was meant by its divine author to be read from various angles and in various contexts. Thus, Rav Hamnuna, although certainly aware of the definition of *tzaddik* that disallows even the slightest iniquity, thought that in another "face" or context "a *tzaddik* to whom there is evil" might mean one whose merits outweigh his sins. Elijah's response, however, was that although there may be many facets of righteousness, this is not one of them. *Any* precise definition of *tzaddik* does not allow for a single behavioral failing. The only way in which the term *tzaddik* can be applied to one who has actually sinned is when it is used as a "borrowed term," as the author shall explain.[15]

As for that which is generally said, that one whose deeds and misdeeds are equally balanced is called a *beinoni,* while one whose virtues overweigh his sins is called a *tzaddik*—these are only borrowed terms in regard to reward and punishment, because a person is judged according to the majority of his [deeds] and is deemed *tzaddik* ("righteous") in his verdict when he is acquitted in law.

Several passages in the Talmud and in the works of our sages (for example, Talmud, *Rosh Hashanah* 16b and *Kiddushin* 39b; *Mishneh Torah,* Laws of Repentance, ch. 3) employ the terms *tzaddik, beinoni,* and *rasha* in a way that seems to contradict what the author has established. Here, the term *beinoni* is used to refer to an individual who is half meritorious and half sinful, and the term *tzaddik* to refer to one whose merits outweigh his sins.

The author explains that these are not definitions but metaphors. In language, we have the noun, which connotes the object (for example, man, table); we also have the adjective, which describes an object's quality (for example, wise, strong). Then we have the "borrowed term" (*shem hamush'al*). Ostensibly, the borrowed term is also an adjective, delineating a quality, but on closer examination, we see that it is borrowed: the object itself does not truly possess this quality, only a certain aspect or approximation of it. We have borrowed the adjective from another object to describe a similar but essentially different quality in our object; in other words, we use it figuratively.

Thus, the term *tzaddik* might be used in the definitive sense, to refer to someone who is a *tzaddik,* or it might be employed as a borrowed term: the man himself is no *tzaddik;* he is only *tzaddik* ("righteous") in the sense that he has been exonerated from punishment. Similarly, there is a figurative *rasha* in the sense that he has been convicted in judgment and a figurative *beinoni* in the sense that his merits and sins have been weighed and found equivalent, so that he receives an intermediate verdict when judged. These terms relate solely to the evaluation of a person's deeds, but in no way do they reflect on his essential nature. Evaluating a man on the basis of his deeds should be both quantitative and qualitative, but we have no way of distinguishing between a small *mitzvah* and a big one, a minor transgression and a major one. Therefore, when we judge a person and find him in the right, this in no way indicates that he is a righteous man: he is righteous only as pertains to the specific issue we are considering. A prime example is to be found in the verse "The innocent and the righteous (*tzaddik*) should not be put to death."[16] The verse is stating the law that a person found innocent in a court of law may not to be brought before the court again to face the same charges, even if new witnesses come forth to testify of his guilt (a concept that exists in modern law as the principle of double jeopardy). Obviously, the term *tzaddik* in this verse does not describe this person's internal state nor even his overall behavior, only the very specific fact of his righteousness regarding this specific case.

But concerning the true definition and quality of the distinct levels and ranks of *tzaddik* and *beinoni,*

If we define the *tzaddik* as one with a greater number of merits, no *qualitative* difference exists between a *tzaddik* and a *beinoni.* However, according to the "true definition and quality" of these two levels, the *tzaddik* and the *beinoni* are truly and intrinsically different types of human being.

What the author has done, in effect, is to raise our conception of these terms several notches. The *rasha*, it turns out, is anyone who has commited any transgression or failed to observe any *mitzvah* he was capable of observing and has yet to repent his failing—a state of affairs that is considered quite normal and average by conventional standards. The *beinoni*, according to the author, is one who has done every *mitzvah* in his power to observe and has never committed a transgression that he did not repent. This however, begs the question: What, then, is a *tzaddik?* So the author explains:

our Sages have said that *"Tzaddikim,* their inclination for good [alone] judges them," as it is written, "And my heart is void within me,"[17]—that it is void of an evil inclination, because he had slain it through fasting. But whoever has not attained this level, even if his virtues exceed his sins, cannot at all be reckoned to have ascended to the rank of *tzaddik.*

The heart is the seat of the evil inclination; from it stems desire and gravitation to sin. In the *tzaddik,* this place vacant of evil—his heart—is, in the words of the psalmist, "void within him." Therein lies the essence of the *tzaddik:* he not only behaves righteously (as does the *beinoni*) but is intrinsically righteous, devoid of all inclination to evil.

The difference between the *tzaddik* and the *beinoni* lies not in their deeds, their speech, or even their thoughts. As we shall see, one who sins in thought is a *rasha;* sinful thoughts contaminate the soul in a manner that is even more damaging, in a certain sense, than sinful deeds. The *beinoni* does not sin even in thought, but he has an evil inclination; although he does not allow his negative nature to manifest itself, it is present and keenly felt. The *tzaddik*'s heart, in contradistinction, is void; he has no inclination to evil whatsoever.

This is why our Sages have declared in the Midrash, "The Almighty saw that *tzaddikim* are few, so He planted them in every generation . . . [As] it is written,[18] 'The *tzaddik* is the foundation of the world.'"[19]

Tzaddikim are the foundation of the world: in their merit, the world continues to exist. But because *tzaddikim* are such rare individuals, God distributed them sparingly across the generations so that no generation should be without *tzaddikim* in whose merit the world would be sustained.

This saying by our sages supports what has been said until now: namely, that the *tzaddik* is not merely one whose virtues outweigh his failings—surely many such individuals exist in each generation—but the rare individual who is perfect not only in behavior but also in essence. It also supports Job's contention that being a *tzaddik* is not a matter of choice but a state of being that is a gift from above.

The *Tanya*'s subject, however, is not the *tzaddik*—for the level of *tzaddik* is beyond the reach of the vast majority of people—but the *beinoni*. The author discusses the *tzaddik* only parenthetically, because this category has no practical relevance. He does so mainly to place the *beinoni* within the spectrum of categories ranging from *rashi* to *tzaddik*. Nor does the author spend much time on the *rasha;* he feels that we know such people well enough. The bulk of the book focuses on the *beinoni*, the intermediate individual—a concept that is original to this work. As has been explained, most ethical works failed to improve the behavior and character of their readers because they promoted a human ideal that was virtually unattainable. The *Tanya*'s uniqueness lies in its creation of a new ideal, the *beinoni*, that is within reach of every person.

Until this point, the author has been setting the stage, so to speak, introducing the concepts of *tzaddik, rasha,* and *beinoni* as they derive from a preliminary examination of the sources. From this point on begins the systematic development of the *Tanya*'s thesis: what the three states of *tzaddik, rasha,* and *beinoni* are; how they develop; and how man functions in the context of these three basic states of being.

The explanation [of these questions] is to be found in the light of what Rabbi Chaim Vital writes in *Sha'ar ha-Kedushah* (and in *Etz Chayyim,* Portal 50, ch. 2) that in every Jew, *tzaddik* and *rasha* alike, are two souls (*neshamot*),

The basis of all that the *Tanya* will say is that every Jew possesses two souls. The existence of these two souls is independent of the person's stature: great and small, righteous and wicked are all equal in this regard. The difference lies in how these souls manifest themselves: which of them finds expression in the person's consciousness and behavior, and on which level and in what manner it does so.

The concept of a "good inclination" (*yetzer tov*) and "evil inclination" (*yetzer harah*) in the heart of man abounds in the Talmud and the *Midrashim.* What is unique about Rabbi Chaim Vital's statement is that he speaks of two *souls,* two entire personas, each with a full set of intellectual and emotional faculties. The *yetzarim,* as the author explains in a Hasidic discourse,[20] are actually the traits, drives, and desires (*middot*) of their respective souls.

as it is written, "The souls (*neshamot*) which I have made," [that is,] two souls (*nefashot*).

The author begins by using the Hebrew word *neshamah* for "soul" but concludes with another synonym for soul, *nefesh.* Although the terms are used interchangeably in the Scriptures, each has a distinct meaning in Kabbalistic and Hasidic terminology.

The term *nefesh* actually has two meanings: a general meaning and a particular meaning. In its general sense, *nefesh* is an all-inclusive term for "soul": the entire range of forces and potentials that constitute the spiritual essence of man. Indeed, not only man but every created thing, including an inanimate object, has a *nefesh,* a spiritual essence.[21] The *nefesh* and the body are the two basic components of every physical entity: the *nefesh* is a thing's spiritual substance, and the body is its material substance; the *nefesh* is the life force, the body its vessel and vehicle. But while every material creature has but one body, the *nefesh* is multidimensional and might manifest itself in the body in a great variety of forms. In humans, the general *nefesh* includes five specific aspects or levels of soul: *nefesh, ruach, neshamah, chayah,* and *yechidah. Nefesh* is also the name of a particular aspect of the general *nefesh,* connoting the level of soul that is in most direct contact with the body and is the source of its biological life. The *nefesh* (in the particular sense) can be seen as a sort of intermediary between matter and spirit, the medium by which the metaphysical life force animates the physical body. *Nefesh* is thus the lowest of the five levels of soul: even one who is devoid of anything spiritual or transcendent in his life exhibits signs of *nefesh,* the most basic common denominator of life.

Now we can understand why the author begins by calling the two souls *neshamot,* but then "corrects" this, so to speak, to *nefashot. Neshamot* is the word employed in the verse from Isaiah from which Rabbi Chaim Vital derives the existence of the two souls; as we said, in scriptural Hebrew, *neshamah* often means soul in the most general sense. The *Tanya,* however, employs the terminology of Kabbalah, in which *neshamah* is a particular level of the soul (the highest of its three internal aspects). In this "language," it would not be accurate to say that every Jew, "*tzaddik* and *rasha* alike," possesses two *neshamot;* not everyone achieves the level of spirituality on which the *neshamah*-aspect of his soul is manifest in his life. Every Jew, however, possesses two *nefashot,* in the general sense of the word: two distinct life forces at play in his person.

The Lubavitcher Rebbe offers another explanation for the *Tanya*'s shift of terminology. The verse speaks of the "*neshamot* I [God] have made"; as created by God, every soul is on the lofty level of *neshamah.* But only the level of *nefesh* is actually vested in the physical body; it is up to man to "draw down" the higher dimensions of his soul into his life. So in speaking of how "every Jew, *tzaddik* and *rasha* alike" possesses two souls, the *Tanya* speaks of two *nefashot.*

One soul originates in *kelipah* and *sitra achra.*

One of the two souls of man stems from the negative elements of creation, called *kelipah* ("husk") and *sitra achra* ("other side").

Kelipah and *sitra achra* are subjects that Hasidism does not deal with extensively, for two reasons. First, this aspect of reality is, in any case, all too familiar; evil and selfishness hardly need to be described to us. Second, no great benefit comes from too much discussion and analysis of these elements. Dealing with evil in any way, even to the end of rectifying it, has a detrimental influence; the result is a familiarity and intimacy with evil that both has overt and subtle negative effects.

We might say, without going into too much detail, that the world is divided into two "sides": the side of holiness and the *sitra achra,* which literally means the "other side." The side of holiness is the side that relates to the Holy One, encompassing everything that recognizes Him and submits to Him. The other side, as its name implies, has no intrinsic content or identity of its own, being defined solely by the fact that it is not of the side of holiness.

This implies that there is no neutral ground between holiness and unholiness. Every object, force, or phenomenon is either holy or not; if it is not holy, it is of the *sitra achra.* A person who cleaves to God is of the side of holiness; a person who does not cleave to God has placed himself on the other side. One cannot be neutral in his relationship with God: man is either committed to Him and on His side or on the other side.

This approach is also related to the author's conception of the *beinoni*. As we said, there is no middle ground between righteousness and wickedness. In all that concerns one's actual behavior, one who is not a *tzaddik*—who is not wholly committed to the side of holiness—is, by definition, a *rasha*, one who has crossed the line to the other side. Between a *tzaddik* and the *rasha*—in the sense of "'*Tzaddik* or *rasha*?' is not pronounced [by the angel in charge of conception]"—there can be no *beinoni*. The "intermediate" of the *Tanya* does not relate to anything that a person does but to what God does. It is not a state generated by the deeds of man but a state created by God, who then gives man the choice of directing it either to the side of holiness or to the other side.

This is the Kabbalistic, as opposed to the halakhic, conception of reality. Halakhah ("Torah law") relates to a trifaceted world, recognizing a holy domain (objects or deeds of a *mitzvah*), a forbidden domain (*issur*), and a domain of the permissible or optional (*reshut*). In halakhah is an area of life that is neither *mitzvah* nor *issur*. From the Kabbalistic perspective, however, the halakhic domain of *reshut* is part and parcel of the other side. This is not to say that the Kabbalistic perspective does not distinguish between the *issur* and *reshut*: although Kabbalah recognizes no middle ground between the holy and the unholy, between the sacred and the profane, it sees a fundamental division within the domain of unholiness itself. There is rectifiable unholiness and unrectifiable unholiness. Those unholy elements that cannot be rectified, that cannot be liberated of their unholy state and elevated to a state of holiness, belong to the forbidden domain in halakhah. The rectifiable elements of *sitra achra* belong to the optional or *reshut* domain in halakhah—elements that can, and should, be transferred to the domain of holiness.

Another meaning of the term *sitra achra* is "the external side" (the Hebrew terms for "other" and "back" both derive from the same root). This meaning connects with the other Kabbalistic term for evil: *kelipah* or "husk." The husk is not just a name but also a metaphor for the relationship between good and evil. The fruit is encased in its husk; the fruit is the desirable element, whereas the extraneous husk serves only to protect the fruit and enable its development. The husk itself is inedible, and at a certain point, when the fruit has matured, the husk becomes an impediment, to be cracked open and discarded; now its role is to desist, to not be.

So *kelipah* and *sitra achra* are more than alternate terms for the same phenomenon; rather, these are two perspectives on evil. *Sitra achra* defines the *contrast* between the two sides. There is the Godly side of existence, which recognizes the Almighty and submits to His authority, and the other side, which does not. *Kelipah,* on the other hand, defines the *relationship* between the two sides. It ascribes a concentric structure to reality: reality consists of a sacred core encompassed by an external husk; by penetrating the husk, one attains the core. When we speak in terms of contrasts—holiness and profanity, positivity and negativity, light and darkness—there is no relationship between the two: one does not uncover positivity within negativity; darkness does not yield light. On the other hand, when we speak in terms of fruit and husk, we imply that by breaking open the husk, we reach the fruit. As the author will discuss in later chapters,[22] man is charged with the task of crushing and subduing the *kelipah* and *sitra achra* in order to reveal the light within.

This is the soul that is clothed in the blood of human being, giving life to the body, as it is written, "For the fleshly soul is in the blood."[23]

This soul is the natural or animal soul, the soul that animates the human body, supplying it with all aspects of natural human life, physical and metaphysical alike. This is "the fleshly soul," the force that transforms a mass of flesh into a living thing, a component of the biological stratum of creation.

The animal soul imbues the body as a force that is "clothed in the blood." This is not, of course, an enclothement in the physical sense; to understand the relationship between body and soul, we must envision it as an envelopment that both conceals and reveals. A garment conceals its wearer, but it is also the medium by which he presents himself to others, to those outside of himself. Or to cite an example of a metaphysical enclothement, thought clothes itself in speech: speech is the medium through which one reveals his thoughts to others, but speech also conceals thought, hiding all but an idea's most external, communicable surface. The metaphor of enclothement is also used to describe a certain aspect of the relationship between the divine light and its vessel, which is the Kabbalistic model for the divine forces that sustain and shape our world through the vessels of the divine attributes. The vessel is the medium through which the divine light manifests itself and acts upon our existence; at the same time, the vessel conceals the light.

Thus, we say that the soul enclothes itself in the blood of the human being. It hides itself in the blood and manifests itself in the blood, providing the body with the spiritual force of life and vitality, and hiding behind the body's obscuring veil of corporeality. The blood is the medium through which the animal soul—the spiritual force that supplies the body with physical life—manifests itself.

From it stem all the [person's] evil characteristics, deriving from the four evil elements which are contained in it.

All negative character traits in a person derive from his animal soul. These fall under four general categories, corresponding to the four elements that constitute the animal soul.

The concept that every entity consists of the four elements (fire, water, air, and earth) was widely accepted in the ancient and medieval world, as well as, to a certain extent, in various periods and disciplines of Jewish thought. In any case, the significance of this division lies less in its empirical details than in the logical categorization it represents. Theoretically, we might employ other models to serve the same end, but the author chose to employ the terminology prevalent in his time and place.

These are: anger and pride, which emanate from the element of Fire, the nature of which is to rise upwards;

Pride and anger are intimately related; the one spawns the other. Here, the author focuses on their spatial structure: just as the nature of fire is to incessantly gravitate upward, so, too, anger and pride are functions of self, the elevation and the inflammation of the ego. Pride is the swelling of ego, and anger is the resistance to anything that might impinge upon the ego's assertion that "I am, and nothing else exists."[24]

As a fire's heat feeds its own upward surge, so, too, are the traits of pride and anger characterized by their self-perpetuation. The nature of other passions is that the more they are indulged, the less intense they become, until they diminish and fade away over time. The experience of pride and anger, on the other hand, only increases its intensity: the more they are indulged, the more they grow. This is reflected in the fact that in Hebrew, "to be proud" (*mitga'eh*) and "to be angered" (*mitragez*) are reflexive verbs ("to pride oneself"; "to anger oneself"); the anger or the pride rebounds to act upon the person. A person becomes proud, and his pride acts upon him to make him prouder still; a person gets angry, and his anger acts upon him to make him angrier still. These are actors that gain a life of their own, feeding on their own frenzy, fanning their own flames as a fire that generates the heat that intensifies its own conflagration.

the lust for pleasure from the element of Water, for water makes to grow all kinds of enjoyment;

Some desires derive from other traits (desires motivated by pride, anger, and so on), and then there is "lust for pleasure": desire for the sake of desire. This desire stems from the element of water, which is the element of life, of fertility, of pleasure. In the Godly and positive dimension of reality, water represents benevolence and love. But every holy element has its negative counterpart on the other side; here the element of water spawns negative desires and negative passions— desire for pleasure as an end in itself, whatever form it might take.

frivolity, causticity, boasting, and idle talk from the element of Air;

These traits are mere emptiness, insubstantial as air. These are not traits that have a certain substance to them, such as the egotistical substance of pride or the pleasure-substance of lust. Frivolity, causticity, and boasting are simply a form of letting go, things a person does without thought or responsibility. What we have here is not a lust for greatness or pleasure but mere lust for nothing. These are actions that, as the expression goes, are full of air; they might seem full and purposeful from the outside, but there is nothing in them. (The author distinguishes here between pride and boastfulness, saying that the two are unrelated: pride is of the element of fire, whereas boastfulness is of the element of air. Indeed, there are people who are full of pride but are not boastful, and boastful people who are not full of pride: these are two distinct traits.)

and sloth and melancholy from the element of Earth.

From earth, the lowliest of the four elements, which gravitates downward, stem sloth and melancholy, which weigh down the soul to inactivity. This might be due to simple laziness or to the inertia of depression. Sloth is a feeling of heaviness, of an inability to drive oneself to do what needs to be done and what one desires to do. Melancholy paralyzes a person's will and creativity, to the same result: an inability to act and respond.

This categorization of the animal soul's negative traits by its four elements is not to say that one person cannot possess traits from two or more different elements. Rather, it means that the traits of each category are, in essence, subtraits of one "father attribute" and will always be distinct from a trait that is derived from another of the four "father attributes." In other words, the categorization of four elements of the animal soul is similar to the Talmud's categorization of "Thirty-Nine Father Labors" (Mishnah, *Shabbat*, ch. 7) or "Four Father Torts" (*Bava Kamma* 2b). Each principal labor or tort is a "father" with many "descendants" or derivatives; "descendants" of the same "father" are intrinsically synonymous with each other (though externally different) and are intrinsically different from the "descendants" of other "fathers." Thus, derivatives of two different elements can be found in a single individual, but they will never become a single trait.

A significant feature of the author's conception of these negative traits is that they *derive* from the four elements of the animal soul but are not synonymous with them. Certain religions and moral philosophies have a tendency to equate the good and evil traits with certain elements of the human character, implying that there are good emotions and drives, and bad ones. For example, one common conception is that a dose of melancholy is a good thing, whereas merriment is a moral defect. This view assumes that an ebullient nature leads to sin, while a melancholy and serious disposition is synonymous with responsibility and virtue. Another approach argues the very opposite: that any emotion that drives a person to act and achieve is positive, that joy and merriment are essentially good, and that even anger and pride are not necessarily evil. At any rate, the difference between a positive trait and a negative one does not lie in the classification of certain characteristics as good or bad; the very same traits can be positive in one context and negative in another, depending on where they come from, the role they play, and the way in which they operate. Good and evil traits are not of two types; rather, they are mirror images of each other; in the words of King Solomon, "One mirroring the other, God has wrought."[25] The positive and negative traits of man—just as holiness and the *kelipah* themselves—differ from each other not in their essence and quality but, to a great extent, in the context and manner in which they are applied. Thus, a person of a particular character or temperament is never, by definition, a "good" or a "bad" person: he can be either this or that, depending on the use he makes of his traits and of the opportunities extended to him. Even the trait of melancholy, which all Hasidic masters deplore, can, at times, be used (most carefully, for it can indeed cause great devastation) to a constructive end.[26] In the same vein, a Hasidic master once said of one of his disciples that the man's vanity was the source of his virtue: every time he was tempted by sin, he said to himself, "How can I, being who I am, stoop to such a deed?" Indeed, even the most lethal poisons are not toxic in all circumstances and dosages; certain poisons (such as curare), when used in the right dosage and manner of application, might even serve as a cure.

In character, as in nature, nothing is intrinsically evil, only its particular application in a particular context. Thus, one cannot determine in advance which things to reject and which to embrace; one must judge each case on its own merits, taking in account the context, actors, and specifics of each situation before deeming a feeling or course of action good or bad.

From this soul also derive the good characteristics that are to be found in the innate nature of every Jew,

The animal soul is not necessarily the "evil" element in man; rather, it is what defines his natural self, the array of vital, spiritual, and emotional forces that make the animal man. As we said, every creature has a *nefesh,* a soul. The *nefesh* is not an abstract life force but a multifaceted, complex dynamic that is specific to each particular creature—man, animal, plant, even stone—and imparts to it its particular qualities. In man, the *nefesh* embodies the drives, volitions, preconceptions, and cravings, both physical and spiritual, that constitute his human self. Good or evil are not at issue here; we are speaking of the natural state of man, in the same way that we would speak of the forces that shape the nature of any animal. In this sense, the uniquely human faculties of man, such as intelligence and speech, also derive from the animal soul. Man is a highly developed, complex creature, so his *nefesh* is likewise highly developed and complex: in addition to its base lusts and drives, in addition to its propensity to frivolity and idle talk, it possesses the faculty for thought, reasoning, and cognition. But the philosopher in man is no less part and parcel of his biological self and does not express anything holy, anything that transcends the naturally human, what is zoologically defined as Homo sapiens.

But even in the animal, biological sense, the Jewish soul is a species unto itself. Just as living things are a unique genre in creation, and the human being is a unique species of animal, so is the Jew a unique species of human (and so, as we shall see, is the *tzaddik* a unique species of Jew). Just as man is born human, the Jew is born Jewish. The only question is to what extent he will actualize his unique potential as a Jew; and this is a factor of education, development, and, most of all, will. But the same is true of humans in general: human children raised by animals develop their human potential only to a most limited extent, if at all. (We know that the more highly developed a creature is, the more it must learn and train in order to realize its potential. A fly does not have to be taught anything; it is born with all it needs to know to be a fly, and it won't learn much more. Higher life forms need to learn more, and if they are not taught and trained, or if there be any significant lack in the manner of their training, they will fail to behave like the rest of their kind.)

Because we are speaking of the Jewish animal soul, we are speaking of a *nefesh* whose natural composition includes distinctly positive traits. Every living creature has its distinct character: some are vicious predators, others naturally compassionate; some are audacious, others docile. The animal soul of the Jew, on its most basic level, possesses certain "good" traits. Instinctively, without any moral effort on his part, the Jew does certain things, reacts to certain stimuli, without a further thought, almost automatically. A person does not have to be taught to desire what is pleasurable, nor does the child have to be trained in how to get angry; these traits are instinctive to the natural soul as an integral part of the human character. In the same way, the natural soul of the Jew possesses certain positive traits,

such as compassion and charity.

This, in keeping with the Talmudic statement, "Three distinguishing features mark this people: they are compassionate, bashful, and charitable."[27] So integral are these qualities to the Jewish character that it was said that whoever does not exhibit these traits is not of the seed of Israel.[28] A Jew is charitable not because he has conquered his selfish inclinations or because he is a particularly good person but because it is his nature. Just as certain people have a weakness for certain things, the Jew has a "weakness" for compassion, bashfulness, and charity.[29] Some people have a propensity for music, but this does not make them better or worse persons. In the same way, the Jew is, by nature, bashful, compassionate, and charitable; this is how he was born. It does not make him more righteous; it makes him what he is.

Why, one might wonder, does the *Tanya* only mention two of the traits enumerated by the Talmud—compassion and charity—and omit the third, bashfulness? The Lubavitcher Rebbe explains that only these two are natural, inborn traits. This is not the case with bashfulness; indeed, the Talmud says that, by nature, "Israel is the most brazen of nations."[30] But the experience of the divine revelation at Sinai suppressed their brazen nature and made them docile. Thus, although bashfulness is a trait common to every Jew (to the extent that its lack puts a person's Jewishness in question), it cannot be said to be a natural trait, deriving from the Jew's animal soul.

For in the case of the Jew, this soul of the *kelipah* is derived from *kelipat nogah,* which also contains good,

There are four basic *kelipot:* the three profane *kelipot* and *kelipat nogah* (the "luminous" *kelipat*). The four *kelipot* are alluded to in a passage in the prophet Ezekiel's description of the supernal "chariot": "a storm wind," "a great cloud," and "a flaring fire"; and a "luminousness [*nogah*] about it."[31] "Storm wind," "great cloud," and "flaring fire" refer to the three profane *kelipot;* "and a luminousness about it" refers to the luminous (or translucent) husk, *kelipat nogah.*

Kelipat nogah is the boundary between the utterly dark and negative domain of unholiness and the domain of holiness and light. It is indeed a *kelipah,* a light-obscuring husk, but it is not utter darkness; it is a luminescent darkness, a veil that allows a hint of light to pass through.

As shall be explained, even the three profane *kelipot* are not completely devoid of light. For nothing exists that does not possess a spark of good. Goodness and holiness are, in essence, synonymous with divinity; and because God is the ultimate and exclusive source of existence, it follows that anything that is completely devoid of good is, by definition, absolute nothingness. A thing that is possesses some measure of good.[32] The difference between the three profane *kelipot* and *kelipat nogah* is the accessibility of the good at their core and the ability to "release" it. In nature, we find many examples of this: substance A might contain a particular element, but this element is "locked" within it, whereas substance B might contain the same element but in a manner that readily allows its extraction. Substance B does not necessarily contain a greater quantity of it; it simply contains that element in a more accessible form. For instance, aluminum is one of the most important metals to industry. It is also one of the most plentiful elements in nature; almost all soil contains aluminum. Practically, however, extracting aluminum from the ordinary soil in any gainful way is virtually impossible. Therefore, one must seek rare and precious materials (such as bauxite), not because they contain greater concentrations of aluminum but because they more readily yield it from themselves. This, in a certain sense, is analogous to the difference between the three profane *kelipot* and *kelipat nogah:* the three kelipot, too, contain good, but we have not been granted the ability to extract it from them; *kelipat nogah,* on the other hand, represents those elements of creation in which the good is more discernible and extractable.

The animal soul in the Jew derives from a nonholy source, from *kelipah.* But this *kelipah, kelipat nogah,* possesses certain elements of good, which, with the proper stimulation, will come to light. The Jew exhibits these traits not because he has chosen good and rejected evil but as an almost instinctive reaction. This, as we shall see, is against the natural self of the non-Jew, which derives from the three profane *kelipot.* Obviously, a non-Jew can also be charitable, compassionate, or bashful; in a non-Jew, however, these are not natural traits but traits that must be acquired and cultivated through education and training, just as the Jew must cultivate many positive traits (humility, joy in serving God, and so on) that are not natural to him, for they are not part of his biological self and must be acquired through education and hard work and often only by vanquishing his natural instincts.

The natural traits of man, whether positive or negative, have no objective value as "good" or "evil." A Jew who lives a wholly animal life, following only the dictates of his base instincts, will find compassion and charity among his *kelipah*-deriving traits. And in a certain sense, the natural self of the non-Jew also includes traits that are morally ambivalent. For every negative trait has its positive side: pride is usually accompanied with a certain amount of guarding one's limits; frivolity and boasting usually signify an openhearted and expansive character; and so on.

Thus, the "the good characteristics that are to be found in the innate nature of every Jew" form part of the natural dynamic that defines the relationship between matter and spirit in every living creature. In the Jew, this dynamic might be more sophisticated and possessive of a higher consciousness, but it is essentially similar to that of every other natural soul.

as it originates in the esoteric "Tree of Knowledge of Good and Evil."

The "Tree of Knowledge of Good and Evil" is the matrix and symbol of *kelipat nogah,* of the admixture of light and darkness, good and evil.

The souls of the nations of the world, however, derive from the other impure *kelipot,* which contain no good whatever, as it is written in *Etz Chayyim,* Portal 49, ch. 3,

The essence of *kelipah* is its egocentricity (as opposed to holiness, which is defined by its self-abnegation to God). In *kelipah,* the "I" is the axis about which all revolves, the ultimate reference point being: What's in it for me? Because the natural soul of the non-Jew is wholly *kelipah,* devoid of all manifest holiness, all the good that the non-Jew does derives from egocentric considerations, be it to the aim of priding oneself with one's good deeds or the aim of achieving peace and harmony in the world that the "I" inhabits. It does not turn toward the other; rather,

all the good that the nations do, is done from selfish motives. As the Talmud comments on the verse, "The kindness of the nations is sin":[33] "All the charity and kindness done by the nations of the world is only for their own self-glorification" and so on.

The author is not coming, with these brief sentences, to define the nature of the non-Jew. Whatever he says here about non-Jews is just the background for the issue with which he is dealing—namely, the uniqueness of the natural animal soul of the Jew. For when we say that the Jew is chosen and unique among the peoples of the world, it is in regard to his animal soul and not regarding the Jew's "Godly soul" (see Chapter 2), which the non-Jew does not possess at all. From the stock of the souls of humanity branches out the Jewish animal soul, which has its similarities as well as its uniqueness vis-à-vis the natural soul of the non-Jew.

The process of Israel's becoming a chosen people is described in the book of Genesis not unlike the process of genetic selection in the breeding of plants. From tens of thousands of specimens, one selects three or four seedlings that exhibit certain desirable qualities. These are set aside and repeatedly grafted upon each other until a new species emerges, a species that exhibits the desired quality distinctly rather than vaguely, naturally rather than by change of nature. This is the story told in the book of Genesis: from millions of human beings, God chooses one seedling; from the progeny of this seedling, He again selects one branch, one individual, whom He carefully cultivates into a new breed of human being. As with our agricultural metaphor, this new species is the result of a natural selection and mutation, guided by a conscious volition, out of thousands of possibilities. This new species now possesses certain qualities that have become part of its nature: it does not have to overcome its natural self to be better than its norm, in order to achieve certain things. The other species of its kind are also capable of achieving these things, but this is an extraordinary achievement for them; they require much effort, conscious orientation, and self-transformation before they can produce something of unalloyed goodness.

It is told that during his imprisonment, Rabbi Schneur Zalman was required to answer a great number of questions regarding Hasidic teaching and the Hasidic position on various issues, including various Hasidic customs and matters of Kabbalistic interpretation. One of these questions concerned what Rabbi Schneur Zalman had written here about the natural soul of the non-Jew. As related in the book *Beit Rebbe* (which was published in Russia under czarist censorship), Rabbi Schneur Zalman answered all the questions to the satisfaction of his interrogators, but when it came to this question he merely smiled and said nothing. The *Beit Rebbe* adds, "The significance of his smile is understandable to the wise."

Chapter 2

T he second soul of the Jew is a part of God above, literally. As it is written, "And He breathed into his nostrils the breath of life," "And You breathed it into me"; and it is written in the *Zohar,* "He who exhales, exhales from within him," that is to say, from his inwardness and his innermost, for it is something of one's internal and innermost vitality that one emits through exhaling with force.

So, allegorically speaking, the souls of Israel arose in the [divine] thought. As it is written, "My firstborn son, Israel," and "You are children unto the Lord your God." That is to say, just as a child is derived from his father's brain, so, too, to use an anthropomorphism, the soul of each Israelite is derived from God's (blessed be He) thought and wisdom—He who is wise, but not with any knowable wisdom, because He and His wisdom are one; as Maimonides writes,

Note: And the Sages of the Kabbalah concurred with him, as is stated in Rabbi Moshe Cordovero's *Pardes.* Also according to the Kabbalah of the "Ari," this is substantiated in the mystic principle of the "Clothing of the Light" of the *Ein Sof,* Blessed be He, through numerous contractions within the vessels *ChaBaD* of the world of *Atzilut* ("Emanation"), but no higher than that. For, as is explained elsewhere, the *Ein Sof,* blessed be He, is infinitely exalted over, and transcends, the essence and level of *ChaBaD*, to the extent that the essence and level of *ChaBaD* are regarded as a physical action in relation to Him, as is written, "You made them all with wisdom."

"He is the knowledge, He is the knower . . . and this thing is not within the power of any man to truly comprehend . . . as it is written, 'Can you by searching find God?,' and 'For My thoughts are not your thoughts. . . .'"

And though there are myriads of different gradations of souls (*neshamot*), rank upon rank, ad infinitum, as with superiority of the souls of the Patriarchs and of Moses our Teacher over the souls of our own generations, those of the "heels of the Messiah," which are as the very heels of the feet compared with the brain and head; and so in every generation there are the leaders of Israel, whose souls are in the category of "head" and "brain" in comparison with those of the masses and the ignorant; likewise [are there distinctions] between *nefashot* and *nefashot*, for every *nefesh* consists of *nefesh, ruach,* and *neshamah;* nevertheless, the root of every *nefesh, ruach,* and *neshamah,* from the highest of levels to the lowest of levels embodied within the ignoramus and the least reverent, all derive, as it were, from the Supernal Mind which is *Chokhmah Ila'ah* ("Supernal Wisdom"), as in the analogy of a child who derives from his father's brain, that even his toenails come into being from the very same drop of semen, through its nine-month stay in the mother's womb, descending degree by degree, changing continually, until even the nails are formed from it, yet [the child's body] is still bound and united with a wonderful and quintessential unity with its original essence and being, which was as a drop of the father's brain, and even now, in the child, the nails receive their nourishment and life from the brain that is in the head. As is written in the *Gemara* (*Niddah,* ibid.), "From the white of the father's drop of semen are formed the veins, the bones, and the nails." (And in *Etz Chayyim, Sha'ar haChashmal,* it is likewise stated, in connection with the esoteric principle of Adam's garments in the Garden of Eden, that they were the "nails" derived from the cognitive faculty of the brain.)

And so it literally is, as it were, with the supernal root of every *nefesh, ruach,* and *neshamah* in the community of Israel on high: in descending degree by degree, through the evolution of the worlds of *Atzilut, Beriah, Yetzirah,* and *Assiyah* from His blessed Wisdom—as it is written, "You have made them all with wisdom,"—the *nefesh, ruach,* and *neshamah* of the ignorant and unworthy come into being; yet they remain bound and united, with a wonderful and quintessential unity, with their original essence and entity, namely, the extension of the Supernal Wisdom. For the nurture and life of the *nefesh, ruach,* and *neshamah* of the ignorant are drawn from the *nefesh, ruach,* and *neshamah* of the *tzaddikim* and Sages, the heads of Israel in their generation.

This explains the comment of our Sages on the verse, "And to cleave unto Him": "He who cleaves unto a Torah scholar is deemed by the Torah as if he had become attached to the very *Shekhinah.*" For through their attachment to the scholars, the *nefesh, ruach,* and *neshamah* of the ignorant are bound up and united with their original essence and their root in the Supernal Wisdom, He and His wisdom being one, and "He is the Knowledge. . . ." (As for those who willfully sin and rebel against the Sages, the nurture of their *nefesh, ruach,* and *neshamah* comes from behind the back, as it were, of the *nefesh, ruach,* and *neshamah* of the scholars.)

As for what is written in the *Zohar* and in *Zohar Chadash,* that the essential factor is to conduct oneself in a sanctified manner during sexual union, which is not the case with the children of the ignorant, and so on, what is meant there is that since there is not a *nefesh, ruach,* and *neshamah* which has not a garment from the soul of its father's and mother's essence, and the *mitzvot* that it does are all achieved via that garment, [and so on], and even the sustenance that is given to him from Heaven is all given through that garment, so if a person sanctifies himself, he will draw down a hallowed garment for the soul of his child. Even a great soul requires its father's sanctification. But as for the soul itself, it sometimes happens that the soul of an infinitely lofty person comes to be the son of a despised and lowly man, etc. All this has been explained by Rabbi Isaac Luria, of blessed memory, in *Likkutei Torah,* on *Parashat vaYera,* and in *Ta'amei haMitzvot on Parashat Bereshit.*

COMMENTARY

In Chapter 1, we discussed the natural or animal soul of the Jew. We said that this soul derives from *kelipah,* but that this does not mean that it is to be identified with the person's evil traits or with evil itself. The natural soul is indeed the source of a person's vices and is closely related to them, but it is by no means synonymous with them. The natural soul embodies the life of man and imparts to him all his human qualities, including his intellect and his aesthetic sense, just as the natural soul of the animal imparts to an animal its particular qualities and nature. If man learns to properly activate this soul, he can thereby attain great heights and create many good and beautiful things. However, this is all within the sphere of human capacity, which, great as it may be, has nothing to do with holiness. There is nothing in the nature of man that leads, in and of itself, to holiness; there is no natural process by which man might develop and refine his natural body and soul, step by step, into something holy. Touching upon holiness is a break from, rather than an outgrowth of, one's natural self: a prodigious intellect or an aesthetic sensitivity do not necessarily generate or lead man to holiness. Man has one aspect, and that is his natural, animal soul; there is more to man, but this additional dimension does not constitute a continuum with his natural self. It is this second dimension, the holy dimension, by which man and his world connect to God, that the author discusses in the second chapter of *Tanya*.

The second soul of the Jew is a part of God above, literally.

This is the Godly element in man, the spark of divine essence that manifests itself in his being and experience.

The phrase "part of God above" is from Job (31:2). The author adds the word *mamash* ("tangibly" or "literally") to stress that this is to be understood most literally. The Godly soul in man is not figuratively a part of God but actually and literally so.

The author refers to the Godly soul as "the second soul of the Jew," though it might seem that, in terms of its greatness and loftiness, it might have been more aptly termed the "first soul." One reason for this is that this soul is a person's second: our sages tell us that man is born with his evil inclination and only later acquires his good inclination. As explained in Chapter 1, the evil inclination is the group of emotional traits that stem from the animal soul, whereas the good inclination is that of the emotional traits of the Godly soul. Although the Godly soul is inherent in the Jew and is the ultimate source of his life from the very start, only upon the attainment of the age of maturity (thirteen for a man, twelve for a woman) does it manifest itself in the form of a good inclination, as a drive and desire for attachment to God.[1]

There is a reason for this order. The animal soul must come first because the Godly soul requires a vessel that is sufficiently developed and sophisticated to channel and express it. As long as natural man has not attained this level of development, the Godly soul can exist in him only as a potential for holiness, rather than as an operative force. If a human soul were to be "placed" in a stone, there would be no significance to this combination: no human quality can exist in and manifest itself through such a vessel. Every spiritual force requires a conduit that is fit for it; for the Godly soul, the requisite vessel is a mature animal soul. In order for the Godly soul to manifest itself in the life of man in a meaningful way—that is, in a way that enables its refinement and elevation of the animal soul—it requires that an animal soul should be placed in a human body and that it should develop to the point that the Godly soul can join it and be revealed through it.

The Lubavitcher Rebbe explains that the Godly soul is called the second soul because its investment in the body is due solely to the animal soul. The Godly soul itself is perfect and does not require *tikkun* ("rectification" through the process and achievements of earthly life); it descends into physical life only in order to conquer the evil inclination and refine the animal soul.

As it is written, "And He breathed into his nostrils the breath of life," "And You breathed it into me"; and it is written in the *Zohar*, "He who exhales, exhales from within him," that is to say, from his inwardness and his innermost, for it is something of one's internal and innermost vitality that one emits through exhaling with force

The author now proceeds to explain the concept that the Godly soul is "a part of God above, literally," based on the metaphors that the Torah employs in reference to the soul.

We find the soul repeatedly described as the "breath" of God. Indeed, one Hebrew word for soul, *neshamah*, comes from the same root as *neshimah* ("breath"). In its account of the creation of man, the Torah tells of how God "breathed in his nostrils a breath of life (*nishmat chayyim*)."[2] A similar expression is found in the daily morning prayers, in which we say, "and You have breathed it [my soul] into me."[3] As the *Zohar* points out,[4] *nefichah* ("breathing into"), used in both these citations, implies a most forceful expulsion of air, in which a person expends his innermost reserves of life-sustaining breath.

The metaphor of *nefichah* is the Torah's way of expressing the difference between the soul of man and all other creations. As related in the first chapter of Genesis, all creations—except for man—came into being by divine speech: God said, "Let there be light," and there was light; God said, "Let the earth sprout vegetation," and all plant life came forth from the earth; and so on. As the author explains at length in the first chapter of *Sha'ar haYichud v'haEmunah* (the second book of *Tanya*), these divine "utterances" constitute the creating and animating force that continually sustains all creation. The exception is the soul of man, which was created not by divine speech but by a divine "expulsion of breath."

Obviously, God does not actually speak or breathe. Speech and breath are metaphors: by studying the physical dynamics of these phenomena in ourselves, we gain insight into their purely metaphysical significance vis-à-vis the Creator. In the human being, speech is a relatively external effort: one expends only a small part of the breath in the lungs by uttering words, and one continues to breathe normally as one speaks. Speech thus represents a superficial investment on the part of the speaker, something in which he uses only a small percentage of his ability. On the other hand, with a forceful expulsion of breath, a person gives it his all, expelling all the air in his lungs, expending his very "breath of life" in the effort. Thus, God's "breathing a breath of life" into the nostrils of man implies an entirely different degree of investment on His part compared with His other, "spoken" creations: in all other creations, God involved Himself only on a most external level, whereas in creating the soul of man, He gave of His very self. So man, on his deepest level of being, is animated by a life force that is "a part of God above, literally"—the Godly soul that dwells and operates within him.

One must bear in mind that the *Tanya* does not deal with theoretical ideals but provides models for application in the daily moral life of man. Thus, the fact that the soul of man is "a part of God above" is not some esoteric concept but the underlying idea behind the high standards that *Tanya* holds us to. What the *Tanya* demands of the "intermediate" individual is nothing less than absolute perfection on the behavioral level—what is commonly perceived as the mark of the perfect *tzaddik*. Such a demand can be made only because man is, in essence, "a part of God above." At the very onset, it emphasizes that man should know that the highest, most powerful, and most holy reality— "a part of God above"—is already inherent within him. What remains for him is to ensure that this spark of divinity should be made *mamash*: "literal" and "tangible" in his actual, physical life.

So, allegorically speaking, the souls of Israel arose in the [divine] thought

This expression, taken from the *Zohar*,[5] is another aspect of the metaphor of God's "breathing out" the soul of man. All other creations derive from divine "speech" and thus relate only to the externality of the divine creative force; the soul, on the other hand, "arose in the [divine] thought"—thought being more intimate with, and intrinsic to, its conceiver than speech.

as it is written, "My firstborn son, Israel,"[6] and "You are children unto the Lord your God."[7] That is to say, just as a child is derived from his father's brain, so, too, to use an anthropomorphism, the soul of each Israelite is derived from God's (blessed be He) thought and wisdom—

This allegory is apparently taken from ancient medical science, which believed that the seminal seed originates as an ethereal, near-spiritual substance that comes from the father's brain. As this seed is released from the brain and passes through the body, it gradually coarsens and materializes, until it assumes its physical form as a drop of semen (which then enters the mother's womb and develops into a child). Thus, the child's relationship with his father is more than physical: it extends all the way to the core of their spiritual-psychological being, the child's essence deriving from the father's brain, the seat of his consciousness and identity. In other words, the child originates as a particle of the father's personality; only by a complex process, which unfolds within the father's body and continues in the womb, does the child evolve and materialize into a being that is ostensibly separate from its progenitor. In essence, however, the child remains an integral part of the father's spiritual self.

If a contemporary person were to express this concept in terms consistent with our current understanding of the process of procreation, he might say that the pituitary gland in the father's brain generates the hormones that trigger the reproductive glands' secretion of the sperm. The pituitary gland does not function automatically but is activated by an array of sensory and cognitive stimuli that are consciously assimilated and processed. In this model, we also see the connection between the father's mind and the seminal drop, albeit not in terms of a source for a particular bit of matter that moves from point A to point B but as the originator of causal process that begins with a conscious mind-activity and culminates in the generation of the cell from which a child develops. A chain of cause and effect runs from the metaphysical domain to the physical: from the purely spiritual core of self, through thought and sense, through chemical processes in the brain, through other neurological and chemical processes in the body, to the actual creation of the seminal seed. In truth, the process is far more complex, consisting of many steps across many domains. But regardless of the particulars of whatever model we employ, the point is the same: although on one level of reality father and child are two distinct entities, the higher we go back to the child's source, the more unified they are, until we reach the point at which they are one and the same. Thus, the relationship between father and child is one of quintessential oneness, so that even after they separate into two beings, they remain one in essence.

In this sense, the Jew is a child of God. In its primordial origins, the Godly soul of the Jew is not just a creation generated by the divine will but an integral part of the divine manifestation itself. This is the level of the soul that is called *yechidah* ("singularity"), the point at which all souls of Israel constitute a single unit. On this level of being, the soul has no individual identity: its essence as a "part of God above" is manifest, so all individual souls coalesce and self-abnegate in face of the revealed divine unity.

Hasidic teaching has a concept called *d'veikut* ("attachment"). *D'veikut* is the process by which a person retraces the phases of his own creation until he reaches the point at which he ceases to be a separate entity. This is the state that the *Zohar* refers to as "being drawn into the body of the King":[8] to be "sucked in" and nullified within the divine essence. This is comparable, if such a thing would be possible, to a child retracing the phases of his conception and reverting to be once again a mere thought in the mind of his father.

He who is wise, but not with any knowable wisdom, because He and His wisdom are one;

We said that the Godly soul derives from the "thought and wisdom" of God. The author immediately qualifies this by quoting the *Zohar*, which states that "He is wise, but not by any knowable wisdom";[9] although we refer to God as "wise" and possessing wisdom, this is not a wisdom of the sort that we are capable of understanding or relating to in any way. His is a wisdom of an entirely different sort, the most basic distinction being that "He and his wisdom are one." A human being's wisdom—his knowledge and understanding—is something additional to his self: he knows and understands things that are, for the most part, outside of himself; therefore, his wisdom is also something distinct from him. He relates to it; he is deeply influenced and even transformed by it; but he and it always remain two distinct entities: himself and the wisdom he possesses. God, however, is the sole reality—in the words of the Torah, "There is none else beside Him";[10] everything that He "knows" and "understands" is but an expression of His own being. So God's wisdom is synonymous with His very being.

as Maimonides writes,[11] "He is the knowledge, He is the knower . . .

The quotation continues "and He is the mind itself—all are one." All human knowledge has three distinct components: the known object, the knower, and the mind—the instrument by which the knower knows the known object. In God, writes Maimonides, the three are one and the same.[12]

and this thing is not within the power of any man to truly comprehend. . . .

A person can understand only something that exists, in some form or manner, within himself.[13] Because nothing in man is in any way comparable to the wholly internal, all-embracing self-knowledge of God, it is impossible for him to truly comprehend its nature.

As it is written, 'Can you by searching find God?'[14] and 'For My thoughts are not your thoughts. . . .'"

"My thoughts are not your thoughts" (Isaiah 55:8) does not merely mean that God "thinks" of other, greater, things than we do, but that His very "thought process" is utterly different from ours. In the words of the *Zohar*, His is "not a knowable wisdom": His wisdom bears no resemblance whatsoever to the wisdom we know but is of a different essence entirely and thus incomprehensible to us.

Note: And the Sages of the Kabbalah concurred with him, as is stated in Rabbi Moshe Cordovero's *Pardes*.[15]

Several sages, most notably the Maharal,[16] took issue with this statement by Maimonides, arguing that one cannot describe or define God in any way nor ascribe anything as intrinsic to His being—not even in the most sublime and abstract terms. But most Kabbalists, despite the differences between their worldview and that of Maimonides, agree with Maimonides on two points: (1) that the divine wisdom utterly transcends all levels and all qualities of human wisdom; and (2) that God's wisdom is not separate from Him but one with Him with an absolute unity.

Also according to the Kabbalah of the "Ari," this is substantiated in the mystic principle of the "Clothing of the Light" of the *Ein Sof*,[17] Blessed be He, through numerous contractions within the vessels *ChaBaD*[18] of the world of *Atzilut* ("Emanation"), but no higher than that.

The Lurianic Kabbalah (the Kabbalistic tradition taught by Rabbi Isaac Luria, known as the Holy Ari) discusses dimensions of the divine reality that are loftier and more abstract than what is discussed in the Cordoverian Kabbalah, formulated by Rabbi Moshe Cordovero in his book *Pardes Rimmonim.* Thus, when viewed in light of the Lurianic tradition, Maimonides' statement regarding the identification of the divine wisdom with the being of God is correct only on a particular level of the divine reality, not absolutely. Regarding the very essence of God, Maimonides' statement is indeed inappropriate; here, the Maharal's argument—that wisdom (in whatever form) cannot be ascribed as a divine quality, just as no definitive quality can be ascribed to Him—holds true. But when applied to a particular manifestation of the divine reality—that of the world of *Atzilut* ("Emanation")—it is true that God assumes, to the point of utter unity, the attribute of wisdom. By the means of many *tzimtzumim* ("constrictions"), a ray of the infinite essence of God enclothes itself in the divine attribute *chokhmah* ("Wisdom") of *Atzilut,* and regarding this constricted ray of Godliness, it can be said that "the knower, known, and mind are one."

In context of the greater picture (that is, the divine reality as seen via the Lurianic Kabbalah), Maimonides' statement is only partially correct. Nevertheless, Rabbi Schneur Zalman cites this particular statement in our chapter (qualifying it as a particular truth within a broader truth only in a note), because Maimonides' formula makes the concept under discussion accessible to a wider range of minds.[19] The use of a partial formula, although a broader formula also exists, is common practice in all fields; generally, the reason for this is because the narrower formula optimally describes the concept under discussion, whereas a broader formulation is not only unnecessary but also confusing to the student. The same is true in our case: Maimonides' formula is both adequate and accurate in our context, and it is also a more useful approach to the understanding of the subject at hand. Thus, when the author wishes to also point out the existence of a broader perspective and the relationship of Maimonides' statement to that perspective, he confines his remarks to a note, rather than including them in the chapter proper.

For, as is explained elsewhere,[20] the *Ein Sof*, blessed be He, is infinitely exalted over, and transcends, the essence and level of *ChaBaD*, to the extent that the essence and level of *ChaBaD* are regarded as a physical action in relation to Him, as is written, "You made them all with wisdom."

As we said, "He and His wisdom are one" describes not the relationship of the supernal wisdom to the divine essence but its relationship to the divine emanation that constricts itself to manifest itself in it. As for the relationship of the supernal wisdom to the divine essence—of this we cannot say anything. All we can say is that the supernal wisdom is to the divine essence as physical action is to us. In the spectrum of our reality, *chokhmah* is the highest point and physical action the lowest, and the distance between them is the greatest conceivable distance between two entities in our reality. This being the most extreme model we are capable of conceiving, we use it as an analogy and as a means for conceiving the immeasurably greater distance between the divine essence and supernal wisdom. This analogy the author reads in the verse he quotes from Psalms, "You made them all with wisdom" (*kulam b'chokhmah assita*).[21]

Just as our physical deeds are extrinsic to our quintessential being, such is the supernal *chokhmah*'s relationship to the divine essence. The quintessential being of God transcends the divine attributes and their qualities; it is the essence of all divine manifestations, yet it remains utterly untouched by them.

And though there are myriads of different gradations of souls (*neshamot*), rank upon rank, ad infinitum,

The Godly soul of the Jew is "a part of God above," a spark of the divine essence. Nevertheless, although all souls are rooted in the utterly singular essence of God, the bodied souls of the community of Israel contain many levels and gradations. Regarding every Jew, the Torah says, "You are children unto the Lord your God."[22] This does not mean, however, that all are the same: there are differences between souls just as there are differences between children. The same father might have virtuous children and nonvirtuous children, intelligent children and unintelligent children. But all are equally their father's children, regard-less of their qualitative differences.

As noted in the Compiler's Preface, people differ in character and intelligence—in how they conceive, comprehend, and relate to things. Here, the author is adding that the differences between individuals run even deeper than that: souls differ from each other in their essential nature, for in the earliest stages of their evolution from their source, they subdivide into infinite gradations of holiness and spirituality.

as with superiority of the souls of the Patriarchs and of Moses our Teacher over the souls of our own generations, those of the "heels of the Messiah," which are as the very heels of the feet compared with the brain and head;

"The heels of the Messiah" (*ikveta di'meshicha*) is a common phrase in the writings of our sages, referring to these last generations before the coming of the Messiah, those inhabiting that period of history when the footsteps of the Messiah are approaching. The author sees a deeper meaning in the phrase, interpreting it not only as a figure of speech referring to these generations' proximity to the coming of the Messiah but also to the essential quality of the time and the souls that dwell in it.

Every soul is a *komah sheleimah* ("complete structure") mirroring the organization of the body in which it is enclothed. It has a "head" that consists of its cognitive faculties: conception, comprehension, and application (*ChaBaD*)—the "matrices" that give birth to the emotions (see beginning of Chapter 3). It has, so to speak, arms, a torso, and legs, and it also has heels—the very lowest extremities of the human form, lowest also in the sense that they possess only a marginal degree of vital-ity and sensation. In a more general sense, the souls of a given genera-tion likewise constitute an anthropomorphic organism, including souls that serve as its "head," "arms," and so on. Finally, all souls of all gener-ations also constitute a complete organism—the spiritual organism of Adam, the first man, of whom the *Midrash* says that all souls of all generations are "appendages" of his general soul: "some are appended to his head, others to his arms, others to his feet"[23] and so on.

In this sense, then, the souls in each and every generation are parts of that complete organism. Thus, some generations' souls are of the head, and others whose souls are on the level of the feet, their relative spiritual quality synonymous with the difference between the inner life of the head and that of the feet. The closer one gets to the Messianic era (that is, the further along one goes in the process of history), the lower down are the souls placed within the collective *komah sheleimah.* Thus, these last generations of history are the "heels of the Messiah."

In other places, the author further develops this idea, explaining that just as in the human body each organ and limb has its defined role, so, too, every individual soul has it special role within the complete organism comprising all souls. Thus, different things are expected of different individuals, in accordance with their spiritual quality and their place in the cosmic body. Even when it comes to the actual performance of the *mitzvot,* which are equally binding on every Jew, from Moses to the most despicable Jew, there is a great difference in the manner in which they are expected to fulfill them. (As in the story of the *tzaddik* who said to his coachman: "You place *tefillin* upon your head; I set the *tefillin* within the head.")[24]

These differences between individual and individual and between generation and generation, between the souls of the patriarchs and the souls of our era, between great and small, are not differences in intelligence. When we speak of the level of a great soul versus a minor soul, we are speaking of a particular quality—namely, the soul's receptiveness to holiness. An individual who is neither wise nor learned can nevertheless possess an extremely lofty and holy soul; on the other hand, a very wise and learned man might possess the lowliest of souls. A person can be extremely accomplished in all areas and at the same time be completely dysfunctional in all that pertains to holiness. A holy soul is a soul endowed with the very special sense and capacity of connecting to the divine.

and so in every generation there are the leaders of Israel, whose souls are in the category of "head" and "brain" in comparison with those of the masses and the ignorant;

As we said, each individual generation is also a complete organism and includes souls of varying levels, from the souls of the leaders who constitute its head to the lowly souls whose spiritual stature is analogous to the heel's meager vitality in relation to the head. As we shall see, however, the organism analogy relates not only to the difference in quality between the souls but also to their integration and interdependence: all limbs of the generation are inexorably bound to the head in the same way that the limbs of a physical body are connected to, and vitalized by, the brain in the head.

To summarize, each generation includes many levels of souls, ranging from the lofty head to the lowly heel; this, in addition to a similar difference between generations. Taken together, we indeed have "myriads of different gradations of souls."

likewise, [there are distinctions] between *nefashot* and *nefashot,*

As we said in Chapter 1, the soul of man consists of five aspects or levels: *nefesh, ruach, neshamah, chayah,* and *yechidah*. *Nefesh, ruach,* and *neshamah* are the three lower levels of the soul, those that are more readily manifested in the body. The author's point here is that individuals differ not only on the level of *neshamah*, which is the loftiest of the three immanent aspects of the soul, but also on the level of *ruach*, and even of *nefesh*, the aspect of soul that drives the person's most ordinary faculties, such as his capacity for bodily action.

for every *nefesh* consists of *nefesh, ruach,* and *neshamah*;

Because every male Jew is equally obligated to fulfill the *mitzvot* (for example, every Jew is obligated to put on *tefillin*, regardless of the loftiness or lowliness of his soul), one might think that on the level of *nefesh*, which is the level of deed, there are no differences between souls. Therefore, the author notes that in truth, each level of the soul itself comprises various levels and gradations: the *nefesh* itself includes a sub-*nefesh, ruach,* and *neshamah*. Even on the level of action, we distinguish between the deed itself and the quality, spirit, and soul of the deed: there can be a coarse action or a refined action, a simple action or a profound action. Thus, there are distinctions also between *nefashot* and *nefashot*.

nevertheless, the root of every *nefesh, ruach,* and *neshamah*, from the highest of levels to the lowest of levels embodied within the ignoramus and the least reverent,

The "ignoramus" (*am ha-aretz*) is one who lacks all knowledge and comprehension of the divine. Therefore, in actuality, his soul is on a most lowly level, because its higher elements cannot manifest themselves in his life. The "least reverent" (*kal sheba-kalim*) is one who belittles everything, sins easily, and is utterly indifferent to everything spiritual and holy. But these souls, too, all derive, as it were, from the Supernal Mind which is *Chokhmah Ila'ah* (Supernal Wisdom), as in the analogy of a child who derives from his father's brain,

All souls, from the loftiest to the lowliest, derive from the "mind" of God, each being but another expression of the supernal wisdom, according to the analogy. Just as the child's primordial origin is in the father's mind and brain, so, too, does every Jewish soul derive from the "mind" of God.

that even his toenails come into being from the very same drop of semen, through its nine-month stay in the mother's womb, descending degree by degree, changing continually, until even the nails are formed from it, yet [the child's body] is still bound and united with a wonderful and quintessential unity with its original essence and being, which was as a drop of the father's brain,

The "drop" that passes from the core of the father's being to generate the child (or to employ a modern-day term, the father's genetic code) creates the entire spectrum of the child's being: the child's character and the child's talents, the child's brain and the child's toenails. The very same life force manifests itself on all these levels, assuming a coarser and more material form at each progressively lower level. The toenail is not only further from the brain than the other limbs in the spatial sense but conceptually as well: it is a part of the body with a most minimal degree of vitality and sensation. Nevertheless, it derives from the very same elementary seed that generates the person's spiritual faculties, his musical talents, or his intellect; indeed, if the single cell that comes from the father is flawed, the flaw might also be expressed in a defect in the child's toenail. In other words, regardless of the tremendous qualitative difference between them, the child's toenail is of one essence with the mind of the father, the source of the initial stimulation, the primordial seed, from which the child's entire being, in all its complexity and variance, derives.

and even now, in the child, the nails receive their nourishment and life from the brain that is in the head.

The "brain" we now speak of is the child's brain. In other words, the drop from the father's brain develops into a child, which includes a part that remains visibly identical to its source (that is, the child's brain), as well as parts that are overtly distant from it, all the way down to the child's toenail. Nevertheless, all are quintessentially one with their source, and all retain their manifest connection with it through their integration with that part of the child that remains synonymous with it—the child's brain. In the analogy, this corresponds with the fact that even the "ignoramus and most irreverent" (analogous to the child's toenails) are integral parts of the complete organism, deriving their vitality by way of the leaders (the brain of the child) of their generations, as shall be explained.[25]

As is written in the Gemara (*Niddah*, ibid.), "From the white of the father's drop of semen are formed the veins, the bones, and the nails."[26] (And in *Etz Chayyim, Sha'ar haChashmal*, it is likewise stated, in connection with the esoteric principle of Adam's garments in the Garden of Eden, that they were the "nails" derived from the cognitive faculty of the brain.)

And so it literally is, as it were, with the supernal root of every *nefesh, ruach,* and *neshamah* in the community of Israel on high:

This profound, quintessential relationship between the multifaceted being of the child and the seed of life in the father's mind is the analogy that illustrates the bond between the souls of Israel and their Father in heaven. Just as the many organs and limbs of the child, qualitatively different as they are, all derive from the same drop generated by the core of the father's being, so, too, all souls of Israel, from the loftiest—such as the souls of the patriarchs and Moses—to the lowliest, including the sinner and the heretic, are all, in essence, a "part of God above."

The phrase "and so it literally is, as it were" seems an odd, if not oxymoronic, marriage of idioms: "as it were" (*kivyakhol*) implies that we are speaking figuratively, whereas "and so it literally is" (*v'kakha mamash*) implies the very opposite—that our intention is the most literal sense of our words. Indeed, the author wishes to stress both the literalness of his statement and impreciseness of his metaphor. When we say that every Jewish soul is a part of God above, rooted in the divine wisdom, we mean that it is literally so. On the other hand, we must qualify the metaphor of the father-child relationship with the words "as it were," because the manifest difference between the father's mind and the child's toenail is but a small, insignificant difference compared to the infinite distance between a human soul and the supernal wisdom

of God. The combination of these two expressions comes to emphasize the point that the soul is "a part of God above, literally"; that
although the divine reality is utterly intangible, it is the most real and
literal truth within man, whereas any model or analogy we might conceive will only be "as it were." Indeed, if any model could be a precise
presentation, this would mean that the soul's divinity is only figurative.

**in descending degree by degree, through the evolution of the worlds of
Atzilut, Beriah, Yetzirah, and *Assiyah*[27] from His blessed Wisdom**

The divine essence of the Jewish soul does not manifest itself fully
and equally in each individual. In the father-child analogy, we have
seen that the father's quintessence is not equally manifest in every
organ and limb of the child but rather undergoes a process by which
it evolves and develops, "descending degree by degree," to take the
form of any given cell in the child's body. Similarly, the divine spark
generated by the "Supernal Wisdom" (the attribute of *chokhmah*)
manifests itself in the *yechidah* that is the essence and root of every
Jewish soul (comparable to the "drop" generated by the father), from
which evolve and develop the many gradations of souls, each embodying the same divine essence but manifesting it on its particular level,
down to the souls of the "ignorant and unworthy."

—as it is written, "You have made them all with wisdom,"

The attribute of Wisdom is the key of creation, the first *sefirah*
("divine attribute") in every system, the divine light in the generation
of reality.

**the *nefesh, ruach,* and *neshamah* of the ignorant and unworthy come into
being; yet they remain bound and united, with a wonderful and quintessential unity, with their original essence and entity, namely, the extension
of the Supernal Wisdom.**

Even the lowliest of the low, even the soul that denies its Father in
heaven, is also bound and united with its primal source in divine wisdom. The question of whether a child acknowledges or denies the existence of his father has no bearing on the quintessential bond between
them; it might tell us what kind of a person the child is, but it cannot
change the fact that he is a child of his father's.

For the nurture and life of the *nefesh, ruach,* and *neshamah* of the ignorant are drawn from the *nefesh, ruach,* and *neshamah* of the *tzaddikim* and Sages, the heads of Israel in their generation.

As we elaborated earlier, all souls of a particular generation constitute a *komah sheleimah*—an integral structure and organism. It consists of a head—the souls of the *tzaddikim* who head the generation—and of a great variety of lower organs and limbs, down to those souls whose spiritual station is comparable to that of the feet and toenails of the body of Israel.

Every organ and limb of this body is connected in two ways: (1) with the body's brain (and thereby with all other limbs of the body) in a mutual bond, as parts of an integral organism; and (2) with its source, the generative potential of the father. But although the father's original seed remains the essence of every part of the child's body, it is expressed and manifested in the child's brain in a greater degree than in his feet. Thus, the feet and the hands and all other limbs are subservient to the brain, which is the manifest source of their vitality. In the same way, although all Jewish souls are "children of God" and are related to each other as the component parts of a *komah sheleimah,* they also include among them those souls who are the "heads of Israel": souls who possess a greater awareness of their relationship with God and impart this awareness to the other souls of Israel, each according to its level and capacity.

This connection is not one-sided. Just as, in the brain-body analogy, the brain senses the pain of the foot, so, too, a true leader is deeply affected by what happens to the "feet" of his generation. It is told of a certain *tzaddik* that he was unable to sleep if a woman was in labor five hundred miles away, because he felt the pain she was experiencing. A leader who is insensitive to the woes of each and every individual of his generation is obviously not a true head of Israel.

To a lesser degree, this connection also exists between all the "limbs" of Israel. Biologically, as long as a limb is connected to the body, a mutual bond exists between it and all the other limbs of the body, as the same flow of vitality and consciousness circulates in them all; anything that happens to a particular limb is bound to have some effect on the entire body. The difference lies in the degree of awareness to this flow. The mind is the master of the body because it is the organ that is most conscious of the bond between it and the body, and that is most sensitive to the well-being, or lack thereof, of each and every one of its limbs.

Here lies the basis for the institution of the rebbe in Hasidic teaching. The rebbe or *tzaddik* is not merely an individual who is more learned and pious than his constituents but one whose soul is a head in the body of Israel. Those who strive to achieve a bond (*hitkashrut*) with him are people who see in him a source of spiritual nurture and consider themselves as limbs to his head. The *tzaddik,* in turn, is bound to them as a head is to its body; indeed, a headless body is no more viable than a bodiless head. Thus, when the people of Israel sinned by worshipping the golden calf, God told Moses, "Go, descend, for your people have corrupted";[28] as the Talmud explains, God was saying to Moses, "Descend from your greatness! I have made you great only for their sake; now that they have sinned, of what value are you to Me?"[29] When his people stray, Moses can no longer be Moses. Moses was a great man even without being a leader, but this is not where his utmost perfection lay. His ultimate greatness lay not in his ability to comprehend the loftiest reaches of the divine truth, in his prophecy, or even in his role as a teacher and guide of his people. His greatness lay in his leadership—namely, his relationship with Israel as the "head" of the *komah sheleimah* that is the Jewish nation. Thus, a failing on the part of Israel results in Moses' demotion: "Descend from your greatness!"

On another occasion,[30] the author applies the concept of Israel as a *komah sheleimah* to shed light on the principle, "Love your fellow as yourself."[31] Because every Jewish soul is a part of a single organism, all Jewish souls are interdependent. Therefore, loving one's fellow Jew is indeed synonymous with, and an expression of, a person's intrinsic self-love. A sane person does not hate his own hand, nor does he shrug off a pain in his foot by saying, "That's my foot's problem, not mine."

Another implication of this vision of the community as an integrated organism is the recognition that every individual has a distinct function and role—in keeping with his unique qualities as a head, hand, foot, and so on—that he must fulfill. Among the most basic questions that a person must ask himself are: What is my role? In what area lie the achievements that are specifically incumbent upon me to attain? The story is told of a wealthy but tightfisted Hasid who devoted his time to the study of Torah. One day, his rebbe said to him: "You should know that you are in grave danger." "Why?" asked the Hasid. "In every army," replied the rebbe, "there are various units. A soldier who abandons his unit and joins up with another unit is considered a deserter—a crime punishable by death, God forbid. God has given you the capacity and resources to give charity on a large scale, but you have chosen to desert your unit and join the unit of Torah scholars. Know that your very life is in jeopardy!" This story shows that even a person who performs *mitzvot* and good deeds may not be doing what he should do.

Surely, this is not to imply that a millionaire is not obligated to study Torah or that a scholar is absolved from the *mitzvah* of charity. As we mentioned earlier, each individual soul itself also comprises a *komah sheleimah*—a soul that is a hand or foot in the communal organism also embodies all limbs and organs of the soul in its own being. Indeed, our sages have said that every soul must return to earth as many times as is necessary, until it fulfills all 613 *mitzvot* of the Torah. At the same time, each soul also has a specific area in which it is empowered and expected to excel; this is the deeper significance of our sages' words, when they asked various individuals, "Which [*mitzvah*] did your father fulfill most diligently?"[32] Each soul has a specific role, unique to it alone, which it should set as its highest priority and to which it should devote itself with an extra measure of diligence and care, with the awareness that he is absolutely indispensable to this role—no other soul could possibly take his place in regard to it. This is the special role that he is to play within the *komah sheleimah* of the entire Jewish people.

This explains the comment of our Sages on the verse, "And to cleave unto Him": "He who cleaves unto a Torah scholar is deemed by the Torah as if he had become attached to the very *Shekhinah*." For through their attachment to the scholars, the *nefesh, ruach,* and *neshamah* of the ignorant are bound up and united with their original essence and their root in the Supernal Wisdom,

The Talmud quotes the verse, "You shall choose life . . . to love the Lord your God, to obey His voice, and to cleave to Him,"[33] and asks: Is it possible for a person to cleave to God? The Talmud replies that "he who cleaves to a Torah scholar is deemed by the Torah as if he had become attached to the very *Shekhinah* ['divine presence']."

This esoteric statement is readily understood in light of what has been said until now: that the collective body of Israel is comparable to the body of the child, which consists of a great variety of parts, from the brain down to the toenails. All evolve from a drop that is an offshoot of the very essence of the father, but they differ greatly in the degree in which they have been coarsened and distanced from their source. Nevertheless, the lowly toenail is one with the lofty brain, for the entire body of the child is a single, integrated whole; and because the child's brain retains its synonymy and identification with its paternal origin, the toenail, by virtue of its bond with the brain, is also one with its source.

Thus, even the most ignorant and simple of folk, whose souls are incapable on their own of perceiving, experiencing, and identifying with the divine, are one with God by virtue of their connection with those souls who constitute the head of Israel. By binding their lives to those of the *tzaddikim*, they too receive the divine life force that flows from the "Supernal Mind," the source of the "part of God above" that is the Jewish soul.

He and His wisdom being one, and "He is the Knowledge. . . ."[34]

Thus, even a person who is an ignoramus, the simplest of the simple, when he cleaves to the "heads" of his generation, he receives through them the vitality that flows through them, which originates in the "part of God above" of the supernal wisdom.

(As for those who willfully sin and rebel against the Sages, the nurture of their *nefesh, ruach,* and *neshamah* comes from behind the back, as it were, of the *nefesh, ruach,* and *neshamah* of the scholars.)

But what about those who do not cleave to the heads of their generation? Or those who explicitly disavow any such connection, who even actively hate the leaders of Israel?

Nothing can exist in a state of total disconnection from God; certainly not a Jewish soul, which is one, in essence, with the heads of Israel. The only difference possible is in the quality of the connection. One person can enjoy a conscious and willful bond with the leader of his generation—to the one whom he regards as the "head of thousands of Israel"—and be nourished by this bond in a forward manner. Another person might be connected, as it were, backwardly.

The distinction between a forward and backward relationship exists in a variety of contexts. For example, we have the concept of *teshuvah* ("return"). What does it mean to return to God? Is not "the entire world filled with His glory"[35]? If man is always in the presence of God, how can he return to Him? Yet, to quote the prophet, man can be in a state in which "they have turned their backs to Me and do not face

Me."[36] When a person turns his back on someone, he might be in close proximity to that person—they might even be pressed against each other back to back—yet they are as far apart from each other as they can possibly be. *Teshuvah,* then, is a shift in orientation: a person turning to God, after having spurned Him.

The individual who "willfully sins and rebels against the Sages," though he expressly demonstrates that he does not see himself as a "limb" to their "head," nevertheless cannot sever his connection to them. He is inexorably bound to them by virtue of who and what he is, for his spiritual sustenance—indeed, his very life and being— reaches him through them, as a body's limbs are vitalized by the brain. He might disdain his bond with them and thus turn his back on them, but he continues to be nourished by them. Such a person is nourished "from behind the back"—sustained despite his lack of recognition of, and willful connection with, the source of his sustenance.

Another way of looking at the distinction between front and back is in the context of giving and receiving. Here, "front" represents the purpose of a thing, whereas the "back" is the secondary, auxiliary element that must exist to serve the "front." Thus, we have the front of the knife, which does the cutting, and the back of the knife, which exists solely because a front must have a back. Hasidic teaching cites the analogy of a king who throws a banquet for all his ministers and servants. The king's objective is to honor his chief ministers and pleasure them with food and drink, but in order to maximize the honor, he must invite numerous people and feed and entertain them. These people are receiving from the "back" of the king's desire, whereas the chief ministers are receiving from its "front" or "inner" element. A more abstract analogy is when two people listen to the same lecture, and one of them remembers the content whereas the other remembers the illustrations, analogies, and jokes. Both received, but the first received the front, or inner intent of the lecture, whereas the second received the "back" of the lecture—things that the lecturer said for the sole purpose of conveying the content.

As for what is written in the *Zohar*[37] and in *Zohar Chadash,*[38] that the essential factor is to conduct oneself in a sanctified manner during sexual union,

The *Zohar* seems to be implying that the quality of a person's soul is determined primarily by his parents: who his parents are and the nature of their intentions—sacred or profane—at the crucial moment of the union that produced him. According to this, the essential nature of a person is hereditary, in the sense that a holy soul can be conceived only by holy parents,

which is not the case with the children of the ignorant, and so on,

These are destined to also be coarse and ignorant. This seems to contradict what the author said in this chapter, that every Jewish soul is "a part of God above, literally," deriving from the same source.

Explains the author:

what is meant there is that since there is not a *nefesh, ruach,* and *neshamah* which has not a garment from the soul of its father's and mother's essence,

One must distinguish between two things: the essence of the soul and the "garments" of the soul. The essence of the soul is "a part of God above, literally" and completely independent of a person's heredity, conditioning, and environment. But the "garment" of the soul—the manner of its manifestation and expression—depends on the person's parents and, later on, on how he is raised and educated.[39]

The child receives his traits and talents from his parents but not his soul. Yet this garment that the parents provide for the soul is extremely important. It includes spiritual as well as physical talents, qualities, and abilities, which combine to provide the person with the personality by which he lives and operates. At the same time, one must bear in mind that this personality is not the soul (though it greatly influences its operation) and that the soul can override it or even transform it.

and the *mitzvot* that it does are all achieved via that garment, etc.,

The soul cannot perform a *mitzvah* on its own, for *mitzvot* are not performed in a vacuum but only by way of elements with which the soul has no direct relation. Thus, the soul requires intermediaries in the form of psychological and physiological tools with which to operate in the world. These tools are the garments of the soul: intelligence, a mind-set and value system, social and physical skills, and so on. All this comes from the parents, mostly by inheritance and partly by conditioning and training.

and even the sustenance that is given to him from Heaven is all given through that garment,

The soul requires "garments" not only to achieve but also to receive. When a person receives a gift from above—an illumination, a spiritual awakening—it is for the purpose of drawing this gift into his being and existence; and it is his soul's garments that translate it into something that he experiences and applies to his life.

so if a person sanctifies himself, he will draw down a hallowed garment for the soul of his child. Even a great soul requires its father's sanctification.

The garments that parents generate for their child's soul are more than a set of physical qualities; as we said, they form the totality of the child's personality. So the parents' inner sanctity, not only their specific traits and talents, is extremely important for the child. Even a great and lofty soul requires a holy garment to aid its realization of its own holiness, and such a garment can only be generated by parents who have sanctified themselves. It is told that the *tzaddik* Rabbi Uri of Starlisk (the Seraph) once said that if only his father would have immersed in a *mikveh* (ritual bath) once in his lifetime, Rabbi Uri's service of God would have been immeasurably easier.[40] No person—even the greatest *tzaddik*—can ever completely disassociate himself from the garments he inherited, and any deficiencies they contain will be a perpetual challenge to him. Conversely, a person who merited to inherit a hallowed garment is thus empowered to achieve great heights in holiness, even if his own soul is of a lesser spiritual quality.

This concept is the basis for the importance traditionally accorded to *yichus,* "ancestry and lineage." A soul is not inherited, but its garments are. These garments impart certain qualities to the soul, such as nobility, refinement, and talent. This garment is passed on from parent to child even if the child is of an entirely different caliber. A lofty garment can be bestowed upon the lowliest of the lowly, in which case, even if he chooses to descend to the depths of depravity, his holy garment will interfere with his lifestyle. It is not that people of an exalted lineage sin less; it is that they cannot enjoy their sins as much as a sinner of lesser parentage. Their lofty garments get in the way; their holy ancestry burdens them and robs them of their capacity to transgress with abandon. There is no guarantee that a person of holy ancestry will be a great person, but somehow, something always remains. If we study this phenomenon closely, we see that this is not only a matter of education but also of the personality that one is born with, a sort of brand burned into his soul. Our generation abounds with such individuals—people whose soul's garment gives them no rest and does not allow them to sin easily or with pleasure, who are driven by mysterious internal forces, often against their conscious will. Try as they may, they cannot shed the garment that garbs their soul by virtue of their lineage.

But as for the soul itself, it sometimes happens that the soul of an infinitely lofty person comes to be the son of a despised and lowly man, [and so on]. All this has been explained by Rabbi Isaac Luria, of blessed memory, in *Likkutei Torah*, on *Parashat vaYera*, and in *Ta'amei haMitzvot on Parashat Bereshit.*

Not only is this possible, but some great and lofty souls cannot be born any other way. Jewish history has many examples of great figures of dubious ancestry. The Mishnaic sage Rabbi Meir seems to have been a descendant of Roman royalty (a quite decadent lineage, from the perspective of holiness); his was said to be the soul of Esau the son of Isaac—a great soul (Jacob's twin!) that had fallen to the depths of *kelipah* and could be reclaimed by holiness only by a Roman convert to Judaism. Rabbi Akiva stemmed of coarse and simple stock and had non-Jewish ancestors; it was said that such a great soul, which shared many features with the soul of Moses, could only be born out of such circumstances. The birth of Moses himself has a certain profane element to it: Moses was born from the marriage of Amram with his aunt, Yocheved; although this was a permissible union at the time, following the giving of the Torah, it is counted among the most severe of incestuous relationships. But the most markedly dubious ancestry is that of the Messiah. His is an ancestry that includes the unions of Judah and Tamar, Boaz and Ruth, David and Bathsheba, Solomon and Naamah the Amonite. The soul of David, which is the fourth leg of the "divine chariot," and the soul of the Messiah, which is "lofty, exalted, and exceedingly high,"[41] are the loftiest of souls but are imprisoned in the depths of *kelipah* and have to pass through the twilight zone between holiness and profanity to be extracted from captivity. They are like pearls that lie buried in refuse heaps. *Tzaddikim* do not frequent refuse heaps, not even in the search for pearls; that's not their line. It is people who seek filth and wallow in filth who dig there, and, for the most part, they come away with filth. But if a pearl is there, they might come up with a pearl.

The parents, then, do not create the soul; they only provide it with a garment. In the words of the Talmud, "There are three partners to [the creation of] a person. . . . His father germinates the white element. . . . His mother germinates the red element. . . . And God places within him a spirit and soul."[42] God provides the soul, and He does not always ask the other partners which soul they want. Some parents might be just as unsatisfied with a lofty soul as other parents might be with a lowly one, as in the famous parable of the hen who hatches the eggs of a goose. Some parents may be unhappy with a holy son, just as others may be rendered miserable by an unholy one—but, as we said, the question of which soul should enter which body does not depend on them.

Every Jew, including the smallest of the small and the lowliest of the lowly, is "a part of God above, literally" and is included in the statement "You are children unto the Lord your God." People differ in what they inherit from their parents, in the garments of their souls—in the manner in which their souls manifest themselves and realize their potential. People also differ in the soul they receive from God, regarding its source in the supernal "chain of evolution." There are great souls— souls with a tremendous scope of achievement in the realm of holiness (with an equally tremendous capacity for corruption, as our sages have said, "Whoever is greater than his fellow, his evil inclination is likewise greater"[43]); and there are lesser souls—souls that, regardless of whether they are righteous or sinful, remain lesser souls. Altogether, there are, as our chapter states, "myriads of different gradations of souls, rank upon rank, ad infinitum." But ultimately they are all equally "a part of God above, literally," all "children unto the Lord your God." A family might contain an accomplished brother and a ne'er-do-well, a wise brother and a foolish one, but they all share a common denominator: all are children of the same father. This fact is unaffected by the deeds of man or by the loftiness or lowliness of his soul.

Chapter 3

N ow, each of these three aspects and levels—*nefesh*, *ruach,* and *neshamah*—consists of ten attributes, corresponding to the ten supernal *sefirot* from which they evolve, which are subdivided into two categories, namely, three "matrices" and the seven "multiples," to wit: *chokhmah, binah,* and *daat;* and the "seven days of construction"—*chessed, gevurah, tiferet,* and so on. So is it with the human soul, which is divided in two—*sekhel* and *middot.* The *sekhel* includes *chokhmah, binah,* and *daat,* whilst the *middot* are love of God, fear and awe of Him, glorification of Him, and so forth. *ChaBaD* are called "matrices" and the sources of the *middot,* for the *middot* are the offspring of *ChaBaD.*

The explanation of the matter is as follows:

The *sekhel* of the rational soul, which is the faculty that conceives any thing, is called *chokhmah*—"the potentiality of 'what?'" (*koach mah*). When [a person] brings forth this potential into actuality, that is, when he cogitates with his intellect in order to understand a concept which he has conceived in his intellect to its ultimate truth and depth, this is what is called *binah.* These are the father and mother which give birth to love of God, and awe and fear of Him.

For when the intellect in the rational soul deeply contemplates and immerses itself exceedingly in the greatness of God, how He fills all worlds and encompasses all worlds and how all is as naught before Him—there will be born and aroused in his mind and thought the emotion of exalted awe, to be awed and humbled before His blessed greatness, which is without end or limit, and to have the fear of God in his heart. In turn, his heart will glow with an intense love like burning coals, with craving, desire, passion, and a yearning soul, towards the greatness of the Blessed Infinite. This is the "dissolution of the soul" (*kelot hanefesh*) of which Scripture speaks: "My soul longs and goes out . . . ," "My soul thirsts for God," "My soul thirsts for You." This thirst is derived from the element of Fire in the Godly soul. As the students of natural science write, and so it is in *Etz Chayyim,* the element of Fire is in the heart, whilst the source of [the element of] Water and moisture is in the brain, which is explained in *Etz Chayyim,* Portal 50, to refer to the faculty of *chokhmah,* which is called the "water" of the Godly soul. All other *middot* are all offshoots of awe and love and their derivations, as is explained elsewhere.

Daat implies attachment and union, as in the verse, "And Adam knew (*yada*) Eve." That is, one binds his mind with a very firm and strong bond to, and firmly fixes his thought on, the greatness of the Blessed Infinite, without diverting his mind [from Him]. For even one who is wise and understanding of the greatness of the Blessed Infinite will not produce in his soul true love and awe, but only vain fancies, unless he binds his mind and fixes his thought with firmness and perseverance. Therefore *daat* is the basis of the *middot* and the source of their vitality; it contains *chessed* and *gevurah,* that is to say, love with its offshoots and fear with its offshoots.

COMMENTARY

Chapter 2 discussed the Godly soul itself, defining it as a "part of God above" and describing its evolution from the supernal mind. This chapter discusses the "attributes" (*bechinot*) of the soul, its various qualities and faculties.

Elsewhere,[1] the author explains that these attributes are not, as might be understood here and in other places in *Tanya,*[2] "the essence and being of the Godly soul." The soul itself is not a composite entity but an abstract force that cannot be dissected or categorized. Any conception of the soul as constituted of various parts would preclude its being a distinct and singular entity, for this would mean that there is no such thing as a soul per se, only a cluster of various faculties. The vitalizing force we call the soul is inherent to every person; as such, it is singular, self-defined, and unchanging. On the other hand, the attributes of the soul—the intellect and emotions—are constantly developing and changing in the course of a person's life.

Ultimately, the soul itself cannot be definitively grasped, understood, or known; the soul is a "part of God above," and like the divine reality of which it is a part, no mind can achieve a "comprehension of its essence" (*yediat hamahut*), only a "comprehension of its existence" (*yediat hametziut*)—the recognition that a soul exists, whose nature is beyond comprehension. Thus, Hasidic teaching does not attempt to define the essential nature of the soul, confining itself to the study of its various faculties and the interrelation between them.

The soul's qualities and faculties are all manifestations of its being. The soul reveals itself in numerous ways, each essentially different from the others. The intellect is one manifestation of the soul, as are its feelings, its speech, and its deeds. Hasidic teaching calls manifestations *levushim*, "garments" in which the essence of the soul clothes itself in order to express itself in a certain way, whether internally (to formulate an idea or feeling) or externally (to communicate to others or affect its surroundings). In the broader sense of the term, all manifestations of the soul are garments, but the term is usually used more narrowly to designate the three most external faculties of soul: thought, speech, and action. Despite all the differences between the garment of thought, which is internal, and the garments of speech and action, which are external, they are equal in that there is no real and essential connection between wearer and garment. The garment reveals something of the inner essence of its wearer, yet garment and wearer always remain two distinct and separate entities (and to the extent that the garment does affect the wearer, it is not because it is a garment, but because it is an entity). Thus, the garments of thought, speech, and action serve the soul and reveal its powers, but they are never identified with it; all they do is lend form and expression to an idea, desire, or drive coming from the soul. This is true even of the most intimate of the three external garments, the faculty of thought, which only translates the soul's conceptions, wants, and feelings into the language of conscious thought (that is, thought is the soul's medium of expressing itself to its conscious self; see Chapter 4).

However, another level of manifestation exists: expressions of the soul that are more intimately related to the soul's being. Although these are also, at times, referred to as *levushim,* they are more specifically termed *tikkunim* ("fixtures"),[3] connoting a type of garment or decoration that becomes an integral part of the personality and identity of its wearer. In this sense, the soul's attributes—its intellect and emotions—are its *tikkunim:* they not only express something of the soul's but also unite with it to a certain extent, to the point that, at least to the outside observer, the soul comes to be identified with its attributes.

The *tikkun* has two dimensions. In and of itself, it is extrinsic to the soul, distinct of the essence it expresses. But from the perspective of what exists outside of the soul—other human beings, or even its own external garments of thought, speech, and action—the *tikkun* is virtually synonymous with the soul itself. For the *tikkun* is more than a medium for the soul's contact with the outside world; the connection between them runs deeper than that. When the soul manifests itself by way of one of its attributes, it takes that attribute on as its "personality"; its mode of manifestation becomes its current identity. So although the soul might alternately manifest itself through any one of its attributes, nevertheless, at the time that it actually assumes a certain attribute as its personality, a true identification has taken place, in the same way that certain garments become a fixture of the body that is wearing it.

Now, each of these three aspects and levels—*nefesh, ruach,* and *neshamah*—consists of ten attributes,

As we elaborated in Chapter 1, the soul (*nefesh,* in the broader sense of the term), includes three basic levels: *nefesh, ruach,* and *neshamah.* These three levels are in fact three distinct "personalities," as different from each other as two people might differ in mind-set and character. Each of these three levels has a full array of intellectual and emotional faculties.

corresponding to the ten supernal *sefirot* from which they evolve,

The ten *sefirot* are the ten basic components of reality: of the divine manifestation, of the divine creative forces that create and sustain the universe, and of the essence of the creation.[4] Every creature likewise possesses ten basic components to its being, corresponding to and evolving from these ten divine attributes. This is especially true of the human soul; as a "part of God above" and a creation forged in the "divine image and form,"[5] the soul of man possesses ten basic attributes, mirroring the ten supernal *sefirot*.

which are subdivided into two categories, namely, three "matrices" and the seven "multiples,"

This categorization of the *sefirot* is from *Sefer Yetzirah*, a Kabbalistic work that employs the model of the twenty-two letters of Hebrew, the Holy Tongue, in its description of the divine reality and the essence of creation.[6] In keeping with this approach, it divides the ten *sefirot* into "three matrices" and "seven multiples." The three "matrices," represented by the three letters *alef, mem,* and *shin,* are the three basic *sefirot,* the foundation of the entire edifice of reality. In terms of the human psyche, these are the three components of the mind, the faculties that enable our perception of things and determine its substance and scope. As we shall explain, these are more than tools for intellectual conception and understanding; they represent the soul's capacity to perceive, assimilate, and relate to things. For this reason, they are the "matrices," because no function of the soul, no thought, and no affection is possible without a prior conception of its subject.

The "seven multiples" are the *middot,* the "traits" or "affections" (*chessed, gevurah, tiferet, netzach, hod, yesod, malkhut*), represented by the letters *bet, gimel, dalet, kaf, peh, resh,* and *tav.* Phonetically, these seven letters serve a double function: each has both a hard and soft pronunciation (*dagush* and *rafeh*), reflecting the fact that the seven latter *sefirot* are bilateral, lending themselves to holy and Godly expressions as well as to expressions in the "other side" of *kelipah.*[7] These *sefirot* have a definitive nature and manner of operation, but no intrinsic direction; for example, *chessed* ("attraction," "love," "benevolence") can be holy or corrupted into profane passion.

to wit: *chokhmah, binah,* and *daat;*

That is, the three matrices are the *sefirot* of *chokhmah, binah* and *daat.*

Kabbalah gives two versions as to which *sefirot* are to be regarded as the first and matriarchal three. Often, they are identified as *keter, chokhmah,* and *binah,* as opposed to the *chokhmah, binah,* and *daat* enumerated here. The two versions are the result of differing schools of Kabbalistic thought, which include variant perspectives on the nature of the *sefirah* of *keter* ("crown"; see Chapter 6). Indeed, the author of the *Tanya* himself counts *keter, chokhmah,* and *binah* as the first three *sefirot* in his discussions of the ten *sefirot;* on the other hand, when ten *sefirot* are referred to in the context of the inner life of man (as here in the opening chapters of *Tanya*), the formula is *chokhmah, binah, daat.*

One might gain an understanding of this differentiation, in part, by examining the three matrices. In the human psyche (our model and vantage point for all discussion of the *sefirot*), the *sefirah* of *keter* embodies all that is transcendent and suprarational. Its external aspect is the power of will, and its internal aspect, the faculty of pleasure. These two most basic faculties exist beyond the pale of the person's consciousness, beyond his understanding, and certainly beyond his control. This whole range is thus never consciously sensed; all awareness and self-knowledge begin at the point of *chokhmah,* the faculty of perception.

On the subjective level, *chokhmah* is the genesis of all that transpires within man. An outside observer might suppose that forces beyond a person's conscious perceptions influence his thinking, emotions, and behavior; but no such recognition exists within one's own subjective realm of awareness. On this level, the "three matrices" of every thought, feeling, and deed are, first and foremost, *chokhmah* ("conception"), followed by *binah* ("comprehension"), followed by *daat* ("will"), which is *keter* ("crown") in its subrational, as opposed to suprarational, form—will that is a derivative of perception and understanding, as opposed to will that transcends the conscious and imposes itself upon it.

and the "seven days of construction"—*chessed, gevurah, tiferet,* and so on.

Chessed is "loving-kindness"; *gevurah* is "power" or "strength"; *tiferet* is "beauty." The other four are *netzach* ("victory" or "eternity"), *hod* ("splendor" or "glory"), *yesod* ("foundation"), and *malkhut* ("kingship").

These seven latter *sefirot* are called "the seven days of construction" because these are the building blocks of creation, as embodied by the seven days in which God created the world (and that constitute the ongoing cycle of creation by which He continually creates and sustains it). The first day of creation embodies the divine attribute of *chessed* and is the source of all *chessed* elements in creation; the second day embodies the attribute of *gevurah;* and so on.

(This is not to say that each *sefirah* is confined to its particular day in physical time, because each *sefirah* contains elements of all others. Thus, the first day of creation (and every Sunday since) embodies the *sefirah* of *chessed*, as well as *gevurah*-of-*chessed*, *tiferet*-of-*chessed*, and so on). The entirety of creation is, in essence, an amalgam of these seven divine manifestations, which generate the various dimensions and facets of reality.

So is it with the human soul, which is divided in two—*sekhel* and *middot*.

"Three matrices" and "seven multiples" are Kabbalistic terms for the *sefirot* as they exist as manifestations of the divine. This division also exists in the attributes of the human soul, only here they are described in the human terms of *sekhel* and *middot*, "mind" and "heart." The three matrices are the faculties of the *sekhel*, the mind and intellect; and the seven multiples are *middot*, "affections."

Sekhel, as we said, is the capacity for perception. The word is often translated as "intellect," but intellect and cognition are only part of this capacity, not its sum, which is the mind's ability to recognize, grasp, and be aware of anything, in a great variety of fashions (intellectual deduction, intuitive conviction, sight, hearing, and so on).

Middot is usually translated as "emotions," but this, too, is somewhat imprecise. The *middot* are seven drives, seven forces that motivate human behavior and elicit an emotional response in the person. Emotions (such as love or fear) are a *middah*'s imprint on a person's thought and awareness. The *middot* are fundamental elements that operate in certain ways but only when combined with the power of thinking do they form actual emotions. An emotion is, in fact, a composite entity (*komah sheleimah*) that includes perceptive elements, sensual elements, and tactile responses. The emotion of fear, for example, includes, in addition to the actual feeling of fear, a perception and recognition of a cause for the fear, as well as the reactions and responses spawned by the fear. In our experience, we never encounter a pure *middah*, or even a pure emotion, but a compound of emotions (just as chemical elements do not exist in nature in a pure form but in various compounds). The *middah*, then, is only the drive, the vector of a certain emotive direction in the heart of man. As such, *middot* are not to be found in reality; they do, however, operate in it within certain emotional structures.

The *sekhel* includes *chokhmah, binah,* and *daat,* whilst the *middot* are love of God, fear and awe of Him, glorification of Him, and so forth.

Because we are speaking of the Godly soul, whose exclusive point of reference is its relationship with God, its love (that is, the emotion that derives from its *middah* of *chessed*), its fear and awe (the emotions that derive from its *gevurah*), its sense of majesty and glory (from *tiferet*), and so on, are the love, fear, and awe of God and the other emotions that delineate its feeling toward its divine source.[8]

"Awe" (*yir'ah*) and "fear" (*pachad*) are two different emotions. Awe is more of a sensation in the mind, the awareness that there is something great and awesome and intimidating, whereas fear is a feeling in the heart, often accompanied by physiological responses. Indeed, a person might fear something without understanding the reason for his fear.[9] This explains why here, in its enumeration of the *middot,* the *Tanya* mentions fear before awe, whereas further along in the chapter, while discussing the manner in which the *sekhel* gives birth to the *middot,* awe is mentioned first.[10]

ChaBaD are called "matrices" and the sources of the *middot,* for the *middot* are the offspring of ChaBaD.

A *middah* must be preceded by a perception and knowledge generated by the "ChaBaD" (acrostic of *chokhmah, binah, daat*) of the soul. Unless there is such a perception—not necessarily in the strict intellectual sense but in the sense of an awareness of the subject to which the soul is relating—there can be no emotional relation. This does not mean that every emotion must be rationally thought through: an emotion can be silly or irrational, but a person must at least be aware of the thing he desires or dreads. Even a baby's muddled affections could not exist without some form of consciousness to elicit them.

It must be emphasized that although the author states that "the *middot* are the offspring of ChaBaD," this is not to say that the mind "begets" them from within itself. The mind generates the subject of the person's affections, an awareness without which no affection can exist, but this does not mean that the mind creates them. Rather, the mind activates the affections, causing their emergence from a prior state of total implicitness. The *sekhel* and the *middot* each have their own source in the soul, as evidenced by the vast differences between them, both in their nature and their essence. Elsewhere,[11] in more extensive analyses of the human psyche, the author even explains that although on the conscious level the mind precedes and dominates the *middot* (as expressed here), in their subconscious root, the *middot* are primary to, and more potent than, the faculties of the *sekhel*.[12]

The relationship between the mind and the *middot* might be thus more accurately described as the mind being the "midwife" that facilitates the birth of the *middot*. The *middot* exist within the soul but in a latent, potential form. The mind does not give birth to the *middot;* it serves as the agent of their emergence into actuality.

The mind is fundamentally the faculty to perceive and comprehend reality, whether external or internal. The *middot* originate as potential impulses: the possibility to love or hate, to be attracted to or repelled by something (to feel drawn to, or away from, certain things). But these impulses, in and of themselves, are blind, having no objects to which to apply. One cannot simply love or hate; one loves or hates something that exists as a perceived reality in one's mind. Only when the mind has assimilated a certain reality and has, by a complex process, established an initial intellectual relationship to it (*daat*), can the emotional impulses be activated and begin to materialize in the heart, clothe themselves in thought, and take shape in words and ideas, aspirations, and endeavors; only then do they become actual *middot*.

The explanation of the matter is as follows:

Now, the author proceeds to define the three faculties of the mind: *chokhmah, binah,* and *daat.* These, however, are extremely complex, and this chapter does not contain a comprehensive treatment, only the most basic outline necessary at this point for the development of the author's thesis.

The *sekhel* of the rational soul, which is the faculty that conceives any thing, is called *chokhmah*—"the potentiality of 'what?'" (*koach mah*).

When we perceive something, whether by way of a sense perception or an intellectual perception, we first experience a general perception—a grasp of the gist of the thing, in which the entire breadth and depth of the thing is encapsulated in a single, dimensionless "point." This point is the first step in the process of perception and is called *chokhmah* (commonly translated as "wisdom"; more accurately, in this context, rendered "conception"). *Chokhmah,* explains the *Zohar,*[13] is a composite of the two words *koach mah*—"the potentiality of 'what?'"

To define the various faculties of *sekhel* and delineate where one ends and the other begins—especially as regards the faculties of *chokhmah* and *binah*—is no simple task. First of all, these processes take place within the mind at such great speed that it is extremely difficult for a person to contemplate what exactly his mind is doing at any given point. In addition, his mind is, by definition, occupied by the object of his cognition rather that by its own processes. A person also grows accustomed to the dynamics of his own mind and comes to accept them as integral to his own experience; and the more a phenomenon is part of us, the more difficult it is for us to analyze or define it. Furthermore, the two faculties of *chokhmah* and *binah* are, in essence, indivisible; in the language of Kabbalah, they are "two inseparable mates" whose union is axiomatic and unceasing. Every reality derives from this union, as does every activity of the soul, intellectual or emotional. The distinction between them is purely theoretical, because, in actuality, the one never exists without the other: the *chokhmah*-kernel of an idea is, in and of itself, inconceivable, as the qualities that facilitate its conception have yet to be developed by *binah. Binah,* on the other hand, the faculty for analysis and comprehension, operates only when presented with an object to analyze and understand—the object being the concept conceived by *chokhmah.* So there can be no *chokhmah* without *binah,* and no *binah* without *chokhmah.*

Nevertheless, these are two distinct phases in the process of *sekhel,* and they can be isolated under certain conditions, when the process has been slowed. For example, when a person wakes from very deep slumber or emerges from the influence of a general anesthetic: as consciousness returns, the brain realizes that it is receiving data (*chokhmah*), but it still has no understanding what this data is or means, not having yet passed on to the phase in which concepts are processed into something meaningful (*binah*). Another example, often cited in the literature of Chabad Hasidism, is the case of a person struggling with an extremely difficult concept, one that necessitates a concentrated effort to grasp and comprehend. At first, the concept is completely elusive, the mind an utter blank. Then, suddenly, there comes in a flash the sense that "Eureka! I got it!" If, at this point, we were to stop this person and ask him, "What did you 'get'? What have you understood?" he would be unable to explain anything to us, except to tell us that he has grasped the concept. This is *chokhmah* before *binah*. The conception at this point is complete, just as pure intuition; he *has* grasped the concept, in its entirely, but he has yet to comprehend it and is thus incapable of articulating it to others or even to himself.

This description of *chokhmah* as a flash in the mind echoes Maimonides' use of this metaphor to describe the essence of prophecy. Maimonides envisions mankind groping in the darkness, and the prophet as one individual who receives a flash of enlightenment and perception, granting him a knowledge of absolute truth. According to the *Tanya*'s description of *chokhmah,* the experience of such a flash is not the exclusive prerogative of prophets but is the initial step of every process of perception, on all levels: every perception begins as a flash in the dark. *Chokhmah,* then, is the essence of the concept, the idea in a purely potential form, from which all subsequent organized development of the idea derives.

The role of *Chokhmah* in the cognitive process corresponds to the manner in which the senses (sight, hearing, and so on) perceive the physical reality. The senses perceive pure data, data devoid of all significance and direction, but this is the initial, all-inclusive link to the perceived object. In the same way, *chokhmah* delivers the intellectually perceived object to the perceiving "I," and without it, none of the other attributes (*sefirot*) can be activated.

The metaphor of the flash also expresses the all-inclusive nature of *chokhmah.* A flash is something that transpires in an unquantifiable, indivisible iota of time, an experience that cannot be broken down into phases. Similarly, *chokhmah* grasps a truth as a singular entity, not as a collection of details. It relates to the substance of the idea, as if intuitively, seeing its various components as an integral whole. People who experience a moment of pure *chokhmah* describe an all-inclusive perception that is devoid of all cognition. They see the thing as one might see an abstract painting: patches of light and color with no perceivable relation to any known object; one perceives an idea here, a truth, though one does not yet understand what it is. *Chokhmah* is perception without cognition; it is not strictly a faculty of mind but the link between the mind and what lies beyond the mind.

Thus, *chokhmah* is *koach mah*—"the potentiality of 'what?'" "What?" (*mah*) is more than an expression of query and quest; it is an expression of nothingness, of the point at which being ends and nullity begins. (Thus, it is the question that rises to one's lips when one is confronted with total ignorance and incomprehension.) Moses says

"We are what?"[14]—to wit: we are nothing. *Chokhmah,* then, is the faculty of "what?"—the faculty that grasps nothingness and that also *is* nothingness. *Chokhmah* is the first of the faculties of the soul, the point at which perception begins from a prior state of nonconception, the transition from nothingness to something.

Hasidic teaching speaks of *chokhmah* as the faculty for self-abnegation. For the capacity to perceive is the capacity to nullify oneself: the more a person abnegates himself, the more he can receive on the level of *chokhmah.* One who is unable to divest himself of ego cannot perceive anything. *Chokhmah* is thus like the dark chamber of the camera or the black pupil of the eye: empty and utterly devoid of light, it is the optimal vessel for absorbing the light entering into it from the outside. This is the connection between wisdom and humility. One who lacks humility cannot absorb anything. One who is full of himself, certain that he knows everything, cannot learn anything. It is no accident that Moses, who merited the loftiest revelations ever revealed to man, whose entire life was a continuous flash of *chokhmah,* was also "the most humble man on the face of the earth."[15] Moses' unparalleled humility is but the other face of his unparalleled wisdom.

The flash of *chokhmah* is also the touchstone of every idea. Ultimately, a person's conviction of the truth of something derives not from its analysis or its comparison to other things (which are part of the *binah* process) but from its *chokhmah*-flash of perception, where a person recognizes: this is true. This capacity of *chokhmah* to distinguish between one thing and another, as well as between truth and falsehood (*gevurot d'abba,* in the terminology of Kabbalah), is also the source of the concept that "*chokhmah* defines"[16] and is the force that distinguishes good from evil and separates them.

When [a person] brings forth this potential into actuality, that is, when he cogitates with his intellect in order to understand a concept which he has conceived in his intellect to its ultimate truth and depth, this is what is called *binah.*

Chokhmah, in itself, is "what?": not an understanding of something, only the potential for understanding. The realization of this potential through a process of dissection, analysis, and synthesis— breaking down the concept to its particulars, identifying its fundamental elements, and building upon them units of meaning—is *binah.* All perception thus comprises two stages: the appearance of the flash point of *chokhmah* and the development of this point by the *binah* process into a full-fledged concept that one can relate to.

Chokhmah absorbs the full picture in a flash. This picture includes a full array of objects and relations but as a single, indivisible point. Thus, the picture perceived by *chokhmah* is unintelligible; intellect, in the common sense of the word, begins with *binah*.

The difference between *chokhmah* and *binah* is analogous to the difference between sight and hearing. Sight takes in the entire picture, with all its details, in a single instant, whereas hearing receives it piece-meal, one detail at a time. Hearing cannot grasp a thing as a singular, all-inclusive whole, only as a series of points presented in a specific order and structure. By the same token, *chokhmah* is the mind's direct sighting of a concept as an all-embracing "picture" of all its principles and particulars; the picture then passes from *chokhmah*, by way of "the thirty-two paths of wisdom" that "tell the story" to *binah*. Thus, *binah* not only receives its information secondhand but also receives it in a form that is essentially different from the manner of *chokhmah*'s reception, as a stream of particles rather than a snapshot image.

These are the father and mother

Chokhmah and *binah* are often referred to as father and mother, respectively, because their interrelationship and interaction resembles that between father and mother in procreation. This refers to both their mutual relationship (*binah* receiving from *chokhmah*) and to their relationship to the *middot*. *Chokhmah*, as the father, provides the seed, the basic nucleus, that *binah*, the mother, develops into a many-faceted entity (*komah sheleimah*). The nucleus is not merely a miniature of the offspring that needs only to be enlarged to its full size but a DNA-like code that concentrates an entire organism in a single cell. For this cell to develop into a multifaceted organism requires a process similar to pregnancy in the mother's womb, so it may grow qualitatively as well as quantitatively, each component part evolving, diversifying, and correlating with the other parts. It needs a mother. The physical development of a fetus thus resembles the spiritual development of an idea, from the stage of conception (achieved by the mating of *chokhmah* and *binah*), through the stages of pregnancy (which, like the physical pregnancy of nine months, requires a duration of time— as much as forty years or more,[17] in the spiritual womb of the mind), and breast-feeding, until it reaches full maturity.

Physical pregnancy has three qualities that are also present in *binah:* duration, construction, and growth. Duration is a factor of time. *Chokhmah,* as we said, is a flash that does not possess a time factor (time might be required for the attainment of conditions conducive for *chokhmah*'s instantaneous enlightenment to occur, but no time elapses in *chokhmah* itself). *Binah,* on the other hand, is a process, and a process requires duration. From the receipt of the first nucleus, through its assessment and development, until a mature and intelligible concept emerges, a period of time elapses—the "months of pregnancy" of the idea.

Binah is also a construction process. *Chokhmah* imparts to *binah* a seed, an abstract point, without "organs" or "limbs." *Binah* extracts the details from this nucleus and builds it into a structure with interrelated components. The various aspects of the concept—which in *chokhmah* existed as pure, formless potential—become an integrated structure with established parameters and dynamic components (each component not only stands in specific relation to its fellows but possesses a content that exerts its influence upon the entire structure). This process involves more than a development of the potential in the nucleus; it also has a creative element: each "organ" of the newborn idea must be "fleshed out" with substance of its own so that it might exist as a distinct and meaningful point in its own right. Only after these constructive processes have been completed can we speak of a "concept," something that a person might comprehend and communicate to others.

And *binah* is also a process of growth. It receives a dimensionless point, which it processes and enlarges into an "object" with a shape and form, into something that can be grasped. The dimensions imparted by *binah* are referred to as the length, breadth, and depth of the understanding. The depth of the understanding is the ability to delve to the roots of the concept. Breadth is the ability to expand the concept, to draw conclusions from the available material. Length is the capacity to extend it, to apply it to other areas and other strata of reality.

In other words, the depth of understanding is the power of analysis, whereas the breadth of understanding is the power of synthesis. *Binah* constructs a concept by first analyzing the "sparks" it gleans from the *chokhmah*-flash and then synthesizing these sparks to form a new, multifaceted structure. Its analytic and synthetic faculties form the two poles of *binah:* giving and receiving—namely, its reception from *chokhmah* and its yield at the culmination of its processing of the concept. When it receives the flash from *chokhmah,* it applies its analytic faculty, breaking down the integral whole of the flash into details, each, to an extent, distinctly intelligible. This is the essence of comprehension.

In mathematical terms, the function of this dimension of *binah* (its depth) is comparable to squaring the circle, which means transforming a system of transcendental numbers into a system of rational numbers. *Binah* dissects the transcendent point of *chokhmah* to a series of graspable, rational concepts. *Binah*'s ability to dismantle the singular snapshot of *chokhmah* and to find in it causation is like the ability to define a beginning and an end of a straight line; *binah*'s ability to distinguish primary and secondary components in *chokhmah*'s homogeneous point is like the ability to scale sections of different lengths in a straight line, something that is impossible to do in a perfect circle.

On the other hand, the element of breadth in *binah* is its capacity for synthesis: it reassembles the extracted details to form a new structure. In this phase, *binah* not only changes the format of the concept but also expands it by adding qualities that it did not previously possess. The wellspring of *chokhmah* is expanded into the broad river of *binah.*

The length of understanding is the ability to explain a concept not only on its own plane of reality but also at more basic levels. Each such descent from level to level requires certain changes of form while preserving the integrity of the content. Indeed, the ability to transmit an idea many levels lower is one of the parameters by which to measure understanding. Elsewhere,[18] the author explains the great wisdom of Solomon, who was able to "speak in three thousand metaphors,"[19] as the ability to convey a concept three thousand levels beneath his own: to translate the concept into a metaphor that expresses its essence on a lower level of intellectual discourse and then retranslate this metaphor into an even more mundane metaphor and so on, three thousand steps down. The ability to bring an idea even a few levels down from its primary level (for example, for a world-class physicist to explain his theorem to a third grader)—let alone three thousand levels—attests to a great clarity of understanding.

Chokhmah is the father, the masculine, active, giving element of the mind; *binah* is the mother, its feminine, passive, receptive element. This, however, is only in regard to their respective roles in their relationship with each other as the "parents" of the *middot;* but when we consider the nature of these two faculties in themselves, the reverse holds true. Our sages define a *chakham* ("one who is blessed with an enhanced faculty of *chokhmah*") as one who is a great receiver of wisdom—one who can "get" the most complex ideas—and a *navon* ("one whose mental prowess lies in his *binah*") as "one who understands one thing from another."[20] A *navon* is thus greater than a *chakham;* his is the more creative mind that not only grasps what is being explained to him but also derives new ideas from what he has learned. These definitions also have their counterpart in Hasidic teaching. As we said, *chokhmah* is *koach mah,* the potential for "what?"—the capacity for self-nullification. In this sense, *chokhmah* is the passive faculty: it does not generate the flash; it is the mind's capacity to surrender to it and thus receive it (*chokhmah* merely passes on to *binah* what it received). This is the essence of *chokhmah;* the greater the mind's capacity for self-abnegation, the greater its *chokhmah.* The *chakham* thus perceives truths but does not generate or develop them; on the contrary, the more "creative" a mind is, the less its capacity to receive. To possess "the potential of 'what?'" one must master the "We are what?" of Moses.

The essence of *binah,* on the other hand, lies not in its inactive reception from *chokhmah* but rather in its capacity to analyze, to dismantle a concept in order to reconstruct it into something intelligible and expand its depth, scope, and reach. Thus the *navon* "understands one thing from another": he dissects a concept in order to create of it something that has not been before. *Binah* thus corresponds to "the world of creation" (the second of the four worlds or dimensions of reality: Emanation, Creation, Formation, and Action), in which reality develops "from nothing to something" and assumes a distinct and tactile form.

Hence, *chokhmah* is the father only in its relationship with *binah,* and *binah* is the mother only in its relationship with *chokhmah.* But insofar as the nature and function of these *sefirot* themselves are concerned, *chokhmah* is the passive recipient, whereas *binah* is the active and creative force.

In every area of achievement—both in art and in the sciences—there is a phase and point at which new discoveries are made. The capacity for this is contingent upon the ability to attain the state of "we are 'what?'"— to know nothing, to be nothing. This is why children are so smart, because they are not full of themselves. This is also the reason why in those fields that require this type of intellectual achievement—such as physics—people often cease to be productive at a relatively young age. One who loses the capacity to receive—to surrender one's mind to what something outside of his conscious self is telling him—can no longer create or make discoveries. On the other hand, some people do not advance beyond the realm of "the power of 'what?'" so their discoveries remain undeveloped intuitive flashes. Such a person may perceive something momentous, but he cannot explain himself. He sees with the eyes of an artist, but he lacks the ability to create art. To articulate one's vision requires the next step: *binah.*

The *chakham,* then, is the one who perceives what comes to him from without, whereas the *navon* is one who develops what he has already internalized, who can dissect and reconstruct a seed into a full-fledged tree. Obviously, no person is exclusively a *chakham* or exclusively a *navon;* these are abstractions. Every mind is a combination of the two, and the relative proficiency of these two faculties defines a person as a *chakham* or a *navon.*

As we said, *chokhmah* and *binah* are the "two inseparable mates" whose union within our reality is perpetual. The bond between them is the soul of existence, and any separation of the two is tantamount to death, for it suspends all renewal, movement, and growth. Life is predicated on consciousness, and consciousness is the product of the union of *chokhmah* and *binah.*

which give birth to love of God, and awe and fear of Him.

Chokhmah and *binah* facilitate an awareness of God's greatness, and the different facets of this awareness generate the respective emotions of love or fear, as shall be explained.

For when the intellect in the rational soul deeply contemplates and immerses itself exceedingly in the greatness of God,

When a person meditates upon God's greatness and achieves a profound comprehension of it, this inevitably triggers an emotional response. To "deeply contemplate and immerse itself exceedingly" is no easy task, but when a person does achieve a true understanding of God's greatness, he can be assured that his *middot,* his capacity for love and awe, will follow suit. The same is true regarding negative contemplations: if a person is constantly confronted with corporeal temptations, this inevitably stimulates desire and transgression. For such is human nature: when there is a persistent awareness and contemplation, emotional responses arise automatically. The problem is that, in practice, envisioning the temptations of this world is far easier than envisioning the greatness of God. The famed Grandfather of Shephulah used to say: "Master of the Universe, You have not made the

world very well. You have put the temptations of the material here
before our eyes, and given men to learn about the *gehinnom* [Gehenna]
in the book *Reshit Chokhmah*. I swear by my beard that had You done
the reverse—if the *gehinnom* was placed before our eyes and the temptations described in that book—no one would sin!"

**how He fills all worlds and encompasses all worlds and how all is as
naught before Him—**

God "fills" all the worlds, giving them life and existence by His
being. He also "encompasses" all the worlds, for His existence extends
beyond the parameter of the created reality. When a person considers
these two facts and the relationship between them—between the
divine presence in creation (Isaiah 6:3: "The world is full of His glory")
and the fact that God simultaneously transcends reality—he realizes
that "all is as naught before Him": relative to the divine being, no thing
is of any consequence whatever.

**there will be born and aroused in his mind and thought the emotion of ex-
alted awe, to be awed and humbled before His blessed greatness, which is
without end or limit,**

Contemplating the unfathomable greatness of God generates an
appreciation of how distant we are from Him, of how exalted and awesome He is. This causes a shriveling of the self, which perceives its
insignificance before what is immeasurably greater than itself.

and to have the fear of God in his heart.

This is the resultant emotion of that awareness: fear of God.

**In turn, his heart will glow with an intense love like burning coals, with
craving, desire, passion, and a yearning soul, towards the greatness of
the Blessed Infinite.**

The same truth, contemplated from a different angle, produces a
love of God: the desire to connect and fuse with His great and mag-
nificent being.

The four expressions the author uses—*chashikah, chafitzah,
teshukah,* and *nefesh shokekah* ("craving," "desire," "passion," and "a

yearning soul")—are various synonyms for love found in the writing of our sages.[21] *Chashikah* implies a striving, a gravitation toward something. *Chafitzah* describes a more internal movement, not desire as it relates to something that is outside of the person but desire as it is to itself. *Teshukah* and *nefesh shokekah* are burning sensations in the soul: longings that fills the soul and compel it to the point that "it cannot be otherwise." (Rabbi Shmuel Grunem quotes Rabbi Hillel from Paritch as explaining the four terms as four aspects of fire in the divine soul, corresponding to the four colors in a flame.)

This is the "dissolution of the soul" (*kelot hanefesh*) of which Scripture speaks:

Love of God at its highest level is called *kelot hanefesh*, "dissolution of the soul." The soul desires to fuse with the divine, despite the fact that such a union would spell the end of its existence as a distinct entity. So great is the soul's love for God that it consumes its very being.

"My soul longs and goes out . . . ," "My soul thirsts for God," "My soul thirsts for You."

These three verses correspond to the three aspects of the contemplation of the divine greatness mentioned earlier: "how He fills all worlds and encompasses all worlds and how all is as naught before Him," which transcends His immanence as well as His transcendence.

This thirst is derived from the element of Fire in the Godly soul. As the students of natural science write, and so it is in *Etz Chayyim,* the element of Fire is in the heart, whilst the source of [the element of] Water and moisture is in the brain, which is explained in *Etz Chayyim,* Portal 50, to refer to the faculty of *chokhmah,* which is called the "water" of the Godly soul.

There is a distinction between two aspects in the soul, one of "fire" and one of "water," which our author bases on the theories of the natural scientists of ancient times and on the Kabbalistic work *Etz Chayyim* that extends the concepts. Fire represents upward movement; ecstasy and emotional arousal in general; and in the Godly soul, the soul's thirst and desire to rise above its material embodiment and merge with the divine. Water is the soul's intellectual element. Like water, the intellect is cold and damp (as opposed to the hot and dry nature of the heart).

Water moves downward, always descending to the lowest possible point in a terrain; this is also the directional flow of *chokhmah,* which descends from the supernal heights to all points of existence.

All other *middot* are all offshoots of awe and love and their derivations, as is explained elsewhere.

Love and awe are the two fundamental *middot* in the soul, the two poles that impel the soul along all its emotive paths. Love is the movement from self outward: the drive for self-expansion, the breaching of the boundaries that separate the self from the other, the will to influence and give without limit. Awe, on the other hand, is an inward movement: the soul's self-contraction, its withdrawal and withholding from others, its capacity to set parameters and confine itself to them. Thus, love and awe define the two directions of the soul: expansion and contraction, giving and refraining from giving. The third primary *middah, rachamim* ("compassion," which is giving to one who needs) is a composite of love and awe, an intermediary between unequivocal giving and not giving at all, and does not constitute a new direction in the soul. The additional *middot* (*netzach, hod,* and *yesod*) are not primary *middot* like *chessed* and *gevurah* but secondary *middot* that are amplifications and mutations of the primary *middot.*

Daat implies attachment and union, as in the verse, "And Adam knew (*yada*) Eve."

Daat is the third of the three matrices listed earlier: *chokhmah, binah,* and *daat.* As we explained, *chokhmah* is the faculty for apprehending the initial flash of perception, whereas *binah* is the faculty for analytic and synthetic thought. *Daat,* on the other hand, is not an intellectual faculty but the capacity to perform connections between the faculties. *Daat* includes a "higher *daat*" and a "lower *daat*"; lower *daat,* discussed here, is the capacity to build a personal relationship with the subject. It is thus the bridge between the mind and the emotions, relating what has been perceived by *chokhmah* and understood by *binah* to the seven *middot,* where it will stimulate emotional feeling. (Higher *daat,* discussed elsewhere,[22] is what connects *chokhmah* and *binah.*)

In Hebrew, the word *daat* (commonly translated as "knowledge") implies relation and connection such as between a man and his wife, as in the verse "And Adam knew (*yada*) his wife Eve" (Genesis 4:1). In

Genesis 18:19, God says of Abraham, "For I know him (*yeda'ativ*)";
Rashi explains that "I know him" is a term of endearment. Also, "Boaz,
our relative (*moda'atenu*)" (Ruth 3:2), meaning someone who is not
a stranger, who is related to us; and similarly, "For you have found
favor in My eyes, and I shall know you (*eda'acha*) by name" (Exodus
33:17). In each of these cases, *daat* implies a knowledge that carries a
distinct relational-emotive element.

In terms of its place in the structure of the *sefirot*, *daat* is of a lesser
stature than *chokhmah* or *binah*. *Chokhmah* and *binah* are not only
sefirot ("attributes") but also *partzufim* ("faces" or "configurations"),
entities with independent and meaningful characteristics. *Daat*, on
the other hand, is only an auxiliary attribute, so to speak, the force that
unites *chokhmah* and *binah*. Yet *daat* plays an extremely important
role in the operation of the attributes in the soul. Although it does not
build awareness, it determines its actual power and influence. What is
perceived by *chokhmah* and understood by *binah* is acquired only by
daat, whose function is the acquisition of knowledge, its relation to
oneself. Hence, the *Midrash* says, "If you have acquired *daat*, what do
you lack? If you lack *daat*, what have you acquired?"[23]

Daat is not just the accumulation of the results of *chokhmah* and
binah; it also has an active function: to summarize and deduce. It fixes
in the soul the picture that is absorbed by *chokhmah* and developed
by *binah*, rendering their constantly changing processes into a
focused awareness.

Daat is thus the faculty to reach conclusions. The perpetual activity of *chokhmah* and *binah* does not yield any conclusive deductions;
at most, *binah* reaches intermediate conclusions between one cycle of
thought and the next, which are without a defined beginning and end
or any specific direction. The perpetual "mating" of *chokhmah* and
binah—whether in the soul of man or in the supernal *sefirot*—does
not generate any definitive deductions, only an awareness. This is
where the pivotal attribute of *daat* comes in: *daat* is the capacity to
reach a conclusion, to impart an intellectual and moral bottom line
to the abstract and undefinitive ideas of *chokhmah* and *binah*.

Without *daat*, there can be no realization of the person's *komah
sheleimah*, his full structure of mental and emotional attributes. A person might have highly potent faculties of *chokhmah* and *binah*, but a lack
of *daat* would prevent him from applying these powers to the direction
and development of his own personality. So although *daat* does not add
anything to a person's perception and understanding, its importance to

the integrity of the soul's inner life is decisive. It provides the link between the various attributes: between the mind and the *middot* (lower *daat*) and between *chokhmah* and *binah* themselves (higher *daat*).

That is, one binds his mind with a very firm and strong bond to, and firmly fixes his thought on, the greatness of the Blessed Infinite, without diverting his mind [from Him]. For even one who is wise and understanding of the greatness of the Blessed Infinite will not produce in his soul true love and awe, but only vain fancies, unless he binds his mind and fixes his thought with firmness and perseverance.

Daat, as we said, is the soul's connection to a subject, the part of the mind that decides "This relates to me," "This is important to me." A person makes this connection by "fixing his mind," by focusing on a certain truth and meditating upon it until it becomes an integral fixture of his soul. This fixing of the mind must be constant; for if one diverts one's mind, there is no longer any *daat,* and the matter is no longer fixed in his soul. The diversion of the mind does not mean that the person's understanding of the matter has disappeared but that the mind is no longer actively relating to it; as soon as this happens, the mind will cease giving birth to any emotions in the soul. But because the person's understanding of the matter still exists, a person might still imagine that he is experiencing love or awe toward it. This, however, is but a fancy, a sterile thought rather than a true emotion. As a purely intellectual feeling, it does not move a person's soul and does not compel his behavior in any way.

Therefore *daat* is the basis of the *middot* and the source of their vitality; it contains *chessed* and *gevurah,* that is to say, love with its offshoots and fear with its offshoots.

Abstract consideration of a piece of data by *chokhmah* and *binah* does not contain any conclusion as to whether it is desirable or undesirable, whether the person should pursue it or disavow it. *Daat* completes the function of the mind by forming such a conclusion, by establishing the relation of the "I" to the subject. This conclusion creates the ability to produce an emotion, either one of attraction (*chessed*) or of repulsion (*gevurah*). Thus, *daat* is the "basis of the *middot*," encapsulating within it, in potential, the emotional attributes, which produce the impulses to love or to hate, to approach something or to withdraw from it.

Chapter 4

━᳁᳁᳁᳁━

In addition, every Godly soul possesses three garments, which are the thought, speech, and action of the 613 commandments of the Torah. For when a person actively fulfills all the precepts which require physical action, and with his power of speech he occupies himself in expounding all the 613 commandments and their practical applications (*halachot*), and with his power of thought he comprehends all that is comprehensible to him in the *pardes* of the Torah—then the totality of the 613 "organs" of his soul are clothed in the 613 commandments of the Torah.

Specifically: the faculties of *ChaBaD* in his soul are clothed in the comprehension of the Torah, which he comprehends in *pardes*, to the extent of his mental capacity and the supernal root of his soul. And the *middot*, namely fear and love, together with their offshoots and derivatives, are clothed in the fulfillment of the commandments in deed and in speech— [that is], the study of Torah which is "the equivalent of all [the commandments]." For love is the root of all the 248 positive commands, which derive from it and have no true foundation without it, since he who fulfills them in truth is one who truly loves the name of God and desires to cleave to Him in truth—for one cannot truly cleave to Him except through fulfillment of the 248 [positive] commandments, which are the 248 "limbs of the King," as it were, as is explained elsewhere. And awe is the root of the 365 prohibitive commands, as one fears to rebel against the Supreme King of kings, the Holy One, blessed be He; or a more inner fear than this—that one feels ashamed in the presence of the Divine greatness to rebel against His glory and do what is evil in His eyes, namely, any of the abominable things hated by God, which are the *kelipot* and *sitra achra,* which draw their nurture from terrestrial man and have their hold in him through [his violation of] the 365 prohibitive commands.

Now these three "garments," consisting of the Torah and its commandments, although they are called garments of the *nefesh, ruach,* and *neshamah,* their quality, nevertheless, is infinitely higher and greater than that of the *nefesh, ruach,* and *neshamah* themselves. As explained in the *Zohar,* the Torah and the Holy One, blessed be He, are one. The meaning of this is that the Torah, which is the wisdom and will of the Holy One, blessed be He, and the Holy One, blessed be He, Himself are one, since "He is both the knower and the knowledge . . . ," as explained above in the name of Maimonides.

And although the Holy One, blessed be He, is called *Ein Sof* ("Infinite"), and "His greatness can never be fathomed," and "No thought can apprehend Him at all," and so are also His will and His wisdom, as it is written: "There is no seeking His understanding," and "Can you by searching find God?" and: "For My thoughts are not your thoughts"—nevertheless, it is in this connection that it has been said: "Where you find the greatness of the Holy One, blessed be He, there you find His humility." For the Holy One, blessed be He, has compressed His will and wisdom within the 613 commandments of the Torah and their laws, and in the combination of the letters of the *Tanakh,* and in the expositions thereof which are to be found in the *aggadot* and *midrashim* of our Sages of blessed memory, in order that each *neshamah,* or *ruach* and *nefesh* in the human body should be able to comprehend them in its mind, and to fulfill them, as far as they can be fulfilled, in act, speech, and thought, thereby clothing itself, with all its ten attributes, in these three garments.

This is why the Torah has been compared to water: just as water descends from a higher place to a lower place, so has the Torah descended from its place of glory, which is the will and wisdom of the Blessed; [for] the Torah and the Holy One, blessed be He, are one, and no thought can apprehend Him at all. Thence it has progressively descended through hidden steps, step after step, with the evolution of the worlds, until it clothed itself in physical things and in matters of this world, which comprise virtually all of the commandments of the Torah and their laws, and in the combinations of physical letters, written with ink in a scroll, namely, the twenty-four books of the Torah, Prophets, and Hagiographa—all this in order that every thought should be able to apprehend them, and that even the faculties of speech and action, which are on a lower level than thought, should be able to apprehend them and be clothed in them. And since the Torah and its commandments clothe all ten attributes of the soul and all its 613 organs from head to foot, it is altogether and literally "bound up in the bundle of life with God," and the very light of God envelops and clothes it from head to foot; as it is written, "God is my rock, I take refuge in Him," and it is also written, "As a shield [Your] will does encircle him," to say, the Blessed's will and wisdom, which are clothed in His Torah and its commandments, [encircles him].

Thus it has been said: "Better is one hour of repentance and good deeds in this world than the whole life of the World to Come." For the World to Come is [that state where] one enjoys the "glow of the Divine Presence" (*ziv haShekhinah*), which is the pleasure of apprehension. No created being, even of the celestial, can apprehend more than some reflection of the Divine light, which is why the reference is to "the glow of the Divine Presence." As for the essence of the Holy One, blessed be He, no thought can apprehend Him at all—except when it is apprehended and clothed in the Torah and its *Mitzvot*. Then [the human being] does literally apprehend, and is clothed in, the Holy One, blessed be He, since the Torah and the Holy One, blessed be He, are one.

And although the Torah has been clothed in lowly, physical things, it is, by way of illustration, like embracing the king: there is no difference, in regard to the degree of closeness and attachment to the king, whether one embraces the king as the latter is wearing one robe or several robes, so long as the royal person is inside them. Likewise, when the king, for his part, embraces one with his arm, even though it is dressed in his robes; as it is written, "And His right hand embraces me," which refers to the Torah which was given by God's right hand, which is the quality of *chessed* and water.

COMMENTARY

In Chapter 3, the author discussed the ten attributes (*bechinot*) of the soul—the three matrices and the seven multiples—corresponding to the ten supernal attributes (*sefirot*). We explained that these are the soul's ten *tikkunim* ("fixtures" or "inner expressions"). The *tikkunim* express the soul and personify it in such a way that, as perceived from without, the soul's inner essence and its expression through its attributes are one. This personality of the soul is how it reveals itself to the outside world, as well as how is manifests itself internally to the soul's *levushim,* "garments." It is the "garments" of the Godly soul that the author discusses in this chapter.

In addition, every Godly soul possesses three garments,

The garments are the means through which the soul expresses itself, like the clothes that a person wears in order to relate to other people. The metaphor of garment stresses the dual nature of every manifestation: to manifest something is both to reveal it and to conceal it. The garment facilitates a person's revelation of himself to others (without his garments, he would not show himself to others), yet at the same time, it conceals the wearer; for one sees not the person but the garments. Another aspect of the analogy is the synonymy between the person and his clothes, the fact that the clothes mirror the person. The clothes are external to the person, yet they duplicate the character of the wearer. Here lies the difference between the garment and other tools that a person uses to a certain end. A tool does not imitate its user, whereas a garment alludes to the shape of its wearer even as it conceals him. Similarly, speech is the garment of thought, expressing the thought even as it veils its deeper dimensions, its words mirroring the "letters" and images of the thought, just as a garment is a kind of copy of the body that wears it.

Unlike the *tikkunim,* the *levushim* constitute the outer expressions of the soul and are distinct from it. The soul has the choice whether to dress itself in them or not, just as a person can clothe himself in a garment or remove it without effecting any change in himself. This is not the case with the more internal *tikkunim,* which, to extend the analogy, are more like a body to the soul. In essence, the body and the soul are two different entities, but the soul embodies itself in the body to the extent that, in many respects, body and soul come to comprise a single entity. A soul cannot remove or change its body without itself changing.[1]

The attributes of the soul are integrally bound to the soul's essence. As the soul's essence is immutable, so are its attributes—*chessed* cannot be transformed into *gevurah,* and so on—just as the soul cannot remove and don its body at will. The garments, on the other hand, are separate from the soul's essence; thus, the faculties of thought, speech, and action can change their function from one extreme to the other, expressing love one moment and fear a moment later. Also, the integral bond between the soul and its attributes means that the very essence of the soul is present in each of them; thus, the extreme stimulation of one of the attributes (love, fear, and so on) can bring about a *kelot hanefesh* ("dissolution of the soul"; see Chapter 3) in the very essence of the soul, something that the soul's garments alone cannot cause.[2]

which are the thought, speech, and action

Thought, the faculty by which a person's soul expresses itself to the conscious self, is the innermost of the garments. Speech is the soul's vehicle of expression to others through words, whereas deed is the expression of the soul by way of the tools of the material world.

of the 613 commandments of the Torah.

The garments of the Godly soul are the 613 commandments (*mitzvot*) of the Torah. Each soul, like every other existence, expresses itself through those garments that facilitate the revelation of its particular nature. The animal soul expresses itself through garments whose content and form are akin to its physical and material nature. The garments of the Godly soul, which belongs to the divine, are the ways of holiness, namely, the thought, speech, and deed of the 613 *mitzvot* of the Torah.

The statement that the manifestation of holiness is through the 613 *mitzvot* of the Torah has a twofold implication, in respect to both what constitutes holiness and what does not. Holiness is attained by observing the *mitzvot,* and it cannot be attained in any other way. This axiom has far-reaching implications: that holiness—that which is absolute good—does not contain anything that is not connected with Torah. There are many important things in the world, but they are not necessarily holy. There is no meaning to such expressions as "the sanctity of the law," "the sanctity of the state," or "the sanctity of labor." People involved in a profession or an ideal acquire a love for it and attribute to it a sort of holiness. But holiness is not merely a matter of extreme regard. Holiness, by definition, is something that pertains to the divine, and the only way to connect with the divine is through Torah and *mitzvot.*

Can holiness be attained in some other way? Is it possible to create new types of holiness other than through Torah and *mitzvot*? We have a letter from the author of *Tanya* (printed in some Chabad prayer books) regarding certain Hasidic groups who, in order to stimulate their souls to prayer, would sit around telling jokes so as to raise their spirits before approaching their prayers. The author sharply condemned this practice, referring to it as "a *mitzvah* that comes through a sin,"[3] "the joy of those who are 'extremely evil and sinful against God,'"[4] and similar expressions. Holiness cannot be manufactured by man. Holiness means relationship with God, the Infinite (*Ein Sof*), but finite man cannot, by his own power, relate to the Infinite, as neither he nor anything he generates can be of intrinsic significance to the Infinite. People tend to relate things they have created to God and then expect Him to regard them as holy. The human being might create something that is very important, very great, very inspiring; that creation might even represent a great sacrifice on his part, in the sense that he has devoted his time and his very self to it; but none of this makes it in any way connected with the Infinite. Between the Infinite and the finite is an infinite gap; between the Infinite and man is a gap that man cannot bridge. However high a man rises, whatever effort he makes, the gap between him and the divine remains. From his side, the gap cannot be closed.

From the time of Adam, the temptation has existed "to become like God, knowers of good and evil."[5] Artists, writers, scientists—all are tempted by the belief that there is some ruse, some hidden way, some new invention, whereby a person can cross a certain line and become divine. But although a person can, by his own efforts, achieve great things—he can even taste of the fruit of the Tree of Knowledge and know good and evil—but he cannot, on his own, touch on the Infinite.

As will be explained, the only way that such contact can be achieved is when God creates this contact, when He extends His hand, so to speak, across the gap to grant man the ability to connect with Him. For the gap that separates the finite from the Infinite can be bridged only by the Infinite.

The hand that God extends to us is the Torah. Torah is not merely words of wisdom. It is beyond all wisdom; it is God's wisdom, and the *mitzvot* are God's commandments. The essence of the Torah is that the Creator of the world communicates to man something that man can hear, comprehend, and do and thereby connect with Him. The essence of the connection is created not by the fact that a certain person studies a lot, prays excessively, or observes the *mitzvot* with great zeal, but by the very fact that one is doing what God wants one to do.

The Torah is thus a manifestation of the divine, a ray of the infinite light penetrating the infinite abyss of the darkness of the finite; it, and it alone, constitutes the garments of the Godly soul, facilitating its contact with the divine.

For when a person actively fulfills all the precepts which require physical action, and with his power of speech he occupies himself in expounding all the 613 commandments and their practical applications (*halachot*), and with his power of thought he comprehends all that is comprehensible to him in the *pardes* of the Torah[6]—then the totality of the 613 "organs" of his soul are clothed in the 613 commandments of the Torah.

The human body consists of 248 members and 365 blood vessels; the soul, too, includes 613 organs, which are the spiritual counterparts of the 613 organs of the body.[7] Each of the 613 organs of the human soul has one of the 613 *mitzvot* of the Torah as its specific garment.

No single individual can actually observe all 613 *mitzvot,* not only because conditions might not allow it, but because there is no individual to whom they all apply. Some *mitzvot* are commanded exclusively to women, others exclusively to men; some apply only to the king or the *kohen gadol* ("high priest"), whereas other people are actually forbidden to observe them. But every Jew has some connection with each of the *mitzvot,* and, in a certain sense, can observe them all. For example, the high priest or the king fulfills his *mitzvot* on his own behalf and on behalf of all Israel. As explained in Chapter 3, all of Israel in a particular generation, and in a broader sense of all generations, constitutes a *komah sheleimah,* a singular unit, just as the human body, consisting of different limbs and organs, constitutes a single organism. Israel, in this sense, is a multidimensional being, in time as well as space, its various generations and communities composing an integrated whole; each generation is a cross section of the greater body, personifying the totality in its specific way. Each individual, therefore, as a part of the whole, shares in the *mitzvot* that every other part observes.

Another way in which a person can fulfill all the *mitzvot* is by realizing those *mitzvot* that he cannot observe physically on another plane, in speech and thought. For example, a person who cannot fulfill the commandments that apply only to kings can still fulfill them, in a way, by thinking and speaking about them. Aside from *mitzvot* that are fulfilled through thought or speech, merely talking and thinking about a *mitvah* does not constitute its true fulfillment. In some cases, it may be enough for a person to develop that part of the garment that clothes the 613 organs of his soul.

Specifically: the faculties of *ChaBaD* in his soul are clothed in the comprehension of the Torah, which he comprehends in *pardes,* to the extent of his mental capacity and the supernal root of his soul.

Comprehension of Torah, at the level at which a person connects and unites it, has two components: "the extent of his mental capacity" and "the supernal root of his soul." There are areas of Torah that many minds are incapable of comprehending strictly because of their limitations. Not every mind can understand the complexities of Talmud with *Tosafot.*[8] Every person has his limits in how much he can comprehend of the four levels of *pardes* or Torah interpretation, limits set by his intellectual ability.

The second factor in the acquisition of Torah is the supernal root of a person's soul. Even one who is intellectually able to deal with a certain area of Torah will not grasp it completely, unless it relates to the root of his soul. Only then will its concepts speak to him and affect him. To comprehend something requires intellectual ability, but it also requires an inner affinity with the concept, which derives from the soul's rootedness in this area of Torah. If a person lacks this inner identification, the matter might be explained to him, or illustrated to him by means of metaphors and analogies, but he will not truly connect to it.

Conversely, some possess a lofty soul, sensitive to great and lofty things, but lack the intellectual talent to fully understand them. Such a person relates to these things intuitively, even without the tools to rationally comprehend them. The Talmud touches on this phenomenon when it speaks of those with the capacity "to derive the [halakhah] ('the legal ruling') from a teaching";[9] this ability is a special talent, almost intuitive, that is not necessarily connected with a person's greatness in the comprehension of Torah. The works of such individuals, who exhibited an acute ability to meet the needs of the time, have become widely accepted and revered, even though they were not among the leading scholars of their generation. The author of *Kitzur Shulchan Aruch* (Abridged Code of Jewish Law) was a great rabbi in his place but was far from being the greatest of his time, either in his own eyes or in the eyes of others. Yet even the most brilliant scholars of the time did not merit to achieve what he achieved. Not only was he able to write in a popular style, but he intuitively knew to isolate the essentials of Torah law that the common Jew of his generation needed to know. When the root of a person's soul is attuned to a certain area of Torah, it leads him there even if he is unable to explain or even understand it.

And the *middot*, namely fear and love, together with their offshoots and derivatives, are clothed in the fulfillment of the commandments in deed and in speech—[that is], the study of Torah which is "the equivalent of all [the commandments]."

The author singles out Torah study as the example of a *mitzvah* fulfilled through the garment of speech (though other examples of such *mitzvot* exist, such as the recitation of the Shema and Grace after Meals) because it is the most prestigious of the *mitzvot*, "the equivalent of them all."[10]

For love is the root of all the 248 positive commands, which derive from it and have no true foundation without it, since he who fulfills them in truth is one who truly loves the name of God and desires to cleave to Him in truth

The 613 *mitzvot* consist of 248 positive commandments (for example, to give charity, put on *tefillin*) and 365 prohibitions (for example, murder, adultery, eating leavened bread on Passover). These correspond to the 248 members and 365 blood vessels of the body and their corresponding organs of the soul, as mentioned earlier.

The 248 positive commandments are the means by which a person expresses his love for God. Thus, the positive *mitzvot* "derive" from the soul's love of God in the sense that love of God is the feeling that motivates and drives their observance. Although a person can observe the *mitzvot* merely out of habit or because he was trained to do so from childhood, this is not a true observance with a "true foundation" but a casual, extrinsic deed, with no relation to the person's inner being. "He who fulfills them in truth" is one who does so out of a genuine inner desire.

—for one cannot truly cleave to Him except through fulfillment of the 248 [positive] commandments,

A frequently recurring question is: How can one cleave to God?[11] We know how to unite with something physical, such as a human being, but how can we unite with something that has no physical form—indeed, no form at all—to something infinite and undefinable? A person can feel love for God, can yearn for God, can proclaim, "My soul thirsts for God!"[12] But this only expresses his yearning; it does not consummate his love; it does not join him to God. At times, a person might feel attached to God, but such a feeling, by definition, is virtually never genuine.

The way to attach oneself to God "in truth" is not by the means of a self-generated feeling of yearning for God but, as our author says here, by fulfilling the 248 positive commandments. Thus, the author will explain in Chapter 40 Isaiah's statement, "Ho, everyone that thirsts, come ye to the waters."[13] On the face of it, the verse doesn't seem to be telling us anything. Obviously, one who is thirsty should go drink water; and if we are to interpret the verse metaphorically as a reference to Torah (per Talmud, *Bava Kamma* 17a: "There is no water save for Torah"), again, one who thirsts for Torah should obviously partake of Torah. Rabbi Schneur Zalman, however, explains that the verse is telling us a profound truth regarding man's efforts to relate to God. "Whoever thirsts" for God, for connection to the divine, "should go to the water," to Torah. One who is physically thirsty knows that he needs water, but one who thirsts for God does not necessarily know that he needs Torah. He yearns for God, and he is told to go and study about "The bull that gored the cow"![14] This approach to relating to God is far from self-evident; indeed, it runs contrary to one's natural inclinations. So Isaiah proclaims: "Let whoever thirsts go to the water!" That is, "one cannot truly cleave to Him except through fulfillment of the 248 commandments."

Hence, just as there is no genuine fulfillment of the *mitzvot* without love of God, so there is no true significance to love of God without fulfillment of the *mitzvot.* A person who yearns to cleave to God and yet is sated with the spiritual experience of yearning for God will never achieve true connection to the divine. When a person merely desires but does not do, even if the desire is genuine and faultless, this alone will never bring about the realization of the desire.

which are the 248 "limbs of the King," as it were, as is explained elsewhere.[15]

The 248 positive *mitzvot* correspond not only to the 248 parts of the human body but also to the metaphorical body of the supernal King. Kabbalistic teaching describes God's sovereignty of the universe—the divine manifestations that reveal God as creator and vitalizer of the world—in terms of an organism (this is also the divine image in which man has been formed, so the 248 parts of the human body mirror the spiritual structure of the divine organism). This organism is the spiritual source of the *mitzvot* that have been commanded to us.

Thus, when a person observes the *mitzvot* in thought, speech, and deed—when he attaches himself and cleaves to them—he thereby cleaves to the 248 limbs of God, so to speak. Human beings express cleaving by embracing and kissing the limbs of the body of the beloved.[16] When a person loves God with great desire and craving, and wishes to come close to Him and cleave to Him, the way to "consummate" this love is by embracing the "limbs of the King," the 248 positive *mitzvot* that are the physical embodiments of the divine revelations in our world.

And awe is the root of the 365 prohibitive commands,

The essence of the emotion of *yir'ah* ("awe") is an inward movement: withdrawal, self-retraction, introversion (in contrast with *ahavah*, "love," which is the movement from the self outward to connect with the other). *Yir'ah* has many forms: awe, fear, shame, humility, and so on. *Ahavah* prompts to action, *yir'ah* to inaction. Thus, there are many reasons that may prevent a person from committing a transgression, but the root of them all is *yir'ah*.

As we said, *yir'ah*, as a feeling, assumes many forms, one of them being

as one fears to rebel against the Supreme King of kings, the Holy One, blessed be He;

A deliberate sin is an act of rebellion, a scorning of the divine authority (compare Numbers 15:30: "And the soul who shall act highhandedly"). Man is prevented from sin out of a fear of rebelling against God, not merely from fear of punishment and reprisal, but because the very thought of rebelling against authority of the supreme King of all kings is frightening to him.

or a more inner fear than this—that one feels ashamed in the presence of the Divine greatness to rebel against His glory

This is a more inner *yir'ah,* in that what affects the person is not the dread of the might of the king but a feeling of awe before God Himself. Because he senses the greatness of God, he is literally ashamed to contravene His will; he feels that God is present, watching him.

Elsewhere the author speaks of yet another type of *yir'ah,* "the awe of loftiness" (*yir'at haromemut*). This, too, is an inner *yir'ah* but of a different character than the "awe of shame" (*yir'at haboshet*) mentioned here. The difference between them is one of personality. "Awe of loftiness" is predicated upon a sense of distance—one is struck by how lofty and removed the awed object is from one's lowly self—so it applies more to people inclined to view things objectively. "Awe of shame," on the other hand, includes an element of connection and intimacy, connoting a relationship within which one experiences the shame of inadequacy. When considering the greatness of the Infinite, some feel overawed and paralyzed; others feel shame. It is told of Rabbi Nachman of Bratzlav that, as young child, whenever he did or thought of doing something wrong, he would blush in shame before God.

and do what is evil in His eyes, namely, any of the abominable things hated by God, which are the *kelipot* and *sitra achra,* which draw their nurture from terrestrial man and have their hold in him through [his violation of] the 365 prohibitive commands.

An evil deed is not merely an act that is contrary to a system of conventions. Evil is evil in essence. The evil deed is a deed that nourishes the cosmic evil, a conduit that feeds power and vitality to *kelipah* (see Chapter 2). The existence of evil is inherent in the nature of the creation, but its nourishment comes from earthly man.

Indeed, man is *kelipah*'s only source of nurture, expansion, and growth. No other creature, spiritual or physical, relates in any way to good or evil. The leopard is no worse than the lamb; both are created with a certain nature that is not definable as good or evil: the leopard that preys on the lamb has committed no transgression of the divine will, nor does the devoured lamb become a martyred saint because it was eaten. In this sense, even the supernal angels, whose holiness (that is, their proximity to God) far surpasses that of man, have the capacity neither for good nor for evil. An angel cannot do good or bad; it is an agent, a messenger, without the capacity for independent choice. To attribute good or evil to an angel is like attributing free choice to a machine. So all creatures, both supernal and ephemeral, are basically objects, neutral matter, to which the concepts of good and evil cannot be applied. Only man, who lives in a world of divine concealment and temptation to evil, has been granted the capacity to choose between transcending them or succumbing to them; only he can act evilly; only he can nourish evil and increase its power. The 365 prohibitions of the Torah delineate the ways in which evil gains a hold on man: when a person transgresses one of the divine prohibitions, he nourishes its corresponding aspect of evil.

Elsewhere,[17] the author describes evil as a parasite that lives off man, coexisting with him in a symbiotic relationship, so to speak. Evil exists wherever man allows it to exist, wherever he allows it to feed off the divine life force that flows to him. The divine vitality is thus diverted from holiness (the soul of man) to *kelipah*. The 365 prohibitions can thus be seen as a sort of "list of parasites," defining the various ways in which man nourishes evil, from those in the mind and heart to those in speech and action.

Now these three "garments," consisting of the Torah and its commandments, although they are called garments of the *nefesh, ruach,* and *neshamah,*

The soul, as we explained, clothes itself in the *mitzvot* it fulfills, each of the 613 *mitzvot* enclothing one of the 613 organs that constitute the human soul. Collectively, the 613 *mitzvot* form an overall garment (which the *Zohar* refers to as *chaluka d'rabbanan,* "the garment of the sage"[18]), enveloping the three levels of the soul—*nefesh, ruach,* and *neshamah*—from every angle. Thus, the *mitzvot* are mere envelopes of the soul, garments that it dons from time to time.

their quality, nevertheless, is infinitely higher and greater than that of the *nefesh, ruach,* and *neshamah* themselves.

Torah and *mitzvot* indeed serve as the soul's garments, as the means by which it expresses its relationship to God. But they are more than auxiliary tools of the soul; qualitatively, they are loftier than the soul itself. As we explained elsewhere, it is precisely because of their loftiness that the soul clothes itself in them in order to connect with God. Because the Torah is higher than the soul, it is able to serve as a bridge between the soul and God.

As explained in the *Zohar*,[19] the Torah and the Holy One, blessed be He, are one. The meaning of this is that the Torah, which is the wisdom and will of the Holy One, blessed be He

The Torah is the supernal wisdom of God (*Chokhmah d'Atzilut*), embodying the totality of the divine relationship with the created reality. The *mitzvot* of the Torah are the divine will, expressing God's desire as to what should be done and what should not be done.

and the Holy One, blessed be He, Himself are one, since "He is both the knower and the knowledge . . . ,"[20] as explained above in the name of Maimonides.

The Torah is God's *chokhmah*, which is synonymous with the divine being Himself. As explained in Chapter 2, God's knowledge is His knowledge of Himself; so all three—the object of his knowledge, the knowledge of it that He has, and He, the Knower—are one and the same. Therefore, the person who studies Torah, fusing his own mind to its concepts, achieves a bond with the divine and thereby with God Himself.

An examination of what the author writes in Chapter 2 raises the question: here we say that the Torah and *mitzvot* are loftier than the soul, because they derive from the divine *chokhmah;* yet in Chapter 2 we said that the soul is "a part of God above, literally" for the very reason that *it* derives from the divine *chokhmah.* So in what way is the Torah superior to the soul?

One explanation is that in Chapter 2 the author speaks of the soul's essence,[21] whereas here he speaks of the soul's ten attributes discussed in Chapter 3. In other words, although the essence of the soul derives from the divine *chokhmah,* the soul's attributes are on a lower level (see our introduction to Chapter 3); its garments, which consist of the Torah and its *mitzvot,* derive directly from the divine *chokhmah.* Thus, the relationship between the soul's attributes and their garments is such that while the garments are extrinsic to the attributes, they constitute, in and of themselves, a loftier manifestation of the divine.

It is said here that the Torah and commandments derive directly from the divine *chokhmah* and are therefore higher than the soul. However, in Chapter 2, it says that the soul, too, derives directly from the divine *chokhmah.*

Rabbi Shmuel Grunem offers the following explanations: First, the soul indeed originates as a generation of the divine *chokhmah.* However, as it passes through the *seder hahishtalshelut* ("chain of evolution"; see Chapter 6), it undergoes a series of metamorphoses, as it descends from the world of Emanation, through the worlds of Creation and Formation, to the world of Action, where it is invested in a physical body. It is now a creature with a character and physical self. Regarding the Torah and *mitzvot,* the reverse is true: the divine will is that the *mitzvot* be observed on physical earth, so it is in the world of Action that the Torah is *most* synonymous with the divine *chokhmah.* Hence, the soul, as it exists in the physical world, is in a state of descent and distance from its source and achieves connection with God by enclothing itself in the thought, speech, and deeds of the Torah.

Accordingly, in Chapter 2, the author refers to the soul as a "part of God above," implying that it has parted and descended from its source in the supernal *chokhmah.* This is not the case with the Torah and *mitzvot,* which are the express will of God as they exist in the physical world.

Second, regarding Torah it is said that "Torah emerges from *chokhmah*" (*oraita michokhmah nafkat*).[22] Hasidic teaching explains that [although] Torah *emerges* from the supernal *chokhmah* (that is, *chokhmah* is the agent of its revelation), its true source is *keter,* which is a higher manifestation of Godliness than *chokhmah.* Thus, the soul descends to the physical world in order to clothe itself in the thought, speech, and action of Torah and thereby elevate its level of connection with God from *chokhmah* to *keter.*

And although the Holy One, blessed be He, is called *Ein Sof* ("Infinite"), and "His greatness can never be fathomed,"[23] and "No thought can apprehend Him at all,"[24]

That is, not only is our earthly intellect an inadequate tool to comprehend God, but no thought at all, not even the spiritual perception of the supernal angels, can possibly comprehend Him, because the Infinite is, by definition, incomprehensible.

and so are also His will and His wisdom

These, as explained earlier, are synonymous with His being.

as it is written: "There is no seeking His understanding,"[25] and "Can you by searching find God?"[26] and: "For My thoughts are not your thoughts"[27]—

The author is raising the question: If God's wisdom and will are as infinite and unfathomable as Himself, how can the Torah, which we do comprehend, be the wisdom of God, and the *mitzvot*, which we enact in our daily lives, be His will? How can we possibly grasp and relate to His wisdom and will?

nevertheless, it is in this connection that it has been said: "Where you find the greatness of the Holy One, blessed be He, there you find His humility." For the Holy One, blessed be He, has compressed His will and wisdom within the 613 commandments of the Torah and their laws, and in the combination of the letters of the *Tanakh*, and in the expositions thereof which are to be found in the *aggadot* and *midrashim* of our Sages of blessed memory,

No man or creature can comprehend the divine wisdom itself. However, as the Talmud states, "Wherever you find His greatness"[28]— wherever His infinity is referred to in the Scriptures—"you find His humility"; in that very same place, you read of how God constricts Himself and defines Himself to a specific place. In every place that you find His power,[29] His infinite power to constrict His own infinity, there you find His humility—there you find Him manifesting Himself in the small details. Where He is described as the "God of gods and Lord of lords" (Deuteronomy 10:17), He is also described as "He who does justice for the orphan and widow" (Deuteronomy 10:18). Where He is described as "the high and lofty One, who inhabits eternity, holy is His name" (Isaiah 57:15), this is followed by "I dwell on high and holy, and with the oppressed and low in spirit, to revive the spirit of the low, and enliven the heart of the oppressed." God, whom "the heavens and the heavens of heaven cannot contain" (1 Kings 8:27), "constricted His presence between the carrying-poles of the ark."[30] This is God's greatness, and this is His power. He is not merely great but infinite; and His infinity and omnipotence enables the expression of His *chokhmah* in finite words and forms. (To say that because God is infinite and without limit He therefore cannot manifest Himself through a finite medium is to impose a limit on Him—that is, to render Him finite! It is specifically His infinity that enables Him to clothe Himself in finite garments. This is what the

Talmud means when its says, "wherever you find His greatness, you find His humility.")[31]

Even if those elements of Torah to which we have access are but "the leavings of *chokhmah*"[32] representing but a paltry fraction of the supernal *chokhmah,* they are nevertheless the written expression of the divine wisdom. It is as if a concept were to be expressed in a series of formulas, each outlining a deeper aspect of the concept; even the most superficial formula is correct, although layer upon layer of deeper formulations exist. Likewise, the Torah is the divine truth at whatever level it appears, in whatever "world" or stratum of reality it is articulated. The letters and words of the Written Torah, the demarcations and categories that define the legal details of each *mitzvah*— this is the wisdom and will of God as expressed in the obscurities, limitations, and contradictions of our material world.

in order that each *neshamah,* or *ruach* and *nefesh* in the human body should be able to comprehend them in its mind, and to fulfill them, as far as they can be fulfilled, in act, speech, and thought, thereby clothing itself, with all its ten attributes, in these three garments.

The contraction of the divine will in the 613 *mitzvot* of the Torah is meant for the soul as enclothed in a physical body and a physical world.

This is why the Torah has been compared to water:[33] just as water descends from a higher place to a lower place, so has the Torah descended from its place of glory, which is the will and wisdom of the Blessed; [for] the Torah and the Holy One, blessed be He, are one, and no thought can apprehend Him at all. Thence it has progressively descended through hidden steps,[34] step after step, with the evolution of the worlds,[35] until it clothed itself in physical things and in matters of this world—which comprise virtually all[36] of the commandments of the Torah and their laws,

In its loftier incarnation, the Torah, being the *chokhmah* of God, is, like Himself, inherently unattainable and incomprehensible. But it does not remain at this level. The entire point of a Torah is that the divine wisdom, while remaining inherently incomprehensible, should progressively be rearticulated, level after level, until it is rendered in a formula to which every human being can in some way relate. We cannot comprehend these formulas fully, because they relate to the divine reality rather than to ours; but we can relate to certain aspects of their bottom line, to their translation into a law and philosophy for physical life.

For an analogy of sorts, we might consider the computer. We can understand a computer on many levels. The most fundamental level, the theory of how the computer operates, is extremely complex and requires specialized expertise that very few people are able to master. But on more superficial levels, one can, with a minimum of mental ability, achieve a certain mastery of the computer. Say that we wish that the computer should multiply a two-digit number to the power of six. The dynamics of this operation are beyond the understanding of the vast majority of people making the calculation on the computer, but the computer has an operating system that translates this process into a simple problem that most everyone can solve: Which keys do I punch?

In a similar way, the Torah is incomprehensible at its elemental level, but a great part of it translates into deeds and rules, do's and don'ts, that anyone can relate to. Were the Torah to remain in the supernal worlds, as abstract *chokhmah,* it could not relate to the ordinary person.[37] But when the Torah successively reformulates itself to the point that, for example, it instructs that we *must* give gifts to the poor on Purim, everyone knows what to do. One need not master the entire array of issues, from the most abstract essence of this law to the final rulings in the *Shulchan Aruch* (Why "gifts"? What is the definition of "gift"? How much would a "gift" be? and so on). All one needs to do is give or receive money on Purim.

Thus, the Torah links the infinite to everyday life. It stretches upward to infinity and extends downward, step by endless step, to a level that anyone can relate to at any time, expressing the divine wisdom within the context of our reality. And our reality is a reality graspable by the body—a reality with which the body can build an involved physical relationship—so that the soul that dwells and operates within the body can experience it, identify with it, and fuse with it. So the Torah, while being the infinite divine wisdom, is at the same time also definitive and intelligible to man. It is the synthesis of God's greatness and His humility, a synthesis that expresses the very essence of the divine.

and in the combinations of physical letters, written with ink in a scroll, namely, the twenty-four books of the Torah, Prophets, and Hagiographa,

Another example of the physical embodiment of Torah (in addition to the physical actions of the *mitzvot*) is the Torah scroll, in which the books of the Written Torah (*Tanakh*) are inscribed. Their content, their wording, the shape of the letters, and even the qualities of the ink (which is governed by a series of *halachot*) in which they are written—are all expressions of the divine will and wisdom.

all this in order that every thought should be able to apprehend them,

As we said before, "no thought can apprehend" the supernal wisdom. But when the supernal wisdom embodies itself, through the Torah, in physical concepts and realities, every mind *can* apprehend it.

and that even the faculties of speech and action, which are on a lower level than thought, should be able to apprehend them and be clothed in them.

The Torah clothes itself not only in conceptions of human reason but also in words we can speak and deeds we can do; thus, we relate to it not only through abstract thoughts but also through concrete speech and deeds. Not only can we understand Torah, we can also speak it and do it, investing our very bodies in the act of a *mitzvah*.

And since the Torah and its commandments clothe all ten attributes of the soul

The ten attributes of the soul constitute a person's inner structure (see Chapter 3), and for each attribute there is a corresponding garment of Torah: *chokhmah*, *binah*, and *daat* clothe themselves in the wisdom of the Torah; *chessed* in the performance of positive commandments; *gevurah* in the observance of the prohibitions; and so with the rest of the soul's ten attributes.

and all its 613 organs from head to foot,

Not only the soul's ten primary attributes but also each of its 613 particular organs has its corresponding *mitzvah* in the Torah: there are 613 *mitzvot* for the soul's 613 components. And because such a perfect correlation exists between the soul and the Torah, the soul can clothe itself in the Torah to the point that

it is altogether and literally "bound up in the bundle of life with God,"38

Entering into the essence of the Torah and becoming utterly united and identified with it is a union that involves the soul's every trait and faculty.

and the very light of God envelops and clothes it from head to foot; as it is written, "God is my rock, I take refuge in Him,"[39]

In turn, the soul is encased in an envelope of divinity. Hence, we have a bilateral relationship between the soul and the Torah: the soul enters into and unites with the Torah, clothing its every limb in a divine command, and the divine light of Torah embraces and envelops the soul on every side like a protective fortress.[40]

and it is also written, "As a shield [Your] will does encircle him,"[41] to say, the Blessed's will and wisdom, which are clothed in His Torah and its commandments, [encircles him].

The Torah originates in the divine will; and the divine will, which is the inner essence of Torah, surrounds the person and envelops him on all sides, as a shield.

The Torah, then, is the divine will and wisdom (the divine will being its higher source, following which it clothes itself in the divine wisdom), and this remains its quintessential nature at every level of its evolution. So although the Torah is not revealed to us in the full scope of its highest level, whatever is revealed to us is of the divine will itself, and its study and observance constitute the true and ultimate attachment to God, even if the form it has assumed is lowly and physical. Furthermore, it is precisely because the divine wisdom and will is expressed in such mundane and physical terms that man, who inhabits a material reality, can truly relate to and unite with it, thereby uniting with the divine wisdom and will, which is fully present in the Torah's earthly manifestation.

Thus it has been said: "Better is one hour of repentance and good deeds in this world than the whole life of the World to Come."[42]

Only in this physical world can one perform a *mitzvah,* and thus unite with the divine will and wisdom, which is a revelation of the divine essence.

For the World to Come is [that state where] one enjoys the "glow of the Divine Presence" (*ziv haShekhinah*), which is the pleasure of apprehension. No created being, even of the celestial, can apprehend more than some reflection of the Divine light,

The "World to Come" is a spiritual world and thus on a higher plane than our physical reality. In the words of our sages, "In the world to come, there is no eating or drinking, no reproduction, no business dealing.... Rather, the righteous sit with their crowns on their heads and enjoy the glow of the [*Shekhinah*] ('divine presence')."[43] "Enjoying the glow of the [*Shekhinah*]," explains the author, is the pleasure derived from the apprehension (grasp, understanding) of divinity. But any apprehension, be it intellectual or emotional, is by definition a finite and definitive thing, even if we are speaking of apprehension by a wholly spiritual being, such as an angel or a disembodied soul that has achieved its ultimate level of purity and refinement.

which is why the reference is to "the glow of the Divine Presence." As for the essence of the Holy One, blessed be He, no thought can apprehend Him at all—

Thus, the spiritual inhabitants of the world to come can only relate to the glow of the divine presence, to a mere reflection of the divine reality, rather than to the essence of the divine light. They cannot apprehend the "luminary" (the source of the light, God Himself) nor even the light (the direct and utter expression of the luminary's essence), only a reflection of the light. This is the most that a created entity of the highest order can grasp, on its own, of the divine reality.

except when it is apprehended and clothed in the Torah and its *Mitzvot*. Then [the human being] does literally apprehend, and is clothed in, the Holy One, blessed be He, since the Torah and the Holy One, blessed be He, are one.

There is, however, one way in which a creature can apprehend, and thus unite with, the divine essence, surmounting the quantum boundary that no level of apprehension can cross: through its assimilation of the concepts of the Torah (see discussion in Chapter 5) and its involvement in the doing of *mitzvot*. When a person does a *mitzvah*, he becomes part of the *mitzvah;* when he studies Torah, he unites with the commander of the *mitzvah,* with the giver of the Torah.

The Torah is not merely God's instructions to man but a manifestation of the divine essence. It is not a reflection of divine light, not even a reflection of divinity, but divinity itself. Apprehending Torah, attachment and union with it, is an apprehension of and union with God Himself.

And although the Torah has been clothed in lowly, physical things,

Again and again, we return to the paradox that to study Torah and fulfill *mitzvot* is to involve oneself with mundane and material things: oxen and donkeys, wool and linen, and so on. Granted that man's connection and identification with the mundane is indeed complete: a person who gives charity becomes at that moment a tool for the *mitzvah* of charity; the man who puts on *tefillin* becomes an implement of the *mitzvah* of *tefillin,* which could not have been fulfilled without a physical, human arm; one who studies a page of Talmud dealing with an ox and a donkey can fully grasp and comprehend his subject— these things are familiar to him, and he can therefore fully identify with the problems under discussion. But however complete his grasp, he has grasped material things. How can we say that this, however profound, is of the essence of the divine wisdom?

The author's answer is that these things, however lowly and material, are indeed the will and wisdom of God. They are not a reflection of His will but are His will itself, translated into the language of the material. The Torah itself does not undergo change; rather, it descends by "hidden steps" from level to level, assuming at each level the garments that relate to that plane of reality. Within these garments, however, is the Torah itself, which is one with God and remains his unadulterated will and wisdom at every level. One can say that the Torah undergoes a series of translations: a translation into the language of the seraphim, a translation into the language of the angels, a translation into the language of the soul that resides in the physical body—languages that are merely garments for the essence of Torah, which remains unchanged at all levels.

The divine *chokhmah* can therefore be envisioned as an extremely abstract, axiomatic formula that embodies within it laws relating to a broad spectrum of systems of all types and forms, yet this formula is so abstract that no particular system can fully express it. Thus, the

Torah descends and is translated into a great variety of languages, including the language of our physical existence. The formula itself is neither altered nor diminished but acquires a definitive and contracted form so that we can comprehend its meaning in our reality.

it is, by way of illustration, like embracing the king: there is no difference, in regard to the degree of closeness and attachment to the king, whether one embraces the king as the latter is wearing one robe or several robes, so long as the royal person is inside them.

One who studies Torah is like one who embraces a king. Is the number of garments that the king is wearing in any way relevant to the degree of intimacy and love that the embrace represents? Obviously not. What is significant is that he is embracing the king. When a person envelops the Torah in his mind, he is in effect embracing God, whose will and wisdom are implicit within it. True, the Torah is draped in many garments, its abstract essence garbed in alien models and euphemisms; but the clothes are only clothes, and the King Himself is inside them.

Likewise, when the king, for his part, embraces one with his arm, even though it is dressed in his robes;

In Chapter 5, the author explains how one who studies Torah not only encompasses it with his mind but is also encompassed by it; thus, it is comparable to one who embraces the king while the king embraces him. He envelops the Torah, while, at the same time, the Torah envelops him.

as it is written, "And His right hand embraces me,"[44] which refers to the Torah which was given by God's right hand,

Deuteronomy 33:2 has: "From His right hand, a fiery law for them."

which is the quality of *chessed* and water.

God's granting us the Torah is an expression of love, a desire to come near to and unite with the loved one; through the Torah, contact, proximity, and ultimately union can occur between man and God. In Kabbalah, the right hand or side is the side of *chessed* and love ("water" is a name for bestowal and love).

In this chapter, the author discussed the garments of the Godly soul. The Godly soul achieves the ultimate realization of its holiness and greatness through its garments, which are the thought, speech, and action of the Torah and *mitzvot*. Furthermore, the Torah and *mitzvot* are not only garments of the soul, they are also the garments of God, within which He is found. Although the Torah and *mitzvot*, as they are revealed to us, do not manifest the divine essence as it is (which is utterly beyond apprehension), God has contracted His will and wisdom within them in a series of "hidden steps" or successive rearticulations, the last of which is the Torah as we know it, formulated as a doctrine and philosophy comprehensible to the physical mind and as a guide to physical life. Thus, on the one hand, the Torah is garbed within mundane and material matters that the soul, vested in the material body, can identify with, clothe itself in, and unite with; on the other hand, "the Torah and God are one." Therefore, when a person immerses his mind in the study of Torah, and when his 613 organs are involved in the doing of the 613 *mitzvot*, he is at that moment cleaving to God Himself, with no intermediary and no partition in between. Thus, although the Torah is garbed in many garments, these are but veiled expressions of the divine essence; these, in turn, become garments for the Godly soul, which itself is literally "a part of God above."

Chapter 5

T o further explain and fully elucidate the term *tefisah* ("apprehension") in the words of Elijah, "No thought can apprehend You . . .":

When a mind conceives and comprehends a concept with its intellect, the mind grasps the concept and encloses it with its intellect, and the concept is grasped, enclosed, and enclothed within the mind that conceived and comprehended it. In addition, the mind is also enclothed within the concept at the time that it comprehends and grasps it with its intellect.

For example, when a person understands and comprehends, truly and fully, any [halakhah] in the Mishnah or *Gemara,* his mind grasps and encloses it and, at the same time, is also enclothed within it. Now this particular [halakhah] is the wisdom and will of God, for it was His will that when, for example, Reuben pleads in one way and Simon in another, the verdict as between them shall be thus and thus. And even if such a litigation never was and never will present itself for judgment in connection with such disputes and claims, nevertheless, since it has been the will and wisdom of the Holy One, blessed be He, that in the event of one person pleading this way and the other pleading that way, the verdict shall be such and such, it follows that when a person knows and comprehends with his mind such a verdict in accordance with the law as it is set out in the Mishnah, *Gemara,* or the Codes, he has thus comprehended, grasped, and enclosed in his mind the will and wisdom of the Holy One, blessed be He, Whom no thought can apprehend, [neither Himself] nor His will and wisdom—except as they are clothed in the laws that have been set out for us. And [at the same time,] the mind is also enclothed within them.

This is a wonderful union, like which there is none other, and which has no parallel anywhere in the material world, whereby complete oneness and unity, from every side and angle, could be attained.

Hence the special superiority, infinitely great and wonderful, that is in the *mitzvah* to know the Torah and comprehend it, over all the *mitzvot* involving action, and even those relating to speech, and even the *mitzvah* to study the Torah through speech. For through all the *mitzvot* involving speech or action, the Holy One, blessed be He, enclothes the soul and envelops it from head to foot with the divine light; but with regard to knowledge of the Torah, apart from the fact that the mind is enclothed in divine wisdom, the divine wisdom is also contained within it, to the extent that one's mind comprehends, grasps, and encloses with its intellect, as much as it can of the knowledge of the Torah, every man according to his intellect, his capacity for knowledge, and his comprehension in *pardes.*

And because, in the case of knowledge of the Torah, the Torah is enclothed within the soul and mind of a person, and is absorbed in them, it is called "bread" and "food" of the soul. For just as physical bread nourishes the body by entering into the person, within his very inner self, where it is transformed into blood and flesh of his flesh, whereby he lives and exists— so, too, it is with the knowledge of the Torah and its comprehension by the soul of the person who studies it well, with a concentration of his mind, until the Torah is absorbed by his mind and is united with it and they become one, and [the Torah] becomes nourishment for the soul, and its inner life, from the Giver of life, the Blessed Infinite, Who is clothed within His wisdom and Torah that are [absorbed] in [the soul].

This is the meaning of the verse, "Your Torah is within my innards." And as it is stated in *Etz Chayyim,* Portal 44, chapter 3, that the garments of the soul in the *Gan Eden* are the mitzvot, whereas the Torah is the food for the souls which, in this world, had occupied themselves in the study of the Torah for its own sake. And as it is stated in the *Zohar, Vayakhel,* page 210.

"For its own sake," means in order to attach one's soul to God through the comprehension of the Torah, each one according to his intellect, as explained in *Pri Etz Chayyim.*

(The food [of the soul] is in the nature of Inner Light, while the garments are in the nature of Encompassing Light. Therefore our Sages, of blessed memory, have said that the study of the Torah equals all the *mitzvot.* For the commandments are but "garments" whereas the Torah is both "food" as well as a "garment" for the rational soul that is enclothed within it during learning and concentration. All the more so when a person also articulates with his mouth in speech; for the breath emitted in speaking [the words of the Torah] becomes an element of Encompassing Light, as is explained in *Pri Etz Chayyim.*)

COMMENTARY

In Chapter 4, the author cited the introduction to *Tikkunei Zohar,* which quotes Elijah as saying of God "no thought can apprehend You at all," and went on to say that, nevertheless, through the Torah and *mitzvot,* a person *can* apprehend and attain the divine essence. In this chapter, the author elaborates by explaining the significance of the word *tefisah* ("apprehension," literally "grasping") in that saying: the meaning of apprehension by thought in general, and the specific nature of the apprehension one achieves through the study of Torah and the unique bond that is thereby created between man and God.

To further explain and fully elucidate the term *tefisah* ("apprehension") in the words of Elijah, "No thought can apprehend You . . .":
When a mind conceives and comprehends a concept with its intellect, this mind grasps the concept and encloses it with its intellect, and the concept is grasped, enclosed, and enclothed within the mind that conceived and comprehended it.

The terms *enclose* and *enclosed* here are used figuratively: obviously the "mind" and the "concept" are not physical objects occupying specific points in space in such a way that one might be placed within the other.

In the process of apprehending a concept, the mind first "grasps the concept," then "encloses it with its intellect," and finally "enclothes" it. The grasping of the concept is the initial contact between the mind and the concept it conceives, the "point of *chokhmah*" described in Chapter 3. The mind's enclosing of the concept—as opposed to merely "touching" the idea on one side—occurs in the stage of *binah* ("comprehension"), in which the object of the mind's interest can be said to exist within the mind and be encompassed by it. *Binah* is not a point but a process: at first, the mind only touches the concept tangentially; and as the comprehension progresses, the mind covers more sides of the concept, until it completely encloses it and relates to its every facet.

When comprehension is complete, so that the idea is totally enclosed by the mind, the idea can now go on to be applied to other ideas. This marks the point at which the idea is "enclothed" by the mind. As we explained in Chapter 3, a garment is the medium by which a thing relates to realities outside of itself. Thus, when we say that the mind enclothes the concept, this means that the concept can now be further extended, that the mind can now serve as the garment by which it is related to other concepts. (This is the basis of the assumption that the inability to explain something well shows a deficiency in understanding. There are other factors, not connected with understanding, that interfere with the ability to pass things on, such as difficulty in communicating. But a true and full explanation is not possible without a full understanding, whereas a person who "truly and fully" understands something will inevitably find a way to pass it on.)

In addition, the mind is also enclothed within the concept at the time that it comprehends and grasps it with its intellect.

At the very same time that the mind enclothes the concept and encloses it within itself, an opposite process also takes place, in which the mind is itself enclothed within the concept. Just as the mind is serving as a garment for the concept (that is, as its medium of expression and relation, as well as the screen that obscures its essence and allows only a certain expression of it to be manifested), so, too, is the concept serving as the garment of the mind. For when a mind is involved and absorbed in a certain subject, it expresses itself at that time through that concept; one can thus say that the mind is enclothed in the concept it is contemplating, for it is now manifesting itself through this particular garment, and the garment is obscuring its quintessential qualities. In other words, the mind is now not a mind per se but a mind as expressed through the particulars of the concept within which it has invested itself. The mind is not only thinking the idea, it is also being "thought" by it, in the sense that the mind is now perceived exclusively in the context of the particular idea.

This is true of every mind and every concept at any level, from the simplest to the most advanced and complicated. The process of thought is always a process in which the mind and the object of its contemplation enclose and are enclosed by each other.

For example, when a person understands and comprehends, truly and fully, any [halakhah] in the Mishnah or *Gemara,* his mind grasps and encloses it and, at the same time, is also enclothed within it. Now this particular [halakhah] is the wisdom and will of God, for it was His will that when, for example, Reuben pleads in one way and Simon in another, the verdict as between them shall be thus and thus.

In this case, the concept enclosing and being enclosed by the mind is no ordinary thought but the wisdom and will of God. The author is not speaking here about the halakhah as practical instruction but about its essence—namely, its being an expression of divine wisdom and will.

And even if such a litigation never was and never will present itself for judgment in connection with such disputes and claims, nevertheless, since it has been the will and wisdom of the Holy One, blessed be He, that in the event of one person pleading this way and the other pleading that way, the verdict shall be such and such, it follows that when a person knows and comprehends with his mind such a verdict in accordance with the law as it is set out in the Mishnah, *Gemara,* or the Codes, he has thus comprehended, grasped, and enclosed in his mind the will and wisdom of the Holy One, blessed be He,

In physics and mathematics, complicated systems are constructed to solve theoretical problems, and the question of whether such a situation could ever arise in practice is considered beside the point. The scientist is seeking to uncover a truth: What is the reality, what is the quintessential state of things, in a given situation? The purpose is not to solve a practical problem but to gain a comprehensive understanding of a truth, to learn the nature of things.

Similarly, when the Talmud discusses a financial dispute between two parties, citing their arguments and counterarguments, it is not necessarily relating an actual case that was or ever will be; rather, it is presenting an abstract, theoretical model. It is endeavoring to discover what God's desire would be in such a situation. The purpose is not to solve a particular dispute between two individuals but to see how this point relates to the universal order, to the inner life of creation; to learn what it is that God wants from His world.

Obviously, the person who comprehends a halakhic ruling does not assimilate the whole of the divine wisdom relating to this matter. Even when he understands the entire array of legal principles and processes that relate to this law and how all this derives from the Torah, he comprehends the subject on only one plane. He does not understand the many strata of meaning that lie beyond the grasp of human reason or even the full significance of the law. But in understanding a particular aspect of it at a particular level, he grasps a point of truth, assimilating if only a particle of the divine truth.

By way of example, the equations $A + B = C$ and $1 + 1 = 2$ say in effect the same thing. The first is general and abstract, and the second is specific; the first sets up a principle, and the second gives a particular example of this principle. When teaching a small child, one teaches the specific case, because the child can learn and understand that thoroughly, but he cannot comprehend the general principle. Yet despite the fact that the abstract equation is beyond the child's comprehension, when he comprehends that an apple and another apple make two apples, he has grasped something of the truth of the formula. By the same token, when a person studies a halakhah about an ox and a donkey,[1] he is assimilating not a mere expression or analogue of the divine wisdom but something of its very essence. When a person listens to a profound lecture and understands only the introductory joke, he has grasped nothing of the wisdom—he has grasped the analogy but not what it relates to, the garment without its content; but one who understands $2 + 2 = 4$ understands something of the concept itself, although not its entirety, its full depth and breadth.

Indeed, this is the only way in which man can grasp something of the divine truth.

Whom no thought can apprehend, [neither Himself] nor His will and wisdom—except as they are clothed in the laws that have been set out for us.

The divine wisdom cannot be attained by contemplating abstract truths. Such contemplation yields, at best, false visions, and in other cases, self-images and self-deception. Apprehending the truth of God's wisdom, if only a tiny grain of truth on a particular level—practical or theoretical—is possible only through the comprehension of Torah.

The laws that have been spelled out to us in the Torah are that aspect of its divine wisdom that is humanly attainable. When a person comprehends a teaching of Torah, even if it is not an inspirational teaching, it is an articulation of absolute truth, a point of divine wisdom related to a particular problem.

And [at the same time,] the mind is also enclothed within them.

When a person's mind grasps and enclothes a concept of Torah, his mind is simultaneously enclothed within the concept, as explained earlier. His mind envelops the divine wisdom, and the divine wisdom envelops his mind. The divine wisdom becomes part of him, and he becomes part of it.

This is a wonderful union, like which there is none other, and which has no parallel anywhere in the material world, whereby complete oneness and unity, from every side and angle, could be attained.

When the thinking mind and the concept of which it is thinking mutually enclothe each other, what happens is not just contact between them but unity and full identification. Whether considering an abstract concept, a story, or a legal ruling, at the moment that the mind is getting to understand it from every angle, it is fused with that thought in a wonderful union—a union that has no parallel in any of the other unions we know. In the material world, we encounter certain intrinsic barriers that we cannot surmount. The encloser and the enclosed, the "I" and the other, cannot be united, because their difference is a part of the definition of material existence. By contrast, in the sphere of conscious ideas, in the relationship between comprehender and the comprehended, the encloser can also be the enclosed, the difference between them becoming diffused until there is union and utter identification from every angle.

Although this is true of every sphere of intellectual activity, the "wonderful union, like which there is none other" contains a uniqueness that one achieves through the comprehension of Torah. Aside from the obvious difference in what the mind is uniting with—the divine wisdom, as opposed to human understanding—the very nature of the union itself is more wonderful in Torah than in other disciplines. When a person understands some other subject, he unites with the idea of the subject but not the subject itself. For instance, when he studies the motion of the stars, his mind unites with the concept of the moving stars and not with the movement of the stars itself. Torah, however, is not merely the understanding of a certain reality but the source of the realities it explains. In the words of our sages, "God looked into the Torah and created the world."[2] So when a mind unites with Torah, it is one not only with the understanding of something but also with the thing itself, because Torah is the essence of the thing's very existence.[3]

Hence the special superiority, infinitely great and wonderful, that is in the *mitzvah* to know the Torah and comprehend it, over all the *mitzvot* involving action, and even those relating to speech,

Although with all *mitzvot* one establishes a connection with God, only the comprehension and knowledge of Torah achieves the wonderful union that occurs between a mind and the object of its contemplation.

and even the *mitzvah* to study the Torah through speech.

The *mitzvah* of Torah study has two aspects. One is the commandment to "speak of them,"[4] to speak words of Torah, to articulate them with one's mouth even if one does not understand their meaning. In this sense, the *mitzvah* of Torah study is akin to other *mitzvot* of physical action (putting on *tefillin*, giving charity, and so on). But another aspect to this *mitzvah* is to know Torah, to study it and comprehend it to the limit of one's intellectual capacity. In this aspect, the *mitzvah* of Torah study possesses a "superiority . . . great and wonderful" over all other *mitzvot*. By comprehending Torah, the person is enveloped by the object of the *mitzvah* and also at the same time encloses it and envelops it. This makes for the "wonderful union, like which there is none other" that is unique to the *mitzvah* of Torah study.

For through all the *mitzvot* involving speech or action, the Holy One, blessed be He, enclothes the soul and envelops it from head to foot with the divine light;

At the time that a person is involved in the performance of a *mitzvah*, this becomes the manner in which he is expressing himself; he thus can be said to be enclothed in the *mitzvah*. When he extends his hand to give charity, the faculty of action implicit in his hand is being manifest in the form of a charitable deed: the *mitzvah* of charity is enclothing his hand. The same applies to all other *mitzvot*: a certain faculty of the soul is being manifested by a particular medium, that of a *mitzvah*. The person, or a certain part of him, is enclothed in the divine will and wisdom.

but with regard to knowledge of the Torah, apart from the fact that the
mind is enclothed in divine wisdom,

The mind is now involved in the wisdom of Torah and is expressing its prowess through this medium. This is the quality that Torah
study shares with all other *mitzvot;* in this sense, there is no difference
if the hand is enclothed in the act of charity, the head in *tefillin,* or the
brain in a Torah idea. But in the *mitzvah* of Torah knowledge, there is
something more:

the divine wisdom is also contained within it,

Here, the divine wisdom not only enclothes the mind that is contemplating it but is also absorbed by it when a person understands
and absorbs a concept of Torah.

to the extent that one's mind comprehends, grasps, and encloses with its
intellect, as much as it can of the knowledge of the Torah, every man according to his intellect, his capacity for knowledge, and his comprehension
in *pardes.*[5]

What is significant is not the magnitude of the concept that the mind
has grasped but the fact that it has grasped Torah. When a person
acquires a knowledge of some item of Torah—a story, a complicated
law, or a small detail thereof—his mind is then clothed in this item of
Torah and enclosed by it; at that time, this item expresses itself through
his mind, is enclosed by his mind, and becomes an integral part of it. A
complete union is formed between the subject of the person's thought
and his thought process. The thinker and the thought become one.

And because, in the case of knowledge of the Torah, the Torah is enclothed
within the soul and mind of a person, and is absorbed in them, it is called
"bread" and "food" of the soul.

At various places in the Scripture, the Torah is compared to bread
(for example, "Come partake of My bread"—Proverbs 9:5). The Torah
that a person learns is absorbed and assimilated by his mind just as
physical food is absorbed and assimilated by the body. The *mitzvot,*
on the other hand, are the clothes of the soul, which enclose the soul
and weave a garment of light that envelops it from end to end. In ful-

filling a *mitzvah,* a person expresses himself in the manner and form of a divine desire. In studying Torah, not only does he express himself through its ideas, but the Torah is also being thought within him, formulated by his mind, molded by its characteristics and qualities.[6]

For just as physical bread nourishes the body by entering into the person, within his very inner self, where it is transformed into blood and flesh of his flesh, whereby he lives and exists—

Food is ingested in two stages. In the first stage, the food "enters within" the person and is digested; in the second, it ceases to be a distinct entity within the person and becomes "blood and flesh of his flesh."

so, too, it is with the knowledge of the Torah and its comprehension by the soul of the person who studies it well, with a concentration of his mind,

This is the first stage, in which the concept enters the mind and is "chewed" and "digested." The idea is transferred from the shape in which it exists outside of that person to the form in which that person absorbs it by being broken down to its particulars and processed by the mind. When a person thus toils over the Torah concept, working it over until his mind grasps it, he achieves the next stage, in which

the Torah is absorbed by his mind and is united with it

The concept has become part and parcel of the structure of his mind and thought process.

and they become one,

The qualities of his mind have also become part and parcel of the concept. Torah study in such a manner

becomes nourishment for the soul, and its inner life, from the Giver of life, the Blessed Infinite, Who is clothed within His wisdom and Torah that are [absorbed] in [the soul].

When a person studies Torah and achieves an intellectual union with it, he not only unites with the revealed Torah as we understand it but also with the essence of the Torah, the divine light of the Infinite.

This is the meaning of the verse, "Your Torah is within my innards."[7]

That is, the Torah becomes like food that I have eaten and digested. It is no longer something distinct from and outside of me but something that has been absorbed by my body and become part of it.

And as it is stated in *Etz Chayyim,* Portal 44, chapter 3, that the garments of the soul in the *Gan Eden* are the *mitzvot,*

The soul's garments are the elements by which it relates to the reality within which it exists. In the physical world, the soul clothes itself in the physical faculties of the body in order to interact with the material reality within which it resides. But in a higher world, in the spiritual reality of *Gan Eden* ("paradise"), it has other garments, appropriate to relating to that environment. These spiritual garments are generated by the *mitzvot* a person performs in this world. Ungraspable by our material senses, these garments become, in a higher and loftier reality, the sole garments of the soul, facilitating its interaction with its spiritual environment.

whereas the Torah is the food for the souls which, in this world, had occupied themselves in the study of the Torah for its own sake. And as it is stated in the *Zohar, Vayakhel,* page 210.

The Torah that a person studies in this world becomes food for his soul in *Gan Eden.* Unlike the garments that the *mitzvot* generate, which fill the extrinsic role of relating the soul to its heavenly environment, the soul's food in *Gan Eden,* generated by the Torah it studied in the physical world, represents what of the supernal reality the soul is capable of internalizing and assimilating into itself.

"For its own sake," means in order to attach one's soul to God through the comprehension of the Torah, each one according to his intellect, as explained in *Pri Etz Chayyim.*[8]

The author has just quoted a passage from the *Zohar* stating that the soul is nourished in *Gan Eden* by food that derives from *Torah lishmah,* "the study of Torah for its own sake." There are various definitions of what constitutes "the study of Torah for its own sake," each expressing the significance of this on a different level. Here, the author presents what, in a certain sense, is the most basic meaning of the term: study for the sake of uniting with God through the comprehension of His wisdom. (Such study is, by definition, an altruistic endeavor. Thus, yearning to unite with God is not to be understood as an exercise in self-fulfillment but as the desire to give pleasure to God, who derives great satisfaction from a soul's reunion with its source—as in the analogy, cited in *Tanya,* Chapter 41, of a king's joy when his only child is freed from captivity.)[9]

(The food [of the soul] is in the nature of Inner Light,

"Inner Light" (*ohr penimi*) is the Kabbalistic term for those divine influences that a person (or other entity) imbibes and internalizes, something he can absorb and integrate into his being. Food is thus the analogy for Inner Light. The reference to Torah understanding as food for the soul expresses the concept that Torah study is an emanation of Inner Light from God.

while the garments are in the nature of Encompassing Light.

Garments are the analogy for what Kabbalah terms "Encompassing Light" (*ohr makif;* also *makifim,* "encompassers"). These are divine influences that are external to the person, not only in the sense that they exist outside of him but also in terms of the manner in which they affect him. These are not internalized and consciously assimilated; their influence on the person is not direct and palpable. A soul's garments, as we said, facilitate the relationship between it and its environment, which affect the soul without being consciously recognized by it and assimilated into itself.

Therefore our Sages, of blessed memory, have said that the study of the Torah equals all the *mitzvot.* For the commandments are but "garments"

The Talmud describes study of Torah as being equal to all the other *mitzvot* put together.[10] This, says the *Tanya,* can be understood in light of what has been said here in regard to the *mitzvot* being garments of the soul. This is not to say that a *mitzvah* is a superficial act: a person can perform a *mitzvah* out of deep, inner feelings—out of love and awe of God, out of *d'veikut* ("deep spiritual attachment") to the Almighty. Yet the *mitzvah* itself remains external to the person, a reality distinct from himself, an encompassing reality. The *mitzvah* is a reality that envelops him and to which he deeply relates, but he cannot internalize it and assimilate its essence. A physical *mitzvah,* such as *tzitzit* or *lulav* or *tefillin,* is an action that a person does but not something that merges with him to become part of his being. For this reason, our sages have said that a *mitzvah* protects a person from harm only at the instant he is performing it,[11] because no perceivable trace of the *mitzvah* remains after the act in the person who performed it.

whereas the Torah is both "food" as well as a "garment" for the rational soul that is enclothed within it during learning and concentration.

In contrast, Torah is food for the soul, entering into the being of the person who studies it and becoming part of his inner self.

Furthermore, Torah is not only food but also a garment to the soul. As we explained at length in this chapter, when a person studies Torah, not only does his mind enclose the concept and make it a part of him, but the concept also clothes and encloses his mind. So the Torah also serves the role of garment—becoming the manner of the soul's expression at the time that one is engaged in its study—as is the case with all *mitzvot.*

All the more so when a person also articulates with his mouth in speech; for the breath emitted in speaking [the words of the Torah] becomes an element of Encompassing Light, as is explained in *Pri Etz Chayyim.*)

In addition to all that has been said about the virtue of knowing and understanding Torah, there is also the *mitzvah* "to speak of them"— to speak words of Torah—as the Torah commands in Deuteronomy 6:7; as Joshua 1:7 states, "This book of Torah shall not cease from your mouth."

Torah acts as a garment to the soul also when it is only being thought, and this is even more so when one articulates it verbally, introducing a dimension of action to the *mitzvah.* Then the physical substance of the breath or air that carries the words at the time of study becomes an Encompassing Light for the soul. When a person performs a *mitzvah,* the material substance of the *mitzvah* is transformed into spiritual light that envelops its performer. When one studies Torah aloud, the *mitzvah* possesses a material substance—the physical air that carries the sound of his learning—which generates the Encompassing Light that derives from the material of a *mitzvah*.

On this basis alone (without even considering the special qualities of Torah study in their own right), we can explain why study of Torah is equal to all the *mitzvot:* all *mitzvot* serve only the role of garment for the soul, whereas Torah is both food and garment. We acquire and grasp Torah through the mind, which, while it is tackling an idea, encloses it and is enclosed by it. Thus, the Torah that a person learns is imbibed as food for the soul, as something that becomes a part of his inner self, and at the same time envelops him as a garment. Furthermore, in studying Torah out loud, the breath that carries the words of Torah become an Encompassing Light, as is the case with all material substances with which a physical *mitzvah* is performed.

Chapter 6

⎯⎯ T his opposite the other, God made."

Just as the Godly soul consists of ten holy *sefirot* and clothes itself in three holy garments, so does the soul which is derived from the *sitra achra*, from *kelipat nogah*, which is clothed in the blood of man, consist of ten profane crowns. To wit: the seven evil *middot* which stem from the four evil elements mentioned above; and the intellect begetting them which is subdivided into three, [namely], *chokhmah, binah,* and *daat,* the source of the *middot.*

For the *middot* are according to the quality of the intellect. Hence a child craves and loves petty things of inferior worth, for his intellect is too immature and deficient to appreciate more precious things. Likewise is he provoked to anger and vexation over trivial things; so, too, with boasting and other *middot.*

Now these ten profane attributes, when a person meditates in them or speaks of them or acts by them, his thought which is in his brain, his speech which is in his mouth, and the power of action which is in his hands and other limbs—all these are now called the profane garments of these ten profane attributes, which clothe themselves in them at the time of the action, speech, or thought. The above constitute all the deeds that are done under the sun—which are all "vanity and striving after the wind," as interpreted by the *Zohar on Beshalach,* in the sense of "a ruination of the spirit . . ."—as well as all utterances and thoughts which are not directed towards God and His will and service.

For this is the meaning of *sitra achra*—the other side—[that is,] not the side of holiness. For the holy side is nothing but the immanence and extension of the holiness of the Holy One, blessed be He, and the Holy One, blessed be He, dwells only on something that abnegates itself completely to Him, whether actually, as in the case of the supernal angels, or potentially, as in the case of every Jew in this world, who has the capacity to abnegate himself completely to the Holy One, blessed be He, by giving his life for the sanctification of God. That is why our Sages have said that "Even when a single individual sits and engages in the study of Torah, the divine presence dwells on him"; and "On each [gathering of] ten Jews, the divine presence dwells" always.

However, that which does not abnegate itself to God, but is a separate thing unto itself, does not receive its vitality from the holiness of the Holy One, blessed be He—that is, from the very inner essence and substance of the holiness itself—but from its back, as it were, descending degree by degree, through the myriads of degrees in the evolution of the worlds by means of cause and effect and innumerable contractions, until the [divine] light and life are so diminished through repeated diminutions that they can be contracted and enclothed, in a state of exile, within that separated thing, to impart to it vitality and existence [out of nothing], so that it does not revert to nothingness and [nonexistence] as it was before it was created.

Consequently, this physical world, with all it contains, is called the world of *kelipot* and *sitra achra.* Therefore all affairs of this world are severe and evil, and wicked men prevail, as explained in *Etz Chayyim,* Portal 42, end of chapter 4.

Note: To be sure, there are contained in it the ten *sefirot* of the holy World of Action, as is written in *Etz Chayyim,* Portal 43, and within these ten *sefirot* of the World of Action are the ten *sefirot* of the World of Formation, and in them the ten *sefirot* of the World of Creation, and in them the ten *sefirot* of the World of Emanation, in which abides the light of the Blessed Infinite. Thus the light of the Blessed Infinite pervades this lower world through being clothed in the ten *sefirot* of the Four Worlds, namely those of Emanation, Creation, Formation, and Action, as explained in *Etz Chayyim,* Portal 47, chapter 2, and in *Sefer haGilgulim,* chapter 20.

The *kelipot,* however, are subdivided into two grades, one lower than the other. The lower grade consists of the three *kelipot* which are altogether

profane and evil, containing no good whatsoever. In the "chariot" of Ezekiel
they are called "storm wind, great cloud. . . ." From these flow and derive the
souls of all the nations of the world, and the existence of their bodies;
the souls of all living creatures that are impure and prohibited for consumption, and the existence of their bodies; the existence and vitality of all
prohibited foods of the vegetable kingdom, such as the fruits of the first
three years of a tree and mixed seeds in the vineyard, etc., as explained in
Etz Chayyim, Portal 49, chapter 6; as also the existence and vitality of all actions, utterances, and thoughts pertaining to the 365 and their offshoots, as
it is explained [in that work], at the end of chapter 5.

COMMENTARY

The previous chapters discussed the Godly soul and its garments.
Now, to complete the picture of the human soul, the author discusses
the other side to the inner being of man, the animal soul and its manners of expression in a person's life.

The author opens this chapter by quoting Ecclesiastes 7:14:

"This opposite the other, God made."

The whole of existence is structured upon a correspondence
between good and evil. Not only is good, as a whole, contrasted with
the phenomenon of evil, but every element and detail in the world of
good has its precisely corresponding negative. For evil is but a shadow,
a duplicate (albeit a negative one) of good.

Just as the Godly soul consists of ten holy *sefirot*

As discussed in Chapter 3, the Godly soul possesses ten attributes
that correspond to, and derive from, the ten supernal *sefirot* ("divine
attributes").

and clothes itself in three holy garments,

As discussed in Chapters 4 and 5, the soul and its attributes manifest
themselves through the three garments of thought, speech, and deed—
these being the ideas, words, and deeds of the Torah and its precepts,
because the Godly soul, being "a part of God above," is exclusively
devoted to the endeavor of cleaving to God and uniting with Him.

so does the soul which is derived from the *sitra achra,* from *kelipat nogah,*

This is the animal soul, which derives from the *sitra achra,* the "other side," and which in the Jew comes from *kelipat nogah,* the "luminescent husk," as discussed in Chapters 1 and 7. Though *kelipat nogah* is a husk—that is, something that obscures the divine light—it is not utterly dark; thus, in a certain sense, it represents an intermediate state between profanity and holiness, as we will discuss in Chapter 7.

which is clothed in the blood of man

As we discussed in Chapter 1, the animal enclothes itself in the blood in order to animate the body. This is the soul that provides man with his physical life, the soul that is in direct contact with the body. In this sense, the animal soul mediates between the Godly soul and the physical body.

consist of ten profane crowns.

In order to distinguish them from the holy attributes of the Godly soul, we do not refer to the attributes of the animal soul as *sefirot* but as "crowns."[1] The term also has a deeper significance: in many ways, the forces of evil operate in the manner of crowns. In the Kabbalistic system of supernal "worlds" and "attributes," the attribute of *keter* ("crown") is not of a piece with the other attributes, but extrinsic to and encompassing them (as in the analogy of a crown that encircles the head). By the same token, the forces of evil do not operate in a manner of internalization and integration but as influences from without. The power that evil holds over man derives not from comprehended and internalized truths but from simple, unconscious drives from the level of *keter* (which includes the faculties of desire and will).

The forces of *kelipah* derive from the world of *tohu,* where the *sefirot* are configured as a series of points or dots one below the other, with no interrelation between them. In other words, only the *keter* of each *sefirah* ("divine attribute") is present, the simple will that is its potential point. In contrast, in the world of *tikkun* ("rectification")— the world of the holy *sefirot*—each *sefirah* is developed as a "face" or configuration (*partzuf*), through the introduction, in a manner of internalized assimilation, of the intellectual attributes, *chokhmah, binah,* and *daat.*

Another reason why the attributes of the animal soul are called crowns is that *kelipat nogah* is a crown in the sense that it is an intermediate level between holiness and *kelipah*. In the same way, the *keter* of each world is the intermediate level between its world and the world above it.[2]

To wit: the seven evil *middot* which stem from the four evil elements mentioned above;

This was mentioned at the end of Chapter 1. The four elements—fire, air, water, and earth—define the qualities of every existence, including the character of the animal soul, which is the essence of physical life.

and the intellect begetting them which is subdivided into three, [namely], *chokhmah, binah,* and *daat,* the source of the *middot.*

As is the case with the holy *middot* of the Godly soul (see Chapter 3), the profane *middot* ("desires") of the animal soul have their rationale. They, too, need a perceptual basis, relative to which they operate.

In order for a *middah*—a drive or impulse—to be manifest in the heart, and, more importantly, in order for it to acquire the characteristics that make it a full-fledged desire for a specific thing, the mind must provide it with certain criteria: What should it desire? Why is the thing desirable? How might it pursue its desire? and so on. There is, however, a significant difference between the relationship between the *middot* and the mind in the animal soul and the relationship between them in the Godly soul. The animal soul, as will be explained, is essentially a creature of impulse; the *middot* constitute the bulk of the animal soul's being, whereas the mind is merely the *middot*'s catalyst and stimulator. Indeed, the *middot*—love, anger, and so on—might manifest themselves on their own initiative, and in this case the role of the mind is merely to give form to their expression. In contrast, in the Godly soul, the *middot* are conceived, developed, and manifested by the mind.[3]

For the *middot* are according to the quality of the intellect. Hence a child craves and loves petty things of inferior worth, for his intellect is too immature and deficient to appreciate more precious things.

A small child will make a small toy, a thing of little value, the object of his desire and jealousy. This is not because his desires are inherently directed toward such things but because his mind is not mature enough to appreciate things of greater and subtler value. The object of his desire is therefore confined to things he can relate to and understand. Things that an adult might desire are not things that appeal to a child.

Likewise is he provoked to anger and vexation over trivial things; so, too, with boasting and other *middot.*

What is true of the *middah* of *chessed* ("attraction," "love," "benevolence") is also the case with the *middah* of *gevurah* ("rejection," "fear," "anger"): a child becomes angry over trivial things, because things that adults perceive as important and real are beyond the range of his understanding. A person will not be attracted to or repulsed by something he has no perception of as desirable or repulsive; such things will all be neutral to him. The same applies to all other *middot* because, as we said, the structure of evil is the same as the structure of good, down to the smallest detail.

Now these ten profane attributes, when a person meditates in them or speaks of them or acts by them, his thought which is in his brain, his speech which is in his mouth, and the power of action which is in his hands and other limbs—all these are now called the profane garments of these ten profane attributes, which clothe themselves in them at the time of the action, speech, or thought.

When a person activates the *middot* of the animal soul, when he actualizes one of these potential impulses through one of the faculties of his body—in thought, speech, or action—the said faculty becomes a vehicle of expression for that profane *middah*. The *middah* is essentially spiritual and abstract; and the person is the means, the vessel, the garment—the medium that expresses it in practice. When a person enclothes the *middah* with his body, mouth, or mind, he becomes at that instant an instrument of the profane, a form of *kelipah*'s expression in the world.

The above constitute all the deeds that are done under the sun

The deeds, words, and thoughts that constitute an actualization of the *middot* of the animal soul include not only things that are commonly considered evil—thoughts, words, and acts of anger, of doing others harm, of rebellion against God, and so on—but in fact "all the deeds that are done under the sun" (an expression from Ecclesiastes 1:14). Everything that is of the material world, everything that relates to the natural reality, is included in the phrase "under the sun."

—which are all "vanity and striving after the wind," as interpreted by the *Zohar* on *Beshallach,* in the sense of "a ruination of the spirit. . . ."—

"I have seen all the deeds that are done under the sun," says King Solomon (Ecclesiastes 1:14), "and they are all vanity and striving after wind." The Hebrew word used here for "striving after" (*re'ut*) also translates as "ruination"; the word for "wind" (*ruach*) also means "spirit." Thus, the *Zohar* interprets the verse to say that "the deeds that are done under the sun" are all "a ruination of the spirit," an expression of *kelipah* and a contrary force to the spiritual and the divine.[4]

as well as all utterances and thoughts which are not directed towards God and His will and service.

Not only blatant evil but also the entire array of material life and all that it entails is "vanity and a ruination of spirit." There might be nothing inherently negative about these things; their fault lies in that they are not directed toward "God and His will and His service."

For this is the meaning of *sitra achra*—the other side—[that is,] not the side of holiness.

Sitra achra is the Kabbalistic term for evil. But the words literally mean "the other side," that is, not the side of holiness. In other words, on the most basic level, there are two aspects to reality: the side of holiness and the other side. The domain of halakhah ("Torah law") contains a broad realm known as *reshut* ("the optional"), which is neither virtuous nor sinful, that lies here between the divinely commanded *mitzvot* and the divinely proscribed *averot* ("transgressions"). However, in the Kabbalistic division of reality, there is no middle ground. Nothing is neutral; anything that does not actively relate to God is automatically of the other side. For there cannot be anything that does not relate, positively or negatively, to God.

The world of holiness is a world of unity, a world that manifests the truth that "There is none else besides Him."[5] The conception of God as "the Infinite" (*Ein Sof*) does not merely imply that He is infinitely great but that He is Infinite Being: being without limit and definition, being that embraces everything so that there can be nothing else. In contrast, the other side is rooted in the world of disunity, in which the light of the Infinite is not manifest, so the exclusive reality of God is not recognized. Thus, the essence of *sitra achra* is that there *is* (so to speak) something else besides Him. In its initial, most basic form, the other side does not deny the existence of holiness, nor is it hostile to it. It merely deigns to define holiness, to confine it within a set of parameters. It is willing to accept the existence of a lofty and superior realm of holiness; what it does not accept is the exclusivity of holiness, based on the assumption that there are other things of significance as well.

For the holy side is nothing but the immanence and extension of the holiness of the Holy One, blessed be He,

There is no inherent "holiness" other than that of God. Something might be of value in the practical sense, but it is not holy. Holiness belongs exclusively to God, and "the side of holiness" contains no realities that are inherently holy, only realities that derive their holiness from God.

and the Holy One, blessed be He, dwells only on something that abnegates itself completely to Him,

In *Iggeret haKodesh* (Part IV of *Tanya*), sections 23 and 25, the author explains that "the dwelling of the divine presence" (*hashra'at haShekhinah*) is not present in everything. The divine presence is everywhere, for "the entire world is filled with His presence"[6]—there are no boundaries or limits to the truth that "There is none else besides Him"; but when speaking of the *hashra'ah* or "dwelling" of the divine presence, we are speaking of a manifest revelation of Godliness, of a thing becoming a vessel of divinity, something that visibly relates to God. The dwelling of the divine presence in a certain object or reality implies that the divine presence is not only there but that it operates and manifests itself through that thing. Not everything can serve as a conduit of the divine; it must have a certain quality that makes it a vessel. This quality is utter self-abnegation to God.

Rabbi Isaac Meir of Gur (author of *Chiddushei haRim*) once asked his Hasidim: "Where is God?" *What a question,* wondered the Hasidim. *God is everywhere!* Their rebbe replied that this is not precise: God is only where He is allowed to enter. This story is a characteristically sharp and concise formulation by Rabbi Isaac Meir of the concept discussed here: that God dwells only wherever there is self-abnegation to Him. Where there is no unequivocal subordination to God, where He is confined to a specific date and time or to certain conditions, God does not enter at all. The Infinite Being pervades every corner of reality, leaving no place for any other existence, so the only way to relate to the Infinite Being is from a standpoint of utter self-abnegation. The closer to Him one approaches, the more meaningful one's relationship to Him is—the more one's own being is negated—and the more the supernal holiness dwells and manifests itself in one's life.

whether actually, as in the case of the supernal angels,

The angels are holy because, being higher creatures, they are exposed directly to the divine light; they have no identity of their own and exist in a perpetual state of complete abnegation to God.

or potentially, as in the case of every Jew in this world, who has the capacity to abnegate himself completely to the Holy One, blessed be He, by giving his life for the sanctification of God.

The Jew, as a physical being on earth, might not be in such a state of self-abnegation at all times, but he possesses the potential to utterly negate his very existence to God.

For this reason, and for this only, a Jew is a holy being: not because the Jew is more clever, more compassionate, or more successful, but because he has the capacity to negate himself to God. Further on in *Tanya* (Chapters 18 and 25), the author defines a Jew as one who, at a "moment of truth," will be prepared to sacrifice his life rather than disrupt, even for a moment, his bond with God. A Jew is one in whom union with God and self-abnegation to Him are implanted in his soul; should anyone ever attempt to separate him from God, this latent bond will be invoked in all its intensity, to the point of self-sacrifice. From this potential for utter self-abnegation, implicit even in the most wicked and sinful Jew, the holiness of the Jew derives.

That is why our Sages have said that "Even when a single individual sits and engages in the study of Torah, the divine presence dwells on him"; and "On each [gathering of] ten Jews, the divine presence rests" always.

Because every Jew possesses the potential for self-abnegation to God, he is a fit vessel for the divine presence to dwell in. When he actually studies Torah, he realizes this potential, nullifying himself to the divine wisdom that enclothes itself within and clothes itself with his mind; at such a time, the divine presence actually "dwells in him." (This is the case particularly with Torah study, for although a person also actively subordinates himself to God while praying, this is not an utter self-abnegation, because in prayer one also asks God for one's personal needs.)[7] The Mishnah (*Avot* 3:6) therefore states that if even a single individual sits alone and studies Torah, the divine presence rests upon him.

To this, the Talmud (*Sanhedrin* 39a) adds that whenever ten Jews gather, the divine presence dwells upon them, even if they are not actually negating themselves to God by studying Torah. Ten Jews constitute a minyan, which is not just a quorum for prayer but a number that constitutes an *eidah*, a "community of Jews." Wherever ten Jews congregate, even if they are unaware of their holiness, even if they defile it, the divine presence (*Shekhinah*, which is also the *Kenesset Yisrael*, the supernal "community of Israel") dwells upon them.[8]

However, that which does not abnegate itself to God, but is a separate thing unto itself,

How it defines itself is irrelevant—whether it considers its own worth as great or insignificant, as lofty or lowly. As long as it relates to itself as a distinct entity, as something other and separate from God, it

does not receive its vitality from the holiness of the Holy One, blessed be He—that is, from the very inner essence and substance of the holiness itself—but from its back, as it were,

Ultimately, it *does* receive life and being from God. For there is no force that is not sustained by His power, no existence that does not derive from His existence. God is the sole source of existence in all its forms and manifestations. Yet there is a profound difference between existences that are sustained from the inner holiness of God—because they desire God and God desires them—and existences that do not desire a bond with God and the complete self-abnegation it requires, and therefore receive their vitality not from the core of the divine will but from its external element or "back."

The back of God's will are the things that He wants not because He desires them in and of themselves but because they are the requisite accessories to the realization of what He truly desires. A container has an inside and an outside. We don't need the outside of the container in and of itself; the purpose of the container is filled by the part containing its contents, the inside. Yet no container can possibly consist only of an inside. By necessity, the inside will always have an outside. The desired part of a knife is its cutting edge.

In other words, the inside of a thing is where its function and purpose lie; the outside is required for the said purpose. In order to realize a goal, we often need to build an entire organization, which includes many auxiliary elements; the auxiliary elements might be far greater, quantitatively, than the part of the organization that actually realizes the purpose. A great and complex system might exist for the sake of a minuscule unit. The part of a thing directly related to its purpose is the inner part, or core, of the will of its manufacturer and user; everything else is the back or external element of his will.

In this sense, the realm of holiness is the inner element of creation, the realm in which is invested the core of the divine will. God relates to the realm of holiness in an intimate manner, because this is His inner will, the essence of His desire. The other, that which is not holy, is the scaffolding and infrastructure, the setting and the background, for the holy core. It is not because God desires it (in the sense of a fundamental will) but because it is necessary to the existence of the universe, which is only the background to the inner desire. This immense structure, the physical world and whatever it contains, is sustained not by the inner will of God but circuitously, by way of its back.

descending degree by degree, through the myriads of degrees in the evolution of the worlds by means of cause and effect and innumerable contractions,

The divine energy that sustains the world derives from the back or external aspect of the divine will, passing through a multiphased process of concealment and diminution known as "the evolution of the worlds" (*hishtalshelut haolamot*). A great number of "worlds" or levels of reality evolve one from another, descending like the links of a chain, the top of one world linked through the bottom of the one above. Each world derives from its predecessor not by a quantum leap but by a link of cause and effect. This serves to even further conceal the divine source of creation. (If each level of reality had no visible connection to its predecessor, this would manifestly point to the presence of a supraexistential Creator. The fact that the worlds follow a traceable path of causational evolution creates the illusion of a natural origin of each world in the world above it, obscuring and distancing the Creator from His creation.)

until the [divine] light and life are so diminished through repeated diminutions that they can be contracted and enclothed, in a state of exile, within that separated thing,

The divine energy that sustains creation is more than a life force; it originates as a ray of divine light, fully expressing the infinite power of God. But each link in the chain of the evolution of the worlds is a screen that dims its light, until at the last screen, only the life force is manifest, whereas its inner divine element is blurred or completely obscured. The divine light is then in "exile"; the existences it sustains do not sense the divine source of their being and life, and might even deny its very existence. A person in exile is one who finds himself where he does not want to be and is forced to remain there and operate under alien and confining circumstances. In this sense, the divine light that sustains the material world is in exile: forced to operate within and provide being and life to a reality that is hostile to it, being dictated to by a reality it should be dictating. This phenomenon is known as *galut haShekhinah,* "the exile of the divine presence."

to impart to it vitality and existence [out of nothing], so that it does not revert to nothingness and [nonexistence] as it was before it was created.

For every being, including the creature that considers itself a thing in its own right, separate from God, requires something of the divine light to keep it alive and grant it its very existence.

God is the essence of all existence, good and evil. The difference between these two categories is wholly a matter of perspective, relating to the perception of the creations themselves. The creations of the side of holiness perceive themselves as naught before God, whereas the creations of the other side do not sense the divine light within them, do not negate themselves, and see themselves as independent entities.

The creations of the side of holiness are thus sustained by the inner essence of the divine will and constitute the core and purpose of creation;

the creations of the other side constitute the external husk, the scaffolding and infrastructure, the setting and background that enables the realization of the inner point of holiness. The other side is of a far greater quantity than the side of holiness because the maintenance of a single being of significance, of a single inner reality, requires an entire world of ancillary structures. Holiness and *kelipah* are not antagonists in essence but are basically two sides of the same reality: a core of self-awareness and an uncomprehending husk.

Consequently, this physical world, with all it contains, is called the world of *kelipot* and *sitra achra*.

As a rule, the physical world and the creatures that inhabit it, including the physical being of humankind, does not perceive or sense itself as subordinate to God. In the spiritual worlds, which are situated at a higher point in the chain of the evolution, the inner core of holiness occupies a greater and more prominent part of that world, so the divine is sensed and manifest. But our world is not only more tactile but also lower, lower down on the chain from the divine source, consisting almost entirely of *kelipah* and *sitra achra*. The other side fills our world in various shades. It may be gray and moderate, or it may be bold and extreme. But overall, this world is mainly a world of the other side, a world in which holiness is not manifest and the other side dominates.

Therefore all affairs of this world are severe and evil, and wicked men prevail, as explained in *Etz Chayyim*, Portal 42, end of chapter 4.

The nature of the physical reality, and the harshness of life in its realm, is a problem that has occupied many thinkers and theologians. Here, the *Tanya* quotes the conception expressed in the Kabbalistic work *Etz Chayyim*, whose general view of our world seems one of hardened realism, even pessimism. Ours is a world characterized by an almost total concealment of the divine, a world whose visible components are overwhelmingly *kelipah* and *sitra achra;* small wonder that it is not filled with brightness and light. In a world that is basically *kelipah*, evil has the natural advantage, and the wicked prevail. But this picture is not necessarily pessimistic, because things can be put right. There is a way to change and transform the world, to fill it with goodness and holiness. But this does not come automatically; it requires diligent and constant work of change and correction.

Note: To be sure, there are contained in it the ten *sefirot* of the holy World of Action, as is written in *Etz Chayyim,* Portal 43, and within these ten *sefirot* of the World of Action are the ten *sefirot* of the World of Formation, and in them the ten *sefirot* of the World of Creation, and in them the ten *sefirot* of the World of Emanation, in which abides the light of the Blessed Infinite. Thus the light of the Blessed Infinite pervades this lower world through being clothed in the ten *sefirot* of the Four Worlds, namely those of Emanation, Creation, Formation, and Action,[9] as explained in *Etz Chayyim,* Portal 47, chapter 2, and in *Sefer haGilgulim,* chapter 20.

As explained earlier, the existence of anything, including *kelipah* and *sitra achra,* can only derive from one source: from God, from the light of the Infinite Himself. The difference between holiness and the mundane lies only in the amount of layers of concealment that shroud the divine essence of a thing. This is determined by the number of steps the divine light has descended along the chain of the evolution of the worlds, as described in the passage from *Etz Chayyim* cited in this note.

The *kelipot,* however, are subdivided into two grades, one lower than the other.

Kelipot ("husks") is an alternate term for *sitra achra* ("the other side"), expressing the concept that the other side is the external, extrinsic element, the element that serves as the husk for the fruit, protecting and preserving the inner content.

When speaking of the various levels in the realm of unholiness, the author refers to it as *kelipah* rather than *sitra achra. Sitra achra* is a generalized description, expressing only the concept that this realm is *not* holy; thus, we cannot speak of various levels in a phenomenon that is defined solely in terms of what it is not. *Kelipah,* on the other hand, is a positive definition, describing the function of the nonholy elements of creation. In this context, we can distinguish between various forms of this function and discuss the two primary levels of *kelipah.*

The lower grade consists of the three *kelipot* which are altogether profane and evil, containing no good whatsoever. In the "chariot" of Ezekiel

A prophetic vision of the divine attributes as perceived by the prophet Ezekiel and recorded in the first chapter of the book of Ezekiel follows:

they are called "storm wind, great cloud. . . ."

The verse ends with and "flaring fire" (Ezekiel 1:4).

From these flow and derive the souls of all the nations of the world, and the existence of their bodies; the souls of all living creatures that are impure and prohibited for consumption,[10] and the existence of their bodies; the existence and vitality of all prohibited foods of the vegetable kingdom, such as the fruits of the first three years of a tree[11] and mixed seeds in the vineyard,[12] etc., as explained in *Etz Chayyim*, Portal 49, chapter 6;

These *kelipot* are totally evil, and they are the root for whatever manifests itself as evil, in whatever way. (In his notes on *Tanya*, Rabbi Levi Yitzchak Schneerson, father of the Lubavitcher Rebbe, points out that although elements from the "three utterly profane *kelipot*" are in three of the four "kingdoms"—the human kingdom, the animal kingdom, and the vegetable kingdom—there are no such elements in the inanimate kingdom. The reason for this is that the inanimate kingdom derives from the divine attribute of *malkhut* ("kingship"), in which there was no "collapse" [in the primordial "bursting of the vessels" that is the source of *kelipah*] but only a "nullification," as stated in the *Zohar:* "earth was nullified.")[13]

Also deriving from and sustained by the "three utterly profane *kelipot*" are

the existence and vitality of all actions, utterances, and thoughts pertaining to the 365 prohibitions and their offshoots, as it is explained [in that work], at the end of chapter 5.

Chapter 7

On the other hand, the vitalizing animal soul in the Jew deriving from *kelipah,* which is clothed in the human blood, as stated above; the souls of the animals, beasts, birds, and fishes that are pure and permitted for consumption; the existence and vitality of all inanimate substances; all of the vegetable world that is permissible for consumption; and the existence and vitality of every act, utterance, and thought in mundane matters that contain no forbidden aspect, being neither root nor branch of the 365 prohibitive precepts and their offshoots, either on the authority of the Torah or by rabbinical enactment, yet are not performed for the sake of Heaven but only by the will, desire, and lust of the body; and even where it is a need of the body, or its very preservation and life, but his intention is not for the sake of Heaven, that is, to serve God thereby, these acts, utterances, and thoughts are no better than the vitalizing animal soul itself—everything in this totality of things flows and is drawn from the second gradation in the *kelipot* and *sitra achra,* namely, a fourth *kelipah,* called *kelipat nogah.* For in this world, called the World of Action, virtually all of [*kelipat nogah*] is negative, and only a little good is intermingled within it (from which come the good qualities contained in the animal soul of the Jew, as explained above).

[*Kelipat nogah*] is an intermediate category between the three completely profane *kelipot* and the category and level of holiness. Thus it is sometimes absorbed within the three profane *kelipot* (as is explained in *Etz Chayyim,* Portal 49, beginning of chapter 4, in the name of the *Zohar*), and sometimes it is absorbed and elevated to the category and level of holiness, as when the good that is intermingled in it is extracted from the bad, and prevails and ascends and is absorbed in holiness.

Such is the case, for example, when one eats fat beef and drinks spiced wine in order to broaden his mind for the service of God and His Torah—as Rava said: "Wine and fragrance . . . "—or in order to fulfill the *mitzvah* to pleasure oneself on the Sabbath and the Festivals. In such case the vitality of the meat and wine, originating in *kelipat nogah,* is distilled and ascends to God like a burnt offering and sacrifice. So, too, when a person tells a joke in order to sharpen his wit and rejoice his heart in God and His Torah and service, which should be practiced joyfully—as Rava was wont to do with his pupils, prefacing his discourse with some witty remark, so that the scholars laughed.

On the other hand, he who is of the egorgers of meat and guzzlers of wine in order to satisfy the lust of his body and animal soul, which is the element of water of the four evil elements contained therein from which comes the vice of lust—in such case the energy in the meat and wine consumed by him is degraded and absorbed temporarily in the utter evil of the three profane *kelipot,* and his body temporarily becomes a garment and vehicle for them, until such time that the person repents and returns to the service of God and His Torah. For, inasmuch as the meat was permissible and the wine was kosher, they can revert and ascend with him when he returns to the service of God. This is implied in the terms *heiter* and *mutar,* that is to say, that which is not tied and bound (*assur*) in the hands of the extraneous forces preventing it from returning and ascending to God. Nevertheless, a trace [of *kelipah*] remains in the body. Therefore the body must undergo the purgatory of the grave, as will be explained later.

So, too, with regard to the vitality of the drops of semen emitted with animal lust by one who has not sanctified himself at the time of his intimacy with his wife in her state of purity.

Such is not the case, however, with forbidden foods and sexual relations, which derive from the three *kelipot* that are entirely profane. These are tied and bound (*assur*) by the extraneous forces forever, and do not ascend from there until their day comes, when death will be annihilated for all eternity, as is written: "And I will remove the spirit of profanity from the land"; or until he repents to such an extent that his willful sins become transformed into merits, which is repentance out of love, coming from the depths of the heart, with great love, desire, and the soul's craving to cleave to God and thirsting for God like a parched desert land. For it is because his soul had been, up until now, in a land of drought and death's shadow—the *sitra achra*—and very far from the light of the divine countenance, that his soul now thirsts [for God] with a greater intensity than the souls of the righteous. As our Sages say: "In the place where penitents stand . . . " It is concerning this sort of repentance out of great love that they have said, "Willful sins become like virtues for him," since it is because of them that he has attained this great love.

But repentance that does not come from such love, though it be a proper repentance, and God will forgive him, nevertheless his sins are not transformed into merits, and they are not completely released from the *kelipah*, until the end of time, when death will be annihilated forever.

However, the vitality which is in the drops of semen that issue wastefully, though it has been degraded and incorporated in the three profane *kelipot*, nevertheless, it can ascend from there by means of a proper repentance and intense concentration during the recital of the Shema at bedtime, as is known from our master Rabbi Isaac Luria, of blessed memory, and is implied in the Talmudic saying: "He who recites the Shema at bedtime is as if he held a double-edged sword . . ." with which to slay the bodies of the extraneous forces that have become garments for the vitality which is in the drops [of semen], so that this vitality may ascend, as is known to those who are familiar with the Esoteric Wisdom.

This is why the sin of wasteful emission of semen is not mentioned in the Torah among the forbidden coitions, although it is even more severe than they, and its iniquity is greater in regard to the enormity and abundance of the impurity and of the *kelipot* which he begets and multiplies to an exceedingly great extent through wasteful emission of semen, even more than through forbidden coitions. But in the case of forbidden coitions he contributes strength and vitality to a most unclean *kelipah*, from which he is powerless to bring up the vitality by means of repentance,

Note: The reason being that this vitality has been absorbed by the female element of the *kelipah*, which receives and absorbs the vitality from the holiness. Not so with wasteful emission of semen, where there is no female element of *kelipah*, and only its powers and forces enclothe the vitality in the semen, as is known to those familiar with the Esoteric Wisdom.

. . . unless he repents with such great love that his willful wrongs are transformed into merits.

Thus one may understand the comment of our Sages: "Which is 'a deformation that cannot be rectified'? Having incestuous intercourse and giving birth to a bastard." For in such a case, even though the sinner undertakes such great repentance, he cannot cause the vitality to ascend to Holiness, since it has already descended into this world and has been clothed in a body of flesh and blood.

COMMENTARY

Chapter 6 began discussion of the *sitra achra:* the "other side" that is contrary to holiness and derives nourishment from the "back" or externality of the divine will and that constitutes the *kelipah* ("husk") of the inner content of creation.

The chapter concluded by establishing that *kelipah* comprises two basic levels. The lower level includes the three thoroughly profane and negative *kelipot*, which contain no good at all. (Though, as we said, it is not possible for anything to exist without any positive content. The meaning of "no good at all" might be understood that, on these levels, the positive content of the *kelipah* is inaccessible to us and thus is of no actual significance.) The higher level, which will be discussed in this chapter, is *kelipat nogah*, the "luminescent husk," in which some good is mixed in.

On the other hand, the vitalizing animal soul in the Jew deriving from *kelipah*, which is clothed in the human blood, as stated above;

The "animal soul," which the author discussed in Chapter 1, is not necessarily animal in the derogatory and base sense of the word. It is meant in the biological sense, in which man, too, is classified as an animal. The drives and desires of this soul, like those of all other animals, are not necessarily evil; they are part of the biological stratum of creation. A human being's brain is larger (relative to his body) and more highly developed than that of other animals. As a result, what we might call the animalism in him differs from that in other creatures, even though he is basically part of the same genera. The animal soul in man is the force of the natural life, infusing him with the basic vitality he shares with all other living things. This soul derives from *kelipat nogah*.[1] Also on the level of *kelipat nogah* are

the souls of the animals,[2] beasts,[3] birds, and fishes that are pure and permitted for consumption; the existence and vitality of all inanimate substances; all of the vegetable world that is permissible for consumption; and the existence and vitality of every act, utterance, and thought in mundane matters that contain no forbidden aspect, being neither root nor branch of the 365 prohibitive precepts and their offshoots, either on the authority of the Torah or by rabbinical enactment,

In other words, *kelipat nogah* includes all the things or actions in existence that have no moral fault or forbidden aspect, on the one hand, but which also do not possess, in and of themselves, any aspect of *mitzvah*, of divine service, on the other. This broad spectrum is not the domain of the dark, the forbidden, or the corrupt, but the sphere of the nonholy and the neutral, that which is neither *mitzvah* nor sin. Anything forbidden, whether biblically or rabbinically, belongs to the world of the three profane *kelipot*, as stated in Chapter 6; something that is not forbidden by Torah does not belong to the utterly profane *kelipot*, but neither is it holy. An old Hasidic saying states: "What is forbidden, one must not; and what is permitted, one need not." What is forbidden is evil, wholly of the other side, but what is permitted is also *kelipah* and *sitra achra*. What is permitted is not holy and there-fore belongs to the other side, for the other side includes all that is not holy. What is not a *mitzvah*, what is not actively holy (that is, sub-servient to and expressive of the divine), is —"husk," something extra-neous to the divine essence of creation. The difference between the forbidden and the permitted is not the difference between holiness and *kelipah* but the difference between levels of *kelipah*, between *keli-pah* that can be rectified and *kelipah* that cannot be rectified.

All the things listed derive from *kelipat nogah* because they

are not performed for the sake of Heaven but only by the will, desire, and lust of the body;

As we already elaborated, there is no middle ground between the holy and the profane, no gray area that is neither one nor the other. A thing is either holy and devoted to God, or it is profane. So all of the acts listed, though kosher and permissible, are *kelipah*, because they are not directly and solely committed to the fulfillment of God's will but to the fulfillment of the will and desire of the body.

and even where it is a need of the body, or its very preservation and life, but his intention is not for the sake of Heaven, that is, to serve God thereby,

Kelipat nogah includes not only luxuries or superfluous pleasures but even the piece of bread that keeps one alive: if a person eats it as other animals do, it does not belong to the side of holiness and thus, by definition, is of the other side. A person can be a glutton without transgressing any law of Torah and even while leading a most simple and modest existence. He need not feast like a king; he can eat a dry crust of bread followed by a sip of water, and this too belongs to the *kelipah*, because any action that is not expressly directed toward holiness belongs to the other side. A person can wear clothes of silk and gold and in so doing be serving God; he can wear sackcloth, yet this can be *kelipah*.

The story is told of a certain learned Jew, very pious in his way, who would fast and inflict all sorts of torments upon himself, wearing sackcloth underneath his clothes. One day, he went to visit a great *tzaddik*. He wanted the *tzaddik* to know how pious he was, so he opened his upper garment slightly so that the sacking would be visible. The *tzaddik* looked at him for a while and then said, "How clever he is! How clever he is!" He repeated this several times until the man had to ask, "Who is so clever?" The *tzaddik* answered, "The *yetzer harah* ('evil inclination'), who took a man such as yourself and put him into a sack!"

A person can live in utter conformity with Torah law, even modestly and ascetically but entirely for himself. In such a case,

these acts, utterances, and thoughts are no better than the vitalizing animal soul itself

As we said, the animal soul does not imply the degradation of man to the level of animals but is the definition of man as an animal: a higher form of animal as the donkey is higher than the worm but no different inherently. Just as the animal soul itself is neither good nor evil, so are its thoughts, speech, and deeds, whether sophisticated or simple, elevated or base, whether connected with essential needs or mere desires. These deeds, if they do not constitute the fulfillment of a *mitzvah* or are not done for the sake of serving God, are, like the animal soul itself, of the realm of *kelipah*.

—everything in this totality of things flows and is drawn from the second gradation in the *kelipot* and *sitra achra,* namely, a fourth *kelipah,* called *kelipat nogah.*

In his vision of the divine chariot, the prophet Ezekiel beheld "a storm wind coming from the north, a great cloud, a flaring fire, and a gleam surrounding it."[4] As we mentioned in Chapter 6, "storm wind," "great cloud," and "flaring fire" refer to the three profane *kelipot.* The fourth *kelipah* is alluded to in the phrase "and a gleam (*nogah*) surrounding it," indicating that this *kelipah* is not completely dark but contains a gleam of light.

Kelipat nogah—literally, "the luminescent husk"—is not as gross as the other husks, but although perhaps more palatable, it is a husk nonetheless. By way of analogy, some fruits come encased in a double covering: a tough outer shell that is completely unfit for consumption and a finer, inner rind that can, with the proper preparation, be eaten.

The desire for *kelipat nogah*—as in the desire of a Jew to eat kosher meat—is described in Chapter 8 as a "Jewish demon." In contrast, the desire to eat pork is an "alien demon," a desire associated with the three profane *kelipot.* But also the Jewish demon, the lust for what is kosher and permitted, is *kelipah.* It is not decidedly evil, but for that very reason it is even more difficult to overcome. Distinguishing between permitted and forbidden is easier than distinguishing between holiness and *kelipah* within the sphere of the permitted. A person can do all that he is obliged to do and avoid every prohibition and still, without realizing it, be immersed in *kelipah* all his life.

For in this world, called the World of Action, virtually all of [*kelipat nogah*] is negative, and only a little good is intermingled within it

Kelipat nogah is the luminescent husk, a veil of darkness that nevertheless has a gleam of light to it. It is a *kelipah* that is not wholly evil but also has some good in it. The extent of this good varies in the four worlds that constitute the primary phases of the *seder hahishtalshelut,* the "chain of evolution" by which our material world evolves from the spiritual essence of creation. In the highest link of the chain, the world of Emanation (*Atzilut*), the good is wholly good; in the world of Creation (*Beriah*), it is mostly good, but something of an obscuring husk has already been formed; in the world of Formation (*Yetzirah*), it is equal parts light and darkness; in our world of Action (*Asiyah*), it is virtually entirely dark, manifesting but the faintest glimmer of divine light.[5]

(from which come the good qualities contained in the animal soul of the Jew, as explained above).

As the author discussed in Chapter 1, the people of Israel possess the traits of bashfulness, compassion, and charity—not as qualities of their Godly souls but as part of their nature, deriving from the animal soul. Just as a certain family or race might hereditarily possess the trait of aggression or a talent for writing poetry, the Jew possesses these traits not as a part of his natural, biological composition and not as a result of the holiness of his Godly soul.

Citing the verse, "Who teaches us from the beasts of the land, and wisens us from the birds of the sky,"[6] the Talmud explains that certain positive traits that, had the Torah not been given, we could have learned from animals: modesty from the cat, respect of another's property from the ant, and so on.[7] Figuratively speaking and in a certain sense, the positive traits of the animal soul of the Jew can be compared to the "positive traits" of these animals. However, the modesty of the cat (which covers its excrement) is not a result of the cat's awareness of the divine omnipresence impelling it to modesty; it is part of the cat's immutable nature. By the same token, one might learn the practice of *netilat yadayim* (ritual washing of the hands) from the raccoon, which seems to wash its hands in water before eating, but the raccoon does not do this because it is mandated by the *Shulchan Aruch*. This is not a practice deriving from a Godly soul's desire to fulfill the divine will but an inherited characteristic in the nature of a particular animal. In a certain sense, the good traits of the Jews are like the good traits of these animals.

[*Kelipat nogah*] is an intermediate category between the three completely profane *kelipot* and the category and level of holiness. Thus it is sometimes absorbed within the three profane *kelipot* (as is explained in *Etz Chayyim*, Portal 49, beginning of chapter 4, in the name of the *Zohar*), and sometimes it is absorbed and elevated to the category and level of holiness,

Note the precise terminology used here. The *Tanya* does not say that *kelipat nogah* is an intermediate between the profanity and holiness but between the three profane *kelipot* and the "category and level of holiness." As elaborated earlier, there is no intermediate level between holiness and *kelipah*: a thing is either one or the other. By definition, the other side includes everything that is not of the side of holiness. *Kelipat nogah* is an intermediate level not because it contains both holy and unholy elements but only in the sense that the elements in its domain are transferable from one side to the other. Namely, with proper preparation and well-aimed action, things that are in the domain of *kelipat nogah* can be elevated to the category and level of holiness.

The difference between *kelipat nogah* and the three profane *kelipot* lies in the potential of those elements that are in the province of *kelipat nogah* to be rectified by man and thus redirected and transferred to the province of holiness, whereas those things that are of the three profane *kelipot* are off-limits to such efforts on our part and are entirely unrectifiable.

as when the good that is intermingled in it is extracted from the bad, and prevails and ascends and is absorbed in holiness.

The elevation of *kelipat nogah* to the level of holiness is achieved by extracting the good implicit within it. "Extracting the good" means, first of all, achieving a distinction between good and evil. For in *kelipat nogah,* the boundary between good and evil is blurred, which leaves room for error. The next stage, after defining what is good and what is evil, is to emphasize the good so that it separates from the evil and ascends to the level of holiness.

Such is the case, for example, when one eats fat beef and drinks spiced wine in order to broaden his mind for the service of God and His Torah— as Rava said: "Wine and fragrance . . ."—

For every individual, there are particular conditions, dictated by his specific nature, under which he can make the most of his potential. When a person is hungry or thirsty, or experiencing some bodily or psychological torment, his ability to operate is obviously impaired. But some individuals require special food and drink, things commonly regarded as luxuries, for their peace of mind; if they lack these things, their concentration and clarity of mind is adversely affected. Thus, the Talmud quotes the Talmudic sage Rava as saying, "Wine and fragrance have made me wise"[8]—that is to say, the effect they had on him was to open his mind to Torah study. A person such as Rava can "eat fat beef and drink spiced wine" and elevate them to holiness, for he does this to the end of broadening "his mind for the service of God and His Torah."

This extreme example illustrates the extent to which a proper intention can elevate elements that are in themselves *kelipah:* a person is not only partaking of the material world but of luxuries, of things that serve not the body's needs but whose only purpose is to give pleasure; nevertheless, because he is doing this for a particular and expressly intended goal, for the purpose of serving God, he raises these elements to the aspect and level of holiness.

Obviously, this does not grant a person carte blanche to indulge in every pleasure with the justification that it is "to broaden his mind for the service of God and his Torah." If a certain act does not truly contribute to one's service of God—for example, if it makes no difference to a person whether or not he eats, and still he eats and enjoys luxuries—this act will never escape the bounds of *kelipah.* An intention "for the sake of Heaven" is not an automatic certificate attesting that this or that thing is kosher; it's not a benediction whose recitation sanctifies everything. There is no simple formula that converts *kelipah* to holiness. For an act to elevate a material substance to holiness, it must be permeated with an awareness that is both thorough and constant.

If the performance of a *mitzvah* requires *kavvanah* ("acute awareness and concentration"), this is even more crucial when attending to one's mundane involvements. With a *mitzvah,* the act itself is holy, so the *kavvanah* is mainly to prevent his thoughts from being distracted by other matters. But in the case of non-*mitzvah* activities, the *kavvanah* itself sanctifies the act. If eating and drinking are to have a holy significance, they require an active elevation into the realm of holiness.

or in order to fulfill the *mitzvah* to pleasure oneself on the Sabbath and Festivals.

To pleasure oneself on the Sabbath and the Festivals with meat and wine and other delicacies is a *mitzvah.*[9] Nevertheless, the *kavvanah* plays a crucial role in elevating the food to holiness. For the *mitzvah* is to enjoy the Sabbath, not simply to experience physical pleasure on the Sabbath. So unless the feasting is accompanied by a constant awareness and intent that one's enjoyment is for the sake of the Sabbath rather than for the pleasure of one's stomach, it remains the pleasure of one's stomach and does not ascend to holiness.

The general rule is that *kelipat nogah* includes those things that are permitted by Torah law[10] and therefore can, by various means, be transferred from *kelipah* to holiness, even if they are not directly involved in the performance of a *mitzvah,* an actual fulfillment of a divine command. When a person "extracts the valuable from the vile" (as in the analogy of metal refining in Jeremiah 15:19), he performs what is one of the greatest acts of holiness and divine service. However, this operation requires an absolute and unequivocal awareness of what one is doing, how he is doing it, and for what purpose. One needs to be conscious at all times of everything that he eats, speaks, or does so that every bite he takes or every word he utters is with an express intention for the sake of heaven.

In the world of *kelipat nogah*, a person eats and enjoys his food because it is his nature, as a biological creature, to eat. In this sense, he is no different from other animals, regardless of his higher level of development. The point of transfer to holiness, the point at which a person truly differs from other creatures, depends on his awareness of the questions: Why am I doing this? What is the significance of my actions? A person who eats but does so for his own reasons, thinking his own thoughts—whether of great or small matters, whether nonsense or the heights of scientific or philosophical theory—belongs at the time to the *kelipah*, even if what he eats is 100 percent kosher according to all the rules of the *Shulchan Aruch*. He has not transcended the material and the biological. For the transfer from the merely natural to the holy requires more than cleverness, more than good faith, more than spiritual experience. Holiness is not cleverness, and it is not a feeling of spiritual elevation; holiness is attachment to God. In holiness, there is no concept or sense of self, only of self-abnegation. The person who negates himself before God and cleaves to Him, transfers himself and everything in his life into the realm of holiness; a person—any person—who does not do so belongs to the other side of existence. Thus, a person might eat dry bread and belong to the *kelipah* or eat all the delicacies of the world and belong to holiness. If the eating is designated to serve as an instrument of holiness, then not only the food but even the pleasure therein become part of what ascends to the supernal holiness, to God Himself.

In such case the vitality of the meat and wine, originating in *kelipat nogah*, is distilled and ascends to God like a burnt offering and sacrifice.

An "offering" (*korban*) is something that is taken from the domain of the ordinary and nonholy and raised to the realm of holiness by being offered to God. Thus, any act involving a mundane object or force that is done toward a holy end is a *korban*, for it elevates a mundane resource and makes it a part of holiness, like the *korbanot* ("offerings") in the *Beit haMikdash* ("Holy Temple"). When a person eats with the intention to serve God with the energy derived from the food, he transfers the food from the domain of *kelipat nogah* to the domain of holiness, even if the act of eating is not itself a *mitzvah* (as long as the food is kosher and permissible for consumption).[11] Such an act of eating is not intrinsically holy, it is *mutar* (which means both "permissible" and "unbound") and is therefore freely transportable by the intent of man to wherever he directs it, whether to holiness or profanity.

When a person performs a *mitzvah,* his awareness and intent (*kavvanah*) affect only the quality of the *mitzvah* but not the fact that it is a *mitzvah;* for a *mitzvah,* by definition, is an act that constitutes the fulfillment of a divine command, an act that is inherently and objectively holy, regardless of the performer's intent. But in the case of an act that is not itself a *mitzvah,* such as eating an ordinary meal, the holiness of the act depends on intent. Without the appropriate intent, it has no holiness and is pure *kelipah.* And the higher the level of the intent, the greater its honesty and sincerity, the higher the level of holiness the act achieves, until it reaches such a high level that it is equivalent to a *korban* offered in the Holy Temple.

The Talmud states that when the *Beit haMikdash* existed, the altar atoned for a person, and now a person's table atones for him.[12] Hence, the customs to place salt on the table as a reminder of the salt that was brought with every offering[13] and to remove the knives before Grace after Meals, because the knife profanes the altar.[14] However, for the table to atone, placing salt on it is not sufficient. One must maintain a constant, active awareness that one is eating for the sake of heaven.

So, too, when a person tells a joke in order to sharpen his wit and rejoice his heart in God and His Torah and service,

Even something that appears to be closer to the profane than eating, such as telling a joke, can be an offering to God. If a person tells a joke for his own enjoyment, because he cannot resist displaying his wit, then his act indeed belongs to a very lowly *kelipah;* but if he does this for God, so as to raise his spirits and open his heart the better to serve the Almighty and is conscious of this at the time, he elevates the very words of the joke to holiness.

which should be practiced joyfully—

A cardinal principal in the service of God is that it must be done with joy. It is said in the name of many Hasidic masters that there is something that is not listed in the Torah as a sin yet is worse than any sin and something that is technically not a *mitzvah* yet is greater than all *mitzvot*. Nowhere does the Torah expressly forbid sadness and depression, yet this is the most virulent of sins, for it stifles the heart and mind, closing them to the service of God. Joy is not an express *mitzvah* but is the greatest of *mitzvot*, for it opens a person's heart and mind, enabling him to perform all the *mitzvot* and to make a *mitzvah* of everything.

The Talmud relates that Rabbi Baroka was standing in the market-place, and Elijah the prophet was standing next to him.[15] Rabbi Baroka asked Elijah: "Is there anyone here who is worthy of the world to come?" Elijah answered, "No." As they spoke, two men entered the marketplace, and Elijah said that these two were worthy. Rabbi Baroka ran after them and asked what their profession was. They told him that they were comedians, whose job was to cheer the downhearted. And this is what made them worthy of the world to come.

as Rava was wont to do with his pupils, prefacing his discourse with some witty remark, so that the scholars laughed.

The Talmud relates that it was Rava's custom to preface his discourse with a joke.[16] Then, after his students had laughed in merriment, he would wrap himself in his *tallit* (prayer shawl) and begin to teach them in a most solemn and awe-inspiring manner. Precisely because he wanted them to receive the words of Torah with awe and reverence, he felt the need to first lighten the atmosphere and arouse their minds with a witticism.

So it is possible for even a joke to be a matter of holiness. The same applies to every permissible act, word, or thought: if a person's intention is to serve God, he is taking something that belonged to the *kelipah* and elevating it to holiness. He is offering a *korban*, with the full implication of the word as used regarding offerings made to God upon the altar in the Holy Temple.

One *tzaddik* said that it is easier to study an entire tractate of Talmud than to eat a single meal. Navigating one's way through the Talmud is easier: the boundaries are clearly marked, and one walks along a well-trodden and clearly defined path. Eating is far more complicated, requiring a concentrated effort of perpetual awareness of what one is doing. It is not only harder work than studying Torah or performing a *mitzvah* but also more dangerous, because one is involved with *kelipah,* the other side. Notwithstanding the loftiness of the endeavor to elevating material things to holiness, should one fail to do so, his act remains *kelipah* and is even further degraded, as will be discussed.

Kelipat nogah differs from profane *kelipot* in that it is not unilateral. The elements in this domain are not categorically defined but can be interpreted and manipulated in various directions. Man determines the direction, significance, and implications of his every act. But whatever a person does unthinkingly, without conscious intent, automatically belongs to the realm of unholiness. For this reason, the neutral state of *kelipat nogah* is profane.

Some levels of *kelipah* are lowlier than *kelipat nogah,* but there is a negative aspect to *kelipat nogah* that does not exist even in the "utterly profane" *kelipot,* the disappointment of something that could have been better but has been degraded into something worse. When a human being who possesses the potential to attain holiness is content instead to be a type of intelligent ape, the failure is far more acute than the failure of an animal to be more than an animal. In order that a person not so disappoint his divine potential, his every deed, his every bite of food, and his every experience of pleasure must be governed by a conscious endeavor to direct it toward holiness.

Can this degree of awareness and control be demanded of every man? The *Tanya* insists that, yes, this is humanly possible. This is the essence of the *beinoni,* the "intermediate," about whom the book revolves. By no means is it easy, but it is within the realm of the possible for every individual. A person does not have to be an exceptional human being in order to achieve that; however, this involves a constant effort of unceasing awareness, that whatever we do must be toward this aim. And the higher the degree of awareness, the higher the levels of holiness that one can attain.

The *Midrash* relates that Enoch used to sew leather into shoes;[17] with each stitch he would say, "Blessed be the name of the glory of His kingship for ever and ever."[18] This *Midrash* has many levels of meaning, the most basic of which is that when an ordinary shoemaker, a simple man engaged in the mundane pursuits of material life, dedicates each and every stitch for the sake of heaven, he "ascends to God," as did Enoch.[19] Such an individual becomes an angel in his lifetime (as is told of Enoch), because he is living like an angel already, even in this world: the materiality of the world is transparent to him; he sees through it to its divine function.

We know of individuals who led such an existence, whose every movement was filled with the awareness of what they were doing and whose every deed, word, and thought were directed heavenward. Such service of God is not the exclusive prerogative of the *tzaddik,* who is a special type of person, but something that basically, if not as fully, pertains to everyone. Everyone can attain a certain degree of awareness of his individual existence and direct it to the service of God.

On the other hand, he who is of the egorgers of meat and guzzlers of wine in order to satisfy the lust of his body and animal soul, which is the element of water of the four evil elements contained therein from which comes the vice of lust—

As the author discussed in chapter 1, the animal soul comprises four elements, corresponding to the four elements of fire, air, water, and earth. The element of water in the animal soul is lust, that is, desire that is not directed to a higher goal but is an end in itself, desire for the sake of the pleasure that comes from the fulfillment of desire. In other words, lust itself is *kelipah:* even if the desired object is not negative, the desire for it is negative if it has no higher objective that its self-satiation.

in such case the energy in the meat and wine consumed by him is degraded and absorbed temporarily in the utter evil of the three profane *kelipot,*

The vital essence of permitted food derives from *kelipat nogah,* but when a person eats it merely to satisfy his desire for food, he degrades himself, and the food he has eaten, to the level of the utterly profane *kelipot.* In this sense, he goes even lower than the food itself. A man who, possessing the potential to transcend the animal, chooses to eat like an animal, is worse than the animal that can only be what it is, and he imposes this subanimal status upon the flesh of the animal he has eaten.

and his body temporarily becomes a garment and vehicle for them,

One who eats and drinks merely to satisfy his bodily desires (or acts similarly in other respects) becomes a vehicle, an instrument and expression, of the forces of evil.

In this sense, there is no difference between desire for what is permitted and desire for what is forbidden. The demarcation between

holiness and profanity is not the demarcation between the permitted and the forbidden. Holiness is all that, and only that, which
relates to God. Everything else, everything that is motivated by
and relates to anything other than Him, belongs to the realm of *kelipah.*
Thus, when a person indulges in his desires, even if permitted, he
does not at that time relate to God. When a person decides, consciously or unknowingly, that he belongs to the world of *kelipah,* he
becomes a "garment and vehicle" for the profane husks that obscure
the divine essence of reality.

It is told of the Holy Grandfather of Radoshitz that in his youth,
before he became a rebbe, he was terribly poor and often had nothing
to eat. One year, after he had eaten nothing from Yom Kippur to the
day before Sukkot, his wife sold a jewel she had and bought candles,
challah, and potatoes for the festival. When he saw the candles and
challah on his return from the synagogue, he was very happy, recited
the *Kiddush,* washed his hands, and sat down to eat. Being very hungry, he ate ravenously, until he suddenly stopped and said to himself:
"Berl, you are not sitting in the *sukkah* but in the plate!" Someone can
be tending to the most basic needs of his body and with conscious
intent be observing the *mitzvah* of eating in the *sukkah,* yet still be sitting in the dish and not in the *mitzvah.*

All the same, even when a person eats to satisfy his lust, his body
becomes a vehicle for *kelipah* only temporarily,

until such time that the person repents and returns to the service of God
and His Torah. For, inasmuch as the meat was permissible and the wine
was kosher, they can revert and ascend with him when he returns to the
service of God.

The meat that he eats and the wine he drinks become part of his
body, part of the vital force that empowers him to function and
achieve. So when he subsequently involves himself with Torah and
mitzvot, he does this with the body and the energy that the meat and
wine generate. Thus, when he elevates his life to holiness, all that has
sustained his life is elevated along with him. In the same way that he
previously served as a garment and vehicle for *kelipah,* he can now
revert to being a garment and vehicle for holiness, redirecting the
material substances he has previously ingested to serve his Torah study,
prayer, and performance of *mitzvot.* This can be done despite the fact
that, at the time, he did not ingest these substances for this purpose

(which is why, at the time, he was a vehicle of *kelipah*), provided that the food was *mutar,* "permissible" for consumption by the Torah.

This is implied in the terms *heiter* and *mutar,* that is to say, that which is not tied and bound (*assur*) in the hands of the extraneous forces[20] preventing it from returning and ascending to God.

Assur, the Hebrew word for "forbidden," literally means "bound" and "tied"; *heiter* and *mutar,* the terms for "permitted," literally mean "unbound," "untied," "free." The permissible is that which is not bound to *kelipah,* that which can be freed and separated from the negative husk. The permissible may serve as an instrument of *kelipah;* it may serve as a vehicle of expression for evil but is not bound to it and is always free to move and change direction from the realm of the profane to that of the holy and vice versa. The permissible is not intrinsically tied to either sphere, although it may appear in either sphere at any time, if man places it there.

For this reason, although a person who lives like an animal in satisfying his desires becomes a part of the *kelipah,* he can subsequently transfer himself and all of his eating, drinking, and other worldly pleasures to the realm of holiness, as long as his satisfaction of his desires did not involve anything forbidden.

The difference between permitted and forbidden is between what can and what cannot be separated from *kelipah.* By way of analogy, useful minerals are found in nature in various forms and compounds. Some can be used as they are; some require extraction, processing, and refinement; and others cannot be used at all, because the useful element cannot be extracted from its ore. The latter are analogous to things that are *assur,* forbidden and bound by Torah law. A halakhic ruling on whether something is forbidden or permitted determines whether it is bound forever to the domain of *kelipah* or is unbound and extractable. When a substance of *heiter,* initially belonging to the realm of *kelipat nogah,* is used toward a holy purpose, it is transferred to the realm of holiness; even when one's motives are only partially holy, some rectification of the *kelipah* has been achieved. By contrast, that which is forbidden is bound to its evil embodiment and cannot ever be freed and rectified.

This explains why there are so many more halakhic prohibitions nowadays than there were in earlier periods, such as the time of the Talmud. One certainly cannot say that the Talmud scholars ate forbidden food and that only we eat what is truly kosher. Permitted and forbidden, as explained, are functions of our capacity to extract the positive essence of a thing from its negative embodiment. A lesser person has a lesser capacity, so, for him, there are fewer things that can be elevated and set free from the bounds of *kelipah*.[21] Hence, the lower the spiritual stature of a generation, the more things are forbidden to it. And the greater a person is, the greater his capacity to elevate things that lie in the twilight zone that borders on the forbidden.

But particularly in this zone, one must exercise extreme caution. The relation between one who influences and one who is influenced is never one-sided. When a person eats, he transforms the food, and the food transforms him. When a person tells a joke, the joke has an effect upon its teller. The more ambiguous the line between the permissible and the forbidden, the greater the danger that, instead of the person elevating the object or force with which he involves himself, the object or force will drag him down. The greatest people of history are no exception. Rabbi Elazar ben Arakh, of whom the Talmud attests, "if all the sages of Israel were to be on one side of a balance scale, and Rabbi Elazar ben Arakh on the other, he would outweigh them all,"[22] is also reputed to have forgotten all his learning because he pursued a life of luxury.[23] Not that he became involved in anything that is definitively negative, but indulging, as he did, in Phrygian wine and Roman baths, although permitted, is dangerous. All influence is bilateral, and the more a person is involved with a particular thing, the more he is drawn to it, so that he often fails to maintain the approach to it he had when he first began his involvement. We say of God, "You extend Your hand to sinners,"[24] because only God can extend a hand to an iniquitous person without being sullied by the contact; a human being cannot. The problem with all contact with *kelipah* is that a relationship is never one-sided: the influenced influences, and the influencer is influenced.

Because of these dangers, safety fences, in the form of ordinances and prohibitions, must be established. Things that are not negative in themselves must be forbidden because not everyone is capable of dealing with them. The need for these fences varies: in certain generations, many things in the twilight zone of *kelipat nogah* must be declared out of bounds. At other times, the spiritual state of the generation is such that some can go so far as to involve themselves with matters that are on the borders of holiness and still remain within the realm of holiness.

Nevertheless, a trace [of *kelipah*] remains in the body.

Eating like an animal has its positive aspects. Animals only eat as much as they need; they do not overeat and do not eat anything harmful. All the same, when a person eats like an animal, eats for no other purpose than to sustain his physical existence, he belongs to the other side, to the universal order of the profane. At that moment (or hour or day), he is part of the other, nonholy world. This moment creates a vacuum in his holy existence, a vacuum that leaves its mark even when he subsequently returns to the service of God. The lapse can be put right, the wound can be cured, but the scar it leaves behind can never be erased or can be erased only with great difficulty. Practically everything can be repaired—a broken dish can be fixed, a torn limb reattached—but it is much more difficult, if not impossible, to remove all trace of the fact that, sometime in the past, something had been in a state of disrepair.

Therefore the body must undergo the purgatory of the grave, as will be explained later

Chapter 8 takes up this issue.

A corpse is a preprimary source of *tumah* ("ritual impurity"), yet our sages say that the bodies of the righteous do not contaminate.[25] For the source of impurity lies not in the human body itself but is generated in the course of a person's lifetime. Every mundane act, bite of food, or uttered word that is not intended for a holy purpose—even if later elevated to holiness—leaves its imprint on the body. In the words of the prophet Ezekiel, "their iniquities are in their bones."[26] This residue of *kelipah,* which accumulates in the body, must eventually be cleansed. A bucket used to carry out slops can be emptied, cleaned, and used for other purposes; but when it is used time and again, the grime and stench become absorbed in its walls, and it must be thoroughly scoured. "Purgatory of the grave" is this scouring, as Chapter 8 will discuss more fully.

So, too, with regard to the vitality of the drops of semen emitted with animal lust by one who has not sanctified himself at the time of his intimacy with his wife in her state of purity.[27]

Again we speak of a permissible act, relations with one's wife during the clean days of her menstrual cycle. Yet if the sole purpose is the satisfaction of one's physical desire, this, too, is an act that belongs to *kelipah,* though one that can be subsequently elevated to holiness.

Such is not the case, however, with forbidden foods and sexual relations, which derive from the three *kelipot* that are entirely profane. These are tied and bound *(assur)* by the extraneous forces forever, and do not ascend from there

An object that is *assur* is something that cannot break free of its connection with the other side. The possibility of severing this bond and attaining a connection with holiness belongs only to the permitted, which is freely transportable from level to level by the way in which one uses it. The prohibited, however, remains profane. If a person eats a forbidden food, deliberately or accidentally, it remains in its state of profanity, regardless of the person's intentions and subsequent actions.

What is forbidden remains *kelipah* even if a person then uses it to perform a *mitzvah.* A *mitzvah* is a *mitzvah,* and a transgression is a transgression, and the one cannot be offset against the other. A person cannot align his transgressions and *mitzvot* as two columns of figures that amount to a deficit or surplus of virtue. Each occurs on a different plane and has its effect upon the person regardless of what transpires on the other plane. A virtuous act does not reduce the negativity of a sinful act that preceded it, nor is it reduced by it. So even the most wicked of the wicked, even a heretic or an apostate, is duty bound to fulfill every commandment of the Torah. The fact that he is an unrepentant sinner who "even in his lifetime is regarded as dead"[28] is true on one plane, and the fact that he is capable of performing *mitzvot,* and fully obligated to realize this capacity, is equally true on another plane.

until their day comes, when death will be annihilated for all eternity, as is written: "And I will remove the spirit of profanity from the land"[29];

Because that which is forbidden is, by definition, irretrievably bound to evil, its rectification and elevation can come about only with the destruction of evil in the messianic era, when God will transform the very nature of creation.

or until he repents

There is one exception to the rule that the positive essence buried within those objects and acts expressly forbidden by the Torah cannot be extracted by man. The exception is *teshuvah*, "repentance" (literally, "return"), which, on its highest level, has the power to elevate elements that derive from the three utterly profane *kelipot* to holiness.

to such an extent that his willful sins become transformed into merits,

The Talmud speaks of two levels of *teshuvah:* a level on which "one's willful sins are regarded as unintentional sins" and a higher level on which "one's willful sins are regarded as merits."[30]

On the first level, a person's repentance achieves that his sins, even if done deliberately, should be regarded as no more than a mistake. One of the explanations of this phenomenon is that when a person does *teshuvah,* he attains a higher level of awareness,[31] he now knows what he did not know previously, so a deed that, relative to his prior state of mind might be considered willful, is a deed bereft of knowledge and understanding if measured against his current state of awareness. Our sages say that, "A person only sins when a spirit of insanity enters him."[32] The *baal teshuvah* ("penitent") is one who cures himself of this insanity, who now realizes that he performed his previous actions without a true understanding and awareness of their significance. With such repentance, he severs himself from his past and attains new perspective on himself and his life, on his past and his future.

However, this level of *teshuvah* only transforms the person's status vis-à-vis his deed, from deliberate to unknowing, but not the significance of the deed itself. The act remains wholly negative, an act of rebellion against God, an act of utterly profane *kelipah.*

The second level of *teshuvah* involves a much more radical change, for it transforms the very essence of the deed. There is not merely a change of awareness regarding the sin but a transformation of the sin into a merit. It is not only a change in the degree of the sin, from deliberate to something less than deliberate, but its complete reversal into a positive phenomenon.

To achieve this level of return or repentance, a person has to effect a change in his personal existence that is akin to the universal transformation in the end of days when "I will remove the spirit of profanity from the land." He has to undergo a transformation so drastic that his entire being, and all his deeds and thoughts, acquire a new and different significance. In effect, he passes into a new field of reality, where everything is completely different from what it was.

One of the most complicated problems in symmetry is to transform something right-handed into its left-handed symmetrical counterpart. Effecting a transformation from one configuration to another is nearly always possible, but transforming right to left involves completely dislodging the thing from its coordinates and reversing it. The only way to turn a right-hand glove into a left-hand glove is to turn it inside out. The transformation from the *kelipah* to holiness, from deliberate sin to virtue, likewise involves turning everything in one's personal world completely inside out. Another analogue is "the reversal of the clay under the seal"[33] where there is a reversal from left to right, from engraving to embossing. This is the "secret of the seal" referred to in Kabbalistic writings, the secret of inversion.

With *teshuvah* on this level, a person elevates to holiness not only the permitted elements of *kelipat nogah* but even acts and elements of outright evil. His transgressions are not merely mitigated but are completely transformed to good. Thus, also what is forbidden and utterly profane can, in certain circumstances, be rectified even before the "end of days."

How is such repentance achieved? By rousing oneself to a return to God in a manner

which is repentance out of love,

This is as opposed to the standard repentance, which is motivated by one of the various levels of awe and fear,

coming from the depths of the heart,

The "depths of the heart" is what a person truly desires, as opposed to the things he desires only with the more external aspects of the heart. A person might say, "I want to study"; "I want to pray"; "I want to perform *mitzvot*"; but these might not be what he truly desires. The depths of the heart is what a person would do if nothing were compelling him to act in any specific way, if he were truly free to do whatever he desires. *Teshuvah* from the depth of the heart is a *teshuvah* that reaches to the very core of a person's being, transforming his will all the way down to its deepest essence. In its shallower forms, *teshuvah* achieves a change in the garments of the penitent's heart, redirecting some of the expressions of his will; with *teshuvah* from the depth of the heart, the very essence of his will is transformed.

with great love,

"Great love" (*ahavah rabbah*) is love that is greater than the natural love of the soul, love that is greater than life and before which life itself pales to insignificance. Hasidic teaching speaks of two classes of love for God: *ahavat olam* and *ahavah rabbah. Ahavat olam* (literally, "world love") is love that is related to the created reality, the soul's love for God as Creator, as the essence of creation. *Ahavah rabbah* is greater than *ahavat olam,* greater than reality; it is the soul's striving for the essence of God that transcends creation. This is the love termed by the Torah "with all your might,"[34] the soul's yearning to dissolve its very being within God, its Father, as He is in essence, as He transcends His "pervasiveness of the worlds" (*memale kol almin*) and even His "transcendence of the worlds" (*sovev kol almin*)—the level on which He bears no relationship with the worlds at all. Through such love, which transcends the "chain of evolution," a person transforms his entire nature, negates his very being, and is reborn as an entirely new creature.[35]

desire, and the soul's craving to cleave to God

The love of God in this form of *teshuvah* is in a manner of "desire" and "craving"—that is, in the same way that a person desires material things, with the same fervor that he lusts for physical pleasures.

It is told of Rabbi Levi Yitzchak of Berdichev that he was unable to sleep on the first night of Sukkot because of his anticipation to make the blessing on the *etrog* (citron). All night he gazed upon the *etrog,* which sat in a glass-paned cabinet, waiting for morning so that he could recite the blessing over it. When morning came, he could wait no longer. He ran to the case, plunged his hand through the glass, and took out the *etrog,* oblivious to the blood streaming from his hand. It is said that his animal soul had been transformed into a Godly soul: he had a lust for *mitzvot* in the same way as others lust for worldly pleasures. When a person has a physical lust, he might also lie awake all night with "desire and the soul's craving" and crash through glass to satisfy his desire. Such is the love and desire for God on the level of *teshuvah* out of love.

and thirsting for God like a parched desert land.

A paraphrase of Psalms 63:2: "My soul thirsts for You, my flesh craves for You, in a parched, desolate, waterless land."

The uniqueness of this love, and the reason why it redefines one's previous sins, is

For it is because his soul had been, up until now, in a land of drought and death's shadow—the *sitra achra*—and very far from the light of the divine countenance, that his soul now thirsts [for God] with a greater intensity than the souls of the righteous.

The *tzaddik,* too, yearns and craves to cleave to God, but the *baal teshuvah* who attains a love for God experiences this desire far more intensely. The *tzaddik* is immersed in holiness all his life and can, at all times, satiate his desire to cleave to God, so he cannot truly *thirst* for God; he cannot know the acute craving that is born of lack. Only one who traverses a spiritually arid land, who knows true thirst, can experience the full intensity of the soul's desire for God.

The *baal teshuvah*'s love for God is the product of his distance, the result of his having been in "a land of drought and death's shadow." So one who undergoes such a *teshuvah* has his sins transformed into merits. The very sin he committed, his very disconnection and alienation from God, is what now fuels his greater and more intense love of God.

The Talmud tells the story of a penitent who is an exemplar of such *teshuvah.*[36] Elazar ben Dordia was said to have never encountered a harlot without committing a sin with her, until one of them remarked to him that he was beyond repentance. He took her words to heart and decided that he would repent. First, he approached the hills and mountains and asked them to plead for his sake, but they refused.[37] After receiving similar responses from the heavens and the earth and the sun and the moon, he concluded: "If such is the case, all depends solely upon myself." He dropped his head between his knees and began to weep, and he wailed and wept until his soul departed from his body. A voice from heaven announced that "Rabbi Elazar ben Dordia is destined for the world to come." Rabbi Judah HaNassi cried over him and said: "There are those who acquire their world in many years and those who acquire their world in a single moment."

Elazar ben Dordia's *teshuvah* was a return to God out of "great love" that transformed all his sins into merits. The voice from heaven referred to him as "Rabbi" and proclaimed that he was granted a place in the world to come. In a single instant, he had created for himself a virtuous life. So great was his anguish that he simply could not continue living. His yearning on the one hand and his sense of lack on the other affected him so deeply that in a single explosive moment, with a single wrenching movement,[38] he underwent a complete transformation.

Regarding the *teshuvah* of King David, the Book of Psalms has: "When Nathan the Prophet came to him as he had come to Bathsheba."[39] It does not say that Nathan came to rebuke him "on account of" (*al asher*) his coming to Bathsheba but "as" (*ka'asher*) he came to Bathsheba: true *teshuvah* is when a person craves to return to God with the same intensity, with the same turmoil, as the craving he experienced at the time of his sin. The sin does not then become a *mitzvah,* but the *teshuvah* redirects it to function as a *mitzvah* does, as an impetus of bringing a person closer to God.

In the same psalm, David proclaims: "My sin is before me, always."[40] The ultimate rectification of a sin is not to neutralize it, not to remove it as a factor in the person's life, but to continue to act upon the person, continue to impel him to attain level after level of *teshuvah.* The sin is like a stain that penetrates a multilayered substance; as each layer is peeled away, the stain reappears on a deeper and more inner level. By the same token, after the sin is rectified on one level, one achieves the recognition that it still exists on a deeper, subtler level, and one is driven to achieve yet a greater *teshuvah.*

The story is told of a peasant who once insulted the king, but because he did not understand the gravity of what he had done, he could not properly be punished. So he was invited into the palace and given a position in the royal court. His rank was then gradually raised level after level. Thus, he began to appreciate the significance of royalty and the gravity of his offense. As he rose in rank, his appreciation grew; with each level he attained came a deeper regret over his deed. By the same token, the higher a person ascends in holiness, the more he comprehends the depth of his sin; and the greater his recognition of his sin, the greater its power to elevate him to holiness. *Teshuvah* is thus not a onetime act but a continuing process, and as the *baal teshuvah* attains each higher level of *teshuvah,* he understands—with a greater intensity each time—how he must begin doing *teshuvah* all over again.

As we said, there are different types of *teshuvah.* If a person wants to do *teshuvah* in order to fulfill his obligation to repent for his sins, to become an accepted member of the community or be fit to serve as *shochet* ("one authorized to slaughter kosher animals"), the rules for this sort of repentance are found in the *Shulchan Aruch*. On the other hand, *teshuvah* of the sort that "transforms sins into merits" does not give him any "certificate of respectability"; on the contrary, it only deepens his awareness of his sins, rousing him to yet a higher level of *teshuvah* and yet a greater striving to cleave to God. And the lower he had sunk with his sins, the greater—by the same ratio—is his desire for God.

The higher a dam is built, the greater the pressure of water accumulating behind it. The greater a person's sins, the higher a dam it is, stymieing his soul's desire to cleave to God, thereby increasing its pressure and intensity. The desire for God that, in a *tzaddik*'s life, finds instant and immediate realization, accumulates in the soul of the *baal teshuvah* for ten, twenty, or fifty years of sin; and the pressure of the accumulation of sins is so great that he can never alleviate it, until this unceasing pressure becomes a part of the structure of his soul and its incessant striving toward holiness.

As our Sages say: "In the place where penitents stand . . ."

The quotation ends: "even the perfectly righteous cannot stand there."[41] With *teshuvah* out of great love, the penitent attains a level of love for God that represents a place in which the *tzaddik,* who lacks this particular type of love for God, cannot stand.

It is concerning this sort of repentance out of great love that they have said, "Willful sins become like virtues for him," since it is because of them that he has attained this great love.

Through this repentance, through this endless love and tremendous yearning, his entire life has been transformed; his sojourn in "the land of drought and death's shadow" has become a lever that lifts him to a more profound awakening and a greater closeness to God. All his past failings turn out now to be the instruments of his attainments in holiness. Such repentance is not merely a good deed to counteract past evil but the use of the evil in such a way that each past sin is now an impetus to a greater desire and a greater love for God. And when "willful sins" become the instrument for a love of God that is more powerful than the love of a *tzaddik,* the very laws of reality are transformed. This person has undergone a process akin to that of the end of days; he has not brought redemption to the entire world, but he achieves redemption in his own private world, removing "the spirit of profanity" from his individual pathway through life.

But repentance that does not come from such love,

Indeed, not everyone possesses the spiritual capacity to achieve such repentance,

though it be a proper repentance, and God will forgive him,

As the author writes in the first chapter of *Iggeret haTeshuvah* (Part III of *Tanya*), "the *mitzvah* of *teshuvah* as mandated by the Torah is merely the abandonment of sin: that he resolve in his heart never again to repeat his folly and to rebel against the divine sovereignty." Such a penitent indeed severs himself from his past deeds and is no longer responsible for the evil that he has caused in the world.

nevertheless his sins are not transformed into merits,

But even if his past can no longer cast a shadow on his present, nevertheless, he cannot transform and sublimate it. The evil deed remains evil,

and they are not completely released from the *kelipah,* until the end of time, when death will be annihilated for ever.

Only at the end of time, when there will be an utter annihilation of evil, will every element of creation be rectified: the permissible and the forbidden, the repented sins and the unrepented sins. Until such time, the forbidden and bound remain forbidden and bound. A person can alleviate the gravity of the offense against God, changing his relationship with evil and even setting his iniquitous life on an opposite course, but the evil remains evil. Except, as stated, by *teshuvah* of such great, driving, and potent love that transforms reality in the manner of the messianic era, when death shall be annihilated forever.[42]

To illustrate, the author now cites an exception to this rule that illuminates the general rule:

However, the vitality which is in the drops of semen that issue wastefully, though it has been degraded and incorporated in the three profane *kelipot,* nevertheless, it can ascend from there by means of a proper repentance

The wasteful emission of semen is a grave prohibition, which causes a descent into the "three profane *kelipot.*"

and intense concentration during the recital of the Shema at bedtime, as is known from our master Rabbi Isaac Luria, of blessed memory,[43] and is implied in the Talmudic saying: "He who recites the Shema at bedtime is as if he held a double-edged sword . . ."

The quotation continues: "in his hand . . . as it is written,[44] 'The pious rejoice in glory, they sing upon their beds; exaltations of God in their mouths, and a double-edged sword in their hands.'"[45] That is, those who sing the praises of God on their beds by reciting the Shema before sleep have a double-edged sword in their hands

with which to slay the bodies of the extraneous forces that have become garments for the vitality which is in the drops [of semen], so that this vitality may ascend, as is known to those who are familiar with the Esoteric Wisdom.

Our sages tell us that "a person's descendants are his *mitzvot* and good deeds,"[46] and the same is true of his sins and evil deeds. A person generates deeds that translate into realities both good and evil, all of which are his "children." The spiritual essence of a good deed is an angel, a person's emissary on high; the spiritual essence of a sin is a demon, a corrupter and agent of destruction. Angels or demons, they remain bound to him and dependent upon him. They pursue him and call after him: "You are our father! You created us, and it is your responsibility to sustain us!" All afflictions of man, all his suffering and ills, are demons of his creation. He made them, and he is the source of their vitality; they leech on to him, suck his life, and destroy him step by step. *Teshuvah*—in this sense, any proper repentance—helps to sever this link, and in certain cases, such as the sin of wasteful emission, it even kills these demons and blots them entirely out of existence.

This is why the sin of wasteful emission of semen is not mentioned in the Torah among the forbidden coitions,

The Torah contains a detailed list of forbidden unions but does not mention wasting semen among them. The only reference is in the story of Judah's sons Er and Onan (Genesis 38) and even there not as an explicit law but implicit within a story. (However, some halakhic authorities include this among the 613 *mitzvot*.)[47]

although it is even more severe than they, and its iniquity is greater in regard to the enormity and abundance of the impurity and of the *kelipot* which he begets and multiplies to an exceedingly great extent through wasteful emission of semen, even more than through forbidden coitions.

A fundamental characteristic of evil is waste, destruction, and death; and this element is present in every forbidden union. In this sense, every forbidden union is a destruction of life. Hence, the sin of wasteful emission is worse than any forbidden union, for it entails utter waste. There is no receiving vessel; the vital potential in the drops is wasted completely. So this sin possesses a negativity that is greater and more profound than any forbidden relation.

But in the case of forbidden coitions he contributes strength and vitality to a most unclean *kelipah,* from which he is powerless to bring up the vitality by means of repentance,

The author proceeds to explain this in a note:

Note: The reason being that this vitality has been absorbed by the female element of the *kelipah,* which receives and absorbs the vitality from the holiness. Not so with wasteful emission of semen, where there is no female element of *kelipah,* and only its powers and forces enclothe the vitality in the semen, as is known to those familiar with the Esoteric Wisdom.

The possibility of rectifying the sin of wasteful emission is not because it is less serious a sin; on the contrary, the negativity of this sin is more profound than that of other sexual sins, and it touches on the very essence of evil. However, precisely because this sin entails such utter destruction, precisely because there is no vessel that receives it, it can more readily be rectified. Because it was not absorbed by another being, it also does not become part of any other reality; it does not become part of the complex systems that make up reality. Its severity lies in that it is wholly one-directional, being an emission of life that is not received by any vessel (that is, any female element). It is for that very reason that it does not become rooted in reality; the person can, with a proper repentance, entirely obliterate its negative embodiment, which is spiritual rather than physical. He cannot transform it and redirect it (as *teshuvah* out of great love transforms sins into merits), but he can destroy it and render it utterly nonexistent, as if it never was. On the other hand, regarding other forbidden unions, because they do not entail an utter destruction, because the life force is received by and absorbed within a female element, the sin is etched in reality. There remains a black hole, a blot of evil, and this blot cannot be eradicated with an ordinary *teshuvah*,

unless he repents with such great love that his willful wrongs are transformed into merits.

Thus one may understand the comment of our Sages: "Which is 'a deformation that cannot be rectified'? Having incestuous intercourse and giving birth to a bastard." For in such a case, even though the sinner undertakes such great repentance, he cannot cause the vitality to ascend to Holiness, since it has already descended into this world and has been clothed in a body of flesh and blood.

When it is said of a particular sin that a person cannot do *teshuvah* for it, this does not mean that he cannot repent and be forgiven for his wrongdoing. A person can always repent so that his sins will no longer be recalled to his detriment, and he can always wrench himself from the vicious cycle where "one sin leads to another";[48] but the sin itself is not blotted out.

Thus, the Talmud speaks of sins such as theft and robbery as "a deformation that can be rectified"[49]—what was stolen can be restored—whereas murder and begetting a *mamzer* (a halakhically defined bastard) are examples of what King Solomon calls "a deformation that cannot be rectified"[50] (though there are cases, as in the story of the *baal teshuvah* for whom the work *Pokeach Ivrim* was written,[51] of people who repented so intensely that the children born of their sins died). The existence of a *mamzer* implies that the sin has become rooted in reality, and the sinner cannot uproot it. However lofty his *teshuvah*, however it might elevate him to holiness, the reality of his sin cannot be undone. His deed has taken on a physical, living form and has assumed an objective reality of its own.

The more spiritual a sin is, the uglier and more negative it is likely to be and the more likely to reach to the very essence of evil. Yet at the same time, doing *teshuvah* for such a sin is easier, as nothing physical has to be changed. On the other hand, a sin whose consequences are physically recognizable within our reality remains "a deformation that cannot be rectified." Even if the sinner is rectified and is absolved of all connection with and responsibility for the deed, the deed itself is not rectified.

The author's purpose in this chapter is not to detail types of sin and their appropriate repentance (such is not the subject nor the nature of this book) but to point to junctures in the cosmic map of good and evil. The purpose of the book is to explain the unique role of man in the various realms, in the side of holiness and the other side. But for man to know how to wage the war of life, he requires a map to guide him: here is the holy side; here is the other side. As already explained, one cannot know the demarcation of good and evil solely from the halakhic definitions; there are further definitions that are not derived from these, which need to be grasped and comprehended.

At the heart of our chapter is the distinction between what is forbidden and bound (*assur*) and what is permitted and unbound (*muttar*); between *kelipat nogah* and the three utterly profane *kelipot*. But the latter is for purposes of definition only: the *Tanya* does not deal with what is forbidden; these are "alien demons," not Jewish temptations. The subject of the book is matters that are permitted. These are the problems that face our author's Jew, the hero of the book, the *beinoni*.

Chapter 8

⎯∿⎯ T here is an additional aspect in the matter of forbidden foods. The reason they are called *issur* ("bound") is that even in the case of one who has unwittingly eaten a forbidden food, and he did so for the sake of Heaven, with the intention to serve God with the energy derived from it, and he has, moreover, actually carried out his intention, having studied and prayed with the energy from that food, nevertheless, the vitality contained therein does not ascend and become clothed in the words of the Torah or prayer, as is the case with permitted foods, by reason of its being bound (*issur*) in the hands of the *sitra achra* of the three profane *kelipot*. This is so even when the prohibition is a rabbinic enactment, for "The words of the Scribes are even more stringent than the words of the Torah. . . ."

Therefore, also the evil impulse (*yetzer hara*) and the lust for forbidden things is a demon of the alien demons, which is the evil impulse of the nations of the world whose souls are derived from the three profane *kelipot.* On the other hand, the evil impulse and the lust for permissible things to satisfy a desire is a demon of the Jewish demons, for it can be reverted to holiness, as explained above.

Nevertheless, before it has reverted to holiness, it is *sitra achra* and *kelipah,* and even afterwards a trace of it remains attached to the body, since from each item of food and drink are immediately formed blood and flesh of his flesh. This is why the body must undergo the "purgatory of the grave"—in order to cleanse it and purify it of its profanity, which it had received from the enjoyment of material things and pleasures which are derived from the profanity of *kelipat nogah* and of the Jewish demons; except for one who had derived no enjoyment from this world all his life, as was the case with Our Holy Master.

As for permissible idle chatter, such as in the case of an ignoramus who cannot study, he must undergo a cleansing of his soul, to rid it of the profanity of this *kelipah,* through its being rolled in "the hollow of a sling," as stated in *Zohar, Parashat Beshallach,* p. 59.

But with regard to forbidden speech, such as scoffing and speaking ill [of another] and the like, which stem from the three completely profane *kelipot,* "the hollow of a sling" alone does not suffice to cleanse and remove the profanity of the soul, but it must descend into Gehenna.

So, too, one who is able to occupy himself with Torah, but occupies himself instead with idle chatter, "the hollow of a sling" cannot itself effectively scour and cleanse his soul, but severe penalties are meted out for neglect of the Torah in particular, apart from the general retribution for the neglect of a positive commandment through indolence, namely, in the "Gehenna of snow," as is explained elsewhere.

Likewise, one who occupies himself with the sciences of the nations of the world, this is considered as "idle chatter" insofar as the sin of neglecting the Torah is concerned, as is explained in *The Laws of Torah Study.* Moreover, the profanity of the science of the nations is greater than that of idle chatter. For the latter enclothes and profanes only the *middot* which derive from the element of the holy *ruach* within his Godly soul, contaminating them with the profanity of the *kelipat nogah* that is contained in idle chatter which is derived from the element of the evil *ruach* of this *kelipah* in his animal soul, as mentioned above; but it does not profane the faculties of *ChaBaD* in his soul, for these are but words of foolishness and ignorance, for even fools and ignoramuses can speak that way. Not so in the case of the science of the nations, whereby one clothes and profanes the *ChaBaD* of his Godly soul with the profanity of the *kelipat nogah* contained in those sciences, whither they have fallen through the shattering of the vessels from the hinder parts [*chokhmah*] of holiness, as is known to those familiar with the Esoteric Wisdom. Unless he employs [these sciences] as a useful instrument—that is, as a means for a more affluent livelihood to be able to serve God—or he knows how to apply them in the service of God or His Torah. This is the reason why

Maimonides and Nachmanides, of blessed memory, and their adherents, engaged in them.

COMMENTARY

Chapter 7 discussed the *kelipot* (the "husks," the nonholy elements that are extraneous to the holy essence of creation), particularly the difference between *kelipat nogah* (the "luminescent husk") and the three profane *kelipot*. It explained that the realm of the permitted in *kelipat nogah* and the realm of the forbidden in the three profane *kelipot* do not differ essentially, because permitted things that are not done with active holy intent also belong to *kelipah*. The difference between forbidden things on the one hand and permitted things done without holy intent on the other is only in whether or not they can be subsequently rectified and raised to holiness. At the beginning of this chapter, the author presents another distinction between permitted and forbidden, regarding the case when they *are* done with holy intent.

There is an additional aspect in the matter of forbidden foods. The reason they are called *issur* ("bound") is that even in the case of one who has unwittingly eaten a forbidden food, and he did so for the sake of Heaven, with the intention to serve God with the energy derived from it, and he has, moreover, actually carried out his intention, having studied and prayed with the energy from that food,

Had he done this with a permitted food, this would have been as virtuous an act as can be. As Chapter 7 explained, such an act is akin to the bringing of a *korban*, an "offering" upon the altar in the *Beit haMikdash* ("the Holy Temple"): a mundane object has been elevated to holiness. However, because this was a forbidden act, such as eating nonkosher food, even if he was in error or completely blameless—because he did not know or had no way of knowing that it is forbidden—

nevertheless, the vitality contained therein does not ascend and become clothed in the words of the Torah or prayer, as is the case with permitted foods,

Although there is no willful transgression on the part of the person, the offering to God is not accepted. Regarding the *korbanot* ("offerings"), certain laws govern what is fit and what is not fit to ascend from the altar, and if something that is not fit is offered, even by mistake, even if the one who offers it is completely blameless, God does not accept the offering, for it is contrary to His will. By the same token, the energy within the nonkosher food cannot ascend to holiness,

by reason of its being bound (*issur*) in the hands of the *sitra achra* of the three profane *kelipot*.

Issur ("forbidden," "bound") and *heiter* ("permitted," "unbound") are not subjective concepts; they do not relate to the person, nor does the person define them by his knowledge and awareness. A person's knowledge or ignorance does not alter the basic definition of a thing as *issur* or *heiter*. A positive intention, such as the intent "for the sake of Heaven," for a holy purpose, does not prevent something forbidden from being forbidden. The nature of the forbidden thing is not altered by a person's intentions, because the prohibition is objective, relating to the composition, nature, and characteristics of the thing itself and not to what somebody happens to think about it.

This conception of good and evil rejects the emotional and subjective view many have of these definitions, the outlook by which everything is assessed according to a person's intentions. This view does not recognize the concept of an act that is intrinsically evil, but it does recognize personal sins, acts that derive from the intention to do evil; the act itself, the reality of its being done or not, is devoid of significance. But the concept of *issur* as defined here is not a factor of the person's conscious desire to transgress the divine will but of the fact that he did so, even if unintentionally. An evil intention, a deliberate rebellion against God, is a sin in its own right, but it does not in any way define what is in the realm of the forbidden.

This is not to diminish the significance of intent, as stated in Chapter 7: intent has the power to elevate something merely permitted into the realm of holiness or to degrade it to the lowest levels of *kelipah*. But intent cannot transform forbidden into permitted. A person who intends to take a drink of water but inadvertently drinks poison had no adverse intentions, and the fact that his was a totally blameless mistake (for example, the poison was in a bottle marked as water) might subjectively justify his action, but none of this can alter the fact that he drank poison. The Torah's prohibition of something is a definition of its nature; just as there are healthy foods and poisonous substances, so, too, there are things that are objectively holy and things that are objectively *issur*.

This is so even when the prohibition is a rabbinic enactment, for "The words of the Scribes are even more stringent than the words of the Torah. . . ."

This applies not only to items that the Torah forbids, which we can more readily relate to as an objective definition, but also to rabbinic prohibitions, which appear to be subjective and human definitions. "The words of the Scribes are even more stringent than the words of the Torah," says the Talmud.[1] This is based on the assumption (which the author does not discuss here) that the rabbis have the power to decree that from this point on, this or that thing is *assur*—objectively evil—so that it now belongs to the three completely profane *kelipot*.

Therefore, also the evil impulse (*yetzer hara*) and the lust for forbidden things is a demon of the alien demons, which is the evil impulse of the nations of the world whose souls are derived from the three profane *kelipot.*

The impulse that may drive a person to do an evil act that belongs to the three profane *kelipot*—an act that cannot be rectified—is an alien impulse, an impulse that belongs to a non-Jewish soul, which derives from those *kelipot*. The animal soul of the Jew derives from *kelipat nogah*, so its negative impulses are also *kelipat nogah* impulses—impulses for deeds that, though negative, can be rectified. The essence of the Jew is "rectification" (*tikkun*), so everything Jewish is rectifiable. This is not to say that a Jew cannot sin with something forbidden; the fact is that he can, sometimes even more determinedly and enthusiastically than a non-Jew, but then he is behaving un-Jewishly, embracing tendencies that are unnatural to the Jewish soul.

The Midrash *Tanna deVei Eliahu* speaks extensively of "ugly" sins versus "nonugly" sins, a distinction that is not halakhic but instinctive. By this conception, some sins, in addition to being forbidden, are repulsive, when committed by a Jew. Even in our permissive generation, in which the borderlines between good and evil, right and wrong, are much more blurred, some desires are still considered abnormal. There are normal sins and deeds that are considered aberrant for a human being, as being outside the norms of human behavior. In this sense, "Jewish demons"[2] are temptations that are a part of the struggle within the Jewish soul and the challenges a Jew faces in his service of God—part of normal Jewish life—whereas "alien demons" are nonrectifiable temptations and thus beyond the context of the Jew's mission in life. A Jew who is tempted by them is not normal; he is beyond the definitions of Jewish behavior. A Jew who lives within the Jewish norm, whose struggles and doubts are all within the context of his Jewishness, is one whose lusts and even sins are confined to the sphere of *kelipat nogah*.

On the other hand, the evil impulse and the lust for permissible things to satisfy a desire is a demon of the Jewish demons, for it can be reverted to holiness, as explained above.

Some demons are Jewish demons, products of the Jewish experience. These demons are experts in Torah, acting entirely within the framework of halakhah; this *kelipah* is fully kosher and *heiter,* and its essence is rectifiable and can be elevated to holiness.

One of the problems with demons is that they are usually represented in surreal forms, so we do not recognize them in actuality. Literature and art represent demons in half-comical forms, and therefore, when we look for the chicken's claw or the goat's horns, we fail to identify the very human demons in our life. The truth is that the demon is not a stranger to man; he does not come from without but from within. Man himself produced him, with his thoughts, speech, and actions; and from that point on, the demon is attached to him; it is his offspring; it feeds on him, sucks him dry, and ultimately destroys him.

The verse "Sin crouches at the door and its desire is to you"[3] expresses the complex relationship between a person and his evil. It is not a confrontational relationship but a complex, mutual, love-hate relationship. Evil is a parasite that strives to attach itself to man, for man is its only source of nourishment; evil devours man because it lives and feeds by consuming its host.

This complex relationship exists even when a person rejects evil: even as he strives to do *teshuvah* ("repentance") and rectify his evil deeds, his desire for evil still exists; and if he is not careful, he is liable to sink into the very morass from which he is seeking to extricate himself. Often, in the very midst of the regret, distress, pain, and disgust for evil one experiences while doing *teshuvah,* a person might repeat the very sins he is repenting and with an even greater intensity than before. The demons, "the plague of man,"[4] are created by man, but they then assume an existence of their own, reproducing and multiplying until they strangle a person. This is not because they desire his demise but because they must destroy him in order to continue to exist.

Jewish demons, then, are the demons created by Jews, out of the Jewish *yetzer harah* and Jewish sins, which, as explained, derive not from the three profane *kelipot* but from *kelipat nogah,* which is never completely severed from holiness. Theirs is therefore not a complete profanity,

for it can be reverted to holiness, as explained above.

As explained in Chapter 7, regardless of whether a person eats a forbidden or a permitted food, if he eats it only to satisfy a physical need or desire, he is reduced to *kelipah* in the same degree. The difference is only that the act of eating a permissible food can be rectified.

On a deeper level, however, a rectifiable sin is essentially different from a nonrectifiable sin. It is said in the name of several *tzaddikim* that a Jew never fully sins. The Jewish demon created by his transgressions is always missing one limb or the other. It can never be wholly evil, because the act that generates it is never wholehearted. A Jewish sin always contains an iota of good intent; there is at least an assumption that the matter can subsequently be put right. The author develops this idea later on as one of the foundations of this book. A Jew cannot sin with a complete sense of abandonment of and severance from his God. Indeed, he is capable of sin at all only because he does not do so completely, because he assumes that he is still a Jew and has a way back.

The story is told of two friends who, in their youth, were both the disciples of the same rebbe. In the course of time, one became a commissar in the Communist Party, while the other remained a God-fearing Jew. One day, they met, and the latter asked the commissar, "I wonder, does anything remain with you of all the years that we studied together?" The commissar replied: "Sinning. I sin a lot, but I get no true satisfaction from it."

The fact that a Jew cannot fully enjoy his sins derives from the fact that he cannot fully intend to sin. Paradoxically, what does not allow him to sin completely is what allows him to sin at all. This is his justification, his dispensation for committing a sin. The connecting thread between the Jew and God that is never completely severed, obscure and contradictory as it may be, turns the sin into something else. The sin is never complete, either in pleasure or in pain, for the possibility of rectification always remains.

Nevertheless, before it has reverted to holiness, it is *sitra achra* and *kelipah,* and even afterwards a trace of it remains attached to the body, since from each item of food and drink are immediately formed blood and flesh of his flesh.

In order for a person's eating to be holy, there must be holy intent at the time; otherwise, he allows the *sitra achra* ("other side") to infiltrate his being. When that happens, the fact of his profane eating is impressed within reality; a stain is formed, which is never completely removable. If the deed was permissible, it can be rectified, but the profanity it spawned remains ingrained in the person's body as "blood and flesh of his flesh."

By way of analogy, exposure to radiation above a certain intensity can prove fatal. But also a lesser dose is destructive in the long term. Although the person is not immediately killed, a steady process of deterioration begins, from the time of the exposure and onward. Or, to cite another example, some poisons, such as lead, ingested even in the smallest of quantities, can never be removed. Any immediate damage can usually be overcome, but the cumulative effect over time, as more and more of that material enters the body, can be extremely dangerous. In the same way, every nonholy act, even if permitted, even if rectified and elevated to holiness, leaves a mark of profanity. Thus, a person can degenerate spiritually merely by doing things that are permitted by *Shulchan Aruch.* The steady accumulation of mundane actions is liable to draw him out of the realm of holiness. A decent person who never deliberately commits a sin, who merely allows himself a so-called normal life, can, in the half-hour or afternoon he devoted to activities devoid of holiness, create a mark of profanity in his body that cannot be removed.

This is why the body must undergo the "purgatory of the grave"—in order to cleanse it and purify it of its profanity, which it had received from the enjoyment of material things and pleasures which are derived from the profanity of *kelipat nogah* and of the Jewish demons;

"Purgatory of the grave" (*chibbut hakever*) is the suffering the body endures in death and its deterioration and decomposition in the grave, which is a punishment and atonement for the body.[5]

except for one who had derived no enjoyment from this world all his life, as was the case with Our Holy Master.

"Our holy master" (*Rabbeinu HaKadosh*) is a name for Rabbi Judah HaNassi (second century C.E.), compiler of the Mishnah. Rabbi Judah was an extremely wealthy man and lived his entire life surrounded by luxury and opulence. Yet before his passing, he was able to proclaim: "Master of the Universe! It is known and revealed to You that I have toiled with all ten fingers in Torah, and have never benefited [from the material world] even with the little finger."[6] This was not asceticism and self-denial but the ability not to partake of anything for oneself, to be surrounded by all the pleasure of this world and not enjoy it at all for the sake of satisfying one's own desire and fulfilling one's own will. A person who lives such a life is holy; his body, too, is holy and does not require cleansing or purification after death.

The body is not profane in itself. The body is profane because it is contaminated, because it accumulates the residue of all the profane things that were done with it and that passed through it. These are not necessarily things that are forbidden halakhically but even things that can be, and have been, rectified. But because at some point the act belonged to *kelipah,* a stain of profanity remains, a remnant of filth, even when this point has passed and the act has been elevated. Sewage can be purified to make it drinkable, but a foul smell adheres to the machinery and vessels employed in the purification process. In this sense, the body, through which so much spiritual "sewage" passes in the course of a lifetime due to the animalistic, material existence it leads, is like a sewage-treatment plant and must be scoured to remove the stink that adheres to it. On the other hand, the body of one who leads a wholly sacred life has no reason to be profane. This is why "the bodies of the righteous do not contaminate," as mentioned in Chapter 7. Their bodies no longer contain life, but there is none of the profanity (*tumah*) normally associated with a corpse.

Up to this point, the author has discussed the *kelipah* that arises from physical enjoyments of the body, such as eating and drinking. Now, he turns to nonphysical *kelipot.*

As for permissible idle chatter, such as in the case of an ignoramus who cannot study,

The Jew is commanded to devote every available moment to Torah study, and failing to do so is a grave sin, as the author mentioned in Chapter 1. It would therefore follow that engaging in "idle chatter" (*devarim beteilim*)—that is, talk that serves no purpose—will always constitute a transgression. Here, however, the author wants to cite an example of talk that is *kelipat nogah,* that is, mundane but permissible. So he cites the example of a Jew who is unable to study (for example, due to a lack of literacy or intellectual ability), so that his idle chatter is not a sin, because it does not take the place of Torah study.

he must undergo a cleansing of his soul, to rid it of the profanity of this *kelipah,* through its being rolled in "the hollow of a sling," as stated in *Zohar, Parashat Beshallach,* p. 59.

Just as the body requires a "purgatory of the grave" to cleanse and purify it because it served, albeit temporarily, as a channel of profanity, so must the soul be purified of the profanity arising, for example, from idle chatter, through the "hollow of a sling" (*kaf hakela*). This is a concept taken from the remarks of Abigail to David: "But my lord's soul will be bound in the bundle of life with the Lord your God, and the souls of your enemies will be slung in the hollow of a sling."[7] The Talmud interprets this to say that the souls of the wicked are "bound up, and an angel stands at one end of the universe and another at the other end, and they hurl the souls with a sling from one to the other."[8] In other places,[9] the author explains the "hollow of the sling" as the experience of the soul that is repeatedly confronted with its failings in the course of its lifetime in this world. It is hurled "from one end of the universe to the other" as it is wrenched, over and over again, between its present state as a being aware of the divine truth and desiring to cleave to its source in God and the pettiness and profanity of its past actions.

In our experience, we know this as the agony of memory: remembering and reexperiencing past traumas is a major factor in much of our spiritual suffering. Our ability to forget past suffering is a defense mechanism, enabling us to continue living and carry on in the future. In the "hollow of the sling," the soul is compelled to review its past life and relive it, this time not as a participant but merely as an objective observer. This process, apart from the pain it brings, is a process of purification (as, in a very different way, is psychoanalysis), of recalling and reviewing the past in a new light.

All souls, except for those who never involved themselves in the mundane aspects of this world (such as Rabbi Judah the Prince, Our Holy Master), must undergo the process of being hurled in "the hollow of the sling." This is not a punishment per se but rather a technical, almost automatic, stage in the soul's journey to a higher world. A soul that formed an attachment to frivolous things while in the body remains attached to them also when it leaves it, and in that state it cannot enter *Gan Eden* ("paradise"). The nature of *Gan Eden* is that one "enjoys the glow of the divine presence"[10]; the unpurified soul, even if it were smuggled into *Gan Eden,* would find the experience meaningless, as one cannot enjoy divinity when one's enjoyment still lies in earthly matters.

The author's grandson, Rabbi Menachem Mendel of Lubavitch (known as the *Tzemach Tzeddek*), told the story of a wagon driver who performed a great *mitzvah* and saved the life of a Jew. When this man died, the heavenly court did not know how to reward him. He had performed a great *mitzvah,* but being a boor and a very coarse man, he would not be able to appreciate the spiritual pleasures of *Gan Eden,* as *tzaddikim* do. So they decided to ask him what he would like. He asked for a new wagon with six mighty horses. To this day, he drives this wagon with its six horses along a straight smooth road to infinity.

Without a certain reconditioning, a soul cannot enter *Gan Eden,* because there is nothing for it to do there. A free ticket to a concert is not a present that a person who does not appreciate music can enjoy. Likewise, a soul cannot simply be given a ticket to *Gan Eden.* If it does not have the capacity to appreciate what it will find there, it won't be in *Gan Eden* at all but in limbo. Thus, the "hollow of the sling" is not a punishment or chastisement but a refinement that a soul must undergo in order to proceed to its destination. The soul need not undergo any transformation—it is essentially and inherently divine—only a process of divestment of the experiences of the material world, in order to attain a higher level of existence.

But with regard to forbidden speech, such as scoffing and speaking ill [of another] and the like, which stem from the three completely profane *kelipot,*

When a person scoffs at things that it is forbidden to scoff at—that is, scoffing that insults a fellow human being—this is not just idle chatter but a sin in itself, something that is *assur* and cannot be made right by holy intention. (Thus, this is not the "causality" that Chapter 1 mentioned, which is from *kelipat nogah*—that is, the permissible element of *kelipah.*)[11] Speaking ill of another (*lashon hara*) is another outright prohibition performed through speech. It is a grave sin not only to slander and defame a fellow by means of falsehoods but also to relate a truth that is to his detriment. This, too, is speech that is bound to the evil of the three totally profane *kelipot,* for which "the hollow of a sling" alone does not suffice to cleanse and remove the profanity of the soul, but it must descend into Gehenna.

The only exception is if a person repents the sin.

The author now cites another example of speech that belongs to the three profane *kelipot:*

So, too, one who is able to occupy himself with Torah, but occupies himself instead with idle chatter, "the hollow of a sling" cannot itself effectively scour and cleanse his soul,

As mentioned earlier, for a person who is capable of Torah study, idle chatter is not a permissible mundane act but a prohibition. The Talmud expresses itself is quite vehemently, interpreting the verse "those who forsake God shall perish"[12] as referring to those who leave the books of Torah and go out. This is not just an act of omission, a failure to do something, but rather an act of commission, an active abandonment of the Torah.

but severe penalties are meted out for neglect of the Torah in particular, apart from the general retribution for the neglect of a positive commandment through indolence, namely, in the "Gehenna of snow," as is explained elsewhere.[13]

The assumption is that a person who is able to study Torah and does something else instead acts out of laziness, and the punishment for laziness is the "Gehenna of snow." There are two types of Gehenna: one of fire (intense heat) and one of snow (intense cold). The Gehenna of fire is the punishment for possessing too much ardor, for having wanted too much, having done too much, and having pursued what one should not have pursued. The Gehenna of snow is the punishment for not possessing enough ardor, for not having desired, not having done, and not having pursued all the *mitzvot* that one ought to have desired, done, and pursued.

Likewise, one who occupies himself with the sciences of the nations of the world, this is considered as "idle chatter" insofar as the sin of neglecting the Torah is concerned,

The sin of neglect of Torah is so severe that what a person does instead, whether nonsense or profound intellectual study, does not make any difference. There is no real difference between discussing the price of shoes and delving into philosophy, if it is in place of the pursuit of Torah.

as is explained in *The Laws of Torah Study*,[14]

The Laws of Torah Study (*Hilkhot Talmud Torah*, published in Shklov in 1794) is Rabbi Schneur Zalman's first published work (see "The Title Page" at the front of this book). This slim book is a unique and complete work in itself. It is more stimulating than the Laws of Torah Study section in the original *Shulchan Aruch* (of Rabbi Joseph Karo) and more conceptually complete than even the Laws of Torah Study section in *The Book of Knowledge* (the first book of Maimonides' monumental halakhic work, *Mishneh Torah*). In addition to its halakhic overview of the laws pertaining to Torah study, Rabbi Schneur Zalman's work includes a philosophical overview of the qualities and significance of the Torah. Maimonides, too, considers the theoretical side of the laws, but throughout *The Book of Knowledge*, there is a certain lack of integration between the halakhic aspects and the conceptual aspects of the laws. Rabbi Schneur Zalman's work has a greater unity and coherence, with the particular laws and the conceptions of Torah and Torah study producing an integral, unified structure.

Moreover, the profanity of the science of the nations is greater than that of idle chatter. For the latter enclothes and profanes only the *middot* which derive from the element of the holy *ruach* within his Godly soul, contaminating them with the profanity of the *kelipat nogah* that is contained in idle chatter which is derived from the element of the evil *ruach* of this *kelipah* in his animal soul, as mentioned above;[15] but it does not profane the faculties of *ChaBaD* in his soul, for these are but words of foolishness and ignorance, for even fools and ignoramuses can speak that way.

Idle chatter is profane because it is not for the sake of heaven. As we have elaborated, anything that does not serve a holy purpose is profane. Just as a person can be alive or dead but not in some intermediate state between the two, so, too, whatever is not for the sake of heaven is profane; for the very definition of *kelipah* is its nonholiness. Thus, idle chatter, which is devoid of all meaning and content, belongs to the profane. However, it derives only from the *middot* ("emotional attributes") of *kelipah*, because nonsensical talk is a derivative of the person's emotional self. Idle chatter involves only the base, instinctive faculties of the soul, not its intellect. So when a person occupies himself with idle chatter, he contaminates only the *middot* of his Godly soul, while its faculties of mind—*chokhmah* ("wisdom"), *binah* ("understanding"), and *daat* ("knowledge") (*ChaBaD*)—are not involved, compromised, or contaminated.

Not so in the case of the science of the nations, whereby one clothes and profanes the *ChaBaD* of his Godly soul

However, when a person involves himself in philosophy, science, or any other secular pursuit that uses the intellectual powers of *chokhmah, binah,* and *daat,* his spiritual investment is far deeper. This is not just external involvement, as when someone talks in a superficial way, but involvement of all the highest faculties of the soul, to the extent that the soul is "unified" (as discussed in Chapter 5) with its profane subject matter.

As in the case of idle chatter, the author is speaking of secular studies that do not, in themselves, contain any forbidden element but are halakhically neutral, involving no transgression but also no holy purpose. So as long as they are not used to a Godly end, they belong to *kelipat nogah.* For something to belong to *kelipat nogah,* it need not be evil (in the sense that forbidden things belonging to the three profane *kelipot* are); it suffices that it contains no inner aspect of holiness. Thus, whenever a person involves himself in something that lacks holiness, even if it is intellectually lofty and profound, he contaminates his soul

with the profanity of the *kelipat nogah* contained in those sciences,

Indeed, the more lofty and profound this science is, the more interesting and stimulating to the mind, the more a person invests his soul in it—and the more he contaminates it.

whither they have fallen through the shattering of the vessels from the hinder parts of [*chokhmah*] of holiness, as is known to those familiar with the Esoteric Wisdom

They are those knowledgeable in Kabbalah. The source and nature of nonholy wisdom is a complex Kabbalistic issue, which we cannot thoroughly deal with here. Generally speaking, the consensus in Kabbalah is that "the shattering of the vessels" that generated *kelipah* occurred only in the seven lower attributes—the *middot*—but not in the three higher attributes, the intellectual qualities of *chokhmah, binah,* and *daat* (as alluded by the verse, "They die but not in [*chokhmah*]").[16] According to this, the existence of profane *chokhmah* seems impossible. This is why the author emphasizes that the "sciences of the nations" fell from "hinder parts" of the supernal *chokhmah,* not of its inner element, regarding which there was indeed no death or fall to profanity.[17]

Unless he employs [these sciences] as a useful instrument

A person may pursue a secular science as a profession by which to earn his livelihood, just as another takes up shoemaking as his livelihood. The subject itself is not forbidden, but so long as it serves no holy purpose, it constitutes an independent cause, which is the definition of *kelipah.* So just as eating can be rectified and elevated by using it for holy purposes—that is, serving God—so, too, can a secular science be rectified and elevated when a person uses it to support a life in the service of God.

—that is, as a means for a more affluent livelihood to be able to serve God—

Furthermore, even if such a profession demands a deeper spiritual involvement on the part of the person than, say, a life of shoemaking, nevertheless, it is justified by the fact that it will earn him a more comfortable living, increasing the quantity and quality of the time and energy he will be able to devote to his holy pursuits.

or he knows how to apply them in the service of God or His Torah. This is the reason why Maimonides and Nachmanides, of blessed memory, and their adherents, engaged in them.

Secular sciences can assist in the service of God not only indirectly, such as through providing a livelihood, but also directly, if the knowledge itself is used to serve God. If a person studies philosophy to clarify for himself the ways of serving God, if he studies astronomy to see how "the heavens relate the glory of God,"[18] or if he studies other sciences in order to devise ways of better fulfilling the *mitzvot,* his pursuit of these studies constitutes a part of his service of God. The chapters on astronomy that Maimonides included in the beginning of *The Book of Knowledge* are not a professional study of astronomy but part of his halakhic work, *Mishneh Torah.* Maimonides' astronomy makes him think not of Ptolemy (as was said of Copernicus) but of God. His assumption is that the more one knows about creation, the more one knows about the Creator.

The greatness of the Creator can be inferred not only from astronomy. Once, looking at a tiny worm in the sand, one rabbi remarked: "People think that only 'The heavens relate the glory of God,' but how much divine glory is there in a tiny worm!" There is a saying, attributed to the Gaon of Vilna, that when someone lacks one part in science, he lacks nine parts in knowledge of Torah.[19] Science aids the understanding of Torah, and even the logical comparison of different systems can be a stimulating tool in studying Torah. Thus, when a person pursues secular knowledge in one of the above manners, he does to it what he does to the bread he eats for the sake of heaven: he transforms *kelipah* into holiness.

One can say that this chapter completes the map delineating the boundaries of good and evil, holiness and *kelipah, kelipat nogah* and the profane *kelipot.* In the following chapters, the author considers the person: what transpires and what processes he should initiate within his soul. First, he describes the extreme categories, the *tzaddik* and the *rasha;* then he proceeds to explain the *beinoni,* to whom *Tanya,* the "Book of Intermediates," is primarily directed.

Chapter 9

The abode of the animal soul derived from the *kelipat nogah* in every Jew is in the heart, in the left ventricle that is filled with blood, as it is written, "For the blood is the soul." Thus, all lusts and boasting and anger and similar passions are in the heart, and from the heart they spread throughout the entire body, rising also to the brain in the head, so as to think and meditate about them and become cunning in them, just as the blood has its source in the heart and from the heart it circulates to all organs and limbs, rising also to the brain in the head.

But the abode of the Godly soul is in the brains that are in the head, and from there it extends to all organs and the limbs; and also in the heart, in the right ventricle in which there is no blood, as is written, "The heart of the wise man is on his right." This is the love of God which flares like flaming coals in the heart of the perspicacious, who understand and reflect with the *daat* faculty of their mind on matters that arouse this love; [it is] also the gladness of the heart in the beauty of God and the majesty of His glory [which is aroused] when "the eyes of the wise man that are in his head"— [that is,] the mind-faculties of [*chokhmah*] and *binah*—gaze upon the glory of the King and beauty of His greatness that are unfathomable and without end or limit, as explained elsewhere; as also the other holy affections (*middot*) in the heart that originate from *ChaBaD* in the mind.

It is written, however, "Nation over nation shall strengthen itself." For the body is called a "small city": just as two kings wage war over a city, each wishing to capture it and rule over it, that is to say, to govern its inhabitants according to his will so that they obey him in all that he decrees for them, so do the two souls—the Godly [soul] and the vitalizing animal [soul] that derives from *kelipah*—wage war against each other over the body and all its organs and limbs.

The desire and will of the Godly soul is that it alone should rule over the person and direct him, and that all his limbs should obey it and surrender themselves completely to it and become a chariot for it, and serve as a garment for its ten faculties and three garments mentioned above, all of which should be enclothed within the organs and limbs of the body, and the entire body should be permeated with them alone, to the exclusion of any alien influence, God forbid.

In particular: that the three brains that are in the head should be permeated with the *ChaBaD* of the Godly soul, namely, the wisdom of God and the understanding of Him, by pondering on His unfathomable and infinite greatness. And that from them should be born, through the faculty of *daat*, awe in his mind and fear of God in his heart, and a love of God like burning fire in his heart, like flaming coals, so that his soul shall yearn and long, with craving and desire, to cleave to the Blessed Infinite, with his entire heart, soul and might, from the very depths of the heart, in its right ventricle, so that it is so thoroughly paved, filled and overflowing with love that [the love] spreads also to the left ventricle to subdue the *sitra achra* with its element of evil waters—[that is], the lust stemming from *kelipat nogah*—to change it and transform it from the pleasures of this world to the love of God, as it is written, "'With all your heart'—with both your inclinations."

That is to say, that the person should ascend and attain the level of "great love," [which is] a greater affection than the ardent love that is comparable to flaming coals. This is [the love] that is called in Scripture, "love of delights," which is the experience of delight in God, similar to that [experienced in] the World to Come—"delight" (*oneg*) being in the brain of [*chokhmah*], in the intellectual pleasure of conceiving and knowing God, to the extent that one's intellect and [*chokhmah*] can grasp [Him]. This is the element of water and "seed"—[that is], a sowing of light—in the holiness of the Godly soul, which transforms to good the element of water in the animal soul, from which the lust for mundane pleasures had been previously derived.

Thus it is written in *Etz Chayyim,* Portal 50, chapter 3, in name of the *Zohar,* that the evil is converted into, and becomes, completely good, like the good nature itself, through the shedding of its soiled garments—the pleasures of this world—in which it had been clothed.

[The Godly soul] also [desires] that the other *middot* in the heart, the off-shoots of awe and love, should be dedicated to God alone; and that the faculty of speech that is in the mouth, and the thought that is in the brain, should be entirely and solely filled with the thought and speech garments of the Godly soul, namely, the thought of God and His Torah, which should be the theme of [the person's] speech throughout the day, his mouth ceaselessly studying [it]; and that the faculty of action in his hands, as also in the rest of the 248 limbs, should function exclusively in the action of the *mitzvot,* which is the third garment of the Godly soul.

But the desire of the animal soul which is derived from *kelipah* is the very opposite; [it desires this] for the good of man, that he may prevail over it and vanquish it, as in the parable of the harlot in the holy *Zohar.*

COMMENTARY

The previous chapters described the two souls of man: the Godly soul and its attributes and holy "garments"; and the animal soul, its attributes, and the garments of *kelipah* through which it finds expression. They also described the respective domains of *kelipah* and holiness, establishing the points of reference for this pivotal chapter, which discusses the relationship between the two souls and the struggle between them.

The abode of the animal soul derived from the *kelipat nogah* in every Jew is in the heart, in the left ventricle that is filled with blood, as it is written, "For the blood is the soul."

This follows the ancients' anatomical conception of the heart as consisting of two chambers with different functions: one ventricle receiving air (oxygen) and the other being full of blood. In any case, the *Tanya* is not a book on anatomy, and the author is not suggesting that negative traits can be removed by a surgical operation; the issue at hand is not where the animal soul resides in the anatomical sense but the relation between the two souls and the major role that the animal soul plays in the inner life of a man. In this sense, the animal soul resides in the heart (particularly, in the part of the heart that relates to the blood and therefore the body), for the animal soul is deeply connected with the heart and the emotions. It is true that, as Chapter 6 discussed, the animal soul does not consist only of desires and feelings but is a complete entity containing also intellectual and abstract components, yet the center of gravity of the animal soul is with the emotions, in the heart.

The difference between the two souls is brought into focus by the question: Where lies the center of life? What is the axis of the soul, around which all else revolves? In the animal soul, the axis of existence is the self, which is identified with the body and the physical life of man; that self is the core of all existence and the end that it serves. The animal soul manifests itself in many forms, including some that are extremely refined and complex; but when these manifestations are traced to their source, it is consistently found to be the base instincts of man, the "left ventricle in the heart that is full of blood," the person's identity as a physical being. For in the animal soul, "The blood is the soul" (Deuteronomy 12:23): life is for the sake of life, rather than an instrument for a higher purpose. The blood is the soul, and the soul is the blood. The self is life, and life is the self. The self is the epicenter of being; all derives from it, and all reverts to it.

This self-saturated being is not a holy thing. The experience of holiness is, by definition, separate from the experience of selfhood. Where there is ego, there cannot be holiness; holiness can reside only where there is a surrender of the "I," where the self is nullified before its supernal source. Thus, holiness is never a derivative or outgrowth of the ego.

Thus, the quality and sophistication of the animal soul is irrelevant to its holiness. A person can be small by the criteria of his animal soul yet be a holy person, or he might be great in human-animal terms yet not holy at all. Nevertheless, the animal soul might determine the character of the holiness that is present in a person. For the animal soul embodies the basic structure of the human personality, the "I" that permeates all of the person's faculties and "garments." Thus, the person's holiness, although not itself deriving from the animal soul, assumes the scope and character of his animal soul. With a great person (in the conventional sense), his holiness will manifest itself in his greatness, whereas with a person of modest capacities, his holiness will manifest itself in modest ways. But in and of itself, the animal soul is the antithesis of holiness, embodying the concept that "the blood is the soul," that the center of being is in the body in and of itself.

Thus, all lusts and boasting and anger and similar passions

Not only material lusts but also boasting, anger, and the like derive from the animal soul. Boasting and anger are not desires in the conventional sense, for although a person might enjoy his conceit, and even his anger, pleasure is not their main point. Yet they, too, are quintessential expressions of the animal soul. They are not the fulfillment of a desire but rather an assertion of selfhood, pitting one's ego against the other. In a sense, they both are a sort of idolatry, of self-worship.

are in the heart,

All these are in the heart, in the sense that the heart is their primal cause. When a person's lusts, conceits, and angers are stripped of all rationalizations, what remains is the "left ventricle of the heart," the "blood is the soul."

and from the heart they spread throughout the entire body,

They spread also throughout the entire reality of human existence,

rising also to the brain in the head, so as to think and meditate about them and become cunning in them,

The crude impulse, the simple will that arises from the heart, is the nucleus around which the brain constructs an entire edifice. This edifice has two basic components. The first is "to think and meditate in them." The primal impulse is unformed, indistinct, one-dimensional; indeed, the person is barely aware of what he wants. When the mind thinks of it, contemplates it, and ponders the what and how of desire, the primitive, abstract impulse assumes a form, acquires the sophistication and richness of imagination, and develops into a complex passion.

The second component of the rational edifice constructed around the impulses arising from the heart is that the person "becomes cunning in them," cunning in how to effect his wish. Thus, the mind encompasses the desire to its rear and to its fore, erecting a system of rationalizations to back it up and support it, as well as a methodology to move it forward and realize it. Within this structure, the heart's elemental lust of eating and drinking assumes complex and sophisticated forms, which are given a base upon which they might be justified and a framework within which they can be implemented.

The analogy for this is the manner in which the blood, the metaphor for the animal soul ("For the blood is the soul"), circulates through the body,

just as the blood has its source in the heart and from the heart it circulates to all organs and limbs, rising also to the brain in the head.

The blood that spreads from the heart throughout the body is analogous to the expansion of the heart's desires through the structures of thought, speech, and deed.

The word used for "soul" in the verse "For the blood is the soul" is *nefesh*. As explained in Chapter 1, the *nefesh* is only a limited expression of the soul. The *nefesh* is the part of the soul that most closely relates to the body: the soul as the vitalizing force of physical life. Regarding this aspect of the soul, it is said that "the blood is the soul." The *nefesh* is essentially instinctive; like the blood, its axis and engine is the heart. But like the blood, it also radiates throughout the body, rising also to the brain. In the brain, the instinctive *nefesh* develops a logical structure within which it functions and realizes itself.

But the abode of the Godly soul is in the brains that are in the head,

The brain is the seat of the *"ChaBaD"* (*chokhmah, binah,* and *daat*)—the person's faculties of the mind and intellect, and, in a more general sense, his powers of perception and consciousness.[1] Thus, the "headquarters" of the Godly soul—its point of contact with the body and the life of man—is not in the blood, in the instinctive throb of physical life, but in a different, though no less fundamental, organ: the brain, the faculty of consciousness.

The basic difference between heart and mind is that the heart lives for itself. The self is its ultimate point of reference and the ultimate objective of all its desires. By contrast, the brain, the faculty of perception, is the power to absorb and relate to matters that are outside and beyond the self. Indeed, the basis of all perception is the surrender of the egotistical "I" of the heart. As long as the "I" is defined solely by the self and its own needs, it cannot assimilate any objective truth, anything that is beyond the self. Thus, the "abode" of the Godly soul in the human body is the brain, where there is "abnegation" (*bittul*) of the self to another, higher reality.

Elsewhere,[2] the author defines the ultimate in *kelipah* as Pharaoh's remark, "My Nile is mine, and I created myself."[3] When someone says, "This is mine," this is a certain degree of *tumah* ("profanity"); when he adds, "and I created myself," it is the ultimate profanity. The circuit is closed completely; the *kelipah* is hermetically sealed. If I made myself for myself, then the "I" is the beginning and end of all existence, and this is the ultimate descent from holiness.

In contrast, each level of holiness is a level of self-negation. The highest level of holiness is that of the *merkavah* (literally, "chariot"), a state in which a person's individuality is completely negated and he operates as a vehicle, a mere tool, of the supernal will alone. Holiness is not merely the concept that I did not create myself, but also that the "Nile" (that is, the things that are ostensibly in my domain and control) does not belong to me. At this level, words such as "my" and "mine" are unutterable.

The Bible relates how King David, upon offering an enormous donation to the (future) Temple—"Three thousand gold talents of Ophir gold and seven thousand talents of refined silver"[4]—proclaimed: "But who am I and who are my people that we can donate like this? For all comes from You, and it is of Yours that we give to You."[5] As against the essence of *kelipah* (which is "My Nile is mine, and I created myself") is the essence of holiness: "For all comes from You, and it is of Yours that we give to You."

The faculty for self-abnegation, the ability to be receptive to that which is outside of the self, resides in the brain, in the power of perception, which is the capacity to absorb and receive information. As explained in Chapter 3, *chokhmah* is *koach mah* ("power of 'what?'")—the power of self-negation, of humility, the power to be "what?" to be nothing. *Chokhmah* is thus compared to the faculty of sight: sight is utterly passive; it is the receptiveness of the eyes. *Chokhmah*, too, does not emit light but only receives it. It does not exist by its own devices and presents no barrier to anything entering from without. *Chokhmah* is thus the faculty most suitable to serve as a vessel for holiness.

and from there it extends to all organs and the limbs;

The Godly soul abides and is first expressed in the mind. From there, clothed in consciousness and thought, it can spread to the other organs by way of feeling and action.

and also in the heart,

The Godly soul also has a "residence" in the heart, where its *mid-dot* ("emotional faculties") reside. But this expression of the Godly soul remains latent until aroused by the brain.

in the right ventricle in which there is no blood, as is written, "The heart of the wise man is on his right."

"The heart of a wise man is to his right," says King Solomon, "and that of a fool to his left."[6] Man is not a homogenous creature but a dichotomous being; his heart, too, is divided. In the right ventricle of the heart, where the feelings of holiness are located, are the desires of the Godly soul; these do not manifest themselves in the heart in a direct and spontaneous manner but by means of certain processes in the brain. Then in the left ventricle, which holds "the blood that is the [animal] soul," is the home of the feelings and desires that derive from the person's physical, animal side—from the *kelipah* in man. Because the heart is not one and can contain contradictory drives, a person is perpetually faced with the question of where his true heart lies. Where does his heart of hearts, his ultimate self, reside: to the right or to the left?

So although the animal soul is essentially instinctive and the Godly soul is primarily perceptive, this is not to say that the emotional self is exclusively *kelipah*. For the Godly soul also has another point of residence in the human being, in addition to its abode in the mind, the right ventricle of the heart. The human being has fundamental desires that are of a holy, rather than an animal, nature, which express themselves as feelings of the heart. These are

the love of God which flares like flaming coals in the heart of the perspicacious, who understand and reflect with the *daat* faculty of their mind on matters that arouse this love;

Just as there are emotions and impulses that belong to the animal sphere, there are emotions in the Godly sphere. Love of God, as an emotional impulse, is no different from animal love, as when one person loves another. The difference is that the feeling toward God is not normally aroused by itself. A higher machinery of perception and awareness is required to arouse it. This is not necessarily an intellectual awareness, a knowledge of what it says in the books, but rather a personal awareness—one's individual way of seeing, understanding, and sensing. Every object of love requires some sort of image—visual, aural, or connected with some other sense—so that natural feeling can apply to it. When a person ponders matters that arouse love of God, this awakens a place in the heart ("the right ventricle"). This awareness does not remain a theoretical and intellectual experience but spreads throughout all the organs, including the heart, which has a place open also for such a sensitivity, a love of God burning like flaming coals.

also the gladness of the heart in the beauty of God and the majesty of His glory

This is another holy emotion, connected to the *middah* of *tiferet*,[7] which awakens in a person's heart

when "the eyes of the wise man that are in his head"[8]—[that is,] the mind-faculties of [*chokhmah*] and *binah*—gaze upon the glory of the King and beauty of His greatness that are unfathomable and without end or limit, as explained elsewhere;

The nature of these contemplations—what to meditate upon and how to meditate to evoke a particular emotion in the heart—is explained at length elsewhere. Here, the *Tanya* offers only a broad outline of the point of departure and the final goal, giving us an idea of what we are talking about.

A person's emotions are not all of one type. There are feelings of love and feelings of fear, joy, sadness, compassion, and so on. In the animal soul, different emotions are aroused by different causes: what arouses love is not what arouses awe; what one is afraid of is not what one takes pity on; and so on. In contrast, in the Godly soul, the object of the emotions is always one and the same: God. Love is exclusively the love of God, and fear is always fear of God. Unlike the objects of the animal soul's emotions, the divine essence is infinite, pervading all areas of our experience; the different feelings we have toward Him depend on the manner in which we are relating to Him. Approaching God from one perspective, a person is filled with awe and fear; from another, he is suffused with love and yearning. The subject is always the One God, but depending upon the person's manner of contemplation, God might evoke burning love, heartfelt joy, or fear and contraction.

as also the other holy affections (*middot*) in the heart that originate from *ChaBaD* in the mind.

In later chapters, the author clarifies that this is not to say that the emotions of the Godly soul are never stimulated without prior activity of the three intellectual faculties (*ChaBaD*). Certainly, some people possess innate feelings of holiness and experience natural love and awe of God—feelings inherited with the "genes" of their soul and implanted in their subconscious. Here, however, for various reasons, the author does not speak of this type of holy feelings but of the fundamental structure the Godly soul, in which the emotions are derivatives of *ChaBaD*.

In the animal soul, in which "the blood is the soul," the *middot* derive from the heart. Here, the emotions are of a piece with the biological or animal side of man. True, they do not remain at that simple level as with lower forms of animal life: in animals, impulses are simple desires without thought, refinement, or structure. But man can transform into the stuff that great poetry is made of. Even when they attain a high degree of sophistication and beauty, however, the source and true basis of all emotions of this type is the blood, the vitality that courses through the material body. In contrast, some of the emotions of the Godly soul, although as potent and sweeping as those of the animal soul, derive not from the materiality of man but from the human spirit, whose closest bodily instrument is the brain.

Thus, there are two axes of being in man. One axis is centered upon "the blood is the [*nefesh*]," the animal or biological aspect of man; and the other is most primarily manifested in the brain, within its structures of perception and consciousness. The material brain is by no means a perfect vessel for the Godly soul, but it is the vessel closest to holiness.

It is written, however, "Nation over nation shall strengthen itself."[9]

This expression appears in the Torah in relation to Rebecca's tumultuous pregnancy: "the children were struggling within her"[10]; sensing that something is amiss, Rebecca "went to seek God." The divine response was that "There are two nations in your womb, and two peoples will separate from your innards; and nation over nation shall strengthen itself."

In a sense, this applies to every Jew, at any time. Every person senses that there are two "children" struggling within him. When he passes a house of Torah, Jacob struggles to get out, and when he passes a house of idolatry, Esau struggles to get out. The reason for this is that "there are two nations in your womb." A person has within him not a single personality but "two nations," two personalities, each striving in a different direction and frequently in opposition to one another. The problem is that neither personality is content with concerning itself with its own affairs; each is constantly attempting to encroach upon the domain of the other. Furthermore, the relationship between them is such that "nation over nation shall strengthen itself": any increase in strength of one side produces a reaction that increases the strength of the other.

The result is the extreme, agonizing spiritual upheavals that virtually every soul must contend with. A person attains a certain level of goodness or holiness, and at that very point, when he is anticipating a holy experience and a spiritual elevation, he experiences something that is the very opposite. He was involved in a holy pursuit—he truly was in a holy place—when suddenly a thought invades his mind, or a desire erupts in his heart, that has no relation to the holy world in which he had been, something that expresses the lowest and basest side of his personality.

At such moments, a person tends to see himself as even more base and lowly. It is therefore important that a person understand what is transpiring within him. He should understand that there are "two nations in your womb" and that "nation over nation shall strengthen itself"; that a person is not one but two; and that when one becomes stronger, the other rallies strength in response. It is important for us to know that life is not a smooth and straight progression and that one should be prepared for sudden bursts of energy from one side or the other. As we will explain later, a person whose path in life is straight and smooth is not a normal person; he is a *tzaddik gamur,* "a completely righteous individual." The *tzaddik* is a one-dimensional person: he has but one soul, one heart, which is directed toward heaven. Only in such an individual are there no upheavals caused by the "other side."

This conception of the human soul as consisting of two distinct souls is one of the most important innovations of the *Tanya.* The assumption in other books of *mussar* ("moral teaching") is that a person should be good and pious and show other virtues, according to the holy books. Indeed, a person should be this way. However, he is not always capable of doing so, and when he tries and fails, he feels that he is evil and contemptible. What is even more serious is that he then becomes convinced that the books are not speaking to him, that he is too lowly for the laws and rules by which they operate to apply to him.

One of the classical works of *mussar,* written not long before *Tanya,* is *Mesillat Yesharim* by Rabbi Chaim Moses Luzzatto. The book, written in beautiful Hebrew, describes how someone can proceed from virtue to virtue, from "diligence" to "alacrity," from "alacrity" to "cleanliness," and so on, step by step, until he reaches the level of "the divine spirit" (*ruach hakodesh*). Somewhere between diligence and alacrity, an ordinary person might regress, leaving him completely confused as to what level, if any, he now holds and feeling that what this book says is utterly impossible. In contrast, although the demands made by the *Tanya* may appear somewhat extreme, the book takes into account human nature as we know it, with all its complexities and problems. It explains to the person what is happening to him; how the inner upheavals one experiences are an integral part of oneself, of the basic duality of human nature. It explains that one must accept that this duality will exist within him from the day of his *bar mitzvah* to the day he dies. The duality can be moderated and can take on more refined forms; to some extent, a person can even exploit the conflict within him to his spiritual advantage, but he can never totally uproot it.

Similarly, the Mishnah says, "We have neither the tranquillity of the wicked, nor the sufferings of the righteous."[11] Apart from the very few individuals who happen to be either complete *tzaddikim* ("righteous persons") or complete *resha'im* ("wicked persons"), a person can be sure of one thing: his soul will not give him rest. Peace and tranquillity might perhaps come after death (and even then, we are told, "the righteous have no rest . . . in the World to Come,"[12] whereas the wicked are beaten in the grave and "flung around in the hollow of the sling");[13] in this world, as long as a person lives, he cannot experience tranquillity. At times, one may earn a respite, a temporary cease-fire, but achieving complete and true inner peace is never possible. There is a permanent struggle within, and a person should understand that his is an existence of conflict and that the hope of attaining peace and tranquillity is not realistic. With this knowledge, one is not disappointed about failing to attain peace, nor does one feel that one's life has been wasted if one does not achieve a decisive victory in the battle of life. A person must realize that everything he does involves a struggle, that life is war in which "nation over nation shall strengthen itself." The pendulum swings from side to side, and the task of man is to make every effort to emerge from the struggle in a better state than he entered it. In the course of this struggle, in between battles, he should make sure to move forward. Ultimately, this is all a human being can achieve.

For the body is called a "small city";[14] just as two kings wage war over a city, each wishing to capture it and rule over it, that is to say, to govern its inhabitants according to his will so that they obey him in all that he decrees for them,

That is, their aim is not merely to physically occupy a place but to rule over it and influence it, to mold it and remake it to reflect their will,

so do the two souls—the Godly [soul] and the vitalizing animal [soul] that derives from *kelipah*—wage war against each other over the body and all its organs and limbs.

The body and all its organs, including the heart and the brain, are neutral ground. Body and soul are not the conflicting representations of good and evil or those of holiness and profanity. The body, in and of itself, is not an expression of the evil or the profane, just as the soul does not necessarily represent a higher state of being. Rather, the physical body is an instrument that might serve either the profane forces of *kelipah* or the holy forces of Godliness.

The Jewish conception of the physical is that it is not necessarily lowlier than the spiritual. Whether something is material or spiritual is no criterion by which to determine its worth. If anything, the teachings of Judaism lay the greater emphasis on the practical *mitzvot* that involve the activity of the physical body in the material world. This physical activity is not designed as a means of transcending the material world but as an end in itself; these physical deeds should be enacted in the material sphere. Transcendence of the material state (*hitpashtut hagashmiyut*) is something that occurs in the process of fulfilling a *mitzvah*, but this is an occurrence that does not, in and of itself, possess moral significance. The practical *mitzvot* are not a device for attaining spirituality, love of God, and other spiritual aims. In fact, the *mitzvot* have no purpose, material or spiritual, beyond the single aim of attachment to God. And God is neither material nor spiritual but equally distant from both matter and spirit; the question of whether a person believes in God or denies Him is not of any greater "concern" to God than whether a person smokes on Shabbat.

Furthermore, as far as genuine attachment to God is concerned, it is the body that holds the greater potential for such attachment, because, among other things, the vast majority of the *mitzvot* are physical deeds. The prevalent assumption that the spiritual is better suited to achieve attachment to God stems from the failure to distinguish between attachment and a feeling of attachment. The two are not synonymous; indeed, they can be far apart and at times even opposites. Attachment is an objective truth: a person is one with God, and it makes no difference whether the person experiences an uplifting of the spirit at that time or not. If the criterion is how one feels, if one's feelings determine what is good and what is bad, what is true and what is false, what is right and what is wrong, then this is not attachment to God but attachment to oneself!

Elsewhere,[15] the author explains the two types of love: sisterly love and matrimonial love. The love that one feels toward one's mate is love that comes from choice and is therefore more passionate and more intense. A person does not love his sister the way he loves his wife. However, because marriage is a relationship of choice, it can also be terminated. In contrast, the love felt for a sister is less warm; there is no expression of feeling to the extent that there is toward a wife, but it is a connection that cannot be severed. The connection with a wife is dependent on feeling and lasts as long as the feeling lasts, whereas the connection with a sister is a quintessential one. Siblings are siblings for life, and the bond remains even if the manifest feeling is the very opposite of closeness.

In this sense, love is not synonymous with attachment. Love is a feeling, an expression of the emotions and excitement of the soul, which must not be underrated. Attachment, on the other hand, is not a feeling. It may sometimes be accompanied by deep emotion but may also be present without any emotion at all. The presence or absence of emotion is irrelevant to the reality of the bond.

It is told of one of the great Hasidim that on the first night of Passover, he conducted the *seder* with great excitement, diligently fulfilling all the observances with the appropriate *kavvanot* ("meditations") and felt that he was rising into worlds above worlds. The following day, exhausted by the immense effort of that *seder*, he decided to rest a little before the second *seder*. When he awoke, it was nearly midnight (the deadline for finishing the main part of the *seder*), so he had to rush to arrange the *seder* plate and do whatever had to be done quickly so that he complete all in time. Understandably, he was very upset and depressed. Some time later, he came to his rebbe, who said, "*Nu,* so you held two *seders.* At the first, you were flying around in the heavens—so you were flying around in the heavens. But the second *seder*—the second *seder* was a very good *seder* indeed." When someone has lofty experiences, this might make him feel very good about himself, but it has nothing to do with attachment to God. In a sense, the reverse may be true: someone who is in a state of true attachment has no time to think about how much he loves and how he loves, whereas someone who feels good about himself should, perhaps, cast doubts on the quality of his attachment. The Hasid who had to prepare the *seder* in a hurry had no time to prime himself, to contemplate himself, to ascertain the precise level he had attained. In those moments when he was acting, doing something, he displayed his inner desire, and he was attached from within, genuinely and cleanly, with no superlative of emotion and awareness, which are irrelevant to one's actual attachment to God.

In any case, the body is only an instrument, in the sense that it is morally neutral. The battle between the two souls is therefore over the body: Who should use it and for what purpose? Should it serve the animal soul, which sees the body not as an instrument but as an end in itself? Should the instrument, then, be recast as an objective and thus become an expression of *kelipah?* Or should it serve the Godly soul, which sees it as an instrument through which it can achieve a higher degree of attachment to God than it itself possesses?

The desire and will of the Godly soul is that it alone should rule over the person and direct him, and that all his limbs should obey it and surrender themselves completely to it and become a chariot for it,

In the terminology of Kabbalah, a "chariot" (*merkavah*) is a vehicle, a thing that possesses no will or identity of its own but merely serves a higher will, like a chariot controlled and directed by its driver. The *Midrash* states that the patriarchs (Abraham, Isaac, and Jacob) were the divine chariot, comparing their self-negation before God to that of the horse under its rider.[16] Another aspect of the analogy is that just as the horse takes its rider to a place that he cannot reach on his own, so the body, if it is a vehicle for the Godly soul, can transport it to the place that it cannot reach on its own. This is why the

Godly soul wants the body to act as its chariot, a vehicle that negates itself exclusively to it and serves solely to express its nature and aims within the world.

and serve as a garment for its ten faculties

See Chapter 3.

and its three garments mentioned above

Chapter 4 mentions the thought, speech, and deed of the 613 *mitzvot* of the Torah.

all of which should be enclothed within the organs and limbs of the body, and the entire body should be permeated with them alone, to the exclusion of any alien influence, God forbid.

The Godly soul wants to attain complete control over the totality of human existence.

In particular: that the three brains that are in the head[17] should be permeated with the *ChaBaD* of the Godly soul,

In this way, all of a person's thoughts, and his very manner of thinking, should be in the sphere of holiness.

namely, the wisdom of God

This is the faculty of *chokhmah*, described in Chapter 3.

and the understanding of Him, by pondering on His unfathomable and infinite greatness

This is the faculty of *binah* described there.

And that from them should be born, through the faculty of *daat*,

This is the third mind-faculty described there.

awe in his mind

This is *yir'ah*, the sense of recoil and inadequacy generated in the mind when it is aware of an infinitely greater presence than itself.

and fear of God in his heart,

This is *pachad*, the corresponding emotion in the heart, which is different from the more theoretical sense of awe.

and a love of God like burning fire in his heart, like flaming coals,

We will discuss the concept of "love like flaming coals" (as opposed to "love like tranquil waters") later in the chapter.

so that his soul shall yearn and long, with craving and desire, to cleave to the Blessed Infinite, with his entire heart, soul, and might,

"Heart, soul, and might" is a reference to Deuteronomy 6:5, the second verse of the Shema: "And you shall love the Lord your God with all your heart, with all your soul, and with all your might." "With all your heart," as the Talmud interprets it,[18] means with both ventricles of the heart; the heart should be driven to attach itself to God with the very forces of craving and desire with which it is drawn to *kelipah* (as we will presently explain). "With all your soul" means that one's love of God permeates all attributes of the soul: its three intellectual faculties and seven emotive traits, and its three "garments"—thought, speech, and action. "With all your might," means to the extent of giving up one's very existence. This is the soul's suprarational potential—a potential that transcends its *chokhmah*, *binah*, and *daat* and is the loftiest of its faculties.[19]

from the very depths of the heart,

"The very depths of the heart" is what a person really and truly desires. For a person might desire certain things and act upon these desires only on the periphery of his heart. In the routine of life, distinguishing between the two is not always possible, but in a crisis that upsets the normal balance of his life, a person will divest himself of those things that he values only on the periphery of the heart. Hence the oft-told story of the Jew who rushes to throw his *tallit* (prayer shawl) and *tefillin* overboard when his ship gets caught in a storm and the captain orders the passengers to throw some of their possessions into the sea to lighten the load. Obviously, this fellow had other possessions—including things that are heavier than his *tallit* and *tefillin*—but these, it seems, were of greater value to him; for what a person desires from the depth of his heart, he does not throw away so quickly. As long as his life is running smoothly, he can hold on to everything he has, but when things become difficult, he sheds those things whose connection to him he now shows to have been only peripheral. Conversely, times of extreme freedom—when a person finds himself in a position where everything is permitted—are also indicative of a person's true desires. A certain Jew was once told by his mentor that he was mad. That Jew understood this to mean that, as a madman, he was exempt from all *mitzvot,* and from that time, he threw away all he had of Judaism. The feeling that everything is permitted him could just as well have moved him to start praying for seven or eight hours every day, but this was not what he wanted from "the depth of his heart."

in its right ventricle, so that it is so thoroughly paved, filled and overflowing with love

These are not mere expressions: "paved" and "filled" are two phases in how the Godly soul's love of God fills the right ventricle of the heart until it contains nothing else; "overflowing" is the stage at which this love spills over from its natural place onto the other side.

that [the love] spreads also to the left ventricle

The Godly soul is not satisfied to consolidate its rule over those parts of the person (the brain and the right ventricle of the heart) that are its natural domain. It wants more: that the feelings of love and awe of God should spill over into the other side of the heart, into the realm of the animal soul in the left ventricle, to the human, biological element of man. The desire of the Godly soul is to transform the entire human being to a being of holiness.

to subdue the *sitra achra* with its element of evil waters—[that is], the lust stemming from *kelipat nogah*

Chapter 1 discusses this.

—to change it and transform it from the pleasures of this world to the love of God,

Here, we have two stages in the Godly soul's effect upon the animal soul: (1) "to subdue the *sitra achra*" and (2) "to change it and transform it." "Subduing" (*itkafia*) and "transforming" (*ithapkha*) are basic terms in divine service; as we will explain shortly, there is a major difference between the ability to subdue the "other side" and the ability to transform and change it.

as it is written, "'With all your heart'—with both your inclinations."

In Hebrew, the word "your heart" can assume two forms: (*libkha*), spelled with a single *bet,* or (*levavkha*), spelled with two *bet*s. In the verse from the Shema (Deuteronomy 6:5), the word is written with two *bet*s. The Talmud interprets this as a reference to the human double heart, one's inclination for good and for evil.[20] The Torah is telling us that we should love God with both sides of our heart, with both our wills.

That is to say, that the person should ascend and attain the level of "great love," [which is] a greater affection than the ardent love that is comparable to flaming coals.

The *Tanya* appears to be charting the process by which the level of "great love" (*ahavah rabbah*) can be attained. For although it is true that there is no fixed route or technique in these things, because people operate and develop emotionally in different ways, it is nevertheless possible to speak about a general route that is applicable for a large number of people.

The first stage of this process is perception and contemplation of the divine, which serve to awaken the love that is in the heart. This is a love like fire, a thirst and desire for God that is "a love like flaming coals." As described earlier, this love first develops in the right ventricle of the heart (that is, the heart's Godly emotions), fills it, and then spills over into the left ventricle, subduing the heart's material and animal loves and ultimately transforming them into a love for God. When this is achieved, the person can graduate to a higher level of love, a love that is called in Scripture, "love of delights,"[21] which is the experience of delight in God, similar to that [experienced in] the World to come—

Love, then, has two seemingly contradictory modes of expression: "love like flaming coals" and "love of delights," which (as the author will note several lines on) is also known as "love like water." "Love like fire" and "love like water" seem to be working in opposite ways. True, both are forms of love; both contain the general desire for relationship, contact, and affection. Beyond this, however, they are fundamentally different. "Love like flaming coals" is the love of one who lacks. It is a love that is born out of thirst, a love that drives the lover to the beloved; but as the lover approaches the object of his love, his thirst only grows stronger. This love is never sated, a love that is a quest, a longing, a craving. Predicated upon lack and distance, it generates an ever-growing tension; for the closer one approaches to God, the more one senses how distant one truly is from Him.

Although this is a holy love, a love directed to God, it shares with other loves a certain egotistical element. Most worldly loves are, in essence, the love of self: a person loves himself, and for the sake of his self-love, he needs something. When a person plucks a flower and says that he loves flowers, he doesn't love flowers; he loves himself, and to satisfy his self-love, he needs flowers. The same is often true of love between people, love between husband and wife and between parents and children. Hasidim used to point out that the expression "they love one another" in Yiddish (*zey hoben zich lieb*) also means "they love themselves." In this sense, any love "like flaming coals" is a form of self-love. The object of such love can be a great variety of things and can even be God, but such love of God can be said to be a desire like all other desires, because it is predicated upon a human lack. Obviously, the more mundane the object of the love is, the more pronounced is the lover's lust, and the more the so-called love of the object is shown to be a fallacy. When a person says he loves fish, we know that he means that he loves to eat fish; when he says that he loves wisdom, we tend to view his love in less selfish terms. But even in its finer forms, a person's expression of love toward someone or something might be no more a love for that person or thing than a love of fish is a love for the fish. For as long as a love is driven by lack and need, its dominant feature is the lover's want.

A higher form of love is the second type of love: "love like water" or, as Scripture calls it, "love of delights." The soul achieves this love when it no longer has any struggle between its divine and animal parts, when all the person's desires are directed to God. Unlike "love like fire," which is based on the self and what it lacks, this is a love in which the lover is not aware of himself at all, only of the object of his love. When the self ceases to be significant, its needs, too, cease to be significant and no longer afflict the soul with thirst and yearning. Such love is satisfying because it makes no demands; it does not seek to dominate or exercise ownership over its object. As long as love implies the desire to obtain something for oneself, the lack is only magnified with the intensity of the love. But when love belongs to a totally different type of relationship, in which the beloved is loved for its own sake, unconnected with the self of the one who loves, then the more one loves and the more one thinks about and occupies himself with the object of his love, the more satisfying that love becomes. When a fiery love graduates into a "love of delights," there is a complete transformation: love that was formerly characterized by agony and longing becomes a delightful love, akin to the soul's delight in God in the world to come. No longer is the love dependent upon one's possession or grasp of the beloved; it is sustained by the beloved's very existence.

The seven years that Jacob waited for Rachel were "in his eyes like a few days, because of his love for her."[22] Usually, the reverse is the case: a few days of separation from one's beloved seem like seven years. Indeed, as long as love is what the self is demanding, as long as it is about what one lacks and requires, the time of separation progressively appears to get longer. Every day of separation creates stronger yearnings, which increase the feeling of lack, until a few days seem like several years. But Jacob's love for Rachel was of the other type: a "love of delights" that makes no claims, is satisfied by the mere fact that the object of love is there, and does not desire to possess it. In such love, seven years are the same as a few days.

"Love like flaming coals" is not a delight. It is a painful love, an ever-escalating agony. There is beauty and even a sort of pleasure in the pain, but there is a perpetual lack, a dissonance, an ever-increasing tension. "Love in delights," on the other hand, is of the nature of the world to come, which represents a higher plane of reality:—a reality in which there is no conflict, in which man becomes an integral, harmonious being whose soul is wholly consumed with the love of God. There is no longer the tension of unsatisfied desire but "the nearness of God to me is good":[23] man stands before God and is utterly satisfied in his love for Him.[24]

"delight" (*oneg*) being in the brain of [*chokhmah*], in the intellectual pleasure of conceiving and knowing God, to the extent that one's intellect and
[*chokhmah*] can grasp [Him].

As explained earlier, awareness is what defines feeling. Just as there is
awareness that leads to fiery love, to desire, craving, and longing, so there
is a type of awareness, deriving from the [*chokhmah*] faculty of the mind,
by which the more one contemplates, the more delight one derives.

This is the element of water and "seed"—[that is], a sowing of light—in the
holiness of the Godly soul, which transforms to good the element of water
in the animal soul, from which the lust for mundane pleasures had been
previously derived.

When a person attains the level of "love in delights," he no longer
needs to force himself to abandon worldly matters and desires, for he
no longer desires them. This is the transition from the stage of subduing to that of transforming, from the stage where he has to suppress
the animal soul (*itkafia*) to that where the animal soul itself desires
holiness (*ithapkha*).

"Love in delights" suffuses the soul so completely that it leaves no
room for any other desires; as a result, the desires of the animal soul
are converted into holy desires. This is the ultimate solution to all the
problems of desire, in all its forms and expressions. On this level, the
person has achieved a resolution of the problem of desire at its root,
a solution that eliminates the necessity for all other solutions at all
other levels. In this state of being, the mere existence of God is a source
of delight. From this vantage point, all other pleasures are sterile alter-
natives to the delight in their ultimate source.

We are drawn to worldly pleasures only so long as we are not connected with the source of all things. All the substitutes of second, third,
and lower grades serve only to drown our single, basic need: our
intrinsic love for God. Unwittingly, our thirst for God is contorted into
other lusts, which seem to offer a solution, which seem to quench our
thirst. But once we attain a "love in delights" for God, all these things
cease to attract us; we no longer crave them, and no longer do they
have any existence for us.

The picture seems idealistic. A person has a straight path before
him: he contemplates God's greatness, which leads him to a "love like
flaming coals" for God; the desire increases until it fills his heart and

overflows to its other side, and he then attains "love in delights" and no longer desires and needs anything else. In actuality, however, it is never that simple. Each of these stages can take thirty or sixty years or a whole lifetime of toil, with ups and downs and without a moment's respite. The road itself is full of internal contradictions. For instance, there is in "love like flaming coals" on the one hand a process of self-abnegation and on the other a process of intensification of the ego. For the more a person loves, the more pronounced does the "I" that loves and desires become. Progress is therefore engulfed with crises. Elsewhere, the author says that the road to "love in delights" passes through the stage of "awe."[25] In other words, before a person can experience "the nearness of God to me is good," he first must annul his very "I," abnegating all its desires and aspirations. As long as the "I" desires, it lacks; and the more it desires, the more it lacks. To achieve a love that is more satisfying, a love that fulfills the craving of the soul, one must waive, in a sense, love itself. There is a juncture in the road to higher love that is not a simple transition but involves the annihilation of the initial character of love so that the soul's faculty for love can be reconstructed in a completely different manner.

It is told of the author of *Tanya* that he would stand in meditation and declare before God: "I do not want Your *Gan Eden*, I do not want Your world to come—I only want You!" There is a level on which a person attains a lofty state and desires to delight in God, so he is given the chance to delight in God. But higher than this is the level on which a person desires nothing. He waives even the pleasure that is found in the love of God and wants only "to [be] drawn into the body of the King"[26]—to negate himself completely within God.

The structure, then, is not at all simple. It is rife with paradox, a process characterized by advances and retreats, by front that becomes back and back that turns into front. It is a process in which the very nature of the soul is turned inside out, as one reverses a glove to transform it from right-handedness to left-handedness, from one extreme to the other, in order to take the next step. So the process described in this chapter is only a very general sketch of the battle between the Godly soul and the animal soul and the path to final victory.

Thus it is written in *Etz Chayyim,* Portal 50, chapter 3, in name of the *Zohar,* that the evil is converted into, and becomes, completely good, like the good nature itself, through the shedding of its soiled garments—the pleasures of this world—in which it had been clothed.

The *Zohar* distinguishes between desire itself and the garments of the desire, the negative forms it assumes. Because it is possible to separate the two, to strip the essential desire of the animal soul of its "soiled garments," the desire can therefore be transformed and redirected from one extreme to the other.

This means that one has to change not the essence of one's animal nature and the inner forces operating in the animal soul but only their object. This to some extent explains the ambitious aims put forward by the author and their feasibility: seen in this light, the idea of transforming the animal soul's material lusts into a love for God becomes more conceivable.

In this light, the transformation of the animal soul is not a transformation of its essence but a process of educating, training, and refocusing its will. The will of the animal soul serves as the "evil inclination" (*yetzer harah*) within man only as long as it desires evil, but of itself, inwardly, it is not evil. It desires evil not because it is evil but because it conceives of it as good. A baby who eats garbage does not do so out of a corrupt inner nature but because he thinks that it's a tasty food, because he has not yet been educated.

The ways in which desire expresses itself is the result of education, which begins at the moment a child is aware of himself. Our problem is in these initial stages. Education tends to describe the material world as the only real world, and realities that cannot be visualized are discounted as insignificant and are therefore not desired. Because our initial perception of reality is that only the material is "material," material things automatically become the things that the person wants and desires.

Someone who lives by his desires has difficulty distinguishing between the desire itself and the desired object. However, we all observe in others desires that do not pertain to ourselves, and we can view these objectively, analyze them, and demonstrate the difference between desire as desire and desire's selfish garments. For instance, when a football team wins an "important" match, one can observe people mourning or celebrating something that has no true effect on their individual lives. People dance and rejoice over something that requires a great degree of abstraction to relate to oneself. Why should it matter to Joe the taxi driver which way the ball went? Some say that people are self-centered and only want what they can enjoy and what supplies their own needs, but here we have an example that shows that the situation is not all that simple. This is not to say that this silliness has any virtue, but it can serve us as a model to demonstrate that, with the proper conditioning, people can derive a great deal of satisfaction from something that they never saw and that does not supply them with any material benefit. There is no reason why people should not get equally excited over matters of holiness, if their environment and education impressed them with a different set of priorities.

Once we are able to draw the distinction, it becomes clear that the distortion lies with the "soiled garments" rather than the intrinsic drives of the animal soul. Therein lies the hope, the feasibility of the *Tanya*'s program. For the garments can be changed, and the very same drives that previously fueled the lowliest of cravings can now impel the person in the most lofty pursuits, even to the point of self-sacrifice, with the same passion he had for material things, and often with an even greater intensity.

[The Godly soul] also [desires] that the other *middot* in the heart, the offshoots of awe and love, should be dedicated to God alone;

The bulk of this chapter dealt with the emotion of love. But the same applies to the heart's other emotions: these, too, can be educated and "clothed" with the proper garments, raising them level after level to holiness.

and that the faculty of speech that is in the mouth, and the thought that is in the brain, should be entirely and solely filled with the thought and speech garments of the Godly soul, namely, the thought of God and His Torah, which should be the theme of [the person's] speech throughout the day, his mouth ceaselessly studying [it];

Even if it is not possible for a person's thoughts and speech to be restricted to Torah alone, they can nevertheless be filled with it: namely, that Torah constitutes his true and only desire, a desire that suffuses the innermost part of his heart. If a thought or word is not Torah, then he thinks it or says it only because he must, only because they are essential to his existence (an existence dedicated to Torah), following which he immediately returns to his true and only interest—the Torah. When such is the case, his faculties of thought and speech are indeed filled with Torah.

and that the faculty of action in his hands, as also in the rest of the 248 limbs, should function exclusively in the action of the *mitzvot*, which is the third garment of the Godly soul.

As elaborated in Chapter 4, the soul has three garments by which it expresses itself outwardly: thought, speech, and action. The desire of the Godly soul is that these should be exclusively in its domain: that the person's thoughts, words, and deeds should serve only the Godly soul, making the body the exclusive instrument of its will.

But the desire of the animal soul which is derived from *kelipah* is the very opposite;

The author does not elaborate in the specific ways that the animal soul endeavors that the body's faculties and garments should serve it alone (as he does in the case of the Godly soul), perhaps because we are already all too familiar with these details, and in any case, there is no duty to teach them.

The idea that the animal soul desires the "exact opposite" of the Godly soul implies that there is no room here for compromise. A person might arrive at some sort of compromise between the two halves of his inner self in an attempt to effect a peaceful coexistence between them, but such compromise is inherently partial and temporary. Ultimately, both souls want one thing: complete domination. So inherently, there is no room for compromise.

We emphasize this because a compromise of this sort is one thing that Judaism cannot accept. This is one of the reasons why it is so difficult to be a Jew. If all that were required of a Jew would merely be to go to the synagogue and pray there at certain times, it would be far simpler. But the Jew is also required to leave the synagogue for the outside world, and the real question is: What happens then? It is impossible to make some sort of compromise, cutting life in two, half for holiness and half not, because the spheres of holiness and *kelipah* cannot live alongside each other peacefully. Inevitably, a struggle ensues, in which one soul prevails.

A further problem is that the spheres are not clearly defined. For within the range of the animal soul's desires are also aesthetic, philosophical, and even religious cravings. The aim of the animal soul is to satisfy the ego, and if doing holy things makes a person feel good, the animal soul can also grant him this illusion of holiness. As long as a person wishes to serve God part-time, as a hobby, his animal soul will be fully supportive of the endeavor. It will provide him with all the accoutrements of holiness and holy feelings, as much as he desires, for the essence of the battle, the quintessential point over which the souls are fighting, is who should occupy the innermost point, the epicenter of the person. Rabbi Isaac Meir of Gur used to say that once Satan has taken from a person the point of truth, he is prepared to leave him all the nonsense. If the person wants to wear a *shtreiml* (the Hasidic fur hat), he can wear it; if he wants to pray, let him pray; if he wants to be a Hasid, let him be a Hasid, because even so, he can remain just an animal. Perhaps he is a different animal, somewhat more refined, who enjoys different pastimes, such as attending concerts—perhaps even concerts exclusively devoted to *chazzanut* (Jewish liturgical music)—but an animal nonetheless.

[it desires this] for the good of man, that he may prevail over it and vanquish it,

Here, the author touches on a deeper point. He has apparently defined a dualistic world—holiness on one side, *kelipah* on the other—struggling over the neutral ground in between. But at the root, this is not a true duality. In essence, the animal soul, too, is the creation of God, and it, too, desires holiness. The animal soul struggles against the Godly soul, but its innermost desire is that man should defeat it. The seduction practiced by the animal soul is really a contrived challenge to enable the Godly soul to reach higher levels.

A soul on its own, denuded of the body and the accoutrements of physical life, is a holy being; but it is also a static being, because it has nothing to overcome. Some Hasidic masters would often say that if God had merely desired love or study of Torah, he would have created a few million angels to love God and sit and study; but because there is no challenge in this, He does not desire it. Angels are static; they are what they are and do not change; they are therefore called *omdim,* "those who stand."[27] The pure soul is likewise static; in order that it be truly desirable to God, in order that its service of God should be significant, it requires a challenge, and the animal soul provides this challenge. So the animal soul, in its primal state, is not evil in the destructive and negative sense but a challenge that arises from the duality of human nature and from the possibility of free will, a kind of challenge that enables a person to achieve what even the pure soul cannot achieve.

Our author writes elsewhere that some souls descend to this world for the sole purpose of suffering.[28] From these souls, God desires neither Torah nor divine service, only that they should suffer all their lives. This may seem a cruel idea, but from a different standpoint, it represents a conception of reality that is not oriented to achievement. What is important is not how many pages of Talmud someone has studied or even how many *mitzvot* he has performed in a particular day but the success of the soul in overcoming its problems. What is important is what a person does despite all that challenges him. "Despite it all"— these are the words that Rabbi Levi Yitzchak of Berdichev would interject with great emphasis when he sang the Hosha'ana prayer: "[The people of Israel] are exiled and rebellious, *yet despite it all,* they are [as virtuously beautiful] as date palm."

Our sages have declared that a person is never subjected to a test that he has not been granted the capacity to meet. The more difficult the test, the more emphatic is the implied message: "You have what it takes to overcome this and grow from this." The degree of difficulty of the test is proof of the soul's ability to rise higher. From this perspective, there are no greater or stronger individuals; every person possesses a Godly soul and an animal soul that are precisely matched so that there should be an ongoing challenge and a perpetual struggle that he can meet and persevere in, and constantly achieve what he does—"despite it all."

as in the parable of the harlot in the holy *Zohar.*

The *Zohar* tells a parable of a king who was extremely fond of his only son and out of his love for him instructed him to keep away from promiscuous women.[29] One day, the king decided to test his son. To this end, the king hired a prostitute and instructed her to seduce his son. Now the harlot must try her best to faithfully perform the task for which she was employed, but she knows her greatest reward will come if she fails. She also knows that if the prince successfully resists her, he will rise in greatness, and she would be the cause of this. By the same token, the task of the animal soul is to seduce a person, but it, too, knows that the divine intention is that man should overcome it. The animal soul does everything in its power to seduce the person, but its victories do not please it; on the contrary, its true satisfaction comes from its failures.

Chapter 10

ow when a person fortifies his Godly soul and battles his animal soul to such an extent that he expels and eradicates its evil from the left ventricle—as is written, "And you shall eradicate the evil from within you"—yet the evil is not actually converted to good, he is called "an incomplete *tzaddik*" and "a *tzaddik* to whom is evil," implying that there still lingers in him a fragment of evil in the left ventricle, except that because of its minuteness, it is subjugated and nullified by the good. He therefore imagines that he has "driven it out and it is gone from him," all of it, completely. In truth, however, had all the evil in him entirely passed on and departed, it would have been converted into actual good.

The explanation of the matter is that a complete *tzaddik*, in whom the evil has been converted to good, and who is consequently called "a *tzaddik* to whom is good," [achieves] this by completely removing the soiled garments of evil. That is to say, he utterly despises the pleasures of this world—the enjoyment of human pleasures not for the sake of the service of God but merely to gratify the body's desires—because they are derived from and nourished by *kelipah* and *sitra achra*. For whatever is of the *sitra achra* is hated by the perfect *tzaddik* with an absolute hatred, by reason of the immensity of his love of God and His holiness with a great "love in delights" and utmost affection, as stated above. For the two are antithetical one to the other, as it is written, "I hate them with absolute hatred, they have become my enemies; search me and know my heart. . . ." [Thus,] according to the magnitude of the love toward God, so is the degree of the magnitude of hatred towards the *sitra achra* and the utter abhorrence of evil, since like hatred, abhorrence is the veritable opposite of love.

The incomplete *tzaddik* is one who does not hate the *sitra achra* with an absolute hatred; therefore he also does not absolutely abhor evil. And as long as the hatred and abhorrence of evil are not absolute, there must remain some vestige of love and pleasure in it, [meaning that] the soiled garments have not entirely and absolutely been shed. As a result, [the evil] has not been utterly transformed into good, since it still has some attachment to the soiled garments; it is only that it is nullified because of its minute quantity and is accounted as nothing. Therefore such a person is called "a *tzaddik* to whom the evil [within him] is [subjugated and abnegated]." Accordingly, his love of God is also not ultimate, and he is thus called "an incomplete *tzaddik.*"

Now, this level is subdivided into myriads of degrees in regard to the quality of the minute evil remaining from any of the four evil elements, as well as in regard to its proportionate abnegation by reason of its minuteness, such as, by way of example, one in sixty, or in a thousand, or in ten thousand, and the like. Such are the gradations of the numerous *tzaddikim* in all generations, as mentioned in the Talmud that "Eighteen thousand *tzaddikim* stand before the Holy One, blessed be He."

But regarding the rank of the "complete *tzaddik*," Rabbi Shimon bar Yochai said: "I have seen the ascendant ones (*b'nei aliyah*), and they are few. . . ." The reason they are called "ascendant ones" is that they transform evil and make it ascend to holiness, as is written in the *Zohar,* in the Introduction, that when Rabbi Chiyya wished to ascend to the [heavenly] chamber of Rabbi Shimon bar Yochai, he heard a voice come out and say, "Which of you has transformed darkness into light and bitter taste into sweetness? Otherwise, do not approach here. . . ."

Another reason that they are called "ascendant ones" is that also their service in the category of "do good," in the fulfillment of the Torah and its commandments, is for the sake of the Above, the ultimate of the highest degrees; not merely in order to attach themselves to God so as to quench the thirst of their soul, which thirsts for God, as is written, "Ho, everyone that thirsts, come ye to the waters," as is explained elsewhere, but in the manner described in *Tikkunei Zohar:* "Who is a *chassid*? He who is benevolent towards his Owner—towards His nest—uniting the Holy One, blessed be He, and His [*Shekhinah*] within the nethermost worlds." As also explained in *Ra'aya Meheimna* on *Parashat Tetze:* "In the manner of a son who ingratiates himself with his father and mother, whom he loves more than his own self and his life, spirit, and soul (*nefesh, ruach,* and *neshamah*) . . . and is prepared to sacrifice his own life for them, to redeem them from captivity . . ." and as is explained elsewhere.

(And both interpretations are complementary, for through acts of refinement of the good out of *nogah,* one elevates the feminine waters, causing supernal unions to draw down the masculine waters which are the flow of [divine] benevolence contained in each and every *mitzvah* of the 248 positive commandments, all of which are in the nature of benevolence and masculine waters, that is to say, the flow of holiness of His blessed divinity from above downward, to be clothed within the nethermost worlds, as explained elsewhere.)

COMMENTARY

Chapter 9 spoke of the perpetual battle between the two souls in man, each of which desires to gain total mastery over the body and be the sole ruler of its faculties. It gave a very general description of the Godly soul's aims: to conquer the animal soul, subjugate it, and ultimately transform its nature. The chapter did not, however, discuss how long this can take, how much work is involved, or what the chances of success are in this battle; it merely outlined an ideal—what the Godly soul aims to achieve in its battle with the animal soul. This chapter continues with a more detailed discussion of the Godly soul's aims, not as a battle plan that anyone can implement but as a description of various types of goals that can be gained in the battle, even if one falls short of a complete victory over one's animal nature.

Now when a person fortifies his Godly soul and battles his animal soul to such an extent that he expels and eradicates its evil from the left ventricle—as is written, "And you shall eradicate the evil from within you"[1]—

The literal meaning of this verse is in the social context, referring to the elimination of an evil individual from the community. Here, the author is applying it to the person, as an injunction to eliminate the evil element within oneself.

And when a person indeed eradicates the evil from himself,

yet the evil is not actually converted to good, he is called "an incomplete *tzaddik*,"

This is one of the five types of *tzaddik* ("righteous person") mentioned in the *Tanya*'s opening chapter, which alternatively is referred to as

"a *tzaddik* to whom is evil."

In its most literal sense, the phrase "a *tzaddik* to whom is evil" relates to the issue of reward and punishment and the age-old question, Why do the righteous suffer—why do they experience evil? However, as Chapter 1 already discussed, the phrase also has a deeper meaning, relating to the inner composition of the "incomplete *tzaddik*,"

implying that there still lingers in him a fragment of evil in the left ventricle,

This is the "place of residence" of the animal soul, as Chapter 9 elaborated.

except that because of its minuteness, it is subjugated and nullified by the good. He therefore imagines that he has "driven it out and it is gone from him,"[2] all of it, completely.

There is no outward difference, in deed, speech, or thought, between a complete *tzaddik* and an incomplete one. A person observed to act in full conformity with the divine will might be a complete *tzaddik*, but he might also be an incomplete one or even, as will be explained, not a *tzaddik* at all but a *beinoni* ("intermediate"). The difference is internal and invisible. In fact, the difference might also elude the person himself, for one cannot always know if one has achieved a complete transformation within. (This the author demonstrates in Chapter 1, by citing the case of Rabbah, a complete *tzaddik*, who thought himself a *beinoni*.)

Nor is the difference between an incomplete and a complete *tzaddik* that the one can experience negative desires whereas the other cannot. The definition of a *tzaddik*, complete or otherwise, is someone who has no internal struggle; the *tzaddik* is a person whose Godly soul has achieved a decisive victory over his animal soul, and if this has not happened, one is not a *tzaddik*. One does not need to be a *tzaddik* to be a great person or a holy person and to have "rivers of scented oil" awaiting one in *Gan Eden* ("paradise"), but if one has not achieved victory in one's inner battle, attaining the state of "one who rules in the fear of God,"[3] one is not a *tzaddik*.

The state of *tzaddik* is static and not subject to change. The *tzaddik,* "complete" or "incomplete," is one who senses that his inner evil no longer exists, that he has "driven it out and it is gone from him, all of it, completely"; the incomplete *tzaddik* therefore requires some other sign, some other indication, to tell him he is still not a complete *tzaddik.* The indication is that if he had indeed driven out all evil from within, something more drastic would have occurred: the evil would have been converted to absolute good. Complete victory implies more than mere conquest of *kelipah* by the Godly soul, more than the neutralization of the animal soul's ability to tempt the person with material pleasures. It implies a complete transformation, with animal soul itself becoming a force for holiness. So long as a person has not yet achieved this fundamental change, a residue of evil remains within him, and he is still in the category of "a *tzaddik* to whom is evil."

In order that this should not appear completely divorced from reality, we must understand to whom this book was directed. Rabbi Schneur Zalman's followers included ordinary people but also many who had attained great heights in Torah scholarship and spirituality even before they came to him. To be accepted into the lowest of his *chadarim,*[4] one had to be thoroughly versed in both the Babylonian and Jerusalem Talmuds, *Zohar,* and the basic works of *mussar* ("moral teaching") and Jewish philosophy. A disciple of Rabbi Schneur Zalman did not finish at this level and then become head of a yeshiva; this was the entry point. Such was the caliber of many of the people for whom this book was written; for them, the terms "*tzaddik*" and "complete *tzaddik*" and their own relationship to these terms were not inconsequential matters. Furthermore, although the concept of *tzaddik* as defined in this book might be extremely difficult to attain, it is a state that everyone can study and apply as a standard against which to measure oneself. On the most basic level, one who commits any negative act, in whatever sense, or fails to perform a *mitzvah* cannot be called a *tzaddik*. This is a standard that any person possessing an inner integrity can use to examine himself.

The story is told of one of the great early Hasidim who fell to his deathbed in a strange and distant place where he was totally unknown.

The local Jews approached him and suggested that he perform the deathbed confession. The Hasid replied that he had nothing to confess. But they pressed him: How can a Jew die without first confessing? He finally acquiesced, asked for a prayer book, opened it, and began to recite the confession. *"Ashamnu"* ("We have been guilty"), he began, then paused, thought a little, and said, "No." He then continued, *"Bagadnu"* ("We have been treacherous"), again paused, thought, and said, "No." And so he continued throughout the alphabetical list until he came to *"Latznu"* ("We have scoffed"), and said: "No. And what I have done in making fun of the *mitnagdim* ("opposers" of Hasidism), I do not regret now either." The story is usually told as a joke against *mitnagdim,* but it also shows, from a serious angle, how a person on his deathbed, when every person conducts a true and honest self-assessment, can ask himself, Have I sinned? search his conscience, and answer, No.

On a deeper level, the *tzaddik* defines an inner state that goes beyond behavioral perfection. As the *Tanya* has established in its first nine chapters, a person has within him a consciousness, an inner perception, that directs the primary forces of his soul either toward holiness or toward that which is not holy. Without conscious direction, these mighty preconscious forces, if not consciously directed otherwise, tend toward the unholy: they can easily and freely burst out in a disorganized realm where the ordered forces of mind and consciousness do not operate and where they have free rein to realize themselves uninhibitedly. On the other hand, the ordered and fixed realm of holiness is an environment in which it is far more difficult for these primary forces to express themselves, and only by hard work, by the perpetual struggle of the Godly soul against the animal soul over the consciousness and its rule over the life of the soul, can one direct these forces to express themselves through holiness and not through *kelipah.* This struggle goes on for as long as the two realms exist in a person. But when a person achieves complete victory, so that he no longer has two channels of consciousness but only one—namely, the recognition of the divine—all the forces within him begin to move in only one direction. The primary animal forces have not been suppressed but rather redirected so that they now express themselves, with their full animal intensity, within the realm of holiness.

The existence of evil is like that of falsehood. There is no such thing as an utter falsehood: no lie can be sustained unless it contains a grain of truth. And when the lie is "refined"—that is, an element of truth is extracted from its embodiment of falsehood—the false embodiment disappears completely, and one arrives at a state of full, luminous truth. This is the point of transition from the level of "an incomplete *tzaddik*" to the level of "a complete *tzaddik*," the point at which evil is transformed completely into good. At this point, a person should feel as if vital forces of his soul have been doubled—more than doubled, because the animal soul's drives are more passionate than those of the Godly soul. All that he has done in the past seems only a small part of what he can do now, for now he has found the ultimate resolution to the struggles of life. The very nature of reality is transformed for him, and he functions as a totally different person.

There are two levels in *tzaddikim:* the *tzaddik* that does what God wants and the *tzaddik* whose every action *is* God's will. The latter is the level of the complete *tzaddik.* The state of incomplete *tzaddik* is never without a certain conscious basis: his mind must rule over his being and direct it toward the divine will. The complete *tzaddik* requires no such control: he can give free rein to his desires, because his desires always reflect the will of God. He requires no "direction," for all directions his psyche might take are holy and Godly. Such a person does not inhabit a world where both good and evil are possible, because his entirety is a *merkavah* ("chariot"), a vehicle of Godliness.

Hasidic master Rabbi Nachum of Shtifinshti (son of Rabbi Israel of Rozhin) once entered the study hall on Hanukkah and found his disciples enjoying a game of checkers. He asked them if they knew the rules of the game, but no one ventured a reply. Said Rabbi Nachum: "I will tell you. The first rule is that you give up one in order to take two. The second rule is that you move only forward, but once you reach the end of the board, you can move any way you desire." The implication is that the complete *tzaddik,* who has reached "the end of the board" in the battle of life, can go whichever way he desires, because whichever route he takes is God's will; the *tzaddik* is simply incapable of acting in any other way.

But although the *tzaddik* is utterly free of the internal inclination to evil that plagues the ordinary man, he is not devoid of free will. As long as he is in the human realm, he is free to choose, and he is liable even to err and choose wrongly. Moreover, there are situations in which there is a fault to every available option. These are faults that do not arise from within the *tzaddik* but are inherent in the situation itself. Moses is recorded as having lost his temper on a number of occasions. Moses' anger was certainly a fault, yet the situation made it impossible for him to act otherwise; anger was the only educational means available to correct the problem. The prayer for rain recited on the festival of Shemini Atzeret is composed of verses mentioning the deeds of the leaders of Israel in connection with water. The verse in praise of Moses is that "He struck the rock and water emerged." But was not striking the rock the sin of Moses' life, for which his punishment was that he could not enter the land of Israel?

In his commentary on Torah, Rashi explains Moses' sin: if Moses had spoken to the rock rather than struck it, this would have been a great lesson for the people of Israel. The people would have said, "If the rock, which is deaf and dumb and does not require sustenance, obeys Moses, then we certainly must obey him."[5] Yet Moses did not want to speak to the rock; he knew that if the Jewish people continued to disobey him, even after witnessing the rock's obedience, this would have constituted a great accusation against them, against which there could be no defense. So instead of speaking to the rock, he struck it. Moses, who was close to God more than anyone else before or since, also faced choices. He chose, mistakenly or not, to do something that was counted against him, on the one hand, as his great sin, and counted to his credit, on the other, as one of the great deeds of his life—that "He struck the rock and water emerged."

Situations arise in which perfection is not possible, in which the very structure of reality and the relation between a person, the world, and God are such that no perfect solution exists. In such a situation, even a *tzaddik* can reach an erroneous decision. King David's sin with Bathsheba was a tragedy for Uriah, for David, and for Bathsheba, but from the greater perspective of Jewish history, it gave rise to one of the greatest moments of *teshuvah* ("repentance"). Virtually every person sins, and when a sinner reads Psalm 51, "When Nathan came to him [David] after he went to Bathsheba," he has something to relate to. Considering that David is the fourth leg of the "divine chariot," David's sin might be the only way in which certain people can relate to him. If the great ones of Israel had no faults, it would be impossible to establish any connection with them. In this sense, their falls are our path to elevation.

In our reality, we face problems with no clear, unambiguous solution. The question of whether something is a *mitzvah* or a sin, or a *mitzvah* best neglected, or a sin that it is perhaps necessary to commit, does not always have an answer. The Talmud blames the destruction of the Temple and the exile of Israel on the humility of Zechariah ben

Avkulos.[6] Zechariah wanted to act with complete righteousness and honesty, without deviating in the slightest from truth. However, had he been less rigid in that situation, had he been prepared to sin a little, the Temple might not have been destroyed. The final reckoning—What are *mitzvot* and what are sins?—is not for us to decide, because some factors are beyond reckoning, even for a complete *tzaddik.*

The explanation of the matter is that a complete *tzaddik,* in whom the evil has been converted to good, and who is consequently called "a *tzaddik* to whom is good," [achieves] this by completely removing the soiled garments of evil. That is to say, he utterly despises the pleasures of this world—the enjoyment of human pleasures not for the sake of the service of God but merely to gratify the body's desires—because they are derived from and nourished by *kelipah* and *sitra achra.*

The idea that a person can engage in a physical activity simply to derive enjoyment from it, that a person can eat something simply because it is tasty, is for the complete *tzaddik* an abomination that the mind cannot bear. A Hasid of our own generation traveled to America and wrote back home the profoundly shocking observation that, "Here in America, people actually drink wine and eat meat for pleasure!" A Jew can, then, be shocked by the sight of people simply eating to enjoy themselves, without pangs of conscience and without even pretending that they are doing it for a holy purpose.

For whatever is of the *sitra achra* is hated by the perfect *tzaddik* with an absolute hatred, by reason of the immensity of his love of God and His holiness with a great "love in delights" and utmost affection, as stated above.

See Chapter 9.

For the two are antithetical one to the other, as it is written, "I hate them with absolute hatred, they have become my enemies; search me and know my heart. . . ."[7] [Thus,] according to the magnitude of the love toward God, so is the degree of the magnitude of the hatred towards the *sitra achra* and the utter abhorrence of evil, since like hatred, abhorrence is the veritable opposite of love.

The way to "search me and know my heart," to find out if one's love for God is indeed absolute, is to see whether one's regard of everything deriving from *kelipah* is such that "I hate them with absolute hatred." For the two are antithetical one to the other: a desire, or even the slightest affinity, for *kelipah* indicates a less than complete desire for Godliness.

Such a measure of heart is not limited to complete *tzaddikim*. In every society and in every individual's inner moral scale are certain things that are simply not done, certain limits that are not to be exceeded no matter what, things that are abominated and utterly despised, for they are antithetical to everything that society or that individual understands to be right and desirable. So these things are not only not done, they are unthinkable; these are not temptations to be resisted, for they are so totally abhorred that no possibility of temptation exists. For example, the idea of murdering someone in order to rob him of his money was once unheard of in Israeli society; there were thieves, but to kill for money was taboo. Today, that boundary has been breached, and society has, so to speak, become receptive to the idea that such things are possible. People might still utterly reject the idea of killing for money, but they no longer feel the horror and abomination that the very thought once evoked, because the act has entered the realm of possibility. In our society, the idea of eating human flesh is unthinkable. If we hear of a case of cannibalism, our reaction is one of total abhorrence and extreme hatred and contempt toward the one who did such a deed. Yet there are places in the world where even if people do not practice cannibalism daily, the idea is not unthinkable.

There are things that people would never do, sins they would never commit, yet the possibility is not unthinkable; so the temptation or at least the thought of doing them might occasionally arise in their hearts. But every person has certain sins regarding which his heart is utterly pure, sins he would never even consider as a possibility and for which he does not even feel temptation. This is the complete *tzaddik*'s relation to everything belonging to the sphere of unholiness, in every shape and form. Such things do not touch him; he does not comprehend them; they do not enter his mind. His mind and soul are attuned to Godliness and yearn for God alone; worldly pleasures of any kind are inconceivable to him, and he fails to understand how they can be conceivable to anyone else.

Rabbi Yechiel Michal from Zlotchov, one of the disciples of the Baal Shem Tov, was known as a complete *tzaddik* who possessed *ruach hakodesh* ("the holy spirit," a level of divine perception akin to prophecy), which reputedly had been in his family for ten generations.

A wagon driver in his town once committed a violation of the Shabbat, regretted his sin, and approached the local rabbi to see what amends he could make. The rabbi saw that the man's penitence was sincere and told him that he should donate a pound of candles to the synagogue and his sin would be forgiven. When Rabbi Michal heard of this, he did not approve: How could a pound of candles compensate for a breach of the Shabbat? That Friday afternoon, when the wagon driver came and placed his candles in the appropriate place, a big dog came into the synagogue, snatched the candles, and ate them before they could be used. Seeing what had happened, the wagon driver was brokenhearted. He went back to the rabbi and told him that God has not accepted his atonement. The rabbi assured that it was just an unfortunate coincidence; if he would again bring candles to the synagogue the following week, his sin would be forgiven. On the following week, another mishap occurred, and again the week following, until the rabbi, too, conceded that something was amiss. He sent the penitent to the Baal Shem Tov, who realized that Rabbi Michal had a hand in it, and sent for him. The Baal Shem Tov's home in Medzibezh was only a few hours' journey away, but the horses pulling Reb Michal's wagon turned off the road and got lost in the forest; then an axle broke; and one trouble followed another, so that when Rabbi Michal entered Medzibezh, it was late Friday afternoon, and the sun was setting, and the *tzaddik* feared that he had violated the Shabbat by traveling on the holy day. When he came to the Baal Shem Tov, crushed and broken in spirit and beside himself, his rebbe called to him, "Come here, sinner! Until now you did not know how a Jew who has sinned feels, how brokenhearted he is. Now, you will realize that a pound of candles is sufficient!" Rabbi Michal, who had ascended all the rungs in the ladder of holiness, could not comprehend how anyone could sin, how one could possibly rebel against God. What others know from within themselves, the *tzaddik* has to be taught.

Worldly temptations do not tempt the complete *tzaddik,* not because he is indifferent to them but because they do not exist for him. And because they do not relate to him in any way, because they are utterly incomprehensible to him, he hates and despises them. As long as someone is indifferent to something, he is vulnerable to it, even though he might never actually do it: the very fact that he is not overcome with revulsion at the very thought of the thing—that he can accept its possibility with equanimity—indicates that it is not completely inconceivable to him. If it were truly beyond possibility for him, it would provoke a sharp negative reaction. Thus,

the incomplete *tzaddik* is one who does not hate the *sitra achra* with an absolute hatred; therefore he also does not absolutely abhor evil. And as long as the hatred and abhorrence of evil are not absolute, there must remain some vestige of love and pleasure in it, [meaning that] the soiled garments have not entirely and absolutely been shed. As a result, [the evil] has not been utterly transformed into good, since it still has some attachment to the soiled garments; it is only that it is nullified because of its minute quantity and is accounted as nothing. Therefore such a person is called "a *tzaddik* to whom the evil (within him) is (subjugated and abnegated)."

The incomplete *tzaddik* behaves like a complete *tzaddik* in every way. He, too, has passed the stage of inner doubt, torment, and struggle. He, too, is not tempted by evil and experiences no urge for anything not holy. The difference between them is in their innermost heart of hearts, in the ultimate transformation of evil to good. The incomplete *tzaddik* differs from the complete *tzaddik* in that he has not yet achieved this quintessential transformation. Thus, although he worships God in all his deeds and ways, he worships Him without feeling an utter hatred for evil, not because he is likely to sin, God forbid, but because he still contains the idea of something contrary to Godliness, albeit in the most subtle and diminished of forms. The second channel of possible expression of the forces of his soul still exists within him.

Accordingly, his love of God is also not ultimate, and he is thus called "an incomplete *tzaddik*."

The incomplete *tzaddik* is one who serves God with his every deed, word, and thought, but he is serving him with only part (albeit the greater part) of his soul. The remainder is there but does not participate; it has been silenced but not converted to a positive force in his divine service. His love of God is thus incomplete, for it is fueled by less than 100 percent of his potential, by less than the combined forces of his Godly and animal selves.

Now, this level is subdivided into myriads of degrees in regard to the quality of the minute evil remaining from any of the four evil elements,

Only one type of complete *tzaddik* exists: the person who possesses not the slightest vestige of inner evil, having effected its complete conversion into good. In contrast, the incomplete *tzaddik* still has some evil in himself; evil comes in many types and forms, making for many types and degrees of incomplete *tzaddik*, defined by the quality and quantity of evil still in him. We might differentiate them by quantity:

as well as in regard to its proportionate abnegation by reason of its minuteness, such as, by way of example, one in sixty, or in a thousand, or in ten thousand, and the like.

Our author is employing the terminology of halakhah, where a small amount of forbidden food that is accidentally mixed in with permitted food may in some cases be considered as negligible and nonexistent if it is less than one part in sixty and in some cases if it is less than one part in a hundred, and so on. Halakhically, these might not result in different degrees of nullification; when a thing is nullified, it is nullified (but different substances require different percentages for a nullification to occur at all). Similarly, there is no *practical* difference between an incomplete *tzaddik* whose evil is nullified by sixty and one whose evil is nullified by a thousand; in either case, the evil has been suppressed to the point that it has no effect on his behavior or his inclinations. But in terms of the person's inner truth, in terms of the quality of his love for God and his proximity to his ultimate perfection, there are differences between lesser and greater ratios of nullification.

Such are the gradations of the numerous *tzaddikim* in all generations, as mentioned in the Talmud that "Eighteen thousand *tzaddikim* stand before the Holy One, blessed be He."[8]

This Talmudic statement, says our author, is speaking of incomplete *tzaddikim*.

But regarding the rank of the "complete *tzaddik*," Rabbi Shimon bar Yochai said: "I have seen the ascendant ones (*b'nei aliyah*), and they are few. . . ."

The verse continues: "If they are a thousand, I and my son are among them; if they are a hundred, I and my son are among them; if they are two, I and my son are they."[9] Thus, Rabbi Shimon is not sure that there are more than two complete *tzaddikim* in his entire generation.

The reason they are called "ascendant ones" is that they transform evil and make it ascend to holiness,

The Hebrew word *aliyah* means "ascent." Thus, the term *b'nei aliyah* (usually understood to mean "the lofty ones") literally means "the ascendant ones," which our author here interprets as a reference to those who have achieved more than mastery over evil, actually effecting its ascent to holiness, having transformed the very composition of their souls so that the *kelipah* within it is elevated to holiness.

as is written in the *Zohar*, in the Introduction,[10] that when Rabbi Chiyya wished to ascend to the [heavenly] chamber of Rabbi Shimon bar Yochai, he heard a voice come out and say, "Which of you has transformed darkness into light and bitter taste into sweetness? Otherwise, do not approach here. . . ."

Rabbi Shimon, as stated earlier, was the quintessential complete *tzaddik*; those who wish to enter into his domain must exhibit a similar quality. They must be more than incomplete *tzaddikim*; they must be of the category of "the ascendant ones" who transform the evil within their soul into good, the darkness into light, and the bitterness into sweetness. These *tzaddikim* do not merely sweeten the bitter; they transform its bitterness into a new kind of sweetness. They do not merely drive out the darkness; they convert darkness into light. One who can transform darkness into light has no darkness in his world, and his relationship with the world is totally different. The temptations and pains of the world no longer exist for him; for him, no concealment exists, no partition that separates the divine from the earthly, no gap between the physical and the spiritual.

Rabbi Levi Yitzhak of Berdichev once visited one of the leading Hasidic rebbes of his time. The Hasidim had been notified in advance of the prestigious guest and were enjoined to treat him with due reverence. Rabbi Levi Yitzchak arrived at prayer time wearing his *tallit* and *tefillin*, but instead of joining in the prayers, asked after the whereabouts of the kitchen, where he inquired about what was being cooked and chatted at length with the simple folk employed there. The Hasidim wanted to tell off the strange guest for his improper behavior but waited until the prayers were over. Then, to their amazement they saw their rebbe take the visitor, whom they had considered to be the lowest of the low, sit with him, and eat with him out of the same plate, the greatest of honors. Their rebbe then told them: "What this man does, he does in higher worlds." The difference between the lowly and the lofty, between eating (because one is hungry) and one's spiritual activities vis-à-vis the higher worlds (if one is indeed on that level), that applies to ordinary people does not apply to the complete *tzaddik*. The complete *tzaddik* is one whose every action reaches to the higher worlds, to which he elevates the lowest and most mundane elements of material life, which is why he and the likes of him are called "the ascendant ones." Of this level, attained only by the rare perfect individual, the prophet Jeremiah speaks when he says: "If you return and I bring you back, you will stand before Me; and if you extract the valuable from the vile it will be as if [you have placed it in] My mouth."[11] The ability to extract the valuable from the vile is the unique trait of "the ascendant ones."

Another reason that they are called "ascendant ones" is that also their service in the category of "do good," in the fulfillment of the Torah and its commandments, is for the sake of the Above, the ultimate of the highest degrees; not merely in order to attach themselves to God

This is another distinction between the complete *tzaddik* and the incomplete *tzaddik*. The complete *tzaddik* is one whose yearnings, dreams, and desires are directed not inward to his own spiritual development but upward—to God alone. God is his pleasure and his entire world. He is at such a high level that the basis of his service of God is God Himself; he, the servant, is completely irrelevant. His endeavor to cleave to God is not motivated by any selfish desire to achieve this state but by the fact that God desires it.

Some say that the craving for closeness for God is also a desire; yet in order to truly experience it, one must first annul all other desires. This desire is the most wonderful, the loftiest, and the holiest of all the soul's desires. But the complete *tzaddik* is one in whom even this desire is annulled. It is not that he no longer desires God but that this desire pales to insignificance before his purpose in life: to fulfill the divine will. In his all-consuming drive to serve God, he is utterly without any thought of himself, even of the self at its loftiest and holiest level, which is the yen to quench the thirst of their soul, which thirsts for God, as is written, "Ho, everyone that thirsts, come ye to the waters,"[12] as is explained elsewhere,

Elsewhere,[13] the author explains the verse, "Ho, everyone that thirsts, come ye to the waters" as referring to anyone who is thirsty for God, whom the prophet calls to go to the waters of Torah, for the study of Torah and the observance of its commandments is the only way to quench the soul's thirst for God. So the seeker of God turns to the Torah and the *mitzvot* as a thirsting man pounces upon a brook of fresh, bubbling water; he pursues these manifestations of Godliness, grasping them in every possible way. The complete *tzaddik*, however, is beyond all that; he studies Torah and observes the *mitzvot* not to slake his own thirst for God but for God's sake, because God desires that he do so. The complete *tzaddik* is not only devoid of all material ambitions; he is free of all spiritual ambition as well. His objective is not the elevation of his own spiritual self or the sublime pleasure of being close to God, only the satisfaction of the divine will.

The story is told of two disciples of one of the great Hasidic masters who met after being separated for many years. One asked the other: "Why was man created?" "To refine himself," was the other's reply. Said the first: "Have you forgotten what we learned? Man was created to raise the heavens!" (that is, not to think about himself at all, just to be unified with the divine). In other words, one who serves God in order to attach oneself to God achieves the purpose of self-improvement, but the one who serves to "unite the Holy One with His *Shekhinah*" does so to raise the heavens. He does not think of self-improvement, not because such a thing does not exist, but because it is insignificant, compared to the essence of his mission in life, to raise the heavens.

but in the manner described in *Tikkunei Zohar*: "Who is a *chassid*? He who is benevolent towards his Owner

The Hebrew word *chassid* means "benevolent one." In the Talmud, the term is used to connote an individual of great spiritual stature, equivalent to the complete *tzaddik* of the *Tanya*. The *Tikkunei Zohar* explains that a *chassid* is "one who is benevolent towards his Owner": one whose every act is an act of benevolence toward God, whose motive in everything he does is not for his own sake, to achieve attachment and fusion with God, but to fulfill the divine will.

—towards His nest—uniting the Holy One, blessed be He, and His [*Shekhinah*] within the nethermost worlds."[14]

The word the *Zohar* uses for "his Owner" is *kono* (a common euphemism for God), which also can be rendered "His nest"—that is, the divine place of dwelling. Thus, the *Zohar* further develops its interpretation of *"chassid"* as one whose benevolence toward God is expressed in an endeavor to restore the integrity of God's "nest." The divine "nest," as Rabbi Shmuel Grunem explains in his elucidations of *Tanya*, is the *Shekhinah*, the divine immanence that dwells within the created reality. By creating the world, God, in effect, separated "the Holy One" (the divine reality that transcends creation) from the *Shekhinah* (the divine presence within creation). God's desire is that man should unite the two. Every *mitzvah* performed by man is an act of repairing this so-called breach in the divine reality.

For the complete *tzaddik,* the fulfillment of this divine wish eclipses everything else. He completely forgets his own soul's cravings and desires, indeed his very sense of self, in the endeavor "to unite the Holy One and His *Shekhinah.*"

As also explained in *Ra'aya Meheimna* on *Parashat Tetze:*[15] "In the manner of a son who ingratiates himself with his father and mother, whom he loves more than his own self and his life, spirit, and soul (*nefesh, ruach,* and *neshamah*) . . . and is prepared to sacrifice his own life for them, to redeem them from captivity . . ." and as is explained elsewhere.

A complete *tzaddik* is one who abnegates not only the desires of his animal soul but also those of his Godly soul, because the only desire that drives him is the desire to serve God. Such self-sacrifice is greater than physical martyrdom, in which a person sacrifices his life for a certain cause. When a person gives up his life, he is sacrificing his body; but when a person forgoes the positive and holy desires of his soul for the sake of heaven, the sacrifice is much greater.

At one level, a *tzaddik* desires to withdraw from all worldly affairs and cleave to God, but at a higher level, he is prepared to waive this desire because God wants him to be in the world. This is the highest form of self-sacrifice, sacrifice of the Godly soul's desire to enjoy the closeness of God. This is the conflict that faces the *tzaddik:* not the conflict between the material desires of the animal soul and the holy desires of the Godly soul but the conflict between the Godly soul's desire to unite with God and its duty to fulfill its mission in life of "redeeming" God from His "captivity" in the concealment of creation, of reuniting the "Holy One" with the *Shekhinah,* the Godliness that transcends creation with the divine presence implicit in the world.

The Torah tells of Moses' inner struggle when God appointed him to lead the Jewish people out of Egypt, a struggle experienced by every *tzaddik* who is appointed to a position of leadership. When a man such as Moses becomes a leader of Israel, he sacrifices his very self, not just his time and energy but his very soul. From the moment he undertakes to involve himself with others' problems, with their physical and spiritual ills, he waives the possibility of his soul attaining its own spiritual objectives, and this is the ultimate self-sacrifice. Moses resisted the task of serving as the leader of Israel, saying to God, "I am not a man of words. . . . Send whom you will."[16] Moses enjoyed a state of perfect attachment with God, but he knew that if he accepted the appointment, he would have to deal with Pharaoh, with "the complainants"[17] and "the spies,"[18] and with every sort of physical and spiritual leper. Yet Moses accepted the mission, obliterating the ambition of his Godly soul—for God's sake alone. As he himself expressed it (when Israel committed the sin of the golden calf): "And now, if You forgive their sin—; but if You will not, then blot me out of the book that You have written."[19] The same applies to every *tzaddik* who serves as the leader of his generation. A true leader is one who is capable of the ultimate self-sacrifice: the sacrifice of his very "I"; of his "*nefesh, ruach,* and *neshamah*"; of his soul's yearning to cleave to God.

(And both interpretations are complementary,

Both reasons given here as to why the complete *tzaddikim* are called "the ascendant ones"—(1) that they transform evil into good and darkness to light, raising them to holiness and (2) that their only motivation is toward heaven alone without any self-consideration, even for the Godly soul—are, in essence, two aspects of the same truth.

for through acts of refinement of the good out of *nogah,*

Man's service to God in the physical world consists primarily of what the Kabbalists call "the work of refinement," the extraction of the kernel of divine vitality within *kelipat nogah* and its elevation to holiness (as described in Chapters 7 and 8). The *mitzvot*—physical deeds involving physical objects—are performed within the realm of *kelipat nogah,* in the realm of nonholiness; they reveal the holiness within *nogah,* extracting it from its "husk" and elevating it to its source in God. This is what happens when a physical substance is made into an object of holiness (such as a *tallit, shofar,* or *lulav*)[20] and also what happens to the person's very body and animal soul, when he directs his physical life to a Godly end.

one elevates the feminine waters [*mayin nukvin*], causing supernal unions to draw down the masculine waters [*mayin dechurin*]

The most primary and basic division is the division between upper and lower, a division that appears in the very first stages of creation in the form of the separation of the "upper waters" from the "lower waters."[21] The upper waters belong to the heavenly reality and are what the Kabbalists call "masculine waters" (*mayin dechurin*), waters that provide. The Kabbalists call the lower waters, belonging to the lower reality, that of the created worlds, "feminine waters" (*mayin nukvin*), waters that receive. Creation is the separation of the two; life is the dynamics of their mutual influence, and the purpose of life is their unification. But in order for the upper waters to descend and permeate the lower waters, the lower waters must first ascend. When the lower waters gravitate upward, when they well up in yearning toward their separated mate, the upper waters are drawn downward to effuse divine influence in the world, until complete unification is achieved. The "work of refinement," in which a person takes a piece of the world and reveals its inherent holiness, is a rising of lower waters. At that moment, a spark is unleashed, a flash of holiness that rises to its source on high.

When the lower waters ascend, they cause a "supernal union." They unite with the upper waters, stimulating them to meet their ascent with a descent of their own, a providence of "masculine waters" to the world,

which are the flow of [divine] benevolence contained in each and every mitzvah of the 248 positive commandments, all of which are in the nature of benevolence and masculine waters, that is to say, the flow of holiness of His blessed divinity from above downward, to be clothed within the nethermost worlds, as explained elsewhere.)

Thus, there are two aspects to the *mitzvah*. The first is its elevating effect. The *mitzvah,* as we said, acts upon the lower waters, upon the profane world of *kelipat nogah.* The person performing the *mitzvah* takes a material substance, a part of the lower realm of creation; refines it, wholly or partially; and elevates it to the realm of holiness. In this sense, the act of a *mitzvah* is an "ascending of feminine waters." But this is only one aspect of the *mitzvah.* The elevation of the matter, by which the physical world raises itself on tiptoe, so to speak, in an effort to reach for the heavens, is met by a supernal response—a "descending of masculine waters," an effusion of divine provision to the lower realm of creation.

So the essence of *mitzvah* is a joining (*tzavta*) of the terrestrial with the supernal, a collaboration of the human and the divine in a single act, the act of the *mitzvah.* The *mitzvah,* then, is more than an ascent of the lower; it is also a spurt of divinity from above, in which the divine immanence is revealed within the physical reality. Thus are the supernal and the lowly joined and united. This confluence of forces is the "union of the Holy One and His *Shekhinah*" implicit in every *mitzvah.* Every act of Torah study, prayer, or charity is an ascent of "feminine waters" evoking a descent of "masculine waters." This dynamic is also called "an arousal from below [that] evokes an arousal from above."

The part the lower realm plays is the creation of a will, a conscious desire on the part of lower waters that says: We want to ascend. Then comes the flow and descent of the upper waters, which unite with the lower waters, completing the *mitzvah.* A *mitzvah* is not only a human deed; it is a revelation of Godliness, a flash of divinity in the world. The human deed is the body of the *mitzvah,* the vessel, the physical conductor that attracts and captures the flash of divinity from above.

Every *mitzvah* is a union of the supernal and lowly; every person performing a *mitzvah* raises the lower waters and causes the higher waters to descend. But the degree of ascent depends on the quality of the person. The more perfect the person is, the higher the ascent and the greater and more perfect the divine union with the world. The complete *tzaddik* is a *ben aliyah,* an "ascendant one," in the sense that he raises the profane not only by refining—by sorting and selecting part of it for holiness as one extracts pure gold from the dross—but by a complete transformation of all of reality from bitter to sweet, from darkness to light. The complete *tzaddik* elevates the material world not only with an occasional holy deed but with his very existence, with his every action at every moment, with every step he takes in life. His very contact with any thing, even with evil, effects its complete conversion to holiness. His ascending effect on the world is of the highest degree.

So the two interpretations of the phrase "ascendant ones"—(1) that the complete *tzaddik* elevates the material existence and (2) that his concern lies not with his self-development but with the divine endeavor of "uniting the Holy One with His *Shekhinah*"—are not contradictory but complementary. The occupation of the *tzaddik* in this world, the process of transformation that he generates, is itself the union of the immanent and transcendent aspects of the divine reality. The perfect and absolute nature of his elevation of *kelipah* means that it is for the sake of God and not for his own sake.

The divine service of one who is not a complete *tzaddik* might in fact be an escape from the material, in which the person takes things from the world and runs off with them in flight to closeness with God. But the complete *tzaddik* never runs away from the world, because he takes everything in the world and raises it to holiness. He is not satisfied with gratifying his own soul's craving for God but elevates with him everything with which he comes into contact, because everything he does is an act of transformation.

A *tzaddik* who isolates himself and escapes the world ceases, at that moment, to fulfill his duty as a *tzaddik*. The *tzaddik*'s mission in life, his duty to his fellow man and to God, is to involve himself with the world and elevate it. The story is told of a *tzaddik* who once fell ill and sent a request for a blessing to one of the leading Hasidic rebbes of the time. In response, the rebbe instructed him to eat a large meal of milk products in order to be cured. The rebbe subsequently explained that this *tzaddik* never ate cheese, and it was the cheese's accusation against the *tzaddik*, that he had neglected to elevate it to holiness, that led to his illness. His cure would therefore be to eat cheese, so that the accusation would be withdrawn.

For the *tzaddik*, it is a great act of self-sacrifice not to neglect to elevate even a single corner of his world. The *tzaddik* is free of all internal evil; he has no need for any further transformation, no need for any contact with the bitter and the vile. If he forgoes his state of perfect union with God to involve himself with the mundane and the profane, it is only to rectify God's world, to "unite the Holy One with His *Shekhinah*." This is the meaning of the statement: "Who is a *chassid*? He who is benevolent towards his Owner."

This chapter has discussed the two types of *tzaddik:* the complete *tzaddik* and the incomplete *tzaddik.* Later, the author will explain that one cannot possibly attain these states by one's own efforts. If a person is not born with the unique ability to achieve total mastery of his animal soul, there is no way that he can make himself a *tzaddik.* The station of *tzaddik,* on either level, is beyond the range of the ordinary person; it is even beyond the range of the hero of *Tanya,* the *beinoni* ("intermediate"). Nonetheless, the author describes these states in order to present the larger picture, in relation to which a person can place himself and achieve a true estimate of his inner state. These glorious portraits are not to enable us to analyze or evaluate the *tzaddikim* themselves—something that is beyond our capacity—but to serve as ideals against which we might measure ourselves and attain a true assessment of our own place in the spectrum of human potential.

Chapter 11

T his opposite the other"—the "*rasha* to whom is good" is the corresponding opposite of the "*tzaddik* to whom is evil." This is to say that the good of his God soul which is in his brain and in the right ventricle of his heart is subservient to, and nullified by, the evil of the *kelipah* that is in the left ventricle.

This category, too, is subdivided into myriads of degrees which differ in respect of the extent and manner of the nullification and subservience of the good to the bad, God forbid. There is the person in whom the said subservience and nullification are in a very minor way, and even these are not permanent or recurring at frequent intervals. Rather, on rare occasions the evil prevails over the good and conquers the small city that is the body—and not all of it, but only a part of it—subjecting it to its discipline, to become a vehicle and a garment wherein is clothed one of its three above-mentioned garments. That is, either in deed alone, in the commission of minor transgressions and not major ones, God forbid; or in speech alone, in an utterance that borders on slander or causticity and the like; or in thought alone, in "contemplations of sin, which are more severe than actual sin," or even when he does not contemplate committing a sin but indulges in contemplation on the carnal union between male and female in general, whereby he transgresses the admonition of the Torah, "Keep yourself from every wicked thing," meaning that "One must not contemplate during the day . . . ," or when it is an opportune time to study the Torah, but he turns his heart to vain things, as we have learned in the [Mishnah] in *Avot,* "He that wakes in the night . . . and turns his heart to vanity. . . ." Through any one of these things, and their like, he is called a *rasha* at that moment that the evil in his soul prevails over him, clothing itself in his body, inducing it to sin and profaning it. But then the good that is in his Godly soul asserts itself, and he is filled with remorse, and he seeks pardon and forgiveness from God. Indeed, God will forgive him if he has repented with the appropriate penitence according to the counsel of our Sages, of blessed memory, namely, the [threefold] division of atonement which is expounded by Rabbi Ishmael, as is explained elsewhere.

There is also the person in whom the evil prevails more strongly, and all three garments of evil clothe themselves in him, causing him to commit more severe and more frequent sins. But intermittently he experiences remorse, and thoughts of repentance enter his mind from the quality of good that is in his soul, which gathers strength in the interim. However, he does not have enough strength to vanquish the evil so as to rid himself entirely of his sins and be as one who "confesses and abandons [his evil ways]." Concerning such a person, the rabbis, of blessed memory, have said, "The wicked are full of regrets." These represent the majority of the wicked, in whose soul still lingers some good.

But the person who never feels contrition, and in whose mind no thoughts of repentance at all ever enter, is called a "*rasha* to whom is evil." For the evil that is in his soul alone remains in him, having so prevailed over the good that the latter has already departed from within him, encompassing him, so to speak, from above. Therefore the Sages have said, "Over every gathering of ten hovers the [*Shekhinah*]."

COMMENTARY

Chapter 10 described the two types of *tzaddik:* the complete *tzaddik* (the "*tzaddik* to whom is good") and the incomplete *tzaddik* (the "*tzaddik* to whom is evil"). This chapter describes the corresponding types at the other end of the spectrum: "the *rasha* ["wicked person"] to whom is good," who is not completely wicked because there is still a some good within him, and "the *rasha* to whom is evil," who is a complete *rasha,* for no good remains within him.

"This opposite the other"

This expression, which the author also uses in Chapter 6, is from Ecclesiastes 7:14 ("In the day of good, be joyful; in the day of evil, also consider: this opposite the other, God made") and is often used to express the correspondence between good and evil.

the "*rasha* to whom is good" is the corresponding opposite of the "*tzaddik* to whom is evil."

In Chapter 10, the author described the "*tzaddik* to whom is evil": one who is righteous in essence yet has not completely eradicated the evil within him. This remaining evil, however, is "to him," subservient to and nullified by the good that defines his being. Mirroring the "*tzaddik* to whom is evil" in the realm of *kelipah* ("husk") is the "*rasha* to whom is good."

This is to say that the good of his God soul which is in his brain and in the right ventricle of his heart is subservient to, and nullified by, the evil of the *kelipah* that is in the left ventricle.

Thus, although both good and evil reside in the heart of the "*rasha* to whom is good," he is called a *rasha* ("evil or wicked person") because the evil in him has gained mastery over him and has become the seat of his identity.

This category, too, is subdivided into myriads of degrees which differ in respect of the extent and manner of the nullification and subservience of the good to the bad, God forbid.

Again, as is the case with the "*tzaddik* to whom is evil," the "*rasha* to whom is good" is a broad category that includes a great range of types that differ in the quality of the good in them and the degree to which it is subjugated to the *kelipah*. At one end of the spectrum,

There is the person in whom the said subservience and nullification are in a very minor way, and even these are not permanent or recurring at frequent intervals. Rather, on rare occasions the evil prevails over the good and conquers the small city that is the body

In his description of the various levels of a "*rasha* to whom is good," our author begins at the top, with the least evil *rasha*. A "*rasha* to whom is good" is one in whom the evil rules over the good, but this rule may be temporary, occasional, or incomplete. Such a person may commit a sin, but he does so not wholeheartedly and without pleasure. He is one in whom the balance of good and evil are in a state of unstable equilibrium, so he is prone, every now and then, to be upset.

Furthermore, even when the evil in him does gain mastery over his "small city," it conquers

not all of it, but only a part of it—subjecting it to its discipline, to become a vehicle and a garment wherein is clothed one of its three above-mentioned garments

These are the thought, speech, and action of *kelipah*, discussed in Chapter 6.

That is, either in deed alone,

That is, deed without the premeditation of thought and discussion, which is the process by which a person comes to identify more deeply with his actions.

Furthermore, we are not talking here about severe transgressions; not only might this be a deed that only superficially relates to the inner self of its doer, but the deed itself might be the most subtle of sins, a

commission of minor transgressions and not major ones, God forbid;

A minor transgression is not necessarily one that is without effect; on the contrary, the more righteous one is, the more sensitive one becomes to sin. The Talmud tells how the strap of Rav Huna's *tefillin* once got twisted so that the black side, which should be exposed, was turned inward. To rectify this "sin," Rav Huna fasted forty fasts.[1] This was an extremely minor matter, done inadvertently, and from which he certainly derived no physical or spiritual pleasure or gain; yet to Rav Huna, this minute flaw in the manner of his fulfillment of a *mitzvah* was nothing less than devastating.

Rabbi Elimelekh of Lizhensk was one of the great leaders of the third generation of Hasidism; the whole of the Polish branch of

Hasidism is traced to him and his disciples. (Hasidim would interpret the verse, "A river emerged from Eden to water the Garden,"[2] as follows: "Eden" is the Baal Shem Tov, founder of Hasidism; "A river emerged from Eden"—this is the Baal Shem Tov's disciple and successor, Rabbi DovBer of Mezherich; "to water the Garden"—this is Rabbi Elimelekh.) The author of the *Tanya* once found himself in a synagogue of *mitnagdim* ("opposers" of Hasidism), when he noticed a book lying under a bench. He picked it up and saw that it was a copy of Rabbi Elimelekh's work, *Noam Elimelekh*. When asked to describe the author of that book, Rabbi Schneur Zalman said: "I'll tell you one thing about him: if you had thrown the author of this book under the bench, he too would not have uttered a word in protest." For despite his greatness, Rabbi Elimelekh regarded himself as the lowliest of the low. It is told that he would often go into the forest and sit on an anthill until the ants stopped biting him and would then cry: "Meilekh, Meilekh! See, even the ants no longer want to bite you!" He frequently cried, "I am the most wicked man in the world!" Once, one of his followers said to him: "Rebbe, whom are you trying to fool? You know that is not true!" Rabbi Elimelekh replied: "The finer the needle, the more it pierces." Even for the perfect *tzaddik,* there can be something that he will experience as a sin, and that can be so slight that someone else might not be aware of it, but the finer it is, the more piercing it is to the lofty soul.

The highest level of "*rasha* to whom is good," which the author describes here, is no ordinary individual; indeed, such a *rasha* would nowadays probably be considered a *tzaddik.* Yet if he but once transgressed the divine will, on however slight a matter, and he has not yet repented and rectified it absolutely, he is, at that moment, in the category of a "*rasha* to whom is good."

or in speech alone, in an utterance that borders on slander or causticity and the like;

His transgression might have been in speech. He has not spoken words of actual slander (*lashon hara*), which is a most severe prohibition but only *avak leshon hara* (literally, "the dust of slander"), words from which one might infer something derogatory about someone else.

or in thought alone, in "contemplations of sin, which are more severe than actual sin,"

The Talmud states this in *Yoma* 29a. Commentators offer various explanations of this statement. Rashi comments that the Talmud is not saying that a sinful thought is more severe than an actual transgression but is speaking of the severity of the temptation; the temptation to indulge in a sinful thought is often greater than the temptation to actually commit the sin. What is more, a person always has the opportunity to contemplate committing a sin, so this occurs more often than the actual commission, for which the opportunity does not always arise. The *Ohr haChayyim* suggests that because the contemplation of sin never sates the thinker's desire, he is less likely to experience remorse and repent for it than for a sin actually committed. On a deeper level, it is said that the contemplation of a sin, involving the most intimate of the soul's three garments, affects the soul to a greater extent and, in a certain sense, contaminates the soul even more than actually committing the sin.

or even when he does not contemplate committing a sin

A sinful thought need not involve the thought of actually committing the sin. As the Talmud rules, it is forbidden to contemplate a sin even as an abstract idea and without any intention of actually committing it. As in the case of one who

indulges in contemplation on the carnal union between male and female in general, whereby he transgresses the admonition of the Torah, "Keep yourself from every wicked thing,"³ meaning that "One must not contemplate during the day . . . ,"

The verse continues "lest one come to impurity during the night."⁴ Another example of a transgression involving the garment of thought is

when it is an opportune time to study the Torah, but he turns his heart to vain things, as we have learned in the [Mishnah] in *Avot,* "He that wakes in the night . . . and turns his heart to vanity. . . ."⁵

This is one who has the opportunity to study Torah but instead wastes his time thinking idle thoughts. Though these thoughts are not forbidden in themselves, they constitute a transgression in that they come in the place of Torah study.

Through any one of these things, and their like, he is considered a *rasha* at that moment

Any of these transgressions involving one of the three garments of the soul—thought, speech, or action—or any similar minor sin deems the transgressor a *rasha* at the moment of its commission, irrespective of the severity of the sin or its attendant punishment.

The author has already emphasized that the division of existence into holy elements and *kelipah* elements is a division with no neutral or intermediary ground. Every existence must, by necessity, belong either to holiness or to *kelipah:* if something is not holy, it is profane. So ultimately, the degree or extent of a sin is irrelevant. The moment a person turns to the *sitra achra* ("other side"), the moment that he is no longer within the realm of holiness, he has entered the realm of *kelipah.*

We can compare this to an act of treason, whose ultimate significance is that the person who commits it is no longer on "our side" but has gone over to the enemy. In this, the substance of the act is irrelevant. The person might not have engaged in espionage or sabotage but in something much less consequential. The triviality of the deed may be a consideration for leniency when he is judged and punished for his actions, but in terms of the ultimate significance of his deed, the fact that he has crossed over to the other side, what exactly he did to aid the enemy makes no difference. Similarly, anyone touched by sin, anyone who still carries the imprint of a transgression that he has not yet fully repented, exists at that moment outside of the realm of holiness and constitutes a part of the world of *kelipah.* For the ultimate significance of *any* transgression is

that the evil in his soul prevails over him, clothing itself in his body, inducing it to sin and profaning it.

Because we are speaking of the highest level of a "*rasha* to whom is good," one in whom the supremacy of evil occurs only in a fleeting moment of weakness,

the good that is in his Godly soul asserts itself, and he is filled with remorse, and he seeks pardon and forgiveness from God. Indeed, God will forgive him if he has repented with the appropriate penitence according to the counsel of our Sages, of blessed memory, namely, the [threefold] division of atonement which is expounded by Rabbi Ishmael,

The rabbi writes: "One who transgresses by neglecting to fulfill a positive commandment and then repents, does not move from there until he is forgiven; one who transgresses a prohibition and repents, his repentance holds his sin in suspension, and Yom Kippur atones for it; and one who transgresses [a very serious prohibition for which the penalty is] *karet* or capital punishment, and repents, his repentance and Yom Kippur suspend it and suffering cleanses him of the sin."[6]

as is explained elsewhere.

The author elaborates on this Talmudic passage in Part III of *Tanya, Iggeret haTeshuvah.*

But also after "the *rasha* to whom is good" ceases his act of transgression, also after he repents "with the appropriate penitence" and is completely forgiven for his sin, he is still not a *tzaddik* or even a *beinoni* ("intermediate") but a *rasha*, a "*rasha* to whom is good."

A *rasha*, if he is not a "complete *rasha*" ("a *rasha* to whom is [only] evil"), is not always acting as a *rasha* but only occasionally. Such a *rasha* might, in terms of actual behavior, be great in Torah and good deeds. But in terms of his quintessential identity, he is a *rasha*. In the ultimate sense of the term, a *rasha* is not defined by his deeds but by his psychological state, by his capacity for transgression. A person can be a "*rasha* to whom is good" without actually committing a single transgression. A *rasha* is one in whom the inner balance between the Godly soul and the animal soul is unstable; so even if he actually commits no sin, the possibility for sin always exists.

The definition of "*rasha*" applies not only to the actual *rasha* but also to the potential *rasha*. A person might remain a potential *rasha* all his life without ever having committed a sin, simply because the opportunity never presented itself. Similarly, a person can be a thief in essence, without ever actually stealing anything, simply because he has never seen anything that he really wanted to steal. He only thinks about "big money," which has never come his way, but given an opportunity worth his while, he would steal.

Thus, distinguishing between a *tzaddik* and a *rasha* is no simple matter. In Chapter 30, the author describes a person who sits and studies Torah day and night, never has a single sinful thought, yet, in essence, is a *rasha*. He is "naturally frigid," so he has no negative desires; and on the other hand, he has a natural intellectual bent, so he enjoys studying Torah. He commits no transgressions, not because he overpowers his evil inclinations but because he meets neither the temptation nor the opportunity to sin. Such a person is a *rasha* in essence, because he has done nothing to establish the sovereignty of his Godly soul over his natural, animal self.

It is said that "one who sits and commits no sin has in effect performed a *mitzvah*."[7] Because the Torah includes 365 prohibitions, most of which the vast majority of people do not commit day after day, everyone ought to be credited with countless *mitzvot* in their lifetime. However, the author explains the statement as referring not to just any sin but only to a sin for which one has both opportunity and temptation. For instance, one of the 365 prohibitions is the commandment that "the *choshen* ["jeweled breastplate" worn by the *kohen gadol* or high priest when he served in the Temple] shall not move away from the *eiphod* ["apron," one of the priestly garments]."[8] The Torah is commanding us to make sure that the *choshen* should not budge from its assigned place atop another of the priestly garments. Many of us have never committed this sin, and even many wicked people have never even considered doing so. There are also sins for which one has ample opportunity but virtually no temptation, and vice versa. Normal people do not have to overcome a temptation to put on *tefillin* on Shabbat and therefore do not receive a reward for refraining from succumbing to such a temptation. Likewise, many people are quite prepared to gossip but have no one to gossip with. Such people refrain from the sin of *lashon hara* ("slander") not because they overcome their evil inclination but because they lack an appropriate audience.

To summarize: one might transgress only the most lenient of prohibitions and always repent properly—or might in fact never actually transgress—yet be a *rasha*, because the alignment of forces within his soul is such that he is predisposed to transgress the divine will.

The author goes on to describe a lower level of "*rasha* to whom is good":

There is also the person in whom the evil prevails more strongly, and all three garments of evil clothe themselves in him, causing him to commit more severe and more frequent sins.

Earlier we spoke of a *rasha* who, when he commits a transgression, allows only one of the evil garments of the animal soul to "clothe" itself in his body (that is, to pervade it and use it to its ends)—only the garment of thought, the garment of speech, or the garment of deed. A more severe *rasha* is one who sins with all three garments of the soul, indicating a far greater dominance of the evil within him. For this indicates more than a momentary weakness, more than an occasional succumbing to temptation. This is a sinner who is fully involved with his sin, who primes himself psychologically to it, plans it, discusses it, and subsequently commits it in practice.

However, even this *rasha* is still a "*rasha* to whom is good"—whose inner good is still manifest and active within him. Thus,

intermittently he experiences remorse, and thoughts of repentance enter his mind from the quality of good that is in his soul, which gathers strength in the interim.

Between sins, between waves of the *kelipah*'s domination of his self, the good within him awakens, expressed by the feelings of remorse and repentance that frequent every Jew.

However, he does not have enough strength to vanquish the evil so as to rid himself entirely of his sins and be as one who "confesses and abandons [his evil ways]."[9]

He has thoughts of repentance, perhaps even many such thoughts, but these do not actualize to the extent that the supremacy of the good over the evil becomes the true and permanent state of his soul.

Concerning such a person, the rabbis, of blessed memory, have said, "The wicked are full of regrets."[10]

Such a person repeatedly sins and regrets, sins and regrets. Such regrets are a sign not of hypocrisy or self-deception but of the inner struggle between the two forces that dichotomize his inner self: his Godly and animal souls. The feelings of regret and the thoughts of repentance are not by chance or fluke but the reaction of the Godly soul to the triumphs of the animal soul. It is not arbitrary but inherently necessary that a Jew should experience remorse after he sins, because one part of his soul will never give him rest.

These represent the majority of the wicked, in whose soul still lingers some good.

Most *resha'im* ("wicked persons") belong to the category of "a *rasha* to whom is good": the good within them is still active and is repeatedly roused to combat the evil and influence the person. These surges of good cause the *rasha* to experience thoughts of repentance, and even to actually repent, but they fail to effect a qualitative change in the inner structure of his life.

As the author will explain later, not only a *rasha* but even a *beinoni* can succumb to sin. The difference is whether one happens to weaken and transgress or whether the transgression is a natural result of the makeup of his life. The holy books give advice on how to deal with "alien thoughts" (*machashavot zarot*) that enter the mind during prayer. A *tzaddik* once remarked, half-jokingly, that these thoughts are "alien" to a *tzaddik* but not to other people, who think of them all day; on the contrary, when such a person thinks of praying properly, this, to him, is an "alien thought"! In this sense, to a *rasha*, a sin, even if committed only once, is not alien; it is integral to his nature, a possibility existing within his soul.

The "*rasha* to whom is good" inhabits a life of sins and regrets, in which the sins are sins and the regrets are regrets. The regrets may be sincere, deep, and very painful indeed; nevertheless, he remains a *rasha*, even at the moment of his remorse.

But the person who never feels contrition, and in whose mind no thoughts of repentance at all ever enter, is called a "*rasha* to whom is evil." For the evil that is in his soul alone remains in him,

"A *rasha* to whom is evil" describes a state of being in which the good in man no longer operates and is no longer a factor within his personality. Such a person never experiences regret over his evil deeds. In him, the evil within has

so prevailed over the good that the latter has already departed from within him, encompassing him, so to speak, from above.

In this regard, no absolute symmetry exists between the "*tzaddik* to whom is good" on the one hand and the "*rasha* to whom is evil" on the other. As Chapter 10 explained, the "*tzaddik* to whom is good" is the complete *tzaddik* who has succeeded in utterly driving out the evil within him so that he possesses no evil whatsoever. On the other hand, the complete *rasha* cannot in the same way completely banish his Godly soul so that he no longer possesses any good at all.

There are two ways of affecting the animal soul. The first is to push it into a corner. This is what the "*tzaddik* to whom is evil" does: he still has some evil within him, but he has suppressed it so that it can no longer assert itself or exert any influence over the body. The other way is to turn it around so that it no longer functions as an animal soul but as a Godly soul. The latter is the level of the "*tzaddik* to whom is [only] good," in whom no evil remains, for it has been entirely transformed into good.

In contrast, the *rasha* can repress his Godly soul, reducing it to a state of subordination to the animal soul, but he cannot annihilate it entirely, as the *tzaddik* can do to his animal soul.

In a sense, the "*rasha* to whom is evil" is a purely theoretical concept that cannot exist in actuality, because something that is completely of the other side cannot exist. One can create a small lie or a big lie but not a complete lie. Every lie has some factual component and therefore is not a complete lie. A complete falsehood is something one can talk about theoretically, but in actuality, no such thing exists; it is nil. The same is true of evil. If a person could reach a state of "a *rasha* to whom is evil" in the ultimate sense—a state in which he is wholly evil and possesses no good whatsoever—that would be the point of death. "*Resha'im* are called dead even in their lifetime," says the Talmud,[11] because every degree of evil is a degree of spiritual death. If a person were to reach absolute evil, he would be dead in every respect, as he would no longer have any hold on the essence of life, which is connection to God.[12] The other side is something that is negative in essence; were it to exist in an absolute form, it would be absolute negativity—nothing—and total negativity negates everything, including its very self. In actuality, the "*rasha* to whom is evil," the complete *rasha*, is not really completely evil, for he cannot drive out the last grain of good from himself. As long as he exists, some good is in him. But he has banished it from his internal self so that it "encompasses him from above."

A person's soul is not just at one level but exists at various levels, one above the other. There are five levels to the soul: *nefesh, ruach, neshamah, chayah,* and *yechidah.* As a rule, only the lowest of them, the *nefesh,* operates in the realm of consciousness, whereas the others lie beyond the conscious reach of most people. A person's ascent to a higher level is his ability to consciously identify himself with a higher level or levels of his soul. The highest level a person can reach is an awareness of his *yechidah,* the highest essence of his soul, which at its primary source is the "part of the God above" that is identified with God Himself (see Chapter 2). No one can drive this out completely; man cannot uproot his divine essence, because that would uproot his very existence. A person can, however, reach the stage where he is no longer aware of the existence of the Godly soul, because it has ceased to operate within the realm of his consciousness. When in such a state, the Godly soul encompasses him from above. It still exists, but the person has no conscious connection with it. He can then live an utterly animalistic life, completely disconnected from the higher levels of his soul: he does not encounter them, and they do not interfere with his life.

Thus, every person, *tzaddik* or *rasha,* has levels in his soul that he is not aware of, which "encompass him from above." In the *rasha,* these are the higher levels of the divine soul, and in the *tzaddik,* they are the lower levels of the animal soul. Although the person is unaware of their presence, these levels of self still exist, and at times when he is not in a state of full consciousness, they are liable to affect him. Rabbi Zadok Hacohen of Lublin wrote that *tzaddikim* are of different types, at different levels. Some are righteous in all their conscious deeds and thoughts but cannot remain at that level in their dreams. And a tiny minority has dreams at the same level as their thoughts when fully awake, not only in clarity but also in the connection of the dream to the conscious, controlled level. The "*tzaddik* to whom is evil" may be a complete *tzaddik* in the areas of self of which he is conscious, but his soul also has another part of which he is unaware. This part does not normally express itself, but it is liable to do so when a person does not have complete control over himself. Only the complete *tzaddik* has attained the level on which no difference exists between his perceptions when awake and his dreams when asleep.

It is told of certain great individuals that they would experience a vision that began in a dream, in the middle of which they woke up, and the vision continued while they were awake. Most of the prophets received their prophecy that way. The prophet would enter a state that is beyond consciousness, from which he would slide to the conscious reception of the prophecy. Prophecy is a certain degree of consciousness but one that cannot be attained in the ordinary state of being. The only person who could reach that state from his normal state of consciousness was Moses. He alone could converse with God "mouth to mouth"[13] without departing from full consciousness. Only he did not have to pass through the dream state in order to obtain a divine communication.

In this sense, the "*rasha* to whom is evil" is not one who possesses no good whatsoever but one whose good no longer operates within the realm of consciousness and only "encompasses him from above." Thus, he might still dream about it, be influenced by it under certain circumstances, and theoretically he could even repent. To be sure, because the good no longer exists as a conscious factor within him, he cannot repent by his own initiative. Someone who all his life has thought and done only evil, and has banished all else from his conscious self, has no mechanism with which to act otherwise. But outside circumstances might compel even such a person to new choices. If he is pushed into a situation in which all the circumstances of his life are drastically altered, a doorway may at that time open, offering him a new chance to change himself and his way of life. Even though this is not the result of his own efforts, it is yet possible because of the potential for good that hovers beyond the boundaries of his conscious self.

In 1927, the previous Lubavitcher Rebbe, Rabbi Yosef Yitzchak Schneersohn, was arrested and imprisoned because the Soviet authorities wanted to put a stop to his work in teaching and spreading Judaism. Like many others, he was brought to the cellars of the NKVD (forerunner of the KGB) with his captors' intention of never again letting him see the light of day. When he was brought into the interrogation chamber, he turned to his interrogators, all Jews and members of the infamous Yevsektzia,[14] and said: "This is the first time I have entered a room where there are Jews who do not rise when I enter!" The interrogators were shaken; they did not know what to do with a person whose spirit was not broken. One of them threatened him with a revolver and said, "This toy has already caused many people to change their minds." The rebbe answered: "This toy affects people who have many gods but one world, but it does not affect a person who has one God and two worlds." He then added that he would like to tell them a story. When they objected, he said that when he tells a story even the *mitnagdim* listen. Then he said:

My great-grandfather[15] once said to an apostate Jew: "In the Book of Esther, the word for Jews [*yehudim*] is sometimes spelled with one *yud* after the *daled,* and sometimes with two.[16] This implies that there are two types of *yud* [Jew]—righteous Jews and wicked Jews. Sometimes only Jews of the first type consider themselves Jews; but when there is a decree such as that of Haman, it affects both types, and then they all remember that they are Jews." And my great-grandfather said to that Jew: "If you contract a fever, you, too, will remember that you are a Jew!" Subsequently, that Jew had a fever that lasted a full year, as a result of which he had thoughts of repentance.

Rabbi Yosef Yitzchak then turned to the investigators and said, "And when you will contract a fever, you, too, will remember that you are Jews." One may assume that in the following decade, the years of the great purges (when countless Jews were "removed" by Stalin), the investigators too "caught fever." If any of them remained alive, he must have given weighty consideration to the question of what type of Jew he was.

Even if the Jew's self-awareness is modeled entirely on his animal self, completely uprooting one's Godly self is impossible. One's being a Jew, "a part of the God above," cannot be blotted out, even if one is totally unaware of it, even if it is no longer a component of one's inner being but merely "encompasses from above."

Therefore the Sages have said, "Over every gathering of ten hovers the [*Shekhinah*]."[17]

Wherever ten Jews congregate, says the Talmud, the "divine presence" (*Shekhinah*) rests. The point is that who they are or what they are doing is irrelevant. No matter whether they are ten perfect *tzaddikim* or ten complete *resha'im,* if ten Jews gather, it is impossible for the divine presence not to rest there.

The Talmud, however, stresses that the *Shekhinah* rests *over* these ten individuals. It "hovers" over them but does not necessarily affect them.[18] Otherwise, one would be overwhelmed with holiness when one sits in a café or theater containing more than ten Jews. The divine presence is there, but in order to feel that, a person must be receptive to it. Here is the essential difference between the *tzaddik* and the *rasha:* To what extent is one receptive? To what extent is he open to the divine essence of his own soul?

Yet the Talmud's definition of *tzaddik* and *rasha* in terms of reward and punishment and the *Tanya*'s definition of these terms as indicating essence are interconnected. The complete *tzaddik* is "a *tzaddik* to whom is good" in the literal, material sense as well, for he is a person who is incapable of experiencing anything as negative, whereas the reverse is true of the "*rasha* to whom is evil." Negative things can only be experienced as such by one who is receptive to evil and who reacts to evil. This applies not only to mental suffering but to physical suffering as well. When Rabbi Shmuel of Nicholsberg and Rabbi Pinchas, author of *Hahaflaah,* came to Rabbi DovBer, the Great Maggid of Mezherich, they asked him how it is possible—as the Talmud commands—to "bless God over bad fortune just as one blesses Him over good fortune," and what is more, to do it "cheerfully."[19] The Maggid pointed to Rabbi Zusha of Anipoli, who was sitting in the study hall, and said, "Ask him." They posed their question to Rabbi Zusha, a lifelong pauper, sick in body and afflicted with countless troubles, who replied, "I don't know why the Rebbe sent you to me, a person who has never had a bad day in his life!" This same Rabbi Zusha was once reduced to such poverty as to lack bread, and when he was very hungry, he turned to God and said: "Master of the Universe! Thank you for giving me an appetite."

In this sense, the complete *rasha* is one "to whom is evil" because he is totally nonreceptive to anything good. To receive something good and experience it as such, one has to be in a certain frame of mind; one who has driven out his divine element, driven out the good within him, has also driven out the capacity to enjoy even worldly things. The more of a *rasha* a person becomes, the more he allows the evil within him to pervade his being, the more evil he experiences. Just as the complete *tzaddik* cannot experience evil, the complete *rasha* has destroyed his capacity to experience good.

The good things in life, the things from which we derive pleasure, are not objectively good. Our enjoyment of them depends on how our soul is receptive to their goodness. Pleasure, for the most part, derives from the fulfillment of a need; to feel the pleasure, we must first feel the need. Otherwise, life turns into an ever-escalating cycle of suffering, and even more than that, a growing lack of enjoyment in life. A person to whom God has granted wealth and honor, whose worldly desires are satisfied, finds that the more he pursues them, the less he enjoys and appreciates these assets. The more he exploits them, the more he destroys the vitality they contain, the good that is hidden in them, and their ability to give him pleasure. Such a person develops an increasing tendency toward perversion in everything, in an attempt to reach extremes where he can still build a life that contains good and bad so that he might find some meaning and some enjoyment amid all the emptiness. Such a person may even be led to repent, out of dread of the emptiness of evil, which is self-destructive.

Our author has not dwelt at length on the two levels of *rasha,* just as in Chapter 10 he did not elaborate on their opposites, the two levels of *tzaddik,* because the book is not intended for either of these categories. The Book of *Beinonim* is intended for every man, and not everyone is able to attain the level of *tzaddik,* whereas everyone is expected to avoid the state of *rasha.* If the previous chapter is not relevant to most people, this chapter, we hope, is not relevant to anyone.

Chapter 12

he *beinoni* ("intermediate") is one in whom the evil never gains enough power to capture the "small city," so as to clothe itself in the body and make it sin. That is to say, the three garments of the animal soul, namely, thought, speech, and action of *kelipah,* do not prevail within him over the Godly soul to the extent of clothing themselves in the body—in the brain, in the mouth and in the other 248 organs—to make them sin and to defile them, God forbid.

Rather, only the three garments of the Godly soul—namely, the thought, speech, and actions of the 613 commandments of the Torah—they alone, clothe themselves in the body. [The *beinoni*] has never committed, nor will he ever commit, any transgression, and the term *"rasha"* never applied to him, even for a single hour or moment, throughout his life.

However, the essence and being of the Godly soul, which are its ten faculties, do not hold the exclusive sovereignty and dominion over the small city; except at specific times, such as during the recital of the Shema or prayer, which is a time when the divine intellect is in a state of ascendancy above, and is thus a propitious time below for every man, when he binds his *ChaBaD* to God, to apply his *daat,* in an in-depth manner, to the greatness of the Blessed Infinite, and to arouse the "love like flaming coals" in the right ventricle of his heart to cleave to Him by virtue of the fulfillment of the Torah and its commandments out of love. This, as explained, is an essential quality of the Shema, the recital of which is enjoined by the Torah, and of the blessings which precede and follow it, which are a rabbinical enactment and a preparation for the fulfillment of the recital of the Shema, as is explained elsewhere. At such time the evil that is in the left ventricle is subdued and nullified by the good that is diffused in the right ventricle from the *ChaBaD* in the brain, which are bound to the greatness of the Blessed Infinite.

However, after prayer, when the state of ascendancy of the intellect of the Blessed Infinite departs, the evil in the left ventricle reawakens, and [the *beinoni*] experiences desire for the lusts of the material world and its pleasures.

Yet, because [the evil] has not the sole sovereignty [and judgment] and dominion over the city, it is unable to carry out this desire from the potential into actuality by clothing itself in the organs and limbs of the body in deed, speech, or actual thought—that is, to consciously dwell on the pleasures of the material world as to how to satisfy the lust of his heart—because the brain rules over the heart (as explained in *Ra'aya Meheimna, Parashat Pinchas*) by virtue of its inborn and created nature. For this is how man is created from birth, that each person may, with the willpower in his brain, restrain himself and control the drive of lust that is in his heart, preventing his heart's desires from expressing themselves in action, word, or thought, and divert his attention altogether from the craving of his heart toward the completely opposite direction, particularly in the direction of holiness; as it is written: "I then saw that there is an advantage to wisdom over folly as the advantage of light over darkness." This means that just as light has a superiority, power, and dominion over darkness, so that a little physical light banishes a great deal of darkness, which is therewith inevitably superseded as a matter of course and necessity, so is a great deal of foolishness of the *kelipah* and *sitra achra* (as, indeed, our Sages say, "A man does not sin unless a spirit of folly enters into him") inevitably driven away by the wisdom that is in the Godly soul in the brain, whose desire is to alone rule the city and to pervade the entire body, in the manner already mentioned, by means of her three garments, namely, thought, speech, and actions of the 613 commandments of the Torah, as explained earlier.

Nevertheless, such a person is not deemed a *tzaddik* at all, because the superiority which the light of the Godly soul possesses over the darkness and foolishness of the *kelipah,* wherewith the latter is expelled forthwith, exists only in its aforementioned three garments, but not in its essence and being over the essence and being of the *kelipah.* For in the *beinoni,* the essence and being of the animal soul from the *kelipah* in the left ventricle remains entirely undislodged after prayer, when the love of God "like burning coals" is no longer in a revealed state in his heart, in the right ventricle, which is now only inwardly paved with hidden love, that is the natural love of the Godly soul, as will be explained later. So it is now possible for the folly of the wicked fool to reveal itself in the left ventricle of his heart, generating a lust for all material things of this world, whether permitted or, God forbid, prohibited, as if he had not prayed at all. It is only that, in regard to a forbidden matter, it does not enter his mind to actually violate the prohibition, God forbid; but "sinful thoughts, which are yet more severe than sin itself," are able to affect him, rising to his mind and distracting him from the Torah and Divine service, as our Sages have said, "There are three sins against which a man is daily not safeguarded: sinful thoughts, [lack of] concentration in prayer. . . ."

Yet, the impression [of prayer] on the intellect and the innate awe and love of God in the right ventricle achieve this: [they enable him] to overpower and control this evil craving and not allow it to gain supremacy and dominion over the city and carry out its desire from the potential into actuality by clothing itself in the organs and limbs of the body. Moreover, even in the mind alone, [insofar] as evil thoughts are concerned, the evil gains no supremacy and dominion to compel the mind's volition to entertain willingly, God forbid, any wicked thought rising of its own accord from the heart to the brain, as discussed above; rather, no sooner does it reach there than he thrusts it out with both hands and averts his mind from it the instant he becomes aware that it is an evil thought, refusing to accept it willingly, not even allowing himself to willingly think it, and certainly not to entertain any idea of putting it into effect, God forbid, or even to speak of it. For one who willfully indulges in such thoughts is deemed a *rasha* at such time, whereas the *beinoni* is never a *rasha,* even for a single moment.

So, too, in matters affecting a person's relations with his fellow: as soon as there rises from his heart to his mind some animosity or hatred, God forbid, or jealousy or anger, or a grudge and suchlike, he gives them no entrance into his mind and will. On the contrary, his mind exercises its authority and power over the spirit in his heart, to do the very opposite and to conduct himself towards his fellow with the quality of kindness and a display of extra affection, to tolerate him to the extreme limits without becoming provoked into anger, God forbid, or to revenge in kind, God forbid; but rather to repay the offenders with favors, as taught in the *Zohar,* that one should learn from the example of Joseph towards his brothers.

COMMENTARY

Chapters 10 and 11 discussed the two types of *tzaddikim* ("righteous persons") at one end of the spectrum and the two types of *resha'im* ("wicked persons") at the other. After describing these two extremes—that which cannot be reached (by most people) and that which should not be reached (by anyone)—the *Tanya* will now discuss the level that is "the quality of every man": a state that every person can and ought to achieve. In this chapter, we will read of the *beinoni* ("intermediate man") and of how difficult, yet how possible, it is to achieve this state.

The *beinoni* ("intermediate") is one in whom the evil never gains enough power to capture the "small city," so as to clothe itself in the body and make it sin.

The first thing that defines the *beinoni* is that he never commits a transgression.

That is to say, the three garments of the animal soul, namely, thought, speech, and action of *kelipah,* do not prevail within him over the Godly soul to the extent of clothing themselves in the body—in the brain, in the mouth, and in the other 248 organs

These are the specific parts of the body employed by the three "garments": the garment of thought requires a physical brain in order to manifest itself; the garment of speech, a mouth, and so on; and the garment of action pervades the entire body.

to make them sin and to defile them, God forbid.

Furthermore, not only does the *beinoni* completely avoid transgression but also does good, for

Rather, only the three garments of the Godly soul—namely, the thought, speech, and actions of the 613 commandments of the Torah—they alone, clothe themselves in the body.

In this way, the *beinoni*'s every thought, word, and deed is utterly devoted to fulfilling the divine will as expressed in the Torah's *mitzvot* ("commandments").

Thus, the *beinoni* is one who

has never committed, nor will he ever commit, any transgression, and the term *"rasha"* never applied to him, even for a single hour or moment, throughout his life.

This is not to say that a person who once in his lifetime committed a sin can never become a *beinoni* or even a *tzaddik*. Rather, it means that one who does achieve the level of *beinoni* exists in a state of mind that is utterly removed from transgression, present, past, or future. If he committed any sins in the past, he has repented to such an extent that it is no longer a part of his life. It is as if his negative past belongs to someone else, not him.

Every person experiences examples of such disconnection from the past. Often, something a person did, said, or thought in the past no longer relates to the person he is now. They might belong to his past in the factual and historical sense, but in terms of his present identity and experience, the connection is purely theoretical; these things are no more his than they are someone else's. There is no continuum but a severance from his past self, as if he were two different people. A person might look at things he has written or remember things that he has done and say: These things were done by someone else, not by me. Being what I am now, I could never do such things. Indeed, every person feels this way when he ceases to be a child. As children, we do things, good and bad, that as adults we could not do. We remember things that we saw as children but as the memories of someone else; being adults, we can no longer see things the way we saw them then.

If a *beinoni* has sinned in his past, he has repented to such an extent that he relates to his past in the same way: that was someone else, not me. The same applies to the future. This is not to say that the *beinoni* is inherently incapable of sinning, but his present state is such that actually committing a sin is impossible, inconceivable; it creates no resonance within his soul.

Why is such a person—who has never sinned and never will sin, whose every act is either a *mitzvah* or in service of a *mitzvah*—not a complete *tzaddik*? What is missing? Why is he not even an incomplete *tzaddik* but in an intermediate state between *rasha* and *tzaddik*? To understand this, we must first distinguish between the garments and the essence of the *beinoni's* soul. Everything we have thus far said about the *beinoni* pertains to only the garments of his soul, the manner in which his inner self expresses itself in his behavior.

However, the essence and being of the Godly soul, which are its ten faculties, do not hold the exclusive sovereignty and dominion over the small city;

    The side of holiness rules the *beinoni*'s life in practice, but it does
not change the inner makeup of his soul. The *beinoni* does not sin in
practice, but the conflict in his soul has not been resolved. So the
beinoni is in a perpetual state of tension: the good in him prevails over
the evil only because of his active involvement in the struggle between
them. His victory over the evil within him is never complete but only
de facto; at best, he achieves a temporary cease-fire but never a full
truce. The *beinoni* spends his life in an endless struggle. He cannot
relax his vigil for a single instant, because the moment he does so, the
enemy will rouse itself and destroy his status as a *beinoni*.

    The *beinoni* is one who must constantly guard his frontiers, and he
is one who does so successfully. The *rasha* is one whose frontier has
breaches, whereas the *tzaddik* has no frontiers at all. The *tzaddik* has
achieved a permanent peace: no battles rage within him because there
are no frontiers; there are no two domains, because all is one domain.

    In terms of the *Tanya*'s analogy of the body as a "small city," the
tzaddik has destroyed the enemy so that he no longer poses a threat
and the town need no longer be guarded. The *rasha*, even if he is a
"*rasha* to whom is good," even if he spends most of his life engaged in
Torah study and good deeds, finds that the enemy keeps entering the
city. The *beinoni* rules over the city and does not allow the enemy to
enter, but he has to keep constant vigil because the *sitra achra* ("other
side") besieges his city all the time, looking for a weak spot at which
to force an entry, and is never weakened. In the *beinoni*, the other side
is no less powerful than it is in the *rasha*; but the *beinoni* has full control of the city and never allows the other side entry.

    Externally, the *tzaddik* and the *beinoni* are virtually indistinguish-
able: they both behave the same way. Internally, however, in the inner
structure of their souls, they constitute two very different beings. Here,
the *beinoni* is indistinguishable from the *rasha*: the same array of
forces exist within the two. The *beinoni* can be a great and holy man
by virtually any objective standard and even by his own internal measure, but he can never allow himself to regard himself as such, because
he must never lower his guard in the struggle with his animal self.

    The *tzaddik* and the *beinoni* are not phases of one continuum but
two distinct states of being, like a road that forks into two different

directions. These are not rungs on the same ladder, where one climbs from the rung of the *beinoni* to a higher one in order to become a *tzaddik,* but two different paths through life. The importance of this book lies in its establishment of the state of *beinoni* as an end in itself, to which one should aspire and regard as his goal in life. The *Tanya* tells us that even if we never achieve inner peace and tranquillity, this does not mean that we have not attained anything; that even if we never achieve a full and decisive victory in the battle of life, we can still realize our objective in life, which is to maintain the struggle to the very end and not give ground.

In Chapter 27 of *Tanya,* the author writes that God creates two types of people and makes different demands on each. Only a few people are given the ability to achieve inner peace and tranquillity in their lives, and only they are expected to achieve this. Most people are not granted the possibility, are not required to attain this state, and never will.

(We are not speaking, of course, of the peace and tranquillity a soul gains in the world to come in reward for its labors in this world, regarding which it is said, "according to the pain is the gain."[1] Indeed, the *beinoni* may obtain a greater reward there than the *tzaddik,* because he struggles harder and suffers more pain.)

The *beinoni* is one in whom the struggle between good and evil is constant. Indeed, the moment that there is a lull in the battle, the *beinoni* must grow alarmed, because this is a sure sign that something is amiss. To the *beinoni* applies the Talmudic rule that "one should always incite the good inclination against the evil inclination."[2] For him, the fact that evil is within him against which he must struggle is not a negative sign but an indication that he is a *beinoni,* in whom the existence of a struggle is a positive sign.

The *beinoni*'s Godly soul never gives him a moment's rest. Thus, if the *beinoni* ever experiences peace and tranquillity, he must worry that this is coming from the other side. God neither requires nor desires of him to achieve any such peace; He desires the *beinoni*'s struggles and expects him to continue with the struggle throughout his life. Indeed, the state of *beinoni* is not so much a goal but a path, the path of every man, a way of life to which everyone can aspire and in which everyone can walk.

Such is the *beinoni*'s inner state every moment of his life,

except at specific times, such as during the recital of the Shema or prayer, which is a time when the divine intellect is in a state of ascendancy above,

The set time for reciting the Shema and for prayer is a time of "ascendancy of the intellect" (*mochin d'gadlut*) in the supernal worlds, meaning that the divine attributes of *chokhmah, binah,* and *daat*—the three "intellectual" attributes among the ten divine attributes (*sefirot*) that define God's involvement with our reality—manifest themselves in their utmost radiance and potency. (In contrast, there are times of "diminution of the intellect" (*mochin d'katnut*), in which their manifest effect of the supernal *ChaBaD* is partial and dimmed, connoting a state of reduced consciousness and perception at all levels of creation.)

And when the supernal worlds are in a time of "ascendancy of the intellect," this is also

a propitious time below for every man,

The times deemed by halakhah ("Torah law") as suitable for prayer are thus also the times when prayer is most effective. When there is an "ascendancy of the intellect" above, this is also a propitious time for a person to achieve an "ascendancy of the intellect" on a personal level, that is, to achieve a full awareness of the divine in his own mind and relate to it with his entire being.

when he binds his *ChaBaD* to God, to apply his *daat,* in an in-depth manner, to the greatness of the Blessed Infinite,

ChaBaD is an acrostic for *chokhmah, binah,* and *daat.* As we explained in Chapter 3, the "binding" of the mind (that is, the process of identification with an idea so that it affects and transforms the emotional self as well) is through the faculty of *daat.* When a person meditates upon the greatness of God and applies to it not only his faculties for abstract perception and analysis but also his *daat,* his faculty for personalized and subjective apprehension, he will

arouse the "love like flaming coals"

in its natural physical environment, which is

in the right ventricle of his heart

The author discusses this in Chapter 9.

Prayer is thus a time of arousal of the Godly soul not only through the appropriate meditations but also through the stimulation of the Godly soul's emotional faculties (*middot*) and through the person's basic receptiveness to goodness and holiness. The combination of all these generates the striving

to cleave to Him by virtue of the fulfillment of the Torah and its commandments out of love.

The striving is not only to fulfill the *mitzvot* out of a sense of duty to God but to fulfill them with love, with the desire to come close to God thereby and cleave to Him.

This, as explained, is an essential quality of the Shema, the recital of which is enjoined by the Torah, and of the blessings which precede and follow it, which are a rabbinical enactment and a preparation for the fulfillment of the recital of the Shema, as is explained elsewhere.[3]

The Shema is basically the manifesto of the Godly soul. The first verse—"Hear O Israel, the Lord is our God, the Lord is one"—is the Godly soul's declaration of the awareness that pervades its *ChaBaD*, its faculties of perception; the second verse—"And you shall love the Lord your God with all your heart"—is its declaration of love for God, or at the very least, a declaration that it desires to serve Him willingly and with love. Yet to actually achieve a love of God "with all your heart," a love deriving from both the Godly soul in the heart's "right ventricle" and the animal soul to its left, a "declaration of principles" by the Godly soul is not enough; the animal soul, too, must be affected. For this purpose, the sages instituted the preliminary blessings of the Shema, to prime the soul so that the principles contained in the Shema should take root in it and have their desired effect.

The first blessing, *Yotzer Ohr* ("He who creates light"), describes the greatness of God's creation; the supernal "worlds"; the angels, *ophanim* and *seraphim* that populate them; and the manner in which they all serve their Creator, in order to impress upon the animal soul how even its own source—which is in the level of angels, seraphim, and the like—negates itself before God. The second blessing, *ahavat olam* ("Eternal love") describes God's love to us and comes to arouse our love in response "as water mirrors a face to a face."[4] Thus, the blessings of the Shema are intended to bring a person to a state of awareness and the emotional arousal from which he can truly relate to the truths he expresses when he proclaims, "Hear O Israel, the Lord is our God, the Lord is one."

At such time,

When a person achieves the full arousal of his Godly soul's perceptive and emotive powers,

the evil that is in the left ventricle is subdued and nullified by the good that is diffused in the right ventricle from the *ChaBaD* in the brain, which are bound to the greatness of the Blessed Infinite.

In Chapter 9, the author described the process by which the Godly soul's love for God is stimulated to the point that it spills over into the left ventricle of the heart, transforming the animal soul's passions into a love for God. In the *tzaddik,* this process has been completed and is now the permanent state of affairs; the *beinoni* achieves this only in special times, such as during the prayer.

At such times, the rule of the *beinoni* over the evil in the left ventricle of his heart is not merely external, through control of his actions, speech, and conscious thoughts, but involves the entire soul, alive and ardent in striving for the divine. So the *beinoni* can, at specific times, love God with all his heart. At such times, the passions of the other element in his soul are stilled, and he has no wish or desire other than to give himself completely over to his Creator and pour out his soul to God.

Yet the *beinoni* is no *tzaddik;*

after prayer, when the state of ascendancy of the intellect of the Blessed Infinite departs,

Then, the ascendancy of the mind over the heart within the *beinoni*'s person is likewise diminished,

the evil in the left ventricle reawakens, and [the *beinoni*] experiences desire for the lusts of the material world and its pleasures.

When the time of prayer, and the distinct spiritual opportunity it represents, is over, the *beinoni* again becomes like everyone else. Again the *beinoni* is tempted by worldly pleasures, each according to his tastes, the nature of his animal soul, and the manner in which it reacts to the material world. The time of prayer was a time of slumber and submission for the evil within, a submission that bespeaks not an absolute negation, not an essential transformation, but only a temporary departure. So immediately after prayers, the *beinoni* reverts to his previous state, with the evil within again rising against the good.

Yet, because [the evil] has not the sole sovereignty [and judgment] and dominion over the city,

The *beinoni* "experiences desire for the lusts of the material world," but he is not a *rasha*. There is a basic, quintessential difference between the two. When the *rasha* lusts for something, he actually carries out his desire, if not in deed, then in conscious, willful thought. On the other hand, the animal soul of the *beinoni*

is unable to carry out this desire from the potential into actuality

The arousal, the initial urge, transpires in the *beinoni* with the same intensity and force that it does in the *rasha*; but for the initial urge to be implemented in practice, it must gain control of the person—and the *beinoni* is one who never allows the evil in his heart to gain such control. The "sovereignty," the ultimate verdict of the internal tribunal as to what should actually be done, is not in the hands of evil, so it is unable to carry out its desire into actuality,

by clothing itself in the organs and limbs of the body in deed, speech, or actual thought

Obviously, a person is unaware of the drives and urges rising within him until they somehow express themselves in the form of a conscious thought.

—that is, to consciously dwell on the pleasures of the material world as to how to satisfy the lust of his heart

There is a world of difference between one who willfully thinks sinful thoughts, whether thoughts of actually committing a sin or simply contemplations of the sin itself, and one in whom sinful thoughts arise that he immediately banishes at the moment they enter his awareness.

The *beinoni* is able to exercise such control over his person

because the brain rules over the heart (as explained in *Ra'aya Meheimna, Parashat Pinchas*)[5] by virtue of its inborn and created nature.

This axiom is fundamental to this chapter and to the entire book. It means that the brain (which is the seat of the Godly soul, as explained in Chapter 9) can control the heart, not only as a result of special training or extraordinary effort on the part of the mind but because

this is how man is created from birth, that each person may, with the willpower in his brain, restrain himself and control the drive of lust that is in his heart, preventing his heart's desires from expressing themselves in action, word, or thought, and divert his attention altogether from the craving of his heart toward the completely opposite direction,

A fundamental quality of the human being grants his mind the power to rule over the desires of the heart, even in thought and certainly in speech and action. This does not mean that exercising this innate power is easy, that all one needs to do is to think a certain thought and the heart will automatically follow the mind. It means (in this context) that a person can consciously compel himself not to think certain thoughts. He cannot prevent them from coming to mind—one has no control over this—but he has sufficient control to prevent their realization. If, for instance, someone is told not to think about polar bears, he cannot stop them from coming to mind, but he can prevent himself from thinking about them by immediately turning his mind to something else as soon as the thought arises.

This applies only when the mind is functioning normally, but that in an abnormal situation, once a certain limit of provocation is exceeded, a person loses the ability to control the spread of the heart's desires. Everyone, beyond a certain point, is finally dragged into a complex of emotions that is liable to draw him to anything—for better or worse. In such situations, he might even be aware, sometimes very clearly, that he is about to do something that is self-destructive—something that runs contrary to all that is true, right, and good—yet he is powerless to stop himself.

All the same, the control the mind exerts on the heart is complete and decisive. For the situations in which control is lost do not occur on their own. A person loses control when he allows himself to cross a certain threshold. If he allows an emotion or relationship to develop beyond all manageable proportions, he is liable to reach a point of no return. He then becomes subject to emotions and desires that he can no longer stop.

"The mind controls the heart" does not imply that the mind can stop any activity of the heart or develop it by force of will alone; rather, it expresses the axiom that a person in a state of awareness and consciousness can supervise himself and refrain from certain actions and certain thoughts by not completing every thought that arises within him. This ability not to think through every thought but rather to disrupt it at a certain point is an innate advantage of the mind over the heart, of conscious will over unconscious drives. The *beinoni* is the one who uses this power to repel thoughts that arise from the evil in his soul. The *beinoni*, unlike the *tzaddik*, cannot prevent the eruption of these impulses, but he can prevent them from reaching fruition. They are rejected as soon as they sprout and rise.

particularly in the direction of holiness

In addition to the general power of the mind to control the heart, the Godly soul has an advantage in its struggle to overpower desires originating in the animal soul,

as it is written: "I then saw that there is an advantage to wisdom over folly as the advantage of light over darkness."

The nature of that additional advantage is expressed in the quote from Ecclesiastes (2:13), which compares the superiority of wisdom over folly (that is, of good over evil) to the superiority of material light over darkness:

This means that just as light has a superiority, power, and dominion over darkness,

The advantage of light over darkness is not merely qualitative, in the sense that light is better than darkness, nicer, more useful, and more pleasant, but that a little physical light banishes a great deal of darkness, which is therewith inevitably superseded as a matter of course and necessity,

Light and darkness do not combat each other as equal contestants; rather, light possesses an innate superiority over darkness—the superiority of positivity over negativity. Light need not battle darkness, for with its very appearance, it repels not only an equal amount of darkness but a lot of darkness. When two equally positive substances are brought in contest, such as when a solid is immersed in water, the volume of water displaced exactly equals the volume of the solid immersed. But when one takes a small candle into a dark room, the volume of darkness displaced greatly exceeds the volume of the flame of the candle.

In the same way,

a great deal of folly of the *kelipah* and *sitra achra*

The forces of evil are "folly,"

(as, indeed, our Sages say, "A man does not sin unless a spirit of folly enters into him")[6]

Elsewhere,[7] the author further develops this concept, stating that no one who has any true awareness of what he is doing, however weak-minded he might be, would ever sin, unless a spirit of folly entered him. At such times, he can do things that, when he regains his awareness—perhaps immediately after his deed or even in the midst of his deed—will fill him with shame and self-abhorrence. In retrospect, he cannot bear to think that he has done such a thing, yet he did it because "something came over him"—a spirit of folly.

And because the evil in man is "a spirit of folly," it is

inevitably driven away by the wisdom that is in the Godly soul in the brain,

just as the negativity of darkness naturally gives way before the positivity of light

whose desire is to alone rule the city

The city is the "small city" that is man, over whose control the Godly soul struggles for against the animal soul.

and to pervade the entire body, in the manner already mentioned,[8] by means of her three garments, namely, thought, speech, and actions of the 613 commandments of the Torah, as explained earlier.[9]

The *beinoni* has times of struggle: when he concludes his prayers and goes out into the street, he meets temptations and desires of all types. But because his animal self has not gained control of his soul, he can, by the force of his will, exploiting "the advantage of light over darkness," prevent himself from succumbing to evil, in deed, speech, or thought. He repels all thought of sin, immediately and automatically.

Nevertheless, such a person is not deemed a *tzaddik* at all,

Despite the fact that the *beinoni* never transgresses even the most subtle of sins, he is not a *tzaddik*. There is still a great distance and a most fundamental difference between the two.

because the superiority that the light of the Godly soul possesses over the darkness and foolishness of the *kelipah,* wherewith the latter is expelled forthwith, exists only in its aforementioned three garments, but not in

the Godly soul's

essence and being over the essence and being of the *kelipah.*

The *beinoni* exercises the advantage of light over darkness, of wisdom over folly, only in the *expressions* of his soul, not in the soul itself. When two thoughts of equal magnitude, one of holiness and the other of the foul, struggle for supremacy, the former will oust the latter. But even if a person spends his entire lifetime thinking only holy thoughts, this will in no way banish the underlying forces of evil in his soul. The *beinoni* has transformed the external face of his soul, the manner in which his soul expresses itself outwardly (speech and deed) and inwardly (thought), but the soul itself has not been changed: not its unfathomable depths nor its consciously felt wills, desires, and passions. These exist within the *beinoni* exactly as they exist within the *rasha,* the only difference being that the *beinoni* prevents their implementation and fruition in practice.

For in the *beinoni,* the essence and being of the animal soul from the *kelipah* in the left ventricle remains entirely undislodged after prayer,

At the time of prayer, the *beinoni* was completely engrossed in matters of holiness, completely consumed by his ecstasy, by a single-minded, self-negating bond with his God. The love of God burned in his heart, extinguishing all other loves. The subjugation of evil to good was not merely in practice but in essence. His entire being lay within the realm of holiness. But the *beinoni* does not pray all day. After prayers, when he returns to his own affairs,

when the love of God "like burning coals" is no longer in a revealed state in his heart, in the right ventricle,

At that point, all that he experienced during prayer recedes as if it never was. Earlier, when he was consumed by love and expressed it in his prayers, his experience was genuine: at the time, his heart truly and wholly belonged to God. However, this was not the *beinoni*'s normal state of being but a state brought on by a special effort to arouse in himself an all-consuming love for God. When this special state of arousal passes, all that remains within him is the potential for such love, a potential that exists within him because his heart

is now only inwardly paved with hidden love, that is the natural love of the Godly soul, as will be explained later.

In Chapter 18, the author speaks of an intrinsic love for God that exists within the heart of every Jew. So even when the "revealed love" generated by the *beinoni* through a process of meditation and prayer passes, this hidden love remains, which, though not an emotional experience of love, implies a very deep relationship. It represents a fundamental, quintessential bond between man and God that exists beyond consciousness and, in a certain sense, is deeper and more basic than any experience of love. But because this love is not experienced by the soul, because it does not manifest itself in the form of an actual craving and passion to cleave to God,

it is now possible

now that the "revealed love" the *beinoni* experiences during prayer has receded, for the folly of the wicked fool to reveal itself in the left ventricle of his heart, generating a lust for all material things of this world, whether permitted or, God forbid, prohibited, as if he had not prayed at all.

The experience of holiness can linger in the *beinoni* after his prayers; indeed, the author will yet discuss the various ways in which the *beinoni* might prime and develop himself so that this experience will leave a mark on the soul in the form of a manifest feeling. In essence, however, the arousal of love that the *beinoni* experiences during prayer is confined to a specific time frame, after which it is no longer operative. And when his Godly soul ceases to manifest itself throughout his being, the *beinoni* is again exposed to the arousal of alien passions, which exist within him as they do in the *rasha*. The time of prayer has indeed effected a change in him: at the time, the *beinoni* was truly one with the experience, but the change is temporary; immediately afterward, he reverts to what he has been previously. However great the sincerity, devotion, and love he expressed in his prayer, it does not effect a fundamental change in the *beinoni*'s soul.

It is only that, in regard to a forbidden matter, it does not enter his mind to actually violate the prohibition, God forbid;

One of the definitions of the *beinoni* is that he is so far removed from certain things—the things forbidden outright by the Torah— that they do not occur to him as practical possibilities. Indeed, everyone has certain limits that he will never exceed and that he is unable to even consider the possibility of exceeding, things for which any desire or lust is merely theoretical. These limits vary from individual to individual and from society to society, but every personality structure precludes certain acts as inconceivable. Ibn Ezra, explaining the last of the Ten Commandments, "You shall not covet" (Exodus 20:14), brings an example of a simple peasant who happens to see the king's daughter. He may think of her as beautiful and desirable, but he does not desire her and will never even think of trying to obtain her, because he knows that she is unattainable. To the *beinoni*, anything forbidden by the Torah falls into this category: the thought of something forbidden might arise in the mind of a *beinoni* but not the thought of actually doing it, because he knows that this is something he cannot ever do.

Even though it never occurs to the *beinoni* to actually commit a forbidden act, he nevertheless thinks about it.

but "sinful thoughts, which are yet more severe than sin itself,"[10]

because, as already discussed, they involve the faculty of thought, the innermost and most intimate of the soul's garments.

are able to affect him, rising to his mind and distracting him from the Torah and Divine service,

Thoughts of sin, even if they are devoid of any possibility of execution, are extremely damaging to the soul. For instance, imagining a forbidden relationship with a certain woman, even if the circumstances are such that preclude any possibility of the thought being translated into action, will agitate the basic desire and confuse a person who was occupied at that time with Torah and *mitzvot*.

Such thoughts can plague the *beinoni*,

as our Sages have said, "There are three sins against which a man

—"a man," not necessarily a *rasha*, but also a person in the basic state of man, a *beinoni*—

is daily not safeguarded: sinful thoughts, [lack of] concentration in prayer. . . .

The third sin is "the semblance of slander."[11] "Sinful thoughts" (*hirhurei avaeira*), as we said, are not thoughts of actually committing a sin but merely the contemplation of sinful things. "Concentration in prayer" (*iyyun tefillah*) is the failure to properly concentrate on one's prayers due to distraction. "The semblance of slander" (*avak leshon hara*: literally, "the dust of slander") is not actually speaking ill of others, which is an outright sin that one can and must avoid at all times but the semblance of slander—that is, talk that might, in some roundabout way, imply something negative about someone else—which is virtually impossible to avoid.

These sins are not committed intentionally, and they are extremely difficult to avoid even with a concentrated effort and the exercise of the mind's sovereignty over the heart. Their occurrence is inherent to the state of *beinoni*, whose inner self has not undergone any fundamental change. The evil within him is under the control of the good, but it has not been transformed into good; it continues to ferment within him and gives him no rest. In the same way that the good remains within the *rasha* and "fills him with regrets," giving him no rest, so, too, does the evil in the *beinoni* constantly plague him, exposing him daily to the "three sins."

Yet, the impression [of prayer] on the intellect

When a person studies and prays and attains a state of attachment to God—even if only temporarily—the memory of it remains. Even if he does not repeat the experience, the influence of that occasion lingers within him. An impression remains, and some change takes effect within his soul.

and the innate awe and love of God in the right ventricle

In addition to the impression remaining in the soul of the *beinoni* from the experience of prayer, a latent sense of awe and love of God inherent to the essence of his soul exists within every person, at all times. The combination of the impression left by the experience of love and awe in prayer and the latent potential for love and awe in every soul

achieve this: [they enable him] to overpower and control this evil craving and not allow it to gain supremacy and dominion over the city

The *beinoni*'s power is such that even without an actual experience of love and awe of God (which the *tzaddik* experiences constantly), he can draw the strength from the "impression" left by prayer and from his latent love of God to completely control every aspect of his life, never allowing his animal soul to

carry out its desire from the potential into actuality by clothing itself in the organs and limbs of the body.

Moreover, even in the mind alone, [insofar] as evil thoughts are concerned, the evil gains no supremacy and dominion to compel the mind's volition to entertain willingly, God forbid, any wicked thought rising of its own accord from the heart to the brain, as discussed above;

So great is the power of the *beinoni* that even the "sinful thoughts" (which rise of their own accord from the left ventricle of the heart to the mind; see Chapter 9) never develop into conscious, structured thoughts. These thoughts arise spontaneously within the *beinoni*, because the divided heart with which he was born has not been rectified. His heart is like that of every man; he desires what everyone desires and lusts after what everyone lusts after, each according to his taste and station. Yet though he cannot prevent these thoughts from rising to his mind,

no sooner does it reach there than he thrusts it out with both hands and averts his mind from it the instant he becomes aware that it is an evil thought, refusing to accept it willingly, not even allowing himself to willingly think it, and certainly not to entertain any idea of putting it into effect, God forbid, or even to speak of it. For one who willfully indulges in such thoughts is deemed a *rasha* at such time, whereas the *beinoni* is never a *rasha,* even for a single moment.

Up to now, the discussion has dwelled on sinful desires that relate to man's duties toward God (for example, the desire for a nonkosher food, a forbidden sexual relationship, and so on). The same applies to negative desires and behaviors in all that pertains to man's relationship with his fellows.

So, too, in matters affecting a person's relations with his fellow: as soon as there rises from his heart to his mind some animosity or hatred, God forbid, or jealousy or anger, or a grudge and suchlike, he gives them no entrance into his mind and will.

The *beinoni* is not a person who never gets angry. But he has sufficient control over himself not to indulge his anger and allow it to take root in his mind and develop into a full-fledged emotion.

On the contrary, his mind exercises its authority and power over the spirit in his heart, to do the very opposite and to conduct himself towards his fellow with the quality of kindness and a display of extra affection, to tolerate him to the extreme limits without becoming provoked into anger, God forbid, or to revenge in kind, God forbid;

The Torah forbids this outright in Leviticus 19:18.

but rather to repay the offenders with favors, as taught in the *Zohar*,[12] that one should learn from the example of Joseph towards his brothers.

In summation, the *beinoni* is one whose Godly soul successfully controls his animal soul. Although he experiences all forms of temptation, such as anger, hatred, and lust, in exactly the same way that the *rasha* experiences them, he will not succumb to them, even in thought. In his willful thoughts, and certainly in his speech and deeds, he expresses only the goodness and holiness of his Godly soul.

⟶ Glossary

The purpose of this Glossary is to convey a general sense of what the terms mean and how they are used. Most entries begin with a literal translation in parentheses, followed by a brief definition and one or two relevant ideas from Hasidic thought. Beyond that, we have not attempted to provide a comprehensive discussion or a thorough explanation of the concepts. This material is intended as a hint pointing in the direction of the vast wealth of explanation and understanding in the literature of Hasidism.

Terms preceded by an asterisk have their own entries in the Glossary. All foreign terms are Hebrew unless otherwise indicated.

Acharonim ("the later [scholars]")   A general term for the sages who lived after the appearance of the *Shulchan Aruch* in the sixteenth century.

aggadah ("nonhalakhic material"), pl. *aggadot*   The Talmud and the Oral Torah in general distinguish between *halakhic (legal) material and nonhalakhic material. The nonhalakhic material is called *aggadah,* and it includes "philosophical" discussions, *mussar,* and stories. The *aggadot* of the Talmud contain, in a concealed way, most of the secrets of the Torah.

ahavah zutah ("the small love"); *ahavah rabbah* ("the great love")   Two levels in the love of God, differing in the following ways: (1) the lower level, *ahavah zutah,* has an element of self-interest, because it stems from a person's recognition of the benefits that he received from God and that he is likely to receive in the future. The higher level, *ahavah rabbah,* is an altruistic love, because it stems from a person's awareness of God's intrinsic goodness, without regard to his own benefit. (2) *Ahavah zutah* is an emotion that one experiences like other emotions (in the heart). *Ahavah rabbah,* however, is a function of the Godly intellect, and even its emotional component, called *ahavah beTa'anugim* ("the love that is accompanied by delight"), results from the revelation of the inner aspect of *keter (oneg,* "delight") within the intellect of the Godly soul. (3) *Ahavah zutah* is generated "from below," by a person's meditation, whereas *ahavah rabbah* is a gift "from above."

ahavah mesuteret ("the hidden love")   A love of God that is hidden within the heart of every Jew. Inherent in the Jewish soul, it is a type of spiritual inheritance from the patriarchs. The patriarchs were a *merkavah* to God, and their love for God was such an essential aspect of their being that it could be transmitted to their descendants. The *ahavah mesuteret* is related to *yechidah,* the highest level of the soul. The existence of this hidden love is one of the fundamental ideas of *Tanya.*

ahavat olam ("world love")   *Olam* means "world," and *ahavat olam* is a love of God that stems from the awareness that God is the source of all life and existence in the world. Because it focuses on God as He benefits the world, it is on the level of *ahavah zutah* and not *ahavah rabbah,* which focuses on more essential aspects of God. The term *ahavat olam* can also denote God's love for us, as reflected in the fact that He "limits" His own being in order to permit the existence of a world.

assur ("bound"); *mutar* ("unbound")   *Assur* means "forbidden" or "prohibited," and *mutar* means "permitted." Any action can be assigned to one of three categories: *mitzvah, mutar,* or *assur.* A *mitzvah* is derived from holiness, whereas any other action is derived from *kelipah* ("unholiness"). An action that is *mutar* is derived from *kelipat nogah,* so it contains a divine spark that can be elevated to holiness. Hence, the name *mutar,* which hints that the divine spark is unbound and free to be elevated. An action that is *assur* is derived from one of the *kelipot temeiot,* and the divine spark within it cannot normally be elevated to holiness. Hence, the name *assur,* which hints that the divine spark is bound and cannot be elevated.

Atzilut ("Proximity" or "Emanation")   The first and highest of the four general worlds (*olamot*) created by God: *Atzilut, Beriah, Yetzirah,* and *Asiyah.* Both derivations of the name are relevant. On the other hand, *Atzilut* is regarded as being "together with" (*etzel*) the Creator, unified with God. From the point of view of God's essential being, however, *Atzilut* is regarded as an emanation from and away from divinity.

baal teshuvah ("one who has returned"), pl. *baalei teshuvah*   See **teshuvah*. A person who has returned to God. This may be either a person who sinned and then returned to God through the process of repentance or a **tzaddik* who never sinned, because *teshuvah* can refer to the general process of reconnecting the soul to its source in God.

Most often the term refers to a person who has sinned and repented, and in this sense, our sages teach (*Berachot* 34b) that "*baalei teshuvah* stand on a level where even complete *tzaddikim* cannot stand." The reason is that a *baal teshuvah* has succeeded in elevating aspects of the world and of his own soul that were on a very low level, whereas a *tzaddik* is never directly involved with such low things. In addition, a *baal teshuvah*, having been far away, feels a greater thirst for God than a *tzaddik*. Also, a *baal teshuvah* must transcend his own nature and reveal new powers within himself, while a *tzaddik* serves God with powers that were always available to him.

Baal Shem Tov ("Master of the Good Name")   The title given to Rabbi Yisrael ben Eliezer (c. 1700–1760), founder of the Hasidic movement. He lived in Podolia, an area of the Ukraine, and in Galicia. At the age of thirty-six, after living for many years as one of the hidden (unrecognized) **tzaddikim*, he began to teach a small group of students in the city of Mezhibuzh, and his teachings spread throughout Eastern Europe.

The Baal Shem Tov emphasized that nothing is unrelated to Godliness and that Godliness can be found in all places and in all situations.

Rabbi Schneur Zalman never saw the Baal Shem Tov, but he regarded him as his spiritual grandfather, because the Baal Shem Tov was the rebbe of the Maggid of Mezherich, who was Rabbi Schneur Zalman's own rebbe.

behemah ("beast"), pl. *behemot* ("cattle" or "livestock")   A general term for domesticated animals and, in particular, for animals that can be offered as sacrifices, such as cattle, sheep, and goats.

Although an animal is spiritually lower than a man (according to the way they both exist in the world), nevertheless, the spiritual source of an animal (which is in the world of *tohu*) is higher than the spiritual source of a man (which is in the world of *tikkun*). Hence, when a person offers an animal as a sacrifice, and the animal is elevated to its source, the person receives a "light" from that high source that elevates him spiritually. This is also why a person who eats animals or plants receives vitality from the food. Similarly, when a person elevates his own animal soul (see *korbanot*), his Godly soul receives additional vitality.

The sages often use the terms *behemah* ("animal") and *adam* ("man") to define two categories within the elements of a single entity. For example, within a person, the animal soul is characterized as *behemah,* whereas the Godly soul is characterized as *adam.* Within the Jewish people, an individual who serves God as a "servant" is said to have the nature of a *behemah,* whereas the individual who serves God as a "son" is said to have the nature of an *adam.* And within the *olamot,* the worlds of *Beriah, Yetzirah,* and *Asiyah* are described as *behemah,* whereas the world of *Atzilut* is described as *adam.*

beinoni ("intermediate"), pl. *beinonim*   In general usage, an individual whose fulfillment of the commandments is on a level between that of the *tzaddik* and the *rasha,* a person whose good deeds are equal in importance to his transgressions.

In *Tanya,* the term *beinoni* refers to a person who has an impulse to sin but who always overcomes it and never sins in thought, speech, or action. As such, the *beinoni* represents a distinct and independent category, and a *beinoni*'s endowments and accomplishments are essentially different from those of either a *tzaddik* or a *rasha.* Every Jew has the ability to become a *beinoni,* and he is obligated to work toward that goal. The divine service of a *beinoni* and of the individual who aspires to be a *beinoni* is the primary focus of the *Tanya* and of Chabad Hasidism in general.

Although *Tanya* describes a *beinoni* as "one who never sinned even once in his lifetime," the Lubavitcher Rebbe explains that even a person who has sinned in the past can reach the level of *beinoni.* The *Tanya* means only that a *beinoni,* in his present state, is unaffected by any previous sin, and he is free from any weaknesses that would cause him to sin in the future.

ben aliyah ("ascendant one"), pl. *b'nei aliyah*   Individuals who have reached the highest spiritual levels. In *Tanya*, the term refers to complete *tzaddikim.*

binah ("understanding")   The second of the ten *sefirot. In the soul, *binah* receives the germ of an idea from *chokhmah and develops it to the stage of complete understanding. *Binah* is the central *sefirah* of intellect; it develops implications, ramifications, and applications. It sets limits and builds a structure of understanding that the individual can later express in emotion, thought, speech, and action.

   Binah is also called the "mother of the children" because it generates and directs the emotions and behavioral impulses associated with the lower *sefirot.*

bittul ("nullification")   A fundamental concept in Hasidism. In Jewish law, the term *bittul* refers to the *halakhic ruling that a small substance attached to or contained within a larger entity should be regarded as a part of the larger entity and not as an independent object. Similarly, in Hasidic thought, the term *bittul* refers to the process by which a person's sense of his independent existence is subsumed within and elevated to an awareness of a greater, more inclusive existence, the existence of God. Hasidic thought explains that the existence of every created being is, in truth, subsumed within God's existence; through *bittul,* a person brings his subjective perception into harmony with that objective truth.

   Two general levels of *bittul* exist: (1) a higher level, *bittul haMetziut* ("nullification of existence"), and (2) a lower level, *bittul haYesh* ("nullification of substance"). On the higher level of *bittul,* there is no sense of any separate or independent existence. This corresponds to the way that entities in the world of *Atzilut are unified with God (a level of unity known as *yichuda ila'ah*). On the lower level, a person feels that he has an independent existence but chooses to submit to God's will. This corresponds to the way that created beings in the worlds of *Beriah, Yetzirah,* and *Asiyah* are unified with God (a level of unity known as *yichuda tata'ah*).

Chabad   (Acronym for *chokhmah, *binah, *daat, the three *sefirot associated with intellect.) Chabad is the name of the Hasidic movement founded by Rabbi Schneur Zalman of Liadi toward the end of the eighteenth century in parts of Russia, the Ukraine, and eastern Lithuania. The movement became known as Chabad because it teaches a way of serving God that is based to a great extent on intellectual powers of the soul, the faculties of *chokhmah, binah,* and *daat.* Chabad regards intellectual meditation and sustained, rigorous thought about the nature of God and His relation to the world as the primary tools for the spiritual service of God.

chassid, chassidic   See Hasid, Hasidic.

chayah   The fourth level of the soul, the level above **neshamah. Chayah* is not "clothed" within any of the revealed powers of soul; it stays above them like an **ohr makif* ("a transcendent or surrounding light"). *Chayah* is associated with the "source of **chokhmah,*" which is above intellect; hence, it is related to the *sefirah* of *keter. Chayah* corresponds to the world of **Atzilut.*

chessed ("loving-kindness")   One of the **sefirot, chessed* is the first of the emotional attributes. *Chessed* is expressed as giving or bestowing influence, and the inner aspect of the **middah* is love, which motivates the act of giving. Because *chessed* reflects an expansive, outward impulse, a movement to reach beyond the boundaries of self, it is also called *gedulah* ("greatness").

chokhmah ("wisdom" or "insight")   The first of the ten **sefirot.* In the soul, *chokhmah* is the faculty of intellectual insight. It gives the germ of an idea to **binah,* which develops it to the stage of complete comprehension. Hence, the relationship between *chokhmah* and *binah* is described as that of a "father" and a "mother."

Chokhmah Ila'ah ("supernal wisdom")   The **sefirah* of **chokhmah* in the world of **Atzilut. Chokhmah Ila'ah* reveals God's wisdom itself, before it is clothed in other powers or attributes, as opposed to *chokhmah tata'ah* ("the lower wisdom"), which refers to *chokhmah* as it is clothed in **malkhut* ("kingship").

d'veikut ("attachment")   A state of mind in which all of one's powers of thought and feeling are exclusively directed to and attached to God. In a state of *d'veikut,* the individual becomes attached to God. He is temporarily unaware of himself as a separate being, and his consciousness is filled by an awareness of God's being.

One can attain a state of *d'veikut* in many ways. The **Baal Shem Tov spoke about concentrating in prayer and attaching one's thoughts to the individual letters and words of the prayers.

*Chabad Hasidism emphasizes *hitbonenut,* contemplative meditation in which one thinks deeply and continuously for an extended period of time about a topic explained in Hasidic discourses. Such meditation, together with feelings of love and fear of God, may accompany the Hasid's prayers and may deepen his understanding of the words themselves.

daat ("knowledge" and "connection")   The third of the ten *sefirot.* The word *daat,* as used in the Torah, implies attachment and connection. In the soul, *daat* is the power that allows the intellect to connect with and influence the other powers of the soul, such as the emotions. Similarly, *daat* is the power of intellect that enables it to connect with the idea or subject itself, as it exists independently, above and beyond the intellect of the person who is trying to understand it.

Derush   See *pardes.*

Ein Sof ("the Infinite [One]")   A term in Kabbalah that refers to God as He exists above and beyond every limitation and definition. Although the term is only a negative characterization of God, it constitutes a kind of definition, and hence it cannot be accepted as characterization of God's essential being, which is above all definition, even by negation. Instead, we understand the term as a characterization of the first emanation from God's essential being, an emanation that is sometimes referred to as His Name (see *Likkutei Torah, Devarim* 7b). Because the relation between this first emanation and God's essence is comparable to the relation between the light of the sun and the body of the sun, this first emanation is often referred to as *Ohr Ein Sof* ("the Infinite Light").

Etz Chayyim ("the Tree of Life")   The Torah describes *Gan Eden* (Genesis 2:9) as having an *Etz Chayyim* in the center of the garden and also an *Etz haDa'at Tov vaRa* (a "Tree of Knowledge of Good and Evil"). Based on the words of King Solomon (Proverbs 3:18), the Torah is called *Etz Chayyim,* and the things of the physical world (*kelipat nogah*) are referred to as *Etz haDa'at.* Kabbalah and Hasidism point out that even within the Torah itself, there is a level comparable to *Etz Chayyim* and a level comparable to *Etz haDa'at.* The inner, mystical dimension of the Torah, which is not clothed within the terms and concepts of the lower worlds, is referred to as *Etz Chayyim;* the revealed dimensions of the Oral

Torah, to the extent to which they are clothed within the terms and concepts of the lower worlds and to the extent to which they are studied in order to elevate sparks of Godliness from the *kelipot*, are referred to as *Etz haDa'at*. (See *Iggeret haKodesh*, Chapter 26.)

Etz Chayyim is also the title of one of the most important works of Kabbalah. Based primarily on the manuscripts in which Rabbi Chaim Vital recorded and arranged the teachings of the *Holy Ari, it was compiled and edited by Rabbi Meir Popperos in the seventeenth century.

galut haShekhinah ("the exile of the divine presence")   The *Shekhinah* is the Godly "energy" that fills the universe, giving life and existence to every created being.

This spiritual energy is clothed within the physicality of the world, where it is concealed but also revealed by the fact that it brings about the existence of the world. Nevertheless, when the *Shekhinah* reveals itself this way, it cannot do so in the way it "would like to" but only in the way that the "garment" (*levush*) in which it is clothed permits it to be revealed. For example, a person receives his existence and vitality from the *Shekhinah*. Hence, when a person sins, he is "forcing" the *Shekhinah* to participate in his sin, which is against its will. This situation, in which the *Shekhinah* may be "compelled" to give life and existence to that which is against God's will (that is, to the *sitra achra*), is referred to as *galut haShekhinah*.

An even deeper level of *galut haShekhinah* is caused by the exile of the Jewish people among the nations of the world. The ultimate purpose of that exile is to collect and elevate the "sparks of holiness" that are scattered throughout the world and, in doing so, to rectify the world itself.

Gan Eden ("paradise")   As described in the Torah, *Gan Eden* is the place where Adam and Eve, the first man and woman, lived immediately after they were created. The original intention was that they would serve God by fulfilling His commandments in *Gan Eden*. As a result of their sin, however, they were expelled from *Gan Eden*, and henceforth, their service of God was to take place in a lower, more physical world (in which we live today).

Gan Eden continued to exist as a spiritual world where the soul would be rewarded for its service. Because it is a spiritual world, only the soul can enter *Gan Eden,* and this generally occurs only after the death of the body. (In extraordinarily holy and refined individuals, who can "divest" the soul from its physical involvement, it may also occur even while they are living in the world.) The performance of **mitzvot* and the rectification of character traits does not continue after the soul enters *Gan Eden.* On the other hand, the soul in *Gan Eden* is able to sense the divine pleasure and enjoy the divine light that resulted from the Torah it studied and the *mitvzot* it performed while it was in the material world. That perception and enjoyment are the soul's reward for *mitzvot.*

Gemara (Aramaic: "study" or "completion")   The portion of the **Talmud* that discusses and explains the Mishnah. The term is also used in a more inclusive sense to refer to the entire Talmud.

gevurah ("power" or "strength")   One of the **sefirot,* the second of the emotional attributes. *Gevurah* is the power of restriction and definition, and its inner aspect is fear. *Gevurah* is also called *din* ("judgment") because it places limits and restrictions on all things, and it leads a person to demand exactitude and correctness.

halakhah   The entire body of Jewish law or a particular ruling of the sages. The root meaning of the word is "walking" or "conduct," because Jewish law provides a path and a guide for the conduct of Jewish life.

According to Hasidic thought, God's will and wisdom, which are beyond the comprehension of any created being, are clothed within the laws of halakhah. Because halakhah is comprehensible, we can grasp, in effect, God's supernal will and wisdom. When a person studies any area of the Torah, God's will and wisdom are revealed within his soul, his thought, and his speech. Through the study of the halakhah, however, it is possible to grasp an even deeper and more essential aspect of God's being. Hence, the saying of our sages (*Berachot* 8a) that since the destruction of the Temple, God's only dwelling place in the world is the one provided for Him by the study of halakhah.

hashgachah p'ratit ("supervision of the individual")   Particular Divine Providence. The idea that God controls the affairs of the world has always been a fundamental belief in Judaism. The **Baal Shem Tov* emphasized that Divine Providence applies directly to every individual creature and every detail of creation, without exception. In the words of *Admor haRayatz:* "Not only is every movement of every individual creature an expression of Divine Providence, and not only is that Divine Providence the very life of the individual creature and the source of its existence—in addition, the particular motion of every individual creature is related in a general way to the overall purpose of the entire universe." This "absolutist" view of Divine Providence became one of the few points of genuine philosophical disagreement in the dispute between *Hasidim and *mitnagdim. (See *Igros Kodesh* of the Lubavitcher Rebbe, vol. 1, p. 94).

Hasid, pl. Hasidim   In biblical Hebrew and in the language of our sages, the term *chasid* (often spelled *chassid*) refers to a person who is on an extremely high level of righteousness and spiritual perfection. A Hasid does more than the law requires, and he sacrifices his own interests for the sake of others.

   Since the establishment of the Hasidic movement by the *Baal Shem Tov, Hasid also refers to an individual associated with that movement. In *Chabad Hasidism, the term generally indicates a person who feels a connection to the rebbe, studies the teachings of Hasidism, and conducts himself according to the practice of Hasidim.

hishtalshelut haolamot ("the concatenation of the worlds")   The process by which God creates and sustains the entire system of the worlds—a system known as *seder hahishtalshelut*. (See *olam.) In this process, God restricts His infinite light through a graduated series of limitations and concealments that are known as *tsimtzumim* ("contractions"). The result is a graduated series of worlds, or levels of reality and perception, in which each lower world is characterized by a greater concealment of Godliness. The term *hishtalshelut* is derived from the word *shalshelet* ("chain"), and so it suggests that the worlds are connected like the links of a chain. The interconnection of the worlds is comparable, in the individual, to the interconnection between the realms of intellect, emotion, thought, speech, and action.

hitkashrut ("bond" or "attachment")   A term used to refer to a deep, essential connection between two beings. *Hitkashrut* is a connection based on more than a single aspect of being; it involves all aspects of one's being and even the very essence of one's being.

Hitkashrut differs from **d'veikut* in two ways: *hitkashrut* is an internal connection, one that is revealed within the inner powers of the soul (like an **ohr penimi*). *D'veikut,* on the other hand, is a connection that is not internalized, and it relates to the higher, transcendent powers of the soul (like an **ohr makif*). In addition, *hitkashrut* involves a greater degree of influence (*hashpa'ah*) than *d'veikut* and results in a more significant change in the individual.

Although *hitkashrut* is an internal connection, it transcends **sekhel* and can exist even without a logical justification. Just as there is *hitkashrut* between a Jew and God, one can also speak of *hitkashrut* between a Hasid and his rebbe. A Hasid expresses this when he acts in accordance with his rebbe's teachings, and such *hitkashrut* can also transcend **sekhel.*

hitpashtut hagashmiyut ("divestiture of physicality")   A spiritual state in which soul is able to rise above its involvement with the physical world and devote itself to the contemplation of purely spiritual matters. According to the *Tur,* a fourteenth-century code of Jewish law (**Orach Chayyim,* section 98, "The Laws of Prayer"), Hasidism in the time of the Mishnah would reach this level in prayer, and *Tanya* explains that it is a level close to prophecy. Because the soul is clothed within a body, its perception is generally limited to that which is provided by the physical senses, and its understanding of all topics is generally modeled on its understanding of physical reality. Hence, in order for the soul to perceive and understand purely spiritual entities, entities that exist in a realm that is entirely beyond the physical, the soul must first divest itself from its "physical garment" and transcend its intellectual and emotional involvement with the physical world.

hod ("splendor" or "glory")   One of the **sefirot,* the fifth of the emotional attributes. *Hod* is the power to persevere even when faced with obstacles that seem insurmountable. It is the power of acknowledgment: admitting that God is right even when one does not understand, recognizing that He is the one true reality and giving praise and glory to Him. (See **netzach.*)

Holy Ari (also known as Arizal)   (*Ari* is an acronym for *HaEloki Rabbeinu Yitzchak,* "the Godly Rabbi Yitzchak"; the suffix -*zal* adds the words *zichrono livrocha,* "of blessed memory.") Rabbi Yitzchak ben Shlomo Luria, regarded as the greatest of all the Kabbalists, lived in sixteenth-century Egypt and *Eretz Yisrael* (the Land of Israel). He spent the last two years of his brief life in Tzefat, and only there did he began to reveal his teachings. The Holy Ari himself wrote almost nothing, and his teachings were recorded in the works of his students, particularly his principal disciple, Rabbi Chaim Vital. The Arizal's impact on the entire Jewish world was immense, and Hasidic thought is largely based on his Kabbalistic teachings.

Kabbalah ("that which has been received" or "tradition")   The inner, mystical dimension of the Torah, corresponding to the level of *sod. As indicated by its name, a knowledge of Kabbalah is based on traditions received from one's teachers, who received them, in turn, from their teachers.

Kabbalah is not a separate area of Torah knowledge but rather the hidden, spiritual dimension of the revealed aspects of the Torah. Whereas the revealed aspects of the Torah, such as *halakhah, speak primarily about visible, physical things, Kabbalah speaks directly about spiritual entities. It speaks of the system of *olamot and *sefirot through which God creates, sustains, and directs the universe; and it discusses the interaction between those spiritual entities and the performance of *mitzvot in the physical world. Hence, Kabbalah has been called the soul of the Torah.

All Torah study is based on an acceptance of tradition and on the attitude that because the Torah is a divine gift, a person must make himself into a proper vessel in order to receive it. In the study of Kabbalah, however, these attitudes are even more important. Because Kabbalah is the inner spiritual dimension of the Torah, the individual must study it in a way that engages his inner, spiritual dimension. A person who wishes to study Kabbalah should already have an inner understanding of the ideas, and he must pursue the study of Kabbalah in a spirit of purity and holiness, in order to become a suitable vessel. (See *Holy Ari.)

karet ("excision")   A heavenly punishment for certain very serious sins, in which the soul of the sinner is disconnected from its Godly source in the higher worlds. *Karet* is the most severe form of heavenly punishment.

kav ("line"), pl. *kavim*   The ten *sefirot are sometimes described as being arranged in a single vertical line and sometimes as being arranged in three parallel, vertical lines. The first is a description of the world of *tohu, and the second of the world of *tikkun.

The *Zohar* describes the three lines of the world of **tikkun* as "one long, one short, and one intermediate." The line on the right consists of **chokhmah, *chessed,* and **netzach,* which are long in the sense that they are directed outward; in the soul they are associated with an impulse to give and to exert influence on others. The line on the left consists of **binah, *gevurah,* and **hod,* which are short in the sense that they are directed inward; in the soul they are associated with introspection and self-control. And the middle line consists of **daat, *tiferet,* and **yesod,* which are intermediate in the sense that they blend the attributes of the right and the left and mediate between them. The arrangement in the form of three lines is an expression of the fact that, in the world of **tikkun,* the **sefirot* are interrelated and function as an integrated system.

kavvanot ("meditations"), sing. *kavvanah*   The thoughts and feelings that accompany a person's words or deeds. According to **halakhah,* every **mitzvah* requires certain minimal *kavvanot:* an awareness that the action is a *mitzvah* and an intention to fulfill the *mitzvah.* The *mitzvah* of prayer or the recitation of Shema requires a conscious awareness of the meaning of some words, and during the Shemoneh Esreh prayer, one must be aware that one is standing before God.

*Hasidim in all generations have stressed the importance of serving God with more than these minimal *kavvanot.* According to the **Zohar,* a *mitzvah* performed without love and fear "does not ascend to the higher worlds." *Tanya* explains that a *mitzvah* performed with proper *kavvanot* causes a revelation of God's will that is immeasurably greater than it would be without these *kavvanot.* The increase is comparable to the difference between tremendous light and the vitality of the soul, on the one hand, and limited light and the vitality of the body, on the other.

kelipah ("husk" or "shell")   A term used by Kabbalah and Hasidism to refer to those aspects of the universe that are unholy and conceal God's holiness. Ultimately, the only true existence is that of God, and God's light fills the universe. *Kelipah,* however, conceals that truth. The name *kelipah* is based on a metaphor that compares evil to the inedible shell or husk that covers and protects many kinds of fruit. One has to remove and discard the shell; only then can one enjoy the fruit. Similarly, when evil is subdued and rejected, the Godly essence of creation is revealed. There are several different types of *kelipah*: **kelipat nogah* ("luminous" *kelipat*) contains an element of goodness that can be elevated through Torah and *mitzvot*. The *shalosh kelipot temeiot* ("the impure" *kelipot*) do not have a holiness that can be elevated directly.

kelot hanefesh ("expiry of the soul"   A spiritual rapture so intense that the soul desires to leave the body in order to merge with God. It is associated with a very high degree of **bittul*, and it results from a contemplation of a level of God's Being that transcends all Creation, a level of Godliness in relation to which all of Creation is as nothing. This contemplation generates a fiery love of God, a love known as *rishpei esh* ("flames of fire"), and just as a fire seeks to rise upward and leave the wick to which it is attached, so does the soul wish to leave the body and to become absorbed in God's Being.

keter ("crown")   The highest of the ten **sefirot*. Just as a crown rests on top of the head and encompasses it, so *keter* is above all the other *sefirot* and encompasses them like an **ohr makif*. The outer aspect of *keter* corresponds to the soul's power of will (*ratzon*), and its inner aspect corresponds to the soul's power of delight (*oneg*). The will of *keter* is not a specific will toward any particular goal but the essential, underlying will that is present within and revealed by all the specific powers of the soul. Similarly, the delight of *keter* is not a delight in any particular thing but the essential, underlying delight that is present within and revealed by all the specific powers of the soul.

Keter, the highest *sefirah*, has a special connection to **malkhut* ("kingship"), the lowest of the ten *sefirot*. The fact that a crown is the symbol of kingship and the phrase *keter malkhut* ("the crown of kingship") both hint at this. The meaning of this connection is that God's inner will is revealed and fulfilled through His attribute of kingship and through the fact that the lower worlds accept His authority and perform His will.

In addition, *keter*, the highest level in each **olam*, has a special connection to the lowest level of the world above it, which is *malkhut*; through this connection, *keter* unites each world with the world above it.

komah sheleimah ("a full stature" or "a complete structure")   A spiritual structure that is complete: when considered as a whole, with all its parts and their interrelationships, it mirrors the structure of the human body or the human soul. Only in the world of *tikkun* are the *sefirot* organized in accordance with the principle of *komah sheleimah.* (See **partzuf.*)

The souls of the Jewish people of all the generations also form a *komah sheleimah,* as do the Jewish souls of each particular generation. The souls of the sages and the leaders correspond to the head, whereas the lowest souls correspond to the heels.

korbanot ("offerings" or "sacrifices"), sing. *korban*   As a part of the divine service in the *Beit haMikdash* ("Holy Temple"), animals, birds, and small amounts of flour, wine, and water were placed on the altar as offerings to God. Hasidic thought explains how these *korbanot* brought about an elevation of the material world as a whole and a revelation of Godliness. One aspect of that explanation is that the soul of an animal (like the "animal soul" of a Jew) is derived from **kelipat nogah.* When fire consumed an animal offering on the altar, the animal soul was elevated to its spiritual source within the "animal-like" angels of the **merkavah* of the divine throne. This elevation functioned as *mayin nukvin* and led to the descent of *mayin dechurin,* which was a revelation of Godliness from a level above the divine throne.

The individual can perform the spiritual service of *korbanot* though prayer, because prayer also involves the elevation and purification of the animal soul by means of a "Godly fire": the fiery love of God that burns within the Godly soul. As with *korbanot,* the elevation of the animal soul in prayer leads to a revelation of Godliness within the soul of the worshiper.

lashon hara ("evil speech")   Speech that is derogatory, defamatory, or harmful to another person. Even if the information conveyed is true, such communication is forbidden in all but a few rigorously defined situations, and the sin of *lashon hara* is considered extremely serious.

levushim ("garments"), sing. *levush*   A term used in Kabbalah and Hasidic thought to refer to something that "covers" and conceals a spiritual entity and, at the same time, reveals it and endows it with new powers. Just as a physical garment allows a person to go outside and appear in public, so does a *levush* enable a spiritual entity to go beyond its own limitations into a new realm and to give or receive influence in that realm. The movement may be downward: for example, the soul is clothed within the *levush* of the body and, as a result, gains the ability to express itself and act in the physical world. Or the movement may be upward: for example, in order to receive the spiritual light of the *Shekhinah*, the soul must be clothed within the *levushim* it receives through the study of Torah and the performance of *mitzvot*.

Like a physical garment, a *levush* is separate from the entity that is clothed within it. Nevertheless, the two are closely related, and the *levush* must "fit" the "wearer."

Tanya (Chapter 4) explains that the soul has three *levushim*: thought, speech, and action; these allow the deeper powers of the soul (intellect and emotion) to be expressed.

machashavot zarot ("foreign" or "extraneous thoughts"   Any thoughts that distract an individual from serving God, whether in prayer, Torah, or *mitzvot*. According to *Tanya*, when experiencing such thoughts, an ordinary individual should immediately withdraw attention from those thoughts and redirect it to matters of holiness.

malkhut ("kingship")   The tenth and lowest of the *sefirot*. The *sefirah* of *malkhut* of *Atzilut* is the attribute by which God expresses and exercises His kingship over the lower worlds.

Just as a Jewish king should be completely subservient to God, even as he rules over his subjects from a position of superiority, the attribute of *malkhut* of *Atzilut* is completely subservient to the higher *sefirot*, adding nothing of its own to the divine energy it receives from them. At the same time, when God uses the attribute of *malkhut* to give existence and life to the lower worlds of *Beriah*, *Yetzirah*, and *Asiyah*, He maintains a "distance" from them, which allows the beings of the lower worlds to perceive their own existence as separate from God.

This is related to the fact that a king rules over his subjects with the power of speech. He sends his edict and his name to all parts of the kingdom, but it is not necessary for him to travel there himself. Thus the divine attribute of *malkhut* is referred to as "the Word of God," and in the soul as well, the attribute of *malkhut* is associated with the power of speech, for speech takes intellect and emotion and expresses them (through a process of limitation and concealment) in words (which are separate from the individual) so that they can be communicated to other individuals.

Nevertheless, the letters and words of the divine "speech" are "internalized" by the created beings for whom they provide existence and life, and it is for this reason that *malkhut* of *Atzilut* is frequently referred to as the *Shekhinah ("indwelling").

mamash ("substance" or "matter")   An adverbial expression that is often translated as "literally" or "truly." Related to the word *mishush,* which refers to the sense of touch. The term *mamash* emphasizes that a prior statement is not only true but true in a literal, concrete sense; not only true metaphorically but a fact; not only true in some higher world of ideal forms and abstractions but also in the lowest world. The term appears often in the writings of Rabbi Schneur Zalman and the other rebbes of Chabad.

mayin nukvin ("feminine waters"); *mayin dechurin* ("masculine waters")   To express the dynamics of the relationship between God and Man, *Kabbalah uses a metaphor involving the flow of water. It describes God's flow of benevolence to man as *mayin dechurin,* like rain that descends from above, bringing life to the earth. Similarly, it describes man's service of God, his fulfillment of the commandments, as *mayin nukvin,* like a wellspring that flows upward from within the earth. *Mayin nukvin* can be a "stimulus" to bring forth the divine "response" of *mayin dechurin;* this pattern is called *itaruta deletata* ("an awakening from below"). In addition, *mayin nukvin* prepares the recipient to accept and benefit from the *mayin dechurin.* In a similar way, *mayin dechurin* can be a "stimulus" to bring forth man's response of *mayin nukvin;*— this pattern is called *itaruta dele'eilah* ("an awakening from above"). In addition, *mayin dechurin* endows the recipient with an ability to provide *mayin nukvin.*

memale kol almin ("fills all the worlds"); *sovev kol almin* ("surrounds all the worlds")   Two different ways in which God gives the universe life and existence. He provides an *ohr memale, a divine light that is present within every created being in a manner that is appropriate to its particular nature. At the same time, he provides an *ohr sovev, a transcendent divine light that cannot be "internalized," since it is not adjusted to the particular capacity of each creature.

merkavah ("chariot")   A Kabbalistic term for a thing, person, or spiritual entity that is completely obedient to the divine will. In the physical world, a chariot is a wheeled vehicle drawn by horses and directed by a driver. Because a chariot strictly obeys the will of its driver, it can serve as a metaphor for any entity that is completely subservient to a higher spiritual power.

In the spiritual worlds, some beings are subservient to a higher entity through which they receive their life and existence. Such beings may be called a *merkavah* for the higher entity. (For example, the world of *Beriah* contains angelic beings that are described as a *merkavah* for *malkhut* ("kingship") of *Atzilut*. Other examples are the angelic creatures and "wheels" that are described in the prophetic visions of Ezekiel, Isaiah, and Zechariah.)

In a similar sense, our sages said, "The patriarchs themselves are the *merkavah*." Because Abraham, Isaac, and Jacob were devoted completely and exclusively to performing God's will, they can be called a *merkavah* for God. After the Torah was given, every Jew could acquire the ability to become a *merkavah* for God, though to a more limited extent than the patriarchs. Whenever a Jew performs a *mitzvah,* the limbs of his body that participate in the *mitzvah* become a temporary *merkavah* for God (and the "garments" of his soul, and the Godly soul itself, reach an even higher level of unity with God). On the other hand, if a person sins (in thought, speech, or action), the limbs of his body that participate in the sin may become a *merkavah* to unholiness (and other aspects of his soul may also become attached to unholiness).

middot ("attributes")   The lower seven of the ten *sefirot.* (However, the term often refers only to the first six of these *sefirot,* from *chessed* to *yesod.*) The root meaning of the word *middot* is "measurements" or "parameters," and from these *sefirot* are derived the parameters of the created world: the six "directions" (physical or spiritual) within each world and the six days in which the world was created.

In the soul, the *middot* correspond to the primary emotions of love, fear, and mercy and the behavioral impulses of domination, acknowledgment, and bestowing influence. In the Godly soul, these attributes are entirely holy, but in the animal soul, they are predominantly evil. In the animal soul, for example, *chessed* can become lust, and *gevurah* can become anger.

Midrash ("that which is the product of searching")   One of the major branches of the Oral Torah, *Midrash* consists of homiletic and *halakhic* material, often linked to a linguistic analysis of the biblical text. *Midrash* contains many different collections.

mitnagdim ("opponents")   The opponents of the Hasidic movement in the late eighteenth and early nineteenth centuries. The root of their opposition was a fear that the new movement would generate sects or cults that might eventually break away from the rest of the Jewish community. At the height of the conflict, incidents of physical violence and slander took place, and on a few occasions, the non-Jewish authorities imprisoned Hasidic leaders at the instigation of a few of the *mitnagdim.*

mitzvah ("commandment"), pl. *mitzvot*   In the Torah, God commands us to do specific things; these are the positive *mitzvot.* In addition, He commands us *not* to do specific things, and these are the negative *mitzvot* or prohibitions. According to tradition, there are exactly 248 positive *mitzvot* and 365 negative *mitzvot,* corresponding to the 248 limbs and 365 blood vessels of the human body. By fulfilling the positive *mitzvot* and avoiding the prohibitions, a person brings holiness to every part of his body.

Tikkunei Zohar describes the 248 positive *mitzvot* metaphorically as "the 248 limbs of the King [God]." Just as the limbs of a physical body draw the vitality of the soul into the various structures and activities associated with the limbs, so, too, the *mitzvot* of the Torah draw the divine light and energy into the various levels of the created world.

The 613 *mitzvot* of the Torah and the seven rabbinical *mitzvot* bring the number of commandments to 620, which is the numerical value of the word *keter.* This reflects the fact that the *mitzvot* are derived from the level of *keter,* from God's will, which is higher than His wisdom, and they cause God's will to be expressed within the context of physical reality.

mussar ("moral teaching")   In a general sense, *mussar* is the branch of rabbinical literature that focuses on self-perfection and correct behavior. *Mussar* discusses obligations that *halakhah does not fully specify, such as the need for proper intention in fulfilling the commandments and the obligation to examine one's general priorities in life. In this sense, many works of Hasidism also contain elements of *mussar.*

The term is often used in a more specific sense to refer to the *Mussar* movement, founded by Rabbi Yisrael Salanter in the middle of the nineteenth century. Based primarily in the Lithuanian yeshivas, the *Mussar* movement continues to exert an important influence on the ideals and attitudes taught by those yeshivas.

nefesh ("soul")   In its most general sense, the word *nefesh* refers to the spiritual vitality inherent in every created being. In this sense, it can refer even to the spark of divine energy that is found within inanimate objects.

The word *nefesh* frequently refers to the soul in its entirety, including all of its five levels. This reflects the fact that all the levels of the soul are part of a single spiritual entity that, together with the body, constitutes an *adam*, a man. (Although every soul has five levels, the four upper levels are revealed in an individual only as a result of his efforts and accomplishments in serving God.) The five levels of the soul are *nefesh*, **ruach*, **neshamah*, **chayah*, and **yechidah*. Thus, the word *nefesh* can also refer specifically to the lowest level of the soul.

Nefesh, the lowest level of the soul, is more involved with the body and with giving life to the body than any of the higher levels. In *nefesh*, the soul's power of action is revealed, as well as the power to acknowledge God's greatness and the capacity for **bittul*, by which a person devotes himself completely to doing God's will without any considerations of self-interest or feelings of pride. *Nefesh* corresponds to the world of *Asiyah*.

Tanya explains that on the level of *nefesh*, a Jew has two souls: an "animal soul" and a "Godly soul."

neshamot ("souls"), sing. *neshamah*   Although the singular form often refers to the third level of the soul, the plural form can refer collectively to the Godly souls of the Jewish people. As described in *Tanya*, the Godly soul (*nefesh haElokit*) is a "part of God above" that comes into the world to be clothed within an animal soul (*nefesh haBehemit*) and a body. This descent gives the soul an opportunity for an even greater ascent. *Neshamot* are higher than angels because souls are a part of the "inwardness" of the universe, whereas angels are part of its "externality." In addition, souls can "progress," whereas angels are "stationary."

netzach ("victory" or "eternity")   One of the **sefirot*, the fourth of the emotional attributes. *Netzach* is the will to be victorious, the determination to overcome all obstacles. Although *netzach* and **hod* are, in a sense, opposites, they work together like two aspects of a single entity. Their common purpose is to strengthen the

intellectual and emotional "energy" of the *middot* and to channel it into tangible, practical results, despite any internal or external opposition. One metaphor pictures *netzach* and *hod* as "a pair
of millstones" working together to turn wheat into flour, an image
that expresses their role in "processing" the spiritual energy of the
higher attributes and making it available in a way that will benefit others.

nishmat chayyim ("breath of life")   The soul, which gives life and
breath to the body. In describing the creation of the first man, the
Torah (*Bereshit* 2:7) writes, "And He [God] blew [*vaYipach*] into
his nostrils a soul of life [*nishmat chayyim*]." The word **neshamah*
("soul") is intimately related to the verb *nasham* ("breathe"). One
reason is that the attachment of the soul to the body is both a
cause and an effect of breathing. Also, because physical breath
involves the entry of an invisible entity into the body that is necessary for the maintenance of life, it provides a metaphor for the
soul, an invisible spiritual entity that enters the body and causes
it to live. Because the human soul is associated with breathing, the
Torah writes that the soul that was given to the first man was
placed in his nostrils. In addition, the Torah says that God "blew
the soul" into Adam, which hints that the origin of the soul (*nefesh
haElokit*) is God's "breath," that is, an inner aspect of God's being.

ohr ("light")   A term used in Kabbalah to refer to the divine energy
with which God creates and sustains the universe. The Kabbalists
use the metaphor of light for a number of reasons, including
these: (1) light is the most subtle and incorporeal of all material
things, and (2) light is essential to life. Hasidic thought points out
similarities between the way light is related to its source (for
example, the sun) and the way the divine energy is related to God:
(1) light reveals those aspects of its source that can be revealed;
(2) the divine energy (even as it exists within the **sefirot* and the
*olamot) is united with God just as the light of the sun (when it
is still within the sun) is completely united with the sun itself; (3)
light reveals the sun without causing any change in the sun itself.

Ohr Ein Sof ("The Infinite Light")   The "light" that emanates from
God's essence, at a stage when it is still subsumed within His
essence. To describe this metaphorically, Hasidic thought speaks
of the light of the sun, at a stage when it is still included within
the sun itself. The *Ohr Ein Sof* is not only "a light that *comes* from

the Infinite One" (which would allow the possibility that the light itself might be finite) but also a light that is *itself* infinite.

ohr makif ("an encompassing light"); *ohr penimi* ("an inner light")   Terms that are nearly synonymous with *ohr memale* ("a light that fills") and *ohr sovev* ("a light that surrounds") but differ slightly in usage (see **memale kol almin*): *sovev* and *memale* are generally used to describe God's relation to the worlds and to the **sefirot*, whereas *makif* and *penimi* are usually mentioned in relation to a particular vessel. For example, through the performance of **mitzvot* (and also through study of Torah), the soul receives an *ohr makif,* which is described as a "garment" for the soul, while through the study of Torah (and also the performance of **mitzvot*), the soul receives an *ohr penimi,* which is described as "food" for the soul.

olam ("world"), pl. *olamot*   The word *olam* is related to the word *he'elem* ("concealment"), because the existence of a world in which beings can perceive their own existence and that of other created beings is possible only if God conceals His infinite light. *Olam* can refer to the entire system of graduated levels of reality (known as *seder hahishtalshelut;* see **hishtalshelut haolamot*), in which each lower level involves a greater concealment of God's light, or it can refer to a particular level of that system. Within the system of *seder hahishtalshelut* are four general "worlds": **Atzilut, Beriah, Yetzirah,* and *Asiyah.*

 The relation of these four worlds to the Creator is mirrored in the individual by the relation of the powers of the soul to the soul itself. *Atzilut* corresponds to the faculty of **chokhmah,* the soul's innate selflessness that allows it to receive new insights; *Beriah* corresponds to the intellect; *Yetzirah* corresponds to the emotions; and *Asiyah* corresponds to the soul's power of expression in thought, speech, and action.

omdim ("those who stand); *mehalkhim* ("those who progress)   The term *omdim* generally refers to the heavenly angels, while the term *mehalkhim* refers to souls. According to Hasidic thought, standing in a single place is an expression of **bittul* (self-nullification and subservience to a higher power). (See **Amidah*.) Since angels have a "body" that is refined and spiritual, they perceive the Godly light that is the source of their existence, and hence their own being is completely subservient to Godliness. A soul clothed within a material body cannot perceive the Godly source of its existence, and hence it has less *bittul* than the angels. (However, before a soul is clothed within a body, its perception is not limited in this way, and hence it is sometimes described as "standing before God.")

The term *mehalkhim,* on the other hand, describes a characteristic that makes souls superior to angels: souls can progress— they can ascend from level to level—while angels are limited to a particular spiritual "station." This is because souls are created by God's "thought," while angels are created by God's "speech." As we see by observing the activity of our own minds, thought is characterized by fluidity and change, while speech is a finished product— once a word is uttered, it remains the same.

pardes ("orchard")   In **Tanakh* (Song of Songs 4:13), the word refers to an enclosed garden planted with fruit trees. The sages also use the word to mean a spiritual "place," a level of awareness on which the deepest secrets of the Torah are revealed. The *Gemara* (*Chagigah* 14b) tells of "four scholars who entered *pardes.*"

In a related but slightly different usage, the word is used as an acronym for the four general levels on which the Torah can be understood: *Peshat* ("simple, literal meaning"), *Remez* ("allusion"), *Derush* ("homiletical interpretation"), and *Sod* ("mystical interpretation," the secrets of the Torah). These are not four distinct areas of Torah but four levels on which every topic in Torah can be understood.

partzuf ("face" or "configuration"), pl. *partzufim*   An integrated configuration of **sefirot* in the world of **tikkun.* In the world of **tohu,* each **sefirah* was pure and entirely distinct from every other *sefirah.* In the transition to the world of *tikkun,* the individual *sefirot* acquire a substructure of ten sub-*sefirot,* which endows each individual *sefirah* with the qualities of all the other *sefirot.* The ten sub-*sefirot* of a particular *sefirah* (for example, **chokhmah*) are organized in the form of a *partzuf,* and this allows them to interact with other *partzufim.* There are six primary *partzufim:* the *sefirah* of *chokhmah* together with its sub-*sefirot* is referred to as *Abba* ("father"), and the *sefirah* of **binah* with its sub-*sefirot* is referred to as *Ima* ("mother"). The six **middot* form a *partzuf* with ten sub-*sefirot* that is called *Dukhra* ("the Male"), *Z'eir Anpin* ("the Small Face"), and the *sefirah* of **malkhut* ("kingship"), together with its sub-*sefirot,* is called *Nukvah d'Z'eir Anpin* ("the Female of Z'eir Anpin"). The inner aspect of **keter* forms the *partzuf* of *Atik*

Yomin ("the Ancient of Days"), and the outer aspect of *keter* forms the *partzuf* of *Arich Anpin* ("the Long Face").

Peshat   See *pardes.

rasha ("a wicked person"), pl. *resha'im*   A person who sins. According to the *Tanya*, a *tzaddik* is a person with no desire for sin, and a *beinoni* is one who has a desire for sin but never transgresses. A *rasha*, on the other hand, is a person who actually sins and fails to observe the *halakhah.

Remez   See *pardes.

reshut ("optional" or "nonobligatory")   An activity is described as *reshut* when it does not constitute the fulfillment of a particular *mitzvah* but is also not forbidden, for example, eating kosher food. Every action belongs to one of three categories: *mitzvah* (a fulfillment of God's will), *aveirah* (a violation of God's will), or *reshut* (permissible but not obligatory). To the question of whether to perform a particular action that is *reshut*, the Torah does not provide a clear answer. Instead, it provides general directives, such as the injunction to be holy, which obligates a Jew to practice restraint and avoid indulgence when engaging in permissible activities that involve physical pleasure.

In a related but slightly different usage, the term is also applied to *mitzvah* activities that are not obligatory. For example, according to one opinion in the *Gemara*, "*tefilat arvi—reshut*": "the evening prayer is not obligatory."

Rishonim ("the earlier [scholars]")   A general term for the sages who lived during the six centuries prior to the appearance of the *Shulchan Aruch* in the sixteenth century. (See *Acharonim.)

ruach ("soul")   The second level of the soul, the level above *nefesh. Ruach* is expressed and revealed through the emotional powers of the soul, through love and fear of God. It corresponds to the world of *Yetzirah* (see *olam).

Ruach haKodesh ("the spirit of holiness")   Divine inspiration. A spiritual state in which an individual possesses knowledge and awareness that he could not acquire through intellect or sensory perception. *Ruach haKodesh* is a lesser form of prophecy, a heavenly gift that is usually given only to a person who has perfected his conduct and his character.

Sefer HaGilgulim ("The Book of Reincarnations")   A work that is based on the teachings of the *Holy Ari and edited by Rabbi Meir Popperos.

sefirot (divine "attributes" or "emanations"), sing. *sefirah*   The ten channels of divine energy through with God creates, sustains, and directs the worlds and through which Godliness is revealed. The soul also consists of ten powers or attributes that correspond to the divine *sefirot*. For this reason, by thinking deeply about the powers of the soul, it is possible to comprehend some aspects of the divine *sefirot*.

The *sefirot* consist of *ohrot* ("lights") and *kelim* ("vessels"). The light of a particular *sefirah* is the flow of Godliness within it, whereas the vessel is what restricts the light and gives it a specific identity or quality.

The *sefirot* are divided into two groups: *sekhel* ("intellectual attributes") and *middot* ("emotional attributes"). The intellectual attributes are *chokhmah, *binah, and *daat; and the emotional attributes are *chessed, *gevurah, *tiferet, *netzach, *hod, *yesod, and *malkhut ("kingship").

The *sefirah* of *keter is higher than both *sekhel* and *middot*, but when *keter* is counted as one of the *sefirot, daat* is not counted. Hence, there are only ten *sefirot*.

sekhel ("intellect")   The ten *sefirot and the ten powers of the soul are divided into *sekhel* ("intellectual attributes") and *middot* ("emotional attributes"). *Sekhel* includes the attributes of *chokhmah, *binah, and *daat. In a general sense, *sekhel* gives the "subject" (for example, the thinker) an awareness of the existence or the essential nature of the "object" (the idea or thing). *Middot,* on the other hand, define a relationship between the subject (for example, the lover) and the object of his emotion (for example, the beloved).

Shekhinah ("indwelling")   The divine presence. The Godly "energy" that fills the universe, giving life and existence to each created being in accordance with its particular characteristics. In relation to the worlds of *Beriah, Yetzirah,* and *Asiyah,* the name *Shekhinah* generally refers to the *sefirah of *malkhut ("kingship") in the world of *Atzilut. The *Shekhinah* is also called *Kenesset Yisrael* ("the [supernal] community of Israel") because it is the collective source of the souls of the Jewish people.

By studying Torah and performing *mitzvot,* a Jew can draw a divine light down onto his soul; at the same time, he can unite the Godly source of that light with the Godly source of his soul. This is one meaning of serving God with "the intention to unite the Holy One, blessed be He, and His *Shekhinah.*"

Shulchan Aruch (The Code of Jewish Law; literally, "the set table") Written by Rabbi Yosef Karo of Tzefat in the sixteenth century, the *Shulchan Aruch* is the most important and influential codification of Jewish law. It provides a concise summary of the legal decisions of the *Talmud and later authorities and presents them in a format that is easily accessible, like a table set for a banquet.

Rabbi Shneur Zalman also wrote a code of Jewish law that is known as the *Shulchan Aruch haRav* ("the Rav's *Shulchan Aruch*").

sitra achra (Aramaic: "the other side" or "the side that is not holy")   A general term for evil, including all aspects of the universe that are opposed to Godliness. Synonymous with *kelipah.*

Sod   See *pardes.*

Talmud ("learning")   The most important and fundamental work of the Oral Torah. (The Oral Torah consists of the interpretations and traditions that Moses received at Mount Sinai together with the Written Torah and then transmitted from teacher to student throughout the generations.) Since its completion, the Talmud has been the principal subject for Torah study and the primary authority for all *halakhic decisions.

The Talmud contains Mishnah and *Gemara.* The Mishnah is a concise summary of the teachings of the *Tanna'im* on all topics of Torah, and it was redacted in the second century C.E. In the centuries that followed, the Mishnah was discussed and analyzed by the *Amora'im of the yeshivas of the Land of Israel and Babylonia. The *Gemara* summarizes their discussions and debates, together with stories, *aggadot,* and some explicitly mystical material.

There are two Talmuds: one composed in the Land of Israel and completed in the fourth century (the *Talmud Yerushalmi*) and another composed in Babylonia and completed in the fifth century (the *Talmud Bavli*).

Tanakh   Acronym for the three parts of the Written Torah: Torah (Five Books of Moses), *Nevi'im* (Prophets), *Ketuvim* (Writings, that is, Hagiographa). The sages refer to *Tanakh Mikra* ("that which is read"). The scholars of the Great Assembly, in about the fifth century B.C.E., decided which books would be included in *Tanakh* and thereby accepted as a part of the Written Torah.

Tannai'm ("the ones who teach")   The sages. See *Talmud.

Tanya ("It has been taught")   In the language of the Talmud, the word *tanya* introduces a teaching recorded in a *baraita*, a source that is not part of the Mishnah. One reason that *Hasidim gave Rabbi Shneur Zalman's work *Likkutei Amarim* the name *Tanya* was because it opens with a quote from a *baraita* in the Talmud, and so the first word on the first page is *Tanya*. (See our commentary in the Introduction and in Chapter 1 for additional reasons.)

teshuvah ("return")   *Teshuvah* can mean repentance, the process by which an individual who sinned, and thereby estranged himself from God, gains forgiveness and returns to a state of closeness and attachment to God. Such *teshuvah* requires regret, verbal confession, and a commitment not to repeat the sin. But *teshuvah* can also mean the process by which the soul that is clothed within a body, and thereby separated from God, can deepen its connection to its source, which is God. *Teshuvah*, in this sense, is a divine service that even a *tzaddik can perform.

tiferet ("beauty")   In the order of the *sefirot, it is the third of the emotional attributes. As suggested by its name, which connotes "beauty," *tiferet* involves the harmonious integration of differing and contrasting elements. It is also called *rachamim* ("mercy"), because it integrates the power of love and generosity (*chessed) with the power of fear and restraint (*gevurah). Also referred to as *emet* ("truth"), because a single truth can reconcile and unify many disparate and seemingly contradictory facts.

tikkun ("rectification"); *olam hatikkun* ("the world of Rectification")   The present scheme of creation, which is intended to rectify the spiritual damage that occurred when the world of *tohu ended. The world of *tikkun* is characterized by interinclusion and integration: each *sefirah contains elements of all the others, and a part of the system can reflect the structure of an entire system (see *komah shelemah). The *sefirot are also arranged in three *kavim, with the result that opposing *middot on the right and on the left are integrated and harmonized by the *middot* in the center. Another stabilizing factor is that the *sefirot* of *tikkun* have "weak lights and strong vessels."

Tikkunei Zohar   A section of the *Zohar. The structure of *Tikkunei Zohar* is different from the rest of the *Zohar;* each of its chapters begins with an explanation of a different permutation of the letters of the word *Bereshit* ("In the beginning," the first word of the book of Genesis).

tohu; olam hatohu ("the world of *tohu*")   The original scheme of creation, in which the *sefirot had "strong lights and weak vessels." In addition, each of the *sefirot* had an identity that was pure, indivisible, and entirely distinct from the others. This lack of interinclusion and the consequent lack of integration between the *sefirot* was the deeper reason why the world of *tohu* was unstable and ended with the "breaking of the vessels" of some of the *sefirot.* The world of *tohu* was followed by the present scheme of creation, known as the world of *tikkun.

Torah lishmah ("Torah for its own sake")   Studying the Torah for the proper reasons. On the simplest level, it refers to study that is not motivated by extraneous considerations such as a desire for recognition, honor, or acclaim. The desire to be called a *Talmid chakham* ("Torah scholar") is an extraneous motive, and even the desire to be a *Talmid chakham* is not an entirely pure motive, because it views the Torah as a tool for self-perfection. Rather, a person should study Torah because he loves God and wants to be connected to God by doing His will.

According to Hasidic thought, even study for this reason and study for the purpose of knowing how to perform the *mitzvot are not the highest levels of *Torah lishmah*, because both involve a trace of self-interest. The highest form of *Torah lishmah* is to study the Torah purely for the "benefit" of the Torah itself, without being concerned about how it might affect the individual. The Torah is derived from God's wisdom (the *sefirah of *chokhmah), and a person who studies *Torah lishmah* on this highest level can draw down the *Ohr Ein Sof ("the Infinite Light), which is above *chokhmah, and cause it to be revealed within the Torah. Such study is purely for the "benefit" it brings to the Torah itself.

tumah ("impurity" or "defilement"); *taharah* ("purity")   The Torah generally uses these terms to refer to what might be called *halakhic or "physical" *tumah* and *taharah.* This is defined by a set of laws that specify the physical conditions under which objects (such as food, utensils, or the human body) become halakhically *tamei* or *tahor.* (Although the conditions that determine the status of an object are physical conditions, the difference between the state of *tumah* and *taharah* is not a physical one but a legal and spiritual one.) In general, *tumah* is the result of physical contact with death or of biological events involving a loss of potential life; and the main halakhic significance of *tumah* is that an object that is *tamei* cannot be used for holy purposes; for example, it cannot be brought to the *Beit haMikdash* ("Holy Temple").

In addition, the Torah uses these same terms for what might be called "spiritual" *tumah* and *taharah.* For example, a spiritual *tumah* affects the soul of a person who sins, and spiritual *taharah* results from **teshuvah* and atonement, as well as from the fulfillment of **mitzvot.* Just as physical *tumah* is caused by a lack of physical vitality, by a separation from the source of physical life, so, too, spiritual *tumah* is caused by anything that separates the soul from its source of spiritual life. Thus, sin, anger, and depression are associated with spiritual *tumah*, whereas **teshuvah,* the fulfillment of **mitzvot,* and joy are associated with spiritual *taharah.*

tzaddik ("a righteous person"), pl. *tzaddikim*   In biblical Hebrew and in the language of our sages, a *tzaddik* is an individual whose behavior is just and virtuous, one who will be vindicated in judgment.

According to *Tanya,* a *tzaddik*'s existence is essentially different from that of an ordinary person, and not everyone can expect to become a *tzaddik.* A *tzaddik* has no desire to do anything against God's will, and nothing in the world can weaken his determination to serve God. His inner life—his desires, feelings, and thoughts—are all devoted exclusively to Godliness. In the words of the *Tanya* (*Iggeret haKodesh,* Chapter 27): "The life of the *tzaddik* is not a life of the flesh, but a life of spirituality, [consisting of] his faith in God, his fear of God, and his love of God."

Although the *Tanya* speaks primarily about **beinonim,* it also describes the divine service of a *tzaddik* (see, for example, Chapter 10), because a *beinoni* is, at times, able to function like a *tzaddik.*

tzaddik gamur ("a completely righteous person")   The highest level of **tzaddik,* a *tzaddik* who has not even a trace of evil within himself. *Tanya* identifies the *tzaddik gamur* with the *Gemara*'s category of *tzaddik v'tov lo,* which is interpreted as "a *tzaddik* who possesses [only] good."

yechidah: The fifth and highest level of the soul. Like the level of **chayah, yechidah* is not "clothed" in any of the revealed powers of soul, it stays above them as a *makif* ("a transcendent or surrounding light"), but the *makif* of *yechidah* is even higher than the *makif* of **chayah.* The name *yechidah* can also refer to the essence of the soul, which is even higher than a *makif.* It is unified with God, the *yechido shel Olam*—"the One true Existence of the World."

yesod ("foundation")   One of the **sefirot,* the sixth of the emotional attributes. *Yesod* is the desire of the giver to connect with the recipient, which is an essential aspect of the process by which influence is bestowed. Hence, *yesod* is the power that connects the higher *sefirot* to **malkhut* ("kingship") and allows the divine "energy" of the higher *sefirot* to be transmitted to *malkhut.* Hence, *yesod* is described as a "pillar that joins heaven and earth," and it is called "foundation," because the foundation of a building connects the body of the structure to the earth.

yir'ah ("fear")   Fear of God. The emotion of fear is the inner aspect of the **sefirah* of **gevurah.* Just as *gevurah* is "directed inward," so, too, when a person fears something, he usually retreats from it and withdraws to his own boundaries.

   The fear of God has two general levels: the lower level (*yir'ah tata'ah*) is *yir'at haonesh,* "fear of punishment." Such fear is based on a person's desire to protect his own existence, and it comes from an awareness of an external manifestation of God, namely, "what God might do." The higher level of fear (*yir'ah ila'ah*) is *yir'at haromemut,* an "awe" inspired by an awareness of God's intrinsic greatness, the realization that in comparison to His being, the entire universe is as nothing. Such a fear makes a person feel the insignificance of his own existence, and to the extent to which he is aware of himself at all in God's presence, he is filled with a sense of shame. Hence, it is also referred to as *yir'at haboshet.* This higher fear comes from an awareness of the inner essence of God's being.

Zohar ("Brilliance" or "Splendor")   One of the fundamental texts of Jewish mysticism (**Kabbalah*). The *Zohar* consists of the teachings of the *Tanna,* Rabbi Shimon bar Yochai (second century), as recorded by his close students. Written mostly in Aramaic and arranged according to the weekly Torah portions and the Five Scrolls, it contains both *midrashim* and mystical secrets of the Torah.

⎯ᴗ⎯ Notes

The Title Page

1. *Mipi sefarim u'mipi sofrim;* literally, "From the mouth of books and from the mouth of scribes."
2. In the first two generations of the Hasidic movement, all Hasidim regarded a single leader as their master and teacher: Rabbi Israel Baal Shem Tov and then the Maggid. Following the Maggid's death, by which time the movement had grown and spread throughout Eastern Europe, the movement was basically decentralized, with regional leaders or rebbes each heading another subgroup of Hasidim and teaching his distinct strain of Hasidic thought. Nevertheless, in the first years following the Maggid's death, the Hasidic community acknowledged Rabbi Menachem Mendel of Vitebsk as the greatest Hasidic master, and all the Maggid's disciples, many of whom had established their own branches of Hasidism, regarded him as their rebbe.
3. See *Kitzurim v'He'arot* on *Tanya,* p. 139.
4. *Eruvin* 53a.
5. Talmud, *Shabbat* 31a.

The Approbations

1. The author's colleague and a disciple of the Maggid ("preacher"; see Preface).
2. The author's son-in-law and father of Rabbi Menachem Mendel of Lubavitch, third leader of Chabad.
3. Genesis 1:10, 12.
4. That is, 5556; omitting the millennial is customary.

5. This disciple of Rabbi Dov Ber of Mezherich (the Maggid) was the author's colleague.

6. Ecclesiastes 8:1.

7. The reference is to Rabbi Dov Ber of Mezherich, hinted at also by the word *be'er* ("well" in *be'er mayim chayyim* ("from the well of living waters")).

8. Alluding to Rabbi Israel Baal Shem Tov.

9. See n. 4.

10. Jerusalem Talmud, *Rosh haShanah,* ch. 3, hal. 5.

11. Note that *Sha'ar haYichud v'haEmunah* (pt. II of the *Tanya*) is not mentioned here; neither is it mentioned in the title page.

12. *Nidduy, cherem,* and *shamta* (*NChSh*) are three forms of excommunication.

13. In the Shklov '574 edition appears the date "5[th day (Thurs.)] 22nd of *Iyar* '574," subsequently omitted.

14. Psalms 19:13.

Compiler's Preface

1. Deuteronomy 17:4.

2. Talmud, *Rosh haShanah* 25b.

3. *Midrash Rabbah, Bereishit* 3; and *Shemot* 35.

4. Genesis 1:4.

5. *Baal Shem Tov on the Torah,* 45 and 46.

6. In the text, the word *umit'orer* ("and is aroused") is missing. See the list of text emendations in Rabbi Schneur Zalman, the *Tanya,* ed. R. Menachem M. Schneersohn (Brooklyn, N.Y.: Kehot Publication Society, 1958), beginning on p. 403.

7. Mishneh Torah, "Laws of Fundamentals of Torah," 4:12

8. Psalm 8:4.

9. *Berachot* 58a.

10. *Berachot* 58a.

11. His commentary on the great halakhic work by Rabbi Yitzhak Al-Fasi (known as the RIF).

12. *Ruach hakodesh* has many levels, depending on the spiritual state of the generation and the individual.

13. Talmudic commentator Rabbi Shmuel Eidles (1555–1631).

14. 2 Samuel 23:2.

15. Talmud, *Eruvin* 13a.

16. The text lacks the word *neshamot* ("souls").

17. See *Tanya,* ch. 37.

18. Genesis 16:10 and elsewhere.
19. *Zohar,* pt. III, 73:1.
20. End of the *Shemoneh Esreh* prayer.
21. Deuteronomy 29:28.
22. Talmudic sages (*tanna'im* are the authors of the Mishnah, *amora'im* of the Gemara).
23. *Tzarat ha'bat,* Talmud, *Yevamot* 13b–14b.
24. Talmud, *Eruvin* 13b and elsewhere.
25. In Hebrew, the words *Elokim* ("God") and *chayyim* ("life") are always in plural form, even when the connotation is singular.
26. Commentary on the *Shulchan Aruch* by Rabbi Shabbtai haCohen (1621–1663).
27. "The hidden matters [belong] to God, and the revealed to us and to our children forever, to do all the words of this Torah" (Deuteronomy 29:28). This verse is traditionally interpreted as a reference to the hidden and revealed parts of Torah: the esoteric soul of Torah, dealing with God's relationship with reality, the mysteries of creation, and the inner life of the soul; and the exoteric *halakhot* that deal with the "prohibited and permissible" in everyday life.
28. Pt. I, 103:1 interprets Proverbs 31:23.
29. God and the Jewish soul are repeatedly described as "husband" and "wife" in the Prophets, Scriptures, and *Midrash.*
30. Psalms 135:5.
31. *Tanya,* pt. IV, ch. 22.
32. *Torat Shalom,* p. 56.
33. *Berachot* 33b.
34. *Sanhedrin* 91b, discussing Proverbs 11:26.
35. *Sanhedrin* 92b.
36. Jeremiah 31:33.
37. Isaiah 11:9.
38. *Temurah* 16a, discussing Proverbs 29:13.
39. Deuteronomy 27:17.
40. See Talmud, *Shevuot* 36a.
41. A Talmudic expression that loosely means, "What have I to add, when this has already been said by a much higher authority?" (In *Kiddushin* 6a, the Talmud cites a certain practice in the province of Judah as a precedent for a law and then proceeds to offer a proof from a scriptural verse. This is objected to with the exclamation: "As in Judah and Scripture in addition?" (You're telling me that this is the practice in Judah, and in addition, you're citing Scripture?) If the verse so states, what further proof is needed?

Chapter 1

1. Psalms 109:31.
2. Rashi, ibid.
3. *Bava Batra* 16a.
4. Rashi, ibid.
5. *Niddah* 16b.
6. *Bava Metzia* 86a.
7. *Bava Metzia* 86a tells that a wind blew, making a great noise, and Rabbah, who thought he was hearing horsemen chasing him, preferred to sacrifice himself rather than fall into their hands. Only then could the Angel of Death overpower him.
8. See Talmud, *Kiddushin* 49b.
9. 20a.
10. 12a.
11. 32b.
12. Talmud, *Sanhedrin* 99a.
13. Numbers 15:31.
14. The Hebrew word *panim*, "face," also means "turn" or "angle."
15. From the Lubavitcher Rebbe's expositions on *Tanya*.
16. Exodus 23:7.
17. Psalms 109:22.
18. Proverbs 10:25.
19. Compare Talmud, *Yuma* 38b.
20. *Torah Ohr* 63b.
21. See opening chapter of *Sha'ar haYichud v'haEmunah*, pt. II of *Tanya*.
22. Ch. 29, and ch. 7 of pt. III of *Tanya, Iggeret haTeshuvah*.
23. Leviticus 17:11.
24. Isaiah 47:10 and elsewhere.
25. Ecclesiastes 7:14.
26. See chs. 8, 27, and 31 of *Tanya*.
27. *Yevamot* 79a.
28. *Yevamot* 78b.
29. For instance, from 1 Kings 20:31, it emerges that the gentiles knew well that the kings of Israel—even evil ones, such as King Ahab—were "merciful kings."
30. *Beitzah* 25b.
31. Ezekiel 1:4.
32. See *Likkutei Biurim* on *Tanya*, pp. 27–28.
33. *Bava Batra* 10b comments on Proverbs 14:34.

Chapter 2

1. See *Torah Ohr* 38b.
2. Genesis 2:7; compare Nachmanides' commentary on that verse.
3. Liturgy, Morning Prayer; Talmud, *Berachot* 60b.
4. The Lubavitcher Rebbe points out that this passage (quoted also in pt. IV of *Tanya*, ch. 15) is not in any of the editions of *Zohar* we have today, but it is quoted in many classic Torah works in the name of the sages.
5. Pt. II, 119b.
6. Exodus 4:22.
7. Deuteronomy 14:1.
8. Pt. I, 217b.
9. Introduction to *Tikkunei Zohar*, 12b; also see *Torah Ohr* 13a.
10. Deuteronomy 4:35.
11. *Mishneh Torah*, Laws of the Fundamentals of Torah, 2:10.
12. See *Sha'ar haYichud v'haEmunah*, ch. 7. The author cites only the first two components, "the knowledge and the knower." In ch. 4, he cites these two but in reverse order: "the knower and the knowledge." The previous Lubavitcher Rebbe, Rabbi Yosef Yitzchak Schneersohn, explains these differences in a letter (published in *Kitzurim v'He'arot* on *Tanya*, p. 118).
13. See *Sha'ar haYichud v'haEmunah*, ch. 8.
14. Job 11:7.
15. Cordovero, *Pardes Rimmonim*; see also *Sha'ar Atzmut veKeilim*, ch. 3.
16. Introduction to *Gevurot haShem*. See also *Derekh Mitzvotekha, Mitzvat Haamanat Elokut*, ch. 3, and *Shoresh Mitzvat haTefillah*, ch. 25.
17. *Ein Sof*, the Endless or Infinite, a term frequently used in the *Zohar* and later works of Kabbalah to indicate God.
18. *ChaBaD* is an acronym formed of the initial letters of the Hebrew words *chokhmah* ("wisdom"), *binah* ("understanding"), and *daat* ("knowledge"), the first three of the ten *sefirot*. The corresponding faculties of the soul are defined in ch. 3.
19. See our commentary on ch. 39 (in Hebrew only).
20. See *Tanya*, pt. II, ch. 9, and our commentary there (in Hebrew only).
21. Psalms 104:24.
22. Deuteronomy 14:1.
23. *Sha'ar haGilgulim*, introduction, p. 31.
24. A play on the Talmudic phrase for the head—*tefillin, tefillin sheba-rosh*, which literally translates as "the *tefillin* in the head."
25. From the Lubavitcher Rebbe's glosses on *Tanya*.

340   NOTES

26. Talmud, *Niddah* 31a: "There are three partners to a person: God, his father, and his mother. His father germinates the white [element], which forms the veins, bones, nails, brain, and white of the eye. His mother germinates the red [element], which forms the skin, flesh, hair, and pupil of the eye. And God place within him a spirit and soul, a countenance, eyesight, hearing, speech, walk, understanding, and intellect."
27. Emanation, Creation, Formation, and Action.
28. Exodus 32:7.
29. *Berachot* 32a.
30. *Tanya,* ch. 32. See also *Sefer haMaamarim* 5653, p. 144, and elsewhere.
31. Leviticus 19:18.
32. Talmud, *Shabbat* 118b; see *Iggeret haKodesh,* sec. 7.
33. *Ketubot* 111b quotes Deuteronomy 30:20.
34. See Maimonides, *Mishneh Torah,* Laws of the Fundamentals of Torah 2:10.
35. Isaiah 6:3.
36. Jeremiah 2:27.
37. Compare pt. II, 204b and following; III, 80–82.
38. *Bereshit,* p. 11.
39. Compare Talmud, *Eduyot* 2:9: "The father achieves for his son beauty, strength." The *Alter Rebbe*'s grandson, the Tzemach Tzeddek (in *Hagahot u'Biurim* on *Tanya,* p. 75), suggests that the garment is the *nefesh hasikhlit* ("intellectual soul") discussed in Chabad Hasidism.
40. Immersing oneself in a *mikveh* is an act of purification. Among Hasidim, it is customary to go to the *mikveh* often, to purify oneself in preparation for God's worship.
41. Isaiah 52:13.
42. *Niddah* 31a, cited in n. 27.
43. Talmud, *Sukkah* 52b.

Chapter 3

1. *Torah Ohr* 13c and *Likkutei Torah, VaYikra* 4b.
2. *Tanya,* ch. 12.
3. *Maamar Patach Eliyahu* (introduction to *Tikkunei Zohar*); see the author's discourse on *Patach Eliyahu* (*Torah Ohr* 13c) and that of his great-great-grandson, Rabbi Sholom DovBer of Lubavitch.
4. The author more fully discusses the ten *Sefirot* in pt. IV of *Tanya, Iggeret ha-Kodesh,* ch. 15 and elsewhere.
5. Genesis 1:26.

6. As mentioned in ch. 2, the world was created by divine speech, the letters of which constitute the essence of every created thing. These letters reflect the form of the higher, precreation realities from which they derive, all the way up to the most primordial manifestations of divine light.

7. See *Torah Ohr* 29a.

8. See *Iggeret haKodesh* 15, p. 123.

9. *Kitzurim v'He'arot*, p. 89, and the Rashab's note therein, p. 113.

10. Rabbi Shmuel Grunem Estherman's commentary on *Tanya*.

11. *Torah Ohr* 19b; *Likkutei Torah,* Song of Songs 46d; opening discourse of *Sefer haMaamarim* 5568; and others.

12. See the Rashab's comment in *Sefer haKitzurim*, p. 113.

13. Pt. III, 28a; 34a.

14. Exodus 16:7.

15. Numbers 12:3.

16. *B'chokhmah itbariru.*

17. See Deuteronomy 29:3.

18. *Torah Ohr* 12:3; *Likkutei Torah, vaYikra* 57b; and elsewhere.

19. 1 Kings 5:12.

20. See Rashi's commentary on Deuteronomy 1:13.

21. Compare *Midrash Rabbah, Bereshit* 80.

22. *Iggeret haKodesh* 15, 134a; *Torah Ohr* 75a.

23. *Midrash Rabbah, vaYikra* 1:6.

Chapter 4

1. See *Torah Ohr* 13b and *Derekh Mitzvotekha*, p. 155b.

2. Rabbi Y. Kaidaner's commentary on *Tanya*.

3. Talmud, *Berachot* 47b, and elsewhere.

4. Genesis 13:13, in reference to the people of Sodom.

5. Genesis 3:5.

6. *Pardes* (lit., "orchard") is an acrostic of the four Hebrew words *p'shat, remez, d'rush,* and *sod*, meaning "plain sense," "intimation," "homiletic exposition," and "esoteric meaning," the four primary levels of Torah interpretation.

7. Mishnah, *Ohelot* 4:2; *Tanchuma haKadum, Tetze; Makkot* 24a. See *Tanya,* ch. 51; see also the entry for *mitzvot* in the Glossary.

8. Major commentary and comments on the Talmud, known for its profundity and complexity and dating from the eleventh and twelfth centuries.

9. *Yuma* 26a.

10. Jerusalem Talmud, *Pe'ah* 1:1.

11. As the Torah commands in Deuteronomy 10:20, 11:22, 13:5, and 30:20.

12. Psalms 42:3.

13. Isaiah 55:1.

14. The opening words of ch. 4 of the Talmudic tractate *Bava Kamma*.

15. *Tikkunei Zohar, Tikkun* 30; *Tanya*, ch. 23.

16. The Hebrew is *d'veikut*, used both for human attachment in marriage (Genesis 2:24) and for attachment to God (Deuteronomy 30:20).

17. For example, *Torah Ohr* 74:2.

18. See *Likkutei Torah, baMidbar* 44b.

19. In *Likkutei Torah, Devarim* 46a, the author gives the source of this saying as *Zohar*, pt. II, 60a. See also *Zohar*, pt. I, 24a; *Tikkunei Zohar*, Tikkun 6 and 22. (From the Lubavitcher Rebbe's notes on *Tanya*.)

20. *Mishneh Torah*, Laws of the Fundamentals of Torah, 2:10.

21. *Likkutei Biurim* on *Tanya*.

22. *Zohar*, pt. II, *Parashat Mishpatim* 121a.

23. Psalms 145:3.

24. Introduction to *Tikkunei Zohar* 17a.

25. Isaiah 40:28.

26. Job 11:7.

27. Isaiah 55:8.

28. *Megillah* 31a (the standard Talmudic text reads "His power," but certain manuscripts have "His greatness").

29. *Megillah* 31a.

30. *Midrash Rabbah, Bereshit* 4.

31. Rabbi Y. Kaidaner's commentary on *Tanya*.

32. *Midrash Rabbah, Bereshit* 44:17.

33. Talmud, *Bava Kamma* 17a.

34. Song of Songs 2:14 ("My dove is in the cleft of the rock, in the hidden steps). The steps are "hidden" because each "descent" spells a concealment and constriction *(tzimtzum)* of the Torah's essence.

35. The Torah manifests itself in all "worlds" of the *seder hahishtalshelut:* in *Atzilut* ("Emanation"), *Beriah* ("Creation"), *Yetzirah* ("Formation"), and *Assiyah* ("Action"). Each world reveals another face of the Torah, the divine wisdom as it pertains to the parameters and qualities of that world.

36. Certain *mitzvot* are spiritual in nature (knowing God, prayer), but the great majority are physical, involving physical deeds and physical dynamics.

37. In which case, it would not be God's Torah. For, as we said before, the true mark of infinity is that it is not excluded from any realm, including the realm of the finite; so if the Torah emanates from the truly Infinite, it must

extend to every realm of reality. Indeed, as Hasidic teaching explains on many occasions, the highest level of Torah expresses itself fully only in the lowest world, the world of Action.

38. 1 Samuel 25:29.
39. Psalms 18:3.
40. See *Iggeret haKodesh* 1.
41. Psalms 5:13.
42. Mishnah, *Avot* 4:17.
43. Talmud, *Berachot* 17a.
44. Songs of Songs, 8:3.

Chapter 5

1. For example, Talmud, *Pesachim* 47a; *Hagigah* 4a; and elsewhere.
2. *Zohar,* pt. II, *Parashat Terumah,* 161b.
3. From the Lubavitcher Rebbe's talk of the fifth night of Hanukkah 5717 (1957). See also *Likkutei Biurim* and the second commentary by Rabbi Shmuel Gronem Esterman.
4. Deuteronomy 6:7.
5. See ch. 4, n. 6.
6. See our commentary on pt. II of *Tanya, Sha'ar haYichud v'haEmunah,* p. 70 (in the Hebrew edition).
7. Psalms 40:9.
8. See beginning of *Sha'ar Hanhagat haLimmud.*
9. From Rabbi Shmuel Gronem Estherman's elucidations of *Tanya.*
10. *Pe'ah* 1:1.
11. Talmud, *Sotah* 21a. (unlike Torah, which protects always).

Chapter 6

1. Compare *Zohar,* pt. III, 41a, 70a.
2. From Rabbi Shmuel Gronem Estherman's elucidations on *Tanya.*
3. See ch. 3; Rabbi Shalom DovBer of Lubavitch's notes on *Tanya;* Rabbi Shmuel Gronem Estherman's elucidations on *Tanya.*
4. *Zohar,* pt. II, 59a. See *Likkutei Torah,* [*Devarim*] 63d.
5. Deuteronomy 4:35.
6. Isaiah 6:3.
7. From Rabbi Shmuel Gronem Estherman's elucidations on *Tanya.*

8. See *Tanya,* pt. IV, ch. 23; *Likkutei Torah, [Devarim]* 98b.

9. *Atzilut, Beriah, Yetzirah,* and *Asiyah.*

10. Specified in Leviticus 11 and Deuteronomy 14.

11. *Orlah;* Leviticus 19:23.

12. Deuteronomy 22:9.

13. *Sifra diTzniuta II, Shemot* 176b.

Chapter 7

1. The author's grandson, Rabbi Menachem Mendel of Lubavitch, points out that the *Tanya* does not include the bodies of the Jew and the kosher animals in its list of things deriving from *kelipat nogah,* as it does in the case of the nonkosher animals discussed in Chapter 6, which states that "the souls of all living creatures that are impure and prohibited for consumption, and the existence of their bodies" derive from the three profane *kelipot.* Rabbi Menachem Mendel explains this in accordance with what the author states elsewhere that the body of the Jew is in fact loftier than his animal soul, for the creation of physical matter derives from the "Encompassing Light" of God. (See *Kitzurim v'Hearot,* p. 115; letter by the Lubavitcher Rebbe, published in *Likkutei Biurim,* beginning of ch. 7.)

2. *Chayyot* in the Hebrew.

3. *Behemot* in the Hebrew. *Chayyot* are wild animals, and *behemot* are domesticated animals, though each term also refers to all animals. The Torah (Deuteronomy 14:4–5; see Rashi) lists three species of *behemah* and seven species of *chayyah* as permissible for consumption.

4. Ezekiel 1:4.

5. Rabbi Shmuel Grunem Esterman's elucidations on *Tanya;* see also *Likkutei Biurim.*

6. Job 35:11.

7. *Eruvin* 100b.

8. Talmud, *Yoma* 76b.

9. *Mishneh Torah,* Laws of Sabbath, 30:7; Laws of the Festivals, 6:16. Rabbi Schneur Zalman's *Shulchan Aruch haRav,* 242:1 and 529:1, 3.

10. Some of these things are universal, whereas others may apply to certain individuals but not to others.

11. Such as Shabbat meals or eating *matzah.*

12. *Hagigah* 27a.

13. Leviticus 2:13.

14. Exodus 20:22.

15. *Taanit* 22a.
16. *Pesachim* 117a.
17. *Midrash Talpiot,* section on Enoch.
18. Phrase recited following the first verse of Shema.
19. Genesis 5:22.
20. *Chitzonim,* another term for *kelipah* and *sitra achra.*
21. Compare Talmud, *Pesachim* 49b: "A boor is forbidden to eat meat."
22. Mishnah, *Avot* (Ethics of the Fathers), 2:10.
23. *Shabbat* 47b.
24. Ne'illah prayer.
25. *Zohar,* pt. I, 268a; *Midrash Shocher Tov,* Proverbs 9. This concept has halakhic repercussions as well, as discussed in *Shulchan Aruch, Yoreh De'ah* 372; *Pitchei Teshuvah,* section 2.
26. Ezekiel 32:27.
27. This paragraph does not appear in the standard published text of *Tanya,* but we have inserted it here from a reliable manuscript in the Schneersohn Library. It has also been incorporated into the Yiddish and English editions of *Tanya* (Brooklyn, N.Y.: Kehot Publication Society, 1956 and 1962).
28. Talmud, *Berachot* 18b.
29. Zechariah 13:2.
30. *Yuma* 86b.
31. Attributed to the Baal Shem Tov.
32. Talmud, *Sotah* 3a.
33. Job 38:14.
34. The Shema, Deuteronomy 6:5.
35. See *Torah Ohr* 86b; *Sefer haMaamarim* 5562, p. 222.
36. *Avodah Zarah* 17a.
37. Isaiah 54:10.
38. The Hebrew word for "moment," *sha'a,* that Rabbi Judah HaNassi used, also means "movement."
39. Psalms 51:2.
40. Psalms 51:5.
41. Talmud, *Berachot* 34b.
42. As in Isaiah 25:8.
43. *Pri Etz Chayyim, Sha'ar Keriat Shema SheAl haMittah,* and elsewhere.
44. Psalms 149:5–6.
45. Talmud, *Berachot* 5a.
46. Rashi, Genesis 5:9.
47. See *Derekh Mitzvotekha* 2:2.
48. Mishnah, *Avot* 4:2.

49. *Hagigah* 9a.

50. Ecclesiastes 1:15.

51. Written by Rabbi Schneur Zalman's son, Rabbi DovBer. The story of this *baal teshuvah* is in the introduction to this work.

Chapter 8

1. *Sanhedrin* 88.

2. Compare *Zohar*, pt. III, 253a, 277a, et seq.

3. Genesis 44:7.

4. 2 Samuel 7:14.

5. See *Zohar*, pt. II, 151a, and especially R. Chaim Vital, end of *Sefer haKavvanot*, p. 55b et seq.

6. Talmud, *Ketubot* 104a.

7. 1 Samuel 25:29.

8. *Shabbat* 152b.

9. *Likkutei Torah, baMidbar* 75c, and elsewhere.

10. Talmud, *Berachot* 17a; see *Tanya*, end of ch. 4.

11. *Halekach v'haLibbuv.*

12. *Berachot* 8a interprets Isaiah 1:28.

13. Rabbi Isaac Luria (the Holy Ari), *Likkutei Torah, Shemot.* Compare *Zohar*, pt. I, 62b; 237b; pt. II, 150a–b.

14. First printed in Shklov, 1794, ch. 3, par. 7.

15. See ch. 1.

16. Job 4:21.

17. *Torah Ohr* 110d and elsewhere.

18. Psalms 19:2.

19. See *Sefer haToladot leAdmur haZaken* (1967 ed.), p. 540.

Chapter 9

1. Each of the three intellectual faculties has its corresponding section of the physical brain; hence the *Tanya*'s use of the plural, "brains."

2. See, for example, *Likkutei Torah, Parashat Chukkat* 59a.

3. Ezekiel 29:3.

4. 1 Chronicles 29:4.

5. 1 Chronicles 29:14.

6. Ecclesiastes 10:2.

7. The third of the seven emotional attributes.

8. Ecclesiastes 2:14.

9. Genesis 25:23.

10. Genesis 25:22; and see Rashi's commentary there.

11. Mishnah, *Avot* 4:15.

12. Talmud, end of *Berachot*.

13. 1 Samuel 25:29; see ch. 8.

14. Ecclesiastes 9:14; the Aramaic translation of the same verse; Talmud, *Nedarim* 32b.

15. *Likkutei Torah, Behar* 39c.

16. *Midrash Rabbah, Bereshit,* 47:8.

17. See n. 1.

18. *Berachot* 54a.

19. The Hebrew word for "might," *meod,* in the verse also means "very much" and "beyond."

20. *Berachot* 54a.

21. Song of Songs 7:7.

22. Genesis 29:20.

23. Psalms 73:28.

24. The author discusses the differences between "love like flaming coals" and "love like water" in chs. 15, 16, 18, 40, 41, 46, and 49 of *Tanya*.

25. *Tanya,* pt. IV, ch. 18.

26. *Zohar,* pt. I, 217b.

27. Compare Zechariah 3:7, and commentaries.

28. See, for instance, *Tanya,* ch. 27; *Torah Ohr* 38c.

29. Pt. II, 163a; see also ch. 29 of *Tanya*.

Chapter 10

1. Deuteronomy 21:21.

2. Psalms 34:1.

3. 2 Samuel 23:3.

4. A series of study groups to which Rabbi Schneur Zalman's disciples were assigned in accordance to their scholastic achievements (see *Sefer haToladot leAdmur haZaken,* ch. 11).

5. Rashi, Numbers 20:12.

6. *Gittin* 66a.

7. King David's words in Psalms 139:22.

8. *Sukkah* 45b.

9. *Sukkah* 45b.

10. Pt. I, 4a.

11. Jeremiah 15:19.

12. Isaiah 55:1.

13. *Tanya,* ch. 40.

14. Introduction to *Tikkunei Zohar* 1b. Compare *Zohar,* pt. II, 114b; III, 222b, 281a.

15. *Zohar,* pt. III, 281a.

16. Exodus 4:10, 13.

17. Numbers 11:1.

18. Numbers, 13–14.

19. Exodus 32:32.

20. The *tallit* is the shawl worn during prayer; the *shofar* is the ram's horn, which it is mandatory to blow on *Rosh haShanah;* the *lulav* is the palm branch, one of the "four species" used in the Sukkot festival.

21. Genesis 1:6–8.

Chapter 11

1. Talmud, *Mo'ed Katan* 25a.

2. Genesis 2:10.

3. Deuteronomy 23:10.

4. Talmud, *Ketubot* 46a.

5. Mishnah, *Avot* 3:4.

6. Talmud, *Yuma* 86a.

7. Talmud, *Kiddushin* 39b.

8. Exodus 28:28.

9. Proverbs 28:13.

10. Compare *Nedarim* 9b; *Shevet Mussar,* ch. 25, in the name of our sages.

11. *Berachot* 18b.

12. Compare Deuteronomy 4:4.

13. Numbers 12:8.

14. The Jewish section of the Communist Party.

15. Rabbi Menachem Mendel of Lubavitch, grandson of the author of *Tanya,* known as the Tzemach Tzedek.

16. See Esther 8:1, 7 and 9:18.

17. Talmud, *Sanhedrin* 39a.

18. See *Iggeret haKodesh* 25 for the distinction between divine presence and divine revelation.

19. Talmud, *Berachot* 54a, 60b.

Chapter 12

1. Mishnah, *Avot* 8:23.
2. Talmud, *Berachot* 5a.
3. *Tanya,* ch. 49.
4. Proverbs 27:19.
5. *Zohar,* pt. III, 224a.
6. Talmud, *Sotah* 3a.
7. In chs. 24 and 25.
8. In ch. 9.
9. In ch. 4.
10. Talmud, *Yuma* 29a.
11. Talmud, *Bava Batra* 164b.
12. *Zohar,* pt. I, 201a.

—⟨⟨⟩— The Author

Born in 1937 to a secular family, Rabbi Adin Steinsaltz is internationally regarded as one of the leading scholars and rabbis of his time. According to *Newsweek*:

> Jewish lore is filled with tales of formidable rabbis. Probably none living today can compare in genius and influence to Adin Steinsaltz, whose extraordinary gifts as scholar, teacher, scientist, writer, mystic and social critic have attracted disciples from all factions of Israeli society.

Rabbi Steinsaltz's formal education includes a degree in mathematics from Hebrew University, in addition to his rabbinic studies. At the age of 23, he became Israel's youngest high school principal.

Rabbi Steinsaltz then went on to found the Israel Institute for Talmudic Publications. Under its aegis, he has published more than sixty books on the Talmud, Jewish mysticism, religious thought, sociology, historical biography, and philosophy. These books have been translated into Russian, English, French, Portuguese, Swedish, Japanese, and Dutch. His commentary on Pirkei Avot, the Chapters of the Fathers, has been published in Chinese by the National Academy for Social Studies in Beijing.

Rabbi Steinsaltz is best known for his interpretation, commentaries, and translations of the Babylonian Talmud, a monumental task which he began some thirty-one years ago. Thirty-four of Rabbi Steinsaltz's Hebrew edition of the Talmud have been published; over two million books are in print. The Rabbi expects to complete the project over the next five years.

Since 1989, Random House has published twenty-two volumes of the English edition of the Rabbi's commentary on the Talmud to great critical acclaim, with a combined printing of over 250,000 books.

The Rabbi is also at work on translations into Russian (three volumes to date) published by the Russian Academy of Sciences, French (eight volumes to date), and Spanish (two volumes to date). With these translations, Rabbi Steinsaltz believes that virtually every Jew, any-where in the world, will have access to this great repository of Jewish tradition and culture.

Deeply involved in the future of the Jews in the former Soviet Union, in 1996, Rabbi Steinsaltz assumed the role of Duchovny Nas-tavnik, a historic Russian title which indicates that he is the spiritual mentor of the Jews of the former Soviet Union. In this capacity, Rabbi Steinsaltz travels to Russia and the Republics once each month from his home in Jerusalem, helping to reestablish the foundational insti-tutions of Jewish life.

Rabbi Steinsaltz's other pioneering efforts in Russian include the founding of the Jewish University of Moscow and the Chairmanship of the Jewish University of St. Petersburg. These educational centers provide Hebrew language instruction and classes on Jewish life, his-tory, and philosophy to thousands of Russian Jews each year. The Jew-ish University of Moscow is the first degree-granting institution of Jewish studies ever established in the former Soviet Union. Rabbi Steinsaltz has also founded Lamed, the national teacher's organization with over 1800 members, and Chaverim, a leadership movement com-posed of Russia's leading Jewish intellectuals, activists, and commu-nity leaders.

In Israel, Rabbi Steinsaltz is the Dean of the Mekor Chaim network of schools which encompasses kindergarten through high school. The schools are known for their innovative programming, which goes beyond academics to encourage social responsibility through volun-teerism and military and national service. In 1999, the Rabbi opened the Yeshiva Gavoha (Academy of Higher Learning). The Academy is accredited as a yeshivat hesder and offers an integrated, five-year pro-gram of army service and advanced Jewish learning.

In 1988, Rabbi Steinsaltz received the Israel Prize, the country's highest honor. He has been a resident scholar at major academic insti-tutions in Europe and the United States, among them Yale University and the Institute for Advanced Studies in Princeton and the Woodrow Wilson Center in Washington, D.C. In 1995, he received the Legion d'Honneur, the French Order of Arts and Letters.

Rabbi Steinsaltz's activities in the United States are supported by the Aleph Society, headquartered in New York City.

⟿ Index

A

Abbaye, 47–48

Abraham, Rabbi (the Angel), 6–7

Abraham of Kalisk, Rabbi, xx, 7

Ahavah rabbah ("great love"), 193, 236

Ahavat olam ("world love"), 193, 292

Akiva, Rabbi, 94

Alshech, Rabbi Moses, 28

Animal soul, xxii, 158–170, 174–191

   beinoni and, 287, 294, 297–299, 304

   blood and, 223, 227

   bodily expressions of, 185–186, 189–190, 220–221

   as challenge for Godly soul, 244–245

   and desires, 185–186, 189–190, 222–223, 241–242, 297–298

   differences from Godly soul, 220–227

   and divine energy and creation, 166–168

   effects of Godly soul on, 232–243

   and emotions, 221, 222–223, 225, 226, 227

   and enclothement metaphor, 60–61

   evil and, 66–67, 158–159, 161–163, 168–170, 174, 175, 177, 179, 201, 204–209, 241

   and the forbidden/permissible, 187–191, 201, 204–210

   garments of, 122, 242

   and holiness, attainment of, xxii, 178–191, 205

   holiness and, 59, 165–168, 178–191, 205, 209–210, 221, 243–245

   and *kelipah,* 58–69, 72–73, 169–170, 174, 210–215

   and *kelipat nogah,* 58–69, 72–73, 159, 174–191, 205, 206, 220, 344*n*1

   in left ventricle of heart, 221, 225, 235, 236

   as mediating between body and Godly soul, 73–74, 159

   middot of, 159–162, 214–216, 227

   mind/intellect and, 160–161, 215, 216, 222–223, 227

   negative character traits and four elements of, 61–64, 160, 185

   and nonphysical *kelipot,* 210–215

   and physicality/biology, xxii, 73–74, 159, 168, 174, 220–221

   positive character traits deriving from, 64–68, 178, 338*n*29

   and profane *kelipot,* 66–67, 169–170, 174, 175, 177, 179, 184, 185, 206, 212–213

   selfhood and self-abnegation, 163–165, 221, 243–244

   seven evil *middot,* 160, 216

   sins and, 191–197, 206–210

   and *sitra achra,* 58–60, 72–73, 159, 162–163, 168, 209, 236

   speech and "idle chatter," 210–215

   struggle between Godly soul and, xxii, 227–232, 251

   teshuvah and, 191–201

   and "*tzaddik* to whom is evil," 279, 280

Approbations for the *Tanya,* 11–14

Arakh, Rabbi Elazar ben, 188

Assur/issur ("forbidden," "bound"), 30, 59, 187, 190, 202, 204–205

B

Baal Shem Tov, xiv, xvii, 8, 18–19, 21, 26, 256, 272, 335*n*2